SEX DIFFERENCES IN POLITICAL PARTICIPATION

Processes of Change in Fourteen Nations

Carol A. Christy

Women and Politics
General Editors
Rita Mae Kelly and Ruth B. Mandel

New York
Westport, Connecticut
London

Library of Congress Cataloging-in-Publication Data

Christy, Carol A.
  Sex differences in political participation.

  (Women and politics)
  Bibliography: p.
  1. Political participation—Sex differences.
2. Women in politics. I. Title. II. Series.
JF2011.C56 1987   323'.042'088042   87-9336
ISBN 0-275-92433-5 (alk. paper)

Library of Congress Catalog Card Number: 87-9336
ISBN: 0-275-92433-5

First published in 1987

Praeger Publishers, One Madison Avenue, New York, NY 10010
A division of Greenwood Press, Inc.

Printed in the United States of America

The paper used in this book complies with the Permanent Paper
Standard issued by the National Information Standards Organization (Z39.48-1984).

10 9 8 7 6 5 4 3 2 1

Contents

Figures

Tables

Acknowledgments

Since I became interested in this topic fifteen years ago, my work has taken many different forms: a Ph.D. dissertation, six convention papers, two journal articles, and finally, this book. Along the way I've been helped tremendously by many colleagues' comments on these different versions. I particularly thank my dissertation advisors Bradley Richardson and Kristi Andersen; they suffered patiently through numerous drafts and a six-hundred page final manuscript. I'm also indebted to some excellent anonymous reviews from *Women & Politics* and *Comparative Political Studies*. Finally, the reviewers of this manuscript gave me stunningly brilliant advice. Special thanks to Rita Mae Kelly for engaging these reviewers and to Kate Manzo for her detailed comments.

Many people also helped me gather the information. Joyce Mohler of the Ohio University–Lancaster Library located obscure books. Adam Marsh of the Ohio University Office of Research and Sponsored Programs obtained the surveys from the Inter-university Consortium for Political and Social Research. Barry Garrett of Ohio University–Lancaster, and Chuck Rich, Bob Watkins, and Paul Kierns of the Ohio University Computing and Learning Services all guided me through the intricacies of the computer system. Before Ohio University joined the ICPSR, the Ohio State University Political Science department gave me access to these data through an appointment as adjunct professor. I'm now examining trend data not available through the ICPSR; the Ohio University Research Committee helped finance my trip to the Norwegian and Swedish Social Science Data Services, and the Ohio University–Lancaster Research Committee partially covered my expenses at the Roper Center for Public Opinion Research at Storrs, Connecticut. The Women's Studies Program at the University of Connecticut particularly facilitated my visit to the Roper Center.

Finally, thanks to all those who helped me prepare this manuscript: Eric Heyne for his outstanding advice on composition, Pat Sain for her skill in word processing, and Brad Bates and Gary Lockwood for helping design and draft the figures. The Ohio University–Lancaster Research Committee covered some of the expenses of preparing this manuscript. I'm also deeply grateful to the University for giving me released time to work on this book and to my fellow faculty who shouldered part of my teaching load without complaint.

I dedicate this book to the Women's Caucus for Political Science. Without the encouragement of my fellow caucus members, this book would never have been written. Their granting me the Sophonisba P. Breckinridge Award came at a particularly critical point in my career. Some day a book needs to be written on the instrumental role played by the caucus in promoting research on women and politics.

1

Introduction

This book examines the common assumption that sex differences in political participation are diminishing worldwide, or, in other words, that women's political activity is approaching that of men's. At first glance, this assumption appears correct. Certainly the twentieth century has seen the near universal eradication of legal prohibitions against women's voting and office holding. Traditional attitudes decreeing politics an inappropriate activity for women also appear to be weakening. However, quite large sex differences in political participation still exist. For example, Kim, Nie, and Verba (1974) find that for India, Japan, Nigeria, and Austria, sex is still the most important correlate of political participation, more important than either place of residence or socioeconomic status. Lafferty (1978) reports similar findings for certain types of political participation in Norway. Moreover, elite levels of elective and appointive office everywhere show an enormous discrepancy between the ideals of political equality and the reality of women's massive underrepresentation.

Sex differences in political participation are an important indicator of women's status. Political participation describes a diverse array of activities designed to influence governmental decision making. These activities include voting, working in campaigns and in political parties, local community activity, and even violent protesting. Such activities have instrumental import, promoting or defending individuals' interests and generally giving them more control over their lives. Historically, the West has resisted giving women such power, women's interests being considered identical to those of husband or father. Thus, the barriers to women's voting fell relatively late in comparison to those excluding women from higher education and certain professions. Political participation has normative import as well. Classical democratic theorists saw political participation as a good in itself, and Western democratic culture's idealization of participant citizens reflects this view (Parry 1980; Kendrigan 1984, pp. 9–10). Ultimately, sex differences in political participation touch upon the power relationship between men and women. The broader issue, then, is whether power is becoming more equitably distributed between the sexes.

The corollary to the optimistic assumption that sex differences are diminishing is the belief that they will continue to do so in the future. But any solid predictions must be based on a precise understanding of why change occurs, rather than a vague assumption that past trends will probably continue. The goal of this study is to determine exactly why sex differences in political participation change (or fail to change), so that future trends may be estimated more precisely. This chapter presents several models of how sex differences in political participation diminish, and discusses the methods used to test the accuracy of those models.

The Models and Their Significance

The Development, Generational, and Diffusion Models

Three models detail how sex differences in political participation can diminish. The development model holds that economic development (specifically, urbanization, industrialization, increased affluence and education) reduces these sex differences. The generational model proposes that the sex differences narrow as younger, more egalitarian generations of women replace older, more traditional generations. The diffusion model posits that sex differences shrink as more modern egalitarian attitudes diffuse from urban, higher status, and younger groups out to more rural, lower status, and older populations.

While the political participation literature frequently alludes to these three models, the models themselves represent my synthesis of the literature. Note that all the ways that sex differences in political participation can narrow are not included in the models. All three, however, share common assumptions that distinguish them from other explanations of change: first, that sex differences have diminished regularly in the past; second, that these differences will continue to diminish in the future as economies develop, as younger generations replace older ones, and as egalitarian attitudes spread throughout the entire population.

According to the development model, women's opportunities and resources for political participation are augmented by the processes associated with economic development. Economic development also stimulates more egalitarian attitudes about women's political role. Milbrath and Goel's compendium of research on political participation covers very fully the effects on women of urbanization, industrialization, and the concomitant diminution of the primary sector.

Women from families engaged in primary economic activity (agriculture, forestry, fishing) are much less likely to participate in politics. Women in a primary economy tend to stay close to home and often are involved in production. This not only leaves little time for politics, but also limits social interaction to family members. . . . An additional factor is that primary economies tend to be more tradition-oriented, and it is a strong tradition to think of politics as "man's work." As a greater proportion of the economic activity in a locality becomes secondary and tertiary, the differences in participation between men and women are reduced. (1977, p. 107)

Similar statements as to how urbanization and industrialization narrow sex differences occur in Duverger (1955, p. 42), Verba (1965), Rokkan (1970, p. 378), Haavio-Mannila (1970), R. Inglehart (1977, pp. 228–29), and Haavio-Mannila et al. (1985, p. 49).

Urbanization and industrialization generally correlate with increased affluence, and increased affluence also acts to lessen the physical and cultural constraints on women's political activity. According to Duverger,

It would seem that the preoccupation with family and domestic life, which is over-burdening among women of the poorer classes, forms an obstacle to outside interest and to the development of political consciousness. With a rise in the income level, this economic social pressure lessens, and integration into a social unit larger than the family becomes easier. In the particular case of women, as in general, the emergence of real political freedom is thus linked up with a rise in the standard of living. (1955, p. 154)

Lipset (1963, p. 206) and Lane (1965, pp. 215, 224) also mention that a higher standard of living provides women with resources for political participation such as leisure time.

Finally, education levels rise with economic development, and the literature frequently observes that increased education narrows sex differences in political participation. The explanations imply a distinction (often not explicit) between two different processes. One is that increased education particularly stimulates women's activity, for instance, by fostering more egalitarian attitudes about women's political role. As Duverger remarks, "Women who have had a higher education have much less restrictive and conventional ideas of what is suitable for a woman as regards to political activities." (1955, p. 187) The second possibility is that economic development decreases sex differences in education. Education heightens political interest and political skills and correlates strongly with political activity. Thus a diminution in sex differences in education denotes a more equitable distribution of an important resource for political participation. Those who identify rising education levels as reducing sex differences in political participation include Almond and Verba (1963, p. 399), Di Palma (1970, pp. 133–37), Pomper (1975, p. 70), Barnes (1977, p. 87), Brody (1978), and Baxter and Lansing (1983, pp. 24–27).

In sum, the development model explains the connection between economic development and smaller sex differences in political participation through two corollaries. First, development more equitably distributes participatory resources and opportunities, such as leisure time and education. Second, it weakens traditional cultural norms decreeing that politics is an inappropriate concern for women.

The generational model presumes that women's enfranchisement caused generational differences among women. Specifically, women who became adults before being enfranchised have been schooled in the traditional view that politics is exclusively a male preserve. Consequently, after enfranchisement they resist adopting more egalitarian political attitudes and more participatory roles. In contrast, younger generations of women, less exposed to these traditional norms, feel less hesitant about being active in politics. Thus, as the older, pre-franchise generation dies and is replaced by younger, post-franchise generations, sex differences in political participation will narrow. References to this generational model appear in Duverger (1955, p. 191), Campbell, et al. (1960, pp. 485–88), Butler and Stokes (1969, p. 50), Pomper (1975, p. 70), Brody (1978), M. Inglehart (1979), and Lovenduski and Hills (1981, p. 323).

Broader versions of the generational model allow events other than women's enfranchisement to affect women's political role. Factors hypothesized as having a generational impact include economic development (Di Palma 1970, p. 137), wars (Lansing 1970, pp. 95, 112; Holter 1971), social movements such as feminism (Andersen 1975, among many others), and more general changes in women's role (Rapoport 1981; Rapoport 1982). However, events do not always inculcate more egalitarian political attitudes into impressionable younger generations of women. For example, the German Nazi movement promulgated traditional views of women's role. These broader explanations thus imply that generational turnover does not universally act to reduce sex differences in political participation. However, this study will mainly test the more narrow and optimistic version of the generational model, that focusing on the generational impact of women's enfranchisement.

The diffusion model predicates that change occurs independently of the economic and demographic changes discussed above. *The American Voter* describes this process most precisely. The enfranchisement of women, the authors begin, initiated the diffusion of more egalitarian attitudes about women's political role. Specifically,

We would presume that a shift of role definition of this sort would have its genesis within the most educated strata of society. Subsequently it would ramify slowly downward through the status hierarchy and outward geographically from the more cosmopolitan center to increasingly remote areas of the nation. (Campbell et al. 1960, p. 485)

This explanation simply applies more general diffusion theories developed by social scientists. These theories hold that innovations are first adopted by the young and those at the urban and higher status center of society. Adoption then diffuses outward to the rural and lower status periphery and upward to the older segments of the population. Specification of the precise rate of change involves additional variables dealing with such factors as how the innovations are communicated and whether there exist physical or social barriers to the communications process. (See, for example, Rogers [1983], Brown and Moore [1969], Mahajan and Peterson [1985], and such applications to women's political behavior as Poole and Zeigler [1981] and Hernes [1980].)

There are important similarities between the diffusion model on the one hand and the generational and development models on the other. Specifically, all three models assume that sex differences in political participation are smaller among urban, higher status, and younger populations than among their rural, lower status, and older counterparts. However, the models offer different prognoses for the rate of change. The development and generational models hold that change is a function of their specified economic and demographic changes, while the diffusion model sees change as occurring independently of and at a rate even more rapid than that predicted by economic and demographic factors. Underlying these different prognoses for the rate of change are different assumptions about the constraints on women's political activity. For the diffusion model, traditional attitudes are the primary constraint. However, these attitudes are considered relatively mutable. In contrast, the development and generational models identify the constraints as more than simply attitudinal; they take into account women's lesser resources, skills, and opportunities for political participation. Of course, these models are not mutually exclusive. The two processes can interact— for example, lack of resources and opportunities for political participation can block diffusion effects among certain groups (Campbell et al. 1960, p. 488)—or, change can occur concurrently through both diffusion and economic and demographic changes.

The most significant prediction of all three models is that sex differences will invariably narrow, as ideas spread, newer generations replace older ones, and, over the long run, economies develop. Other theories are less sanguine. For example, women's influx into the work force is often said to be reducing sex differences; but in some countries women's participation in the economy is actually shrinking, which would presumably widen sex differences. Since the diffusion, generational, and development models offer such sweeping and elegant predictions, measuring their accuracy will be the starting point for this book's attempt to make precise predictions about the future.

Modernization Theory and Its Critics

The question of whether economic development, generational turnover, and diffusion do indeed narrow political participation sex differences relates to a broader controversy—that over the impact of economic and social modernization on women's general status. During the 1950s and 1960s the optimistic belief that such modernization elevated women's status pervaded the academic literature. But in the late 1960s feminist scholars began to challenge these assumptions. The feminists have since found allies in Marxist scholars, who do not ascribe to a linear view of progress in the first place, and certain third world scholars, who reject the implicit optimism of development theories. In short, the question of narrowing political participation sex differences has deep roots in more general philosophical and political disagreements.

This section will first describe this general controversy and then specify its relevance to the three models of change. Note that the scholars cited here often do not fit as neatly into either the optimistic camp or a critical camp, as they may appear to do in this necessarily abbreviated discussion.

The optimistic viewpoint stems from what is often called modernization theory (Lapidus 1974; Kelly and Boutilier 1978, chap. 2; Jaquette 1982; and Marshall 1984). This theory, itself an outgrowth of functionalism, contrasts modern and traditional societies in terms of general values. It holds that economic development generally promotes modern values, and some modern values—such as rationality, universalism, and achievement—lessen gender inequality. Modernization theory's discussion of women's status is not elaborate, nor is modernization necessarily envisioned as creating full equality between the sexes. Yet the theory does voice optimistic expectations of women's progress. Moreover, these expectations have a political foundation. As Jaquette notes, modernization theory's treatment of women "reflects the general liberal assumptions about development: that it is a linear, cumulative process, that it is expansionist and diffusionist. . . ." (1982, p. 268). Our three models of change clearly fall in the optimistic tradition of modernization theory.

The social science literature offers two specific explanations of how economic development promotes more egalitarian gender roles. The first is that development reduces the importance of biological differences between the sexes. For example, industrialization and machine technology increase the value of intellectual skills, where the sexes are more similar, while decreasing that of muscular strength. Also, development lessens the need for numerous progeny while simultaneously modern medicine increases women's longevity and allows them greater control over reproduction. Thus women spend less of their lifetime bearing and rearing children.

The second explanation is that economic development changes the institution of the family. The nature of these changes is rather complex and controversial. For example, Goode's thesis that with industrialization the nuclear, conjugal family replaces the extended family has encountered opposition (Osmond 1981). Nor is it certain that the establishment of the nuclear family uniformly raises women's status (Meguro and Morioka 1983; Lovenduski and Hills 1981, p. 321; Oppong 1983). However, some specific changes in family organization do improve women's status. For example, the geographic mobility accompanying development alters patrilocal families into neo-local ones, so that men no longer benefit by proximity to kin. Also, when wealth becomes liquid, inheritance can change from patrilineal to bilateral, flowing down to daughters and not simply to sons (Chafetz, 1980).[1]

The social science literature also may associate development with more general cultural change. For instance, Cavalli (1983) observes that industrialization stimulates egalitarian ideals, such as aspirations for more equality between the sexes and the belief that society should provide equal educational and occupational opportunities. Another correlate of economic development, at least in the West, is individualism. And individualism gives impetus to laws awarding women political and civil rights formerly reserved for male family heads (Stacey and Price 1981, pp. 44, 77). Finally, development is assumed to increase the availability of resources and to diminish threats from the physical environment, creating an increased sense of personal security that may especially benefit women (Masters 1983; Chafetz 1980).

Critics attack the optimistic belief that economic development elevates women's status from several different traditions. For example, Marxists hold that while economic development is a potentially liberating force, capitalist development actually lowers women's status. Starting with the observation that industrialization and the factory system accentuate the male-female division of labor, Marxists see harmful consequences resulting from redefining unpaid domestic labor as women's work and paid labor away from home as men's work. Women's unpaid domestic work becomes devalued, and the low wages women receive for work outside the home reflect this general devaluation (Kaplan 1974; Sacks 1975). However, Marxists say a socialist economy that eliminates this sexual division of labor would allow women to benefit from the fruits of economic development alongside men.

The Marxist theorists also have critics. Some scholars find that culture or government policies strongly affect women's status in socialist economies, so much so that neither economic development nor a socialist economic structure are sufficient for liberating women (Jancar 1978, p. 28; Harasymiw 1980; Wolchick 1981; Lapidus 1974). From a more theoretical perspective, socialist feminists see both economic and cultural forces oppressing women. The oppressive cultural forces are sometimes summed up by the term *patriarchy* (Eisenstein 1979; Rubin 1975; Stacey and Price 1981, p. 177). It is important to note that neither the Marxists nor their critics hold that economic development per se lowers women's status. Rather, both see other factors as more decisively affecting women's status, whether they be the ownership of the means of production, cultural norms, or government policies.

Another strand of criticism comes from recent studies of women's status in third world nations. This new scholarship views modernization theory as Eurocentric, that is, based on Western historical experiences which are not replicable in the third world (Wiarda

1983). Most criticized is the implicit assumption that women's status is higher in the West than in third world nations and that westernization is an emancipating force for third world women. Critics who challenge these assumptions find women's status to be quite elevated in some third world cultures. These studies also document how women's status can decline in third world countries, although explanations for this decline vary, ranging from colonial policy to Western development assistance policies, exploitation by international capitalism, or policies promulgated by indigenous rulers.[2]

The literature on women's position in India and Nigeria illustrates these themes. India and Nigeria are used as examples because I later present survey data on sex differences in political participation for these two nations.

Prior to the colonial era, Nigerian women, along with Western African women in general, enjoyed a relatively high status. Although the situation varied somewhat from tribe to tribe, women usually possessed a great deal of economic autonomy and political power. West African societies were characterized by a strict sexual division of labor. In addition to farming, women in some tribal cultures also controlled trade and the markets. They could either participate directly in politics through their own self-governing institutions or else influence men's institutions through their own representatives and well-developed women's organizations. Although women were certainly not politically equal to men in this precolonial period, their fairly high political status dropped markedly under colonial rule. For example, the British did not recognize female political institutions and also excluded women from all levels of administration. The literature disagrees as to whether independence allowed women to recoup any of these losses, but concurs that women's political influence today is less than in the precolonial era. (Okonjo 1976; Awe 1977; Njoku 1980; Van Allen 1976b; Mba 1982, chaps. 1,2; Howard 1985).

Colonialism had a detrimental effect on other aspects of women's status as well. Women, particularly nonelite women, lost ground economically. While women continued working in subsistence agriculture, men took up cash crops; women were also confined to small-scale trading while men moved into the large-scale distribution and retail trade and into governmental and corporate positions as well. Male migration to urban areas also tended to isolate women in the static, traditional sector of the economy. Urban women, on the other hand, lost the benefits of contact with women's associations and kin and found few job opportunities in the modern sector.

Due to the expenses of schooling and Victorian missionary mores, women were not provided with the Western education necessary for key positions in a modern economy. In short, women became increasingly economically marginalized (Mba 1982, chap. 2; Van Allen 1976b; Remy 1975; Sacks 1982).

Again the literature shows differences in interpretation. For example, Mba (1982, chap. 2) notes some beneficial changes, specifically through the rise of indigenous Christian organizations where women play a leading role and through British-inspired legal reforms. But Sacks (1982) mentions that these legal reforms removed women's access to farmland and increased husbands' authority over wives, and Remy (1975) details the extensive economic exploitation of women continuing today. All writers, nevertheless, agree that women's economic and social status tended to decline with the commercialization of agriculture, industrialization, urbanization, and the introduction of Western education.

In contrast to Nigeria, women's precolonial status in India is usually described as rather low (e.g. Narain 1967). British rule instituted certain legal reforms which clearly benefited women, such as the bans against child marriage and suttee, or widow burning. Western influence sparked the Indian women's suffrage movement and demands for other reforms as well (Everett 1979). However, recent scholarship has uncovered evidence of a deterioration in certain aspects of women's status in the twentieth century, especially among nonelite women. A very disquieting finding is the increase in the ratio of men to women, contrary to the usual tendency observed with economic development. Women's economic value may be declining, reflecting the displacement of women from agricultural, industrial, and trading occupations, the demise of household industries, and the increased incidence and cost of dowrys. Although the data are mixed, sex differences at some levels of education may be increasing as well. (See, for example, Government of India, *Towards Equality* 1974; Mazumdar 1979; Lateef 1981; Mukhopadhyay 1984; D'Souza and Natarajan 1986.)

These examples suggest that different and contradictory processes may be at work across third world nations. One possibility is that the effect of colonialism and westernization varies according to the precolonial status of women. The impact may be largely positive in nations where women's status was generally low but more negative in cultures where women possessed significant economic and political power, such as in West Africa and Southeast Asia (Smock 1977b; Leghorn and Parker 1981, pp. 53–54; Blumberg 1978, pp. 109–10)

Another possibility is that specific processes associated with *late* development lower women's status. According to Sanday (1981), women's status is lowest during periods of cultural disruption and stress; certainly colonialism and contact with Western cultures have greatly stressed third world cultures. Or, it may be that international capitalism's economic exploitation of late developing nations most oppresses women, a tenet of dependency theory which Marshall analyzes (1984).

Governments play a leading social and economic role in late developing nations and may themselves depress women's status. For example, Marshall (1984) finds that regime policies are more important determinants of women's status in North Africa than economic ones. She observes that political problems in these nations tempt political elites to preserve or reinstate traditional gender roles. Plagued by questions of legitimacy or by resistance to extensive social reorganization, elites often find it expedient to retain the "core primordial symbols, such as women and the family," to reassure threatened population groups and to generate national unity (Marshall 1984, p. 517). In a similar vein, Lateef (1981) argues that India's democratization has heightened the political value of communal ties and thus of maintaining community through traditional or ritualistic means. Because women are the primary tool used to maintain group cohesion, through marriage and ritual, their traditional status is preserved or even accentuated. Finally, Howard (1985) observes that leaders tend to scapegoat women in times of crisis.

Neither Marxist nor third world interpretations see declines in women's status as caused by economic development per se but rather by certain correlates of the development process. However, in an analysis too lengthy to summarize here, Ivan Illich perceives economic development as the direct cause of these declines.

[E]conomic development is intrinsically and irremediably gender-destructive—that is, sexist—[and] the sexism can be reduced only at the "cost" of economic shrinkage. Further, the decline of sexism requires, as a necessary albeit insufficient condition, the contraction of the cash nexus and the expansion of nonmarket-related, noneconomic forms of subsistence. (1982, p. 385)

Echoes of this controversy over modernization theory even appear in anthropological studies of preindustrial cultures. There scholars are similarly divided over the determinants of women's status, this division sometimes taking the form of Marxists versus non-Marxists (Atkinson 1982). Specific explanations for variations in women's *political* status also emphasize different factors. Some focus on economic factors, particularly their effect on women's contribution to subsistence and women's control over their production (e.g. Chafetz 1980). Others emphasize the importance of female solidarity groups or various other nonmaterial factors (e.g. Azmon 1981; M. Welch 1983; Ross 1983). The complexity of these explanations increases, Rosaldo (1980) and Whyte (1978) report, because the various indicators of women's status, political or otherwise, are not closely related.

The development, generational, and diffusion models employ processes of change encompassed by modernization theory but only explain one specific indicator of women's status, sex differences in political participation. These differences have not been specifically examined in the debate over modernization theory, for women's status is discussed in much more general terms. Therefore, a test of those models will have important consequences for the larger controversy over the real benefits to women of modernization. As the critics have indicated, any such test must include third world and socialist countries as well as those in the first world. Of course, there are other indicators of power beside political participation, for power can be wielded at both mass and elite levels, and in social, economic, and domestic spheres, as well as political. And power, although important, is only one measure of status. Nevertheless, precisely because the models of change are narrow in scope, they provide a relatively concrete empirical test of the larger claims of modernization theory.[3]

Interestingly, although modernization theory is widely discredited, these three models remain influential. This is probably because they are strongly supported by a cursory glance at the available data. However, as this study will demonstrate, the empirical foundations for the models have never been systematically and comprehensively examined.

In short, this study's critical examination of the development, generational, and diffusion models has important implications not only for predicting the future of women's political participation, but also for the broader controversy over the benefits of "progress." If the models hold up, we may need to take another look at some of the discredited claims of modernization theory. Another possibility is that no general theory can explain all changes in women's status because the various indicators are weakly interrelated. In any event, this study will also have important practical implications. If the models are correct—if women's status is automatically improving through broad demographic and economic changes—then an argument can be made for complacency, for waiting on the inevitable effects of time. If, however, the models are wrong, such complacency could actually widen the gap in political participation, and the proponents of activism have a much stronger case.

The Research Design

Types of Data

Only trend data can adequately test the three models of change. If sex differences in political participation fail to narrow over time, then none of the three models are correct. If differences do narrow, then the trends must be examined among certain sociodemographic groups: age cohorts to investigate the generational model, and groups varying by education, income, occupation, and place of residence to probe the development model. If differences no longer diminish in these sociodemographic groups, then the results support the generational and development models. But if they still continue to narrow, with change occurring first among urban, higher status, and younger groups, then the diffusion model is upheld. This initial test must then be followed by further inquiry into the processes of change. Specifically, trends in attitudes about women's political role and the distribution of participatory resources must be identified and tested for their relevance to the changes in political participation sex differences *within* the various sociodemographic groups.

Reliable trend data, unfortunately, are quite scarce. Most of the publications on trends in sex differences in political participation are limited either to one nation, the United States (e.g. Baxter and Lansing 1983; Andersen 1975; Wassenberg et al. 1983), or to one type of political participation, voter turnout (e.g. Tingsten 1937; Duverger 1955). Yet voter turnout is a unique and unrepresentative type of political participation, as I will later document. There are more obscure sources of information on trends; publications of commercial polling firms do sometimes report political participation broken down by sex. Regrettably, they generally do not break these sex differences down further, either by age or by socioeconomic factors. Thus, these commercial data do not permit any direct test of the three models of change.

This study will examine trend data for several types of political participation and from two nations, the United States and the Federal Republic of Germany. These data are of limited use, because both nations are highly developed economically and enfranchised women early after World War I. No good trend data are currently available from third world nations or nations enfranchising women more recently. Moreover, there is only scanty information on U.S. and German trends in attitudes toward women's political roles and in the distribution of participatory resources. Thus the processes underlying changes in sex differences in political participation cannot be thoroughly explored.

Because of these limits in the trend data, the models will also be tested with nontrend data, which were actually the original basis for the models. Two types of nontrend data were used: variations in sex differences in political participation *across* nations, and variations among certain sociodemographic groups *within* nations. Note that while nontrend data permit the examination of more diverse types of nations and political participation, they also require making certain nonverifiable assumptions about the processes of change over time.

Cross-national variations in sex differences in political participation provide one test of the models. The development model holds that these sex differences are smaller in more economically developed nations. Presumably, differences will diminish as the economies of the less-developed nations become more like those of the developed ones. This reasoning is evident in Milbrath and Goel's compendium of research in political participation. Finding that sex differences are smaller in the United States than in less-developed nations, the authors conclude that "economic and social modernization is slowly eroding this sex difference. . . ." (1977, p. 117). The generational and diffusion models assume that sex differences are smallest in nations enfranchising women earliest. Differences in the late-enfranchising nations will supposedly narrow with generational turnover and diffusion.

Publications employing cross-national data currently provide an inadequate test of the models. Most surveys come from developed nations, such as the United States or those of Western Europe. Yet the literature reviewed above suggests that the processes may work quite differently in third world and even second world nations. For these countries other, less appropriate data are usually substituted for survey data on mass political behavior. For example, two discussions of the impact of economic development on sex differences in political activity, across Latin America (Aviel 1981) and across Western and Eastern Europe (Wolchik 1981), must primarily use data on women's employment, education, and access to elite political positions. Information on mass political behavior is either not available or else fragmentary. Even in first world nations, where survey data are more readily available, comparison may be difficult; only a few studies have been designed to be cross-nationally comparable. Regrettably, the major reports of the specially designed cross-national studies do not systematically test any of the models when discussing sex differences (e.g. Almond and Verba 1963, chap. 13; Verba, Nie, and Kim 1978, chap. 12; Barnes, Kaase, et al. 1979; Jennings and Farah 1980).

This study investigates variations in sex differences across fourteen nations which vary widely in both their economic development levels and the length of time women have been enfranchised. However, these data still provide only a partial test of the three models of change. The sample's imperfections will be discussed later. Moreover, the results may appear to support the models when, in fact, they do not. A correlation between either development or early enfranchisement and smaller sex differences may be spurious, the result of some underlying factor. Also, the situation for early developing or early enfranchising countries may have been quite different from that now encountered by late-developing and late-enfranchising nations. Thus, there is no guarantee that processes of change in the latter countries will imitate those in the former.

Variations in sex differences within nations allow an additional test of the models. In contrast to the cross-national data, comparison within nations reduces the effect of a particular culture and political system. The development model will be indirectly supported by finding that sex differences are smaller among more-educated, affluent, urban, and nonfarm occupational groups. The generational model is supported when differences are smaller among those younger generations in which women have always been allowed to vote alongside their male contemporaries. As these groups grow in size with economic development and generational turnover, sex differences will presumably diminish. Again, however, other factors may be at work. For instance, diffusion processes may temporarily cause sex differences in political participation to be smaller at the urban, higher-status center and among the young. In general, as with the cross-national data, imputing causes on within-nation data taken at one point in time involves certain nonverifiable inferences.

Although data on within-nation variations in sex differences are the most widely available, the published information still tests the models inadequately. Many references to the models use observations from only one nation. Also, the published results are contradictory, for frequently sex differences in political participation fail to diminish as expected by the three models. For example, Verba, Nie, and Kim's study of seven nations differing widely in economic development levels reveals that only in the United States do sex differences diminish uniformly with increased education (1978, pp. 237–45). In Kenya, a survey finds that sex differences are actually larger among higher status respondents (Ross and Thadani 1980). The Commission on the Status of Women in India also reports no relationship between different indicators of modernization and women's participation (Government of India, *Towards Equality* 1974, p. 291). All too often surveys revealing no change or increased sex differences in political activity at the center of society and among the young go unremarked. In fact, some studies allude to the models even when the data fail to support their allusions (Christy 1980, pp. 14–16). This study examines within-nation variations from fourteen nations; this more systematic and comprehensive approach permits a more precise understanding of how the data support or fail to support the models.

In sum, due to limitations in trend data, change over time is inferred from data that actually measure variations across space (e.g. nations, place of residence) or in individual attributes (e.g. education, age). The three models were originally developed on the basis of these within-nation and cross-national data, and unfortunately we are still subject to the same limitations on information.

The Surveys

Table 1.1 presents the nations and surveys examined here. The Inter-University Consortium for Political and Social Research distributes these surveys. The cross-national and within-nation data originate from three types of studies: national election studies from seven nations; the Verba, Nie, and Kim seven-nation study conducted between 1967 and 1971; and the Barnes and Kaase eight-nation study conducted between 1973 and 1976. Altogether 27 separate surveys are examined. The trend data come primarily from fifteen national election studies of the United States and Germany from the early 1950s to 1980. This section will summarize the general methodological points; Appendix A provides additional details.

Ideally, the countries in this study should be selected randomly from all nations. In practice, availability of data largely governed the choice of nations. Because survey data for developing nations are quite scarce, the countries investigated here are disproportionately first world. The cross-national sample does nevertheless

Table 1.1
The Surveys and the Years They Were Administered

The Cross-National and Within Nation Data

	National Election Studies	Barnes and Kaase	Verba, Nie and Kim
The United States	1976 & 1980	1974	1967
Great Britain	1963-64 & 1974	1973-74	
West Germany	1972 & 1976	1974-75	
Italy	1968 & 1972	1975-76	
The Netherlands		1974	1971
Austria		1974	1969
Finland		1975	
Switzerland		1975-76	
Norway	1965		
France	1958 & 1967		
Japan	1967		1967
Yugoslavia			1971
Nigeria			1966
India			1967

The Trend Data (National Election Studies)

The United States	1952, 1956, 1960, 1964, 1968, 1972, 1976, 1980
West Germany	1953, 1961, 1965, 1969, 1972, 1976, 1980

Note: These surveys provide the data for all the tables and figures except Table 2.3. Appendix A further describes the surveys.

include two developing nations, Nigeria and India, and one socialist nation, Yugoslavia. Although this sample is certainly not representative of all nations, Table 2.1 later documents that the selected countries at least have widely different levels of economic development and times of enfranchising women. Moreover, this study does provide a fairly representative sample of first world nations, one that permits generalizations based on the "most similar systems design." Interpretations drawn from studies of second and third world nations must be suggestive only; firm generalizations await more data.

Note that the surveys in the cross-national sample were conducted at different points in time, ranging from 1958 for a French national election study, to 1980 for an election study of the United States. These variations in survey dates should not compromise the test of the models. The measures of the independent variables either come from the same survey or represent the same year the survey was administered. Moreover, trend data indicate that variations across nations are generally larger than those over time in a single nation. Thus, the cross-national variations presented here are probably not greatly discrepant from what might be found with a perfectly contemporaneous cross-national study conducted in the early to middle 1970s.

The sampling frames of the surveys are almost always national in scope. However, the Nigerian sample excludes the Northern Region, where women were not enfranchised at the time of the survey and where Moslem traditions made it hard to obtain interviews from women. Most certainly sex differences in Nigeria would be larger if the Northern Region were included in the sample. The surveys of Yugoslavia and India also exclude certain regions, but, as Appendix A discusses, this exclusion probably did not distort the results presented here.

Several factors enhance the surveys' accuracy. First, the surveys were designed by scholars for research purposes. Thus the sample sizes (reported in Appendix A) are usually more than adequate, and the surveys generally were administered with particular care. The Barnes and Kaase and the Verba, Nie, and Kim studies were intentionally designed to study political participation and are landmarks in the field. Moreover, for eight nations, some survey results are replicated by at least one other survey. Replication permits determining whether the results are unique to a single survey, due to faulty sampling, the influence of events at the time of the interviewing, or other factors. Published results of other cross-national studies, such as those by Almond and Verba, by Inglehart and by Rabier, generally mirror the data presented here. Also, published information on trends usually supports this study's findings.

The Measures of the Variables

Figure 1.1 illustrates the variables examined in this study and the relationships between them as specified by the models. Economic

INDEPENDENT VARIABLES   INTERVENING VARIABLES   DEPENDENT VARIABLES

Economic Development

Industrialization
Urbanization
Increased affluence
Increased education

Sex Differences in
Participatory Resources

Work force participation
Voluntary association
   activity
Education
Affluence

Sex Differences in
Political Participation

Voting
Campaign activity
Communications activity
Unconventional activity
Communal activity
Contacting activity

Women's Enfranchisement

Egalitarian Attitudes
about Women's Political
Role
diffusion
generational turnover

Sex Differences in
Participatory Attitudes

Psychological involvement
   political interest
   partisanship
Political efficacy
   internal
   external

Figure 1.1
The Independent, Intervening, and Dependent Variables

19

development presumably narrows sex differences in political participation in two ways: by more equitably distributing resources for political participation, and by stimulating more egalitarian attitudes toward women's political role. The generational and diffusion models depend only on postulated changes in attitudes toward women's political role after enfranchisement.

This section explains these variables and discusses the important methodological and substantive issues associated with the measures. Appendix B provides additional details on the measures of the dependent and intervening variables, and Appendix C does the same for the independent variables. Two problems require particular attention. First, the variables are often measured by multiple indicators, which complicates analysis of the models. This procedure is required when the variable is composed of many weakly related dimensions, as with political participation. But then it becomes necessary to detail how each specific indicator relates to the models. Second, sometimes measures of the variables are unavailable (especially for the intervening variables). Of course, these two problems are only some of those inevitably encountered in comparative research which uses survey data.

The Dependent Variables: Types of Political Participation

The dependent variable, sex differences in political participation, involves many different and sometimes quite distinctive types of behavior. It may be that the models are more appropriate for some forms of participation than for others.

Electoral activity is the most commonly examined type of political participation. Electoral activities include *voting* and various *campaign activities* such as attending campaign meetings or working for a candidate or party. Since these campaign activities are often connected with political parties, party membership is treated here as another type of campaign activity. But note that political parties are important channels to elective and appointive office and so are more than simply a campaign activity. Examining women's representation in political parties is thus a key to understanding the link between sex differences in mass level activities and women's access to elite positions.

Institutional and political forces affect electoral activities. For example, voter turnout is strongly influenced by partisan organizations, the general political climate, and institutional factors such as registration procedures. In fact, individuals may be mobilized to vote despite their disinterest in politics and their avoidance of all other kinds of political participation. Political parties can mobilize individuals for various other types of electoral activity as well. However, these other types of activity are more difficult than voting and so reflect more closely individuals' psychological involvement levels (Verba, Nie, and Kim 1978, pp. 328–30, chap. 7).

This study will examine whether these political and institutional factors affect sex differences in electoral activity. If so, such factors would be relevant for predicting future trends. The literature does suggest this possibility. For instance, immediately after Italian women's enfranchisement the Catholic Church appears to have stimulated women's turnout. The combination of women's higher rates of church attendance, especially in rural areas, and the Church's active political role acted to produce unexpectedly small sex differences in voter turnout, notably so in the rural sector (Dogan 1959, p. 383; Porter and Venning 1976).

The literature also suggests that the rate of participation affects the magnitude of the sex differences. Tingsten first observed that the higher the turnout rate, the smaller the sex differences in voter turnout (1937, p. 230). Duverger later noted that the more elitist and restricted the political activity, the larger the sex differences (1955, pp. 122–23). However, both Tingsten's law and Duverger's law, as I shall call them, improperly contaminate the independent and dependent variables. That is, sex differences are smallest where turnout levels are highest precisely because electoral forces have mobilized all segments of the population, including the female half. In turn, sex differences are largest in more elitist political activities partly because political forces are not activating most individuals, again including the female half. An uncontaminated version of these laws involves comparing the sex differences with *men's* turnout rate or *men's* participation rate across the various types of electoral activity. Consequently, this study will test whether forces affecting men's rates of electoral activity also affect the sex differences.

Another commonly studied form of political participation is *communications activities*, such as following politics in the media or discussing politics. Since these types of political activity are not channeled through political institutions, they reflect more exclusively individuals' interest and psychological involvement in politics. If economic development, generational turnover, and diffusion processes reduce sex differences in psychological involvement, then these processes should also narrow sex differences in communications activities. Measures of communications activity examined here include: following politics in the broadcast and print media; discussing politics; and, a specialized form of discussion, soliciting votes for one's favored candidate or party.

Again, the models may provide limited or inaccurate explanations
— for variations in sex differences in communications activities. Pro-
— perties of specific types of communications modes may facilitate or
limit women's access. Or perhaps the magnitude of the sex dif-
— ferences may vary according to whether the communications flow is
one way (from media to individual) or two way (among individuals).
Almond and Verba find, for instance, that women are more likely
than men to report feeling constrained in discussing politics (1963,
p. 391). If such factors do affect women's communications activities,
then changes in these factors can affect the trends in the sex differences.

The term *unconventional political participation* includes such
diverse activities as petition drives, boycotts, and legal demonstrations as well as more aggressive types of behavior such as illegal
strikes or violent confrontations (Barnes, Kaase, et al. 1979; Muller
1979). Although women are more opposed to protests and demonstrations than men (Frieze et al. 1978, p. 344), it appears that sex differences in unconventional types of participation are generally
smaller than those in the conventional types (Barnes, Kaase, et al.
1979, p. 184; Jennings and Farah 1980). The sex differences are
smaller, the literature suggests, partly because women are more
highly motivated to participate in certain of these unconventional
types of activity. Also, women's lesser resources, opportunities, and
skills for political participation constrain conventional political activity more than unconventional. Finally, women face less discrimination in unconventional types of activity. Specific explanations
are presented below to indicate more precisely these additional factors not specified by the three models of change.

Some of the less aggressive types of unconventional participation,
such as citizen's movements and community action, frequently address issues quite relevant to traditional female concerns. For example, Japanese women, especially housewives, are very active in direct
action groups dealing with consumer, environmental, and local
issues (Hargadine 1981; Jones 1975; Jones 1976; Pharr 1977). In a
similar vein, North American, British, and Norwegian housewives
are particularly active in ad hoc, direct action movements focusing
on issues of local or community concern (Randall 1982, pp. 40–42, 63).

As for the more aggressive types of political activity, women have
long been active in revolutionary movements in developed and developing nations alike (Benson, Evans, and Simon 1982; Van Allen 1976a;
Rowbotham 1972). Among the nations examined in this book, women
have been very involved in the Yugoslavian partisan movement (Jancar 1978, pp. 113–14), the Indian civil disobedience movement (Luthra

1976; Basu 1976; Minault 1981; Ghosh 1985) and the Nigerian independence movement (Johnson 1982). Nigeria provides the most extraordinary example, the "Women's War" of 1929, a massive, widespread,
lengthy, and sometimes violent confrontation between women and the
colonial administration. This confrontation is only the most striking instance of Nigeria's tradition of women organizing to protect their interests (Mba 1982, chap. 3; Leith-Ross 1965; Van Allen 1976b; Wipper
1982). Explanations offered for women's involvement in these types of
activity range from the remarkable organizational resources of Nigerian women to Indian men's influence over their female kin. More
generally, constraints against women's political activity may break
down during periods of political disarray (Ergas 1982; Jancar 1978).
Also, these unconventional activities may not demand the same high
level of skills and resources necessary for many types of conventional
activity. Gandhi's argument that women are particularly suited for
civil disobedience campaigns because of their patience and ability to
suffer (Basu 1976) underlines this point. That is, smaller sex differences in unconventional political activity need not correlate
positively with a higher status for women in general.

Sex differences in *communal activity*, that is, participation in local
community affairs, may also be relatively small. Partly this is
because the issues considered at local levels, such as education, are
often compatible with traditional female roles (Shaul 1982; Jennings
1979; Reid and Wormald 1982, pp. 187–202). Also, the nonpartisan
and less overtly political nature of these issues may bypass traditional attitudinal constraints against women's political activity. Local
nonpartisan organizations with proportionately large female memberships, such as housewives' organizations in Japan or a variety of
social and cultural organizations in Eastern Europe, often channel
their members toward communal political activity (Jones 1976; Wolchik 1978, p. 122; Denich 1977). Thus, variations in sex differences in
communal political participation may be affected by such factors as
the content and partisan nature of the issues and the types of
organizations stimulating communal activity.

The literature scarcely mentions sex differences in *contacting activity*, that is, contacting government officials about a personal or
political concern. In the United States, sex differences are relatively
small in one form of this activity, particularized contacting, where
the contact involves a narrow concern affecting solely oneself or
one's family (Verba and Nie 1972, p. 99). Moreover, data from two
Latin American cities show no sex differences in particularized contacting (Biles 1983). But it is not known how gender affects social
contacting, that is, seeking assistance for friends or broader groups.

In sum, this section suggests that the three models of change may incompletely explain variations in sex differences in political participation. The additional factors affecting these sex differences vary by the type of political participation under examination. But for most types of participation, these additional factors indicate that sex differences need not diminish over time as the models expect. For example, the political forces particularly mobilizing female voters may weaken over time, or those issues that especially activate women into unconventional direct action movements may become less politically salient. The need is thus evident for more precise specification of the models' relevance to various types of political participation.

The Intervening Variables: Participatory Attitudes and Resources

Attitudes Toward Women's Political Role. All three models specify processes stimulating more egalitarian attitudes toward women's political role. Unfortunately, almost none of the surveys examined here include questions about such attitudes. Thus the models can be tested only indirectly, by using the results of other relevant studies and by inferring the presence of egalitarian attitudes from other attitudes.

Studies indicate that these attitudes are crucial for understanding sex differences in political participation. A belief that politics is an inappropriate concern for women strongly constrains women's political activity (Sapiro 1983; Christy 1980; Hansen, Franz, and Netemeyer-Mays 1976). This belief can be surprisingly widespread, as with a majority of the population in early postwar Germany and Italy (Christy 1980, p. 144). Moreover, traditional norms can remain strong even in nations with officially egalitarian ideologies, such as in Poland (Siemienska 1983). Even in remarkably egalitarian Norway, *latent* traditional attitudes and a more general "female culture" may inhibit women's political participation (Holter 1967; Lafferty 1980).

Very little has been published on how such attitudes change over time. Most studies are of the United States, and these findings will be summarized in Chapter 4. Since the 1970s, however, analyses have been published for the nations of the European Economic Community as well (Commission of the European Communities 1975 and Rabier 1979). Although these studies examine generational and diffusion effects, their analyses often cover factors such as particular social movements, which are not included in the three models of change. Moreover, some imply that economic factors have little relevance for explaining variations in these attitudes. Indirect evidence suggests that variations across Europe reflect events as far in the past as the Reformation (M. Inglehart 1981), and that these attitudes are passed down through succeeding generations by socialization (Jennings 1983).

In this study, *sex differences in psychological involvement* and *political efficacy* will serve as indirect measures of more general cultural norms about women's political role. Women who are taught that politics is a man's concern show less interest in politics and are less politically efficacious, that is, less confident in their being able to influence government decision makers (Christy 1980, pp. 235–41). In turn, psychological involvement and political efficacy correlate strongly with many types of political participation. Thus, more egalitarian attitudes toward women's political role should diminish sex differences in both these participatory attitudes and political activity. The general issue, then, is whether sex differences in psychological involvement and political efficacy are shrinking with economic development, generational turnover, and diffusion.

There are actually several different measures of both psychological involvement and political efficacy. This study examines two components of psychological involvement: one, self-declared interest in politics; and two, partisanship, that is, the extent and strength of identification with a political party. Other aspects of psychological involvement, such as interest in the election campaign and concern over the outcome of the election, are only briefly discussed here. Political efficacy has two components, termed internal political efficacy and external political efficacy. Following Craig and Maggiotto (1982), internal efficacy refers to confidence in one's political understanding and one's general political competence, and external political efficacy denotes confidence in the responsiveness of the political system to one's needs. Also discussed here are attitudes related to political efficacy. Measures of external political efficacy shade into opinions about the fairness, honesty, and competence of government, sometimes termed political cynicism or its obverse, political trust. The Verba, Nie, and Kim measures of efficacy examined here appear to tap aspects of both internal and external efficacy when they ask individuals to rate their political influence in comparison to others.

Resources for Political Participation. The development model holds that economic development also narrows sex differences in those resources that are important for political activity. Regrettably, the surveys examined here contain only some limited measures of such resources. Particularly lacking is information on gender roles, specifically women's domestic and child rearing responsibilities and how they affect leisure time and social interaction outside the family. The surveys include no direct measures of available leisure time and extra-familial contacts. Not many even have data on factors that affect these resources, such as the presence of children in the home, the division of labor in the household, or the adult composition of the household.

The rare studies that have been made on the impact of economic development on women's leisure time and extra-familial contacts are contradictory. Child-rearing responsibilities do depress some types of political activity (Jennings and Niemi 1981, pp. 295–300; Lynn and Flora 1973; McGlen 1980; Sapiro 1983, chap. 3; Lafferty 1980; but also see Welch 1977). However while economic development certainly reduces the years women spend raising children, it may not necessarily free women for political activity. Studies of available leisure time in first and second world nations find little or no relationship between the sex differences and economic development (Wolchik 1981; Nuss 1981). Also, improved household technology has a mixed impact on reducing the time spent on housework (Bose, Bereano, and Malloy 1984).

This study will examine the effect of economic development on four factors frequently identified as stimulating political activity. Sex differences in work force participation and organizational activity are two indicators of the traditional sexual division of labor, one that locates women's work inside the home and men's work outside. Since political activity generally takes place outside the home, women who participate in the work force or organizations may also be more active in politics. The other two factors are education and affluence; the lack of these socioeconomic resources would surely reduce women's political activity.

The literature suggests that in fact some resources have more of an impact on political activity than others. Socioeconomic status, as represented by education and income, is one of the most important determinants of political activity (Verba, Nie, and Kim 1978; Milbrath and Goel 1977). Also, participation in voluntary associations strongly correlates with increased political participation (Verba, Nie, and Kim 1978, chaps. 6 and 7; Almond and Verba 1963, chap. 11; Listhaug and Kindseth 1979). Indeed, given the close ties between interest groups and government in certain nations, such as Norway, organizational participation, per se, is an important form of political participation (Lafferty 1978; Hernes and Voje 1980). However, the impact of work force participation on sex differences in political

participation is less certain. Employment lessens women's isolation
in the home, but it also reduces the time women have available for
political activity, particularly if employed women must shoulder
the double burden of domestic work and paid work. These contradictory effects appear in developing and developed nations alike,
and thus studies can arrive at quite divergent conclusions (e.g.
Devon 1980; Verba, Nie, and Kim 1978, pp. 263–65; Jennings and
Niemi 1981, pp. 301–3; Sapiro 1983, chap. 6; Mossuz-Lavau and
Sineau 1981 and 1983; Thomson and Eichler 1985). My study of
developed nations found that work force participation does narrow
sex differences, but only mildly (Christy 1983).

The literature is ambiguous about the impact of economic development on sex differences in these four resources. For *sex differences in work force participation*, the problem of defining and
measuring women's employment in developing nations is especially
difficult. There women's service as unpaid family workers is not
usually considered as work force participation, although this service is nevertheless important. Women, for example, produce and
prepare virtually all household food (Michel 1977). If employment is
broadly defined in developing nations, women are less represented
in the modern sector of the labor force than in these traditional occupations (Awosika 1981). The growth of the modern sector may
even widen sex differences in work force participation (Boserup
1970; Osmond 1981). Comparing first and third world nations with
standard measures of employment gives a somewhat different picture. Sex differences in work force participation are slightly smaller
in more developed nations than less developed ones (Nuss and Majka
1983). Yet development is only one relevant factor; traditional
cultural norms, regime policies, and the availability of jobs considered compatible with female roles are quite important influences
(Smock 1977a; Nuss and Majka 1983).

The literature also disagrees about the relationship between economic development and *sex differences in education*. Comparing the
proportion of illiterate women to illiterate men indicates that sex
differences are smaller in developed nations. Female illiterates ex-
ceed men by only 2 percent in developed nations but by roughly 20
percent in developing nations (Lindsay 1980). However, among
illiterates the ratio of females to males is greater in developed nations (Finn, Dulberg, and Reis 1979). Also, in developed and developing nations alike the proportion of students who are female drops
dramatically with increased levels of education. Thus, except
perhaps in the Soviet Union and Eastern Europe, women are underrepresented among university graduates and postgraduates (Finn,

Dulberg, and Reis 1979; Nuss 1980). Because the results depend on
the level of education examined, this study will use a measure that
includes all levels of education, namely sex differences in years of
schooling. Whether sex differences in years of schooling diminish
with economic development is still a question. It is certain, however, that regime policies and cultural norms do affect the sex differences independently of development levels (Smock 1977a).

Less is known about the relationship between development and *sex
differences in organizational activity*. Both economic development
and culture stimulate the general rate of associational activity, so
that organizational activity can be quite high in certain third world
nations (Verba, Nie, and Kim 1978, pp. 100–102). There is some in-
dication that culture affects sex differences in organizational activity
as well (Gray 1976; Gustafson, Booth, and Johnson 1979). The well-
developed women's organizations traditional to Nigeria provide one
example (Mba 1982, pp. 290–300; Sklar 1963, p. 14). Traditional cultural norms also affect the nature of women's organizational activity
in first world nations. Studies from these developed nations find that
women belong to different types of groups than men (Booth 1972;
McPherson and Smith-Lovin 1982; Lafferty 1980) and suggest that
women's groups are less likely than men's to stimulate certain types
of political activity (Pollock 1982).

No known data indicate whether *sex differences in income* are
smaller in more developed nations. For employed men and women,
pay differentials do not shrink in the more developed of the first
world nations (United Nations 1980, chap. 4; Jensen 1983). However,
this finding is limited. Theoretically more relevant are the opportunities to participate in politics created by a more affluent life-
style, and such affluence is best measured by family income. Thus
this study examines sex differences in family income.

In conclusion, the indicators of participatory attitudes and
resources used here are limited; they fail to directly tap important
aspects of gender roles. Nevertheless, further examination of these
indicators can still be useful, for they have usually been found to be
strong correlates of political participation. The effect of development, generational turnover, and diffusion on sex differences in
these indicators is still not clear. Thus, this study can at least partially test the processes of change specified by the models.

The Independent Variables: Economic Development
and Generation

This section describes the measures of the independent variables;
later chapters present their variations across nations, within nations, and over time.

Economic Development. As implied in the initial discussion of the development model, four processes are central components of development: urbanization, industrialization, increasing affluence, and rising education levels. The four measures of these components will be urban/rural residence, primary/nonprimary sector occupation, family income, and respondent's education. The actual process of economic development is very complex, involving structural changes and qualitatively different stages of growth (see Flammang 1979). However, such refinements in the measure are not necessary for this initial exploration.

Information on the four indicators of development are not always available for all three types of data. Education and occupation are consistently available, however. For education, the cross-national analysis compares nations by the samples' mean years of schooling; the within-nation analysis compares two groups falling roughly above and below this mean; and the trend analysis compares identically defined educational groups over time. Occupation is consistently defined by that of the head of household, and the primary sector includes forestry and fishing as well as farming (although often the term *farm* is used as an abbreviation for primary sector).

Place of residence and family income are more troublesome. Various surveys can define residence quite differently. For instance, some measure population size of residential units while others measure distance from urban centers. Although these different measures do not preclude comparison of the most urban half of the sample to their rural counterparts in the within-nation data, they do prevent the establishment of a cross-nationally equivalent measure of urbanization. Also, different measures of place of residence for the United States and Germany prevent us from precisely comparing urbanization rates over time. Family income is also easiest to measure in the within-nation data, where the comparison is simply between those above and below the average income. However, comparison of income across nations and over time is complicated by differences in monetary units and variations over time in purchasing power and exchange rates. Thus the cross-national and trend analyses measure income by per capita gross domestic product (GDP), adjusted for inflation. Yet even within-nation analysis encounters measurement problems in these variables, for some surveys simply lack measures of place of residence (e.g., the Barnes and Kaase studies of Switzerland, Finland, and Great Britain) or family income (e.g., the 1958 French election study).

These four indicators of economic development are all closely related. The cross-national variations in the three measures are quite similar, as can be seen in Table 2.1. The intercorrelations, all statistically significant at the .01 level according to Pearson's r, range from .90 (nonfarm households with mean years of schooling) to .79 (per capita GDP with mean years of schooling). Within nations, individuals high on one attribute also tend to fall high on the others. For example, urban, nonfarm, and more affluent people also have more years of schooling. Table 3.1 shows that only once—place of residence and years of schooling for Great Britain—is the relationship negative, signifying that a segment of society assumed more developed is actually less developed by another indicator.

Because of their strong intercorrelations, distinguishing between the four processes associated with economic development is not very important. In fact, the cross-national analysis uses an index of development that simply combines the results of the various indicators. The other types of data do not allow such simplifying strategies.

Generation. The pre-franchise generation is defined as those women not allowed to vote along with their male contemporaries upon reaching adulthood. This measure also varies somewhat across the three types of data. The cross-national analysis compares nations by their proportions of pre-franchise generation women. As Table 2.1 shows, seven nations have few or no pre-franchise generation women remaining in the population. In these nations, within-nation comparison is impossible. Therefore, generational effects among individuals are inferred from variations in sex differences by age instead of generation. If enfranchisement indeed had a generational impact, sex differences in participation should diminish strongly with youth in the seven late-enfranchising nations but not strongly in the seven early-enfranchising nations. (Table 3.1 documents this inference.) The age groups compared are those under 35 and those over 49. This procedure also has the added advantage of standardizing such age-related effects as child bearing status.

The trend data both distinguish a pre-franchise generation, and break the post-franchise generation into groups that may reflect other generational influences such as the women's liberation movement.

The two independent variables, economic development and generation, are positively related. Less-developed nations enfranchised women later, and pre-franchise generation women are less educated, usually lower in income, and more likely to live in farm families. An intriguing issue is the nature and strength of the relationship between development and women's enfranchisement. The development model assumes a positive relationship, while the generational and diffusion models ignore such as possibility. Indeed, the notion of enfranchising women may have simply diffused from more-developed nations to less-developed ones and have no functional relationship to development levels.

Finally, observe that there is no measure of diffusion; its presence can only be inferred from changes in relationships within nations.

The Statistics

This study explores variations in sex *differences*; women's behavior is always compared with that of men because the core issue is equality. Throughout this analysis, gamma is used to measure sex differences in political participation and in participatory attitudes and resources. A positive sign denotes that men participate more than women or are higher in participatory resources and attitudes. And 1.00 indicates that only men are participants, while .00 denotes equality in participation rates. As Appendix D elaborates, gamma is the best measure of conventional concepts of inequality whenever elitist types of political participation are being examined. Note, however, that gamma usually shows larger sex differences than do other commonly employed measures of association. It is also at times more vulnerable to the effects of sampling error. The frequent replications of relationships, however, reduce that problem. Also, although gamma tends to exaggerate the absolute magnitude of the sex differences in comparison to other statistics, the theoretically relevant concern here is not the absolute size of, but rather variations in, sex differences.

Estimates of statistical significance are not presented here, nor are the number of cases upon which the sex differences are calculated. Appendix D explains why tests of statistical significance are not possible with gamma and presents the data base of the calculations. The comparisons across nations and over time come from samples of at least 1000 cases, and usually twice that number. Within-nation variations often involve comparing groups of 500 respondents or more. Tests of statistical significance are tangential to this study's objective of examining variations in sex differences. Yet note that the weak relationships shown here are often not significant by other statistics. Also, in a few instances, even stronger relationships are not statistically significant because they are based upon a relatively small number of cases or strongly skewed marginals. In these latter situations, the results are either not presented or interpreted very cautiously.

With forty-odd surveys and multiple indicators of the variables, this test of the models generates quite a bit of data. The tables and figures in the body of the book usually only summarize the major findings, partly by averaging results from several surveys of the same nation. Also, Chapter 3, which examines variations in sex differences within nations, does not present the original sex differences within each group. Rather, it simply shows changes in sex differences, that is, how much differences increase or decrease among urban, higher status, and younger groups. Appendix D supplies the complete data and explains precisely how they are condensed for presentation in the main text.

Plan of the Book

The following chapters examine variations in sex differences across nations (Chapter 2), within nations (Chapter 3), and over time (Chapter 4). Each chapter presents first the variations in the independent variables (economic development and generation), then those in the intervening variables (sex differences in participatory attitudes and resources), and finally those in the dependent variable (sex differences in political participation). Chapter 5 summarizes the results and discusses their implications for future trends.

Not all the possible processes of change can be explored in each chapter. Evidence of diffusion can only be inferred from trend data. Also, because the measures of the intervening variables are imperfect, as discussed above, the three data chapters cannot fully investigate the development and generational models' assumptions about processes of change. These chapters can, however, explore two aspects of this matter: whether development and generational turnover reduce sex differences in some resources and attitudes important for political activity; and whether sex differences in political participation vary as expected by the models. Explanations for these latter findings can then be deduced from the partial measures of participatory attitudes and resources and from reports of other relevant factors.

Notes

1. *Patrilocal* denotes living with or near the husband's relatives, and *patrilineal* means determining descent or inheritance through the male line. Their respective antonyms are *matrilocal* and *matrilinear*. The terms *neolocal* and *bilateral* indicate no distinction by sex.

2. See, for example, Boserup (1970), Tinker et al. (1976), Rogers (1979), Van Allen (1974 and 1976b), Lindsay (1980), Rendel (1981), and Staudt (1982); reviews of the literature by Jaquette (1982), Staudt (1984), and Marshall (1984); and a bibliography by Danforth (1982).

3. Note that because the models specify certain processes involved in narrowing sex differences in political participation, they do include other indicators of women's status, such as sex differences in education and leisure time.

2

Cross-National Variations

The development model predicts that more economically developed nations have smaller sex differences in political participation. The generational model expects less differences in countries with smaller proportions of pre-franchise generation women. The actual cross-national variations imperfectly meet these expectations and suggest a more complex reality than that portrayed by the models.

The Independent Variables

Table 2.1 presents the cross-national variations for three specific indicators of development: mean years of schooling, proportion of household heads not employed in the primary sector, and per capita gross domestic product (GDP). The economic development index in Table 2.1 represents the sum of the three indicators (after they were standardized to give them equal weight and the signs were reversed).[1] Much of this chapter discusses the correlation between this index and each of the intervening and dependent variables; a positive correlation means that sex differences are smaller in more economically developed nations.

How do the countries vary by this index? As might be guessed, the two third world nations fall very low on this index, and Yugoslavia is about midway between the third world nations and the mean of the first world nations. Perhaps more surprisingly, differences among first world nations are quite marked. The United States measures much higher than any other country, partly because of its high mean years of schooling, but more importantly because of its high per capita GDP. However, the latter figure partly reflects the

Table 2.1
Cross-National Variations in the Independent Variables

Nation	Occupa-tion[a]	Educa-tion[b]	GDP[c]	Economic Development Index[d]	Pre-Franchise[e] Generation
The United States	94%	11.5	$5,130	-4.36	6?
West Germany	95	9.0	3,370	-2.20	4
Great Britain	96	10.0	2,290	-1.81	8
The Netherlands	90	9.5	2,660	-1.60	4
Switzerland	90	7.9	3,350	-1.53	86
Austria	85	9.4	2,080	- .87	0
Finland	82	8.3	2,760	- .83	0
Norway	82	8.4	2,420	- .61	3
Japan	79	10.3	1,490	- .45	52
France	88	7.0	1,870	- .01	71
Italy	80	6.8	1,820	.52	39
Yugoslavia	62	6.4	720	2.41	42
Nigeria	40	2.1	120	5.54	50
India	35	2.2	90	5.78	50

Note: Appendix C more fully describes the measures of these variables, and Appendix A identifies the survey examined here.
[a]Household heads not employed in the primary sector, survey data.
[b]Mean years of schooling, survey data.
[c]Per capita gross domestic product in U.S. dollars, UN data.
[d]Sum of the three preceding variables, after standardization and with signs reversed.
[e]Females not enfranchised upon reaching adulthood, survey data.

fact that U.S. survey data are very current, and per capita GDP has risen over time even in constant dollars. Because the surveys were administered at different times, these rankings do not indicate the exact relationships among these countries either now or in the past. For example, the relatively dated survey data available for France compared to the United States exaggerate the gap between the two countries.

If economic development were solely responsible for narrowing sex differences, then we would expect those differences to be especially large in Nigeria and India, still fairly large in Yugoslavia, and noticeably smaller in the United States. The other first world nations should cluster in the middle, with Germany, Great Britain, the Netherlands, and Switzerland showing somewhat smaller sex differences than Japan and the other European countries. The correlation coefficients at the bottoms of the tables and figures that follow indicate the extent to which the nations fall into this pattern. Of course, because the sample is far from random, tests of statistical significance are not all that meaningful. Thus these statistics are better used as interpretive aids than as definitive tests of the models.

Table 2.1 also presents cross-national variations in the proportion of pre-franchise generation women. The nations fall into two distinct groupings. The seven countries enfranchising women before or immediately after World War I have relatively few women still living who were enfranchised as adults. The other seven countries not enfranchising women until after World War II have roughly half of their samples belonging to the pre-franchise generation. Of course, actual proportions are influenced by the time passed between women's enfranchisement and the survey dates and, to a lesser extent, birth and death rates. If the generational model alone explains sex differences in political participation, then the nations should cluster in two definite groups, with sex differences quite small in the seven early-enfranchising countries and larger in the late-enfranchising ones.

Although Switzerland is a notable exception, more economically developed nations tend to have enfranchised women earlier, the correlation being .44 (Pearson's r). The concluding section of this chapter discusses controlling for variations in economic development, which isolates the direct effect of women's enfranchisement on sex differences in political participation.

Participatory Resources and Attitudes

Participatory Resources

One corollary of the development model is not fully accurate: economic development does not necessarily distribute resources for political participation more equitably. The cross-national variations in sex differences presented in Table 2.2 reveal that: (1) sex differences in family income and work force participation are *not* smaller in more developed countries; (2) differences in education are smaller in first world nations, but not necessarily smaller among the more developed of these nations; and (3) sex differences in organizational activity do tend to narrow at higher levels of economic development. These very mixed results parallel those from other

Table 2.2
Sex Differences in Participatory Resources, by Nation

	Employment (γ)	Education (γ)	Organizational Membership (γ)	Organizational Activity (γ)	Family Income (γ)	Married Women (%)	Women in Single Adult Households (%)
The United States	.56	.04	.17	-.02	.13	63	32
West Germany	.72	.30	.61	.38	.22	64	24
Great Britain	.70	.00	.45	.23	.21	69	...
The Netherlands	.78	.14	.42	.26	.03	74	...
Switzerland	.84	.30	.54	.42	.13	71	...
Austria	.73	.46	.54	.62	.20	67	13
Finland	.4?	-.14	.32	.18	.15	64	...
Norway	.97	.05	.41	...	.09	73	10
Japan	.88	.20	.17	.34	.12	72	4
France	.77	.20	...	...	.09	67	...
Italy	.72	.24	.60	.64	.09	66	...
Yugoslavia	.51	.28	.50	.62	.00	76	6
Nigeria	.30	.56	.39	.35	...	84	3
India	.96	.53	.90	.96	.20	83	2
	Correlation of the Sex Differences with the Economic Development Index[a]						
All nations	(-.13)	.68	.50	.68	(-.09)	.85	-.86
First world nations	(.35)	(.20)	(.35)	.75	(-.28)	(.30)	-.87

Note: Appendix B details the measures of these variables and Appendix A the surveys. The sex differences are measured by gamma, a positive sign indicating men have more of the resource than women. [a]Pearson's *r*, a positive sign denoting that the sex differences or the percentages are smaller in more economically developed nations. Parentheses indicate that the relationship is not statistically significant at the .05 level.

studies on the impact of development on women's status. The development model obviously needs to be supplemented by more detailed explanations for each type of resource and level of economic development.

According to these data, sex differences in family income actually increase slightly with development. This is partly due to increases in the proportion of women in single-adult households (the proportion of men living alone increases less strongly). Some of these women are widows, divorcees, or single mothers without employment, and others are supporting themselves in the work force. Because pensions and other support are often meager and women's wages are lower, women in single-adult households have lower incomes than comparable men.[2] The less developed nations in this study, on the other hand, have few women solely responsible for supporting themselves, due to early and more enduring marriages, extended families, and women's lesser likelihood of outliving men.

However, sex differences in income are not merely a function of female-headed households. Sex differences in India are relatively large despite few women living alone. The Indian survey data show that young and nonfarming women in particular are falling through the protective net of India's joint family system (see Government of India, *Towards Equality*, 1974, pp. 100–101). Moreover, although Nigerian data on family income are unavailable, data on respondent's income and respondent's material possessions reveal a comparatively large gap between men and women. A satisfying explanation of the variations in sex differences in income must consider male-female pay differentials, widow's pensions and general welfare policies, male-female differences in longevity, marriage and divorce rates, and, quite important, family organization.

In short, a mixture of both economic and noneconomic factors affect sex differences in family income. A similar mixture affects family organization as well. Although family size and marriage rates tend to diminish in more industrialized European nations (Stolte-Heiskanen 1975), traditional cultures in these countries are also influential (St. Erlich 1966, pp. 32–53). Moreover, in Japan extended families persist despite the erosive pressures of increased geographic mobility (Morgan and Hirosima 1983), while apartment shortages and the need for child care services may shore up extended family residence in Eastern Europe (Siemienska 1983).

Sex differences in work force participation are also unrelated to economic development. This is clearly demonstrated by the striking contrast between the two third world nations. Among the fourteen nations, Nigeria has the smallest sex differences in employment and India the largest. Most working women in India are low-status agricultural laborers; employment is considered more of a hardship than a privilege (Das 1976, p. 143; Beteille 1975; Bose 1975). Nigerian women have long been active in agriculture and trade; for instance, Wheeler reports that in 1960 the well-known "market women" composed three-quarters of all working women and controlled two-thirds of Nigeria's trade (1967, p. 335).

All kinds of economic and cultural factors affect the cross-national variations in sex differences in work force participation. Women's employment has been encouraged by traditionally favorable attitudes in Finland (Haavio-Mannila 1983, p. 257) and by socialist ideology in Yugoslavia. The growth of the service sector in first world nations promotes women's employment. Also, industrialization facilitates retirement, which in turn reduces men's employment rate and thus the sex differences. However, economic development also reduces the proportion of women employed on farms and in other family enterprises. If not met with the increased availability of other jobs, this reduction in family employment actually increases sex differences in work force participation. In short, economic development is just one factor among many that influence the sex differences, and even that factor reflects complex and sometimes contradictory forces.

Sex differences in years of schooling may in fact narrow in the early stages of economic development. The two third world nations exhibit large differences; when education requires considerable sacrifices by families and a major commitment by government, priorities must be set on whom to eduate, and boys apparently have higher priority. But the introduction of compulsory and universal primary schooling immediately reduces sex differences (Njoku 1980, Wheeler 1967). Moreover, smaller sex differences in education correlate strongly with more years of compulsory schooling (Finn, Dulberg, and Reis 1979). At intermediate stages, however, the development model appears to become less relevant. For example, second world Yugoslavia has moderate sex differences in education not only because it instituted early on eight years of mandatory schooling but also because of its egalitarian socialist values (Springer 1976; Wolchik 1978, pp. 22–44; Jancar 1978, p. 16).

At the later stages of economic development, noneconomic factors better explain the variations in sex differences in education. A particular curriculum may exaggerate or minimize the tendency to prepare boys but not girls for employment. Countries like West Germany and Austria, which have extensive vocational training programs in the public schools, also have large sex differences in years of schooling. Conversely, nations with less extensive vocational training programs have smaller sex differences, although these differences increase when the measure of education includes part-time or private vocational training. Ironically, sex-segregated curricula can decrease differences in years of schooling when girls and boys are being educated for different careers. For example, Japan's modest sex differences reflect its tradition of separately educating girls to be "good wives and wise mothers" and boys for employment (Meguro and Morioka 1983). Besides such long-term cultural traditions, short-term expectations may also affect sex differences in education. For example, labor shortages in less affluent first world nations stimulate demands for women's educational and vocational training (Lovenduski and Hills 1981, pp. 322–23).

Sex differences in the final resource, organizational activity, *do* narrow in more economically developed nations. There are some exceptions, however, most notably Nigeria; and the correlation weakens if one uses organizational *membership* rather than organizational *activity*. Men's organizational membership varies cross-nationally only from 72 percent to 84 percent (except for India and Italy, where the proportion is lower). Therefore, the variations in sex differences between countries are almost entirely dependent on women's organizational membership. A relatively large proportion of employed women obviously facilitates women's access to occupationally related organizations such as trade unions and professional associations. Women's organizational membership is also stimulated when groups particularly appealing to women are well organized, such as neighborhood, school, and religious associations; social, cultural, and leisure organizations; and of course women's organizations. Both factors, women's employment and the types of groups organized, contribute to Nigeria's moderate sex differences in organizational membership (Mba 1982, chap. 6; Wheeler 1967; Nagel 1981) as well as to the large sex differences in India, where male members outnumber females by nine to one. Remnants of Moslem and Hindu traditions of purdah, or the seclusion of women (Government of India, *Towards Equality* 1974, p. 414), probably also constrain Indian women's organizational participation.

Economic development is apparently less likely to provide women with more equal opportunities to join organizations, than it is to facilitate women translating their membership into organizational activity. In the more-developed nations of this study, sex differences are smaller with activity than with membership, whereas in Japan, Italy, Yugoslavia, Austria, and India, the situation is reversed. For organizational activity, thus, the cross-national variations widen and correlate more strongly with economic development.

The influence of development on organizational activity may be felt less through better opportunities than through stronger motivations. The case of Nigeria demonstrates that women in third world countries are not necessarily so preoccupied with child-rearing and household responsibilities that they have no time for associational activity. Indeed, extended families such as those in Nigeria can actually promote the sharing of domestic work and thus facilitate women's activity outside the home. However, as families tend to shrink and scatter with economic development, and more women live alone, social interaction may broaden in compensation, and women's increased organizational activity might be one sign of these social changes.

In sum, women's resources for political participation are generally less than men's. But economic development does not guarantee more equality in the distribution of such resources. Development apparently best narrows sex differences in education (for third world nations) and organizational activity (for all nations), but everywhere the differences reflect noneconomic as well as economic factors.

Participatory Attitudes

Economic development also does not necessarily reduce sex differences in participatory attitudes. Figure 2.1 shows that: (1) sex differences in political efficacy are *not* smaller in more-developed nations; (2) differences in partisanship are larger in less-developed countries but do not become smallest in the most-developed of the first world nations; and (3) differences in political interest do narrow with economic development. The generational model fares worse than the development one. Nowhere is the expected bimodal distribution distinctly evident, and only for partisanship is the correlation of sex differences with generation nearly as strong as that with development. Once again these diverse results demonstrate the need for more refined explanations for the impact of development and generational turnover on gender roles.

All three measures of political efficacy used in this study fail to support the development model. For the Verba, Nie, and Kim measure, sex differences are modest everywhere, and the range of the cross-national variations is quite narrow. Thus there is no need to explain any remaining variations. Data for the other two measures, internal and external political efficacy, are available only

Figure 2.1
Sex Differences in Psychological Involvement and Political Efficacy, by Nation

	POLITICAL INTEREST	PARTISANSHIP	INTERNAL POLITICAL EFFICACY	EXTERNAL POLITICAL EFFICACY	VERBA,NIE & KIM EFFICACY INDEX
CORRELATION OF THE SEX DIFFERENCES WITH THE ECONOMIC DEVELOPMENT INDEX†					
ALL NATIONS	.75	.79	—	—	(.39)
FIRST WORLD NATIONS	.63	(.39)	(.12)	(.10)	(.69)

*Gamma—A positive sign denoting that men participate more than women. Thus nations at the top of the ranges have larger sex differences than those at the bottom.
†Pearson's r-A positive sign denoting that sex differences are larger in less economically developed nations.

for first world countries. Among these countries the cross-national variations widen, but they do not correlate with economic development.

The Verba, Nie, and Kim measure asks respondents to assess their power to influence national government. There are several reasons why sex differences in feeling powerless might not be smaller in developed countries. First, in developing countries women are least likely to answer these questions compared to men. Evaluating their effect on government is evidently not a salient issue to many third world women. Even women who did reply to the question may not be assessing their own power, but rather that of their families. Women have historically been most powerful in both first and third world countries because of family connections (Scott 1978; Aviel 1981). A third reason may relate to the fact that alienation is sometimes stronger among the better-educated, younger, urban, and more-informed segments of society (see Flanagan and Richardson 1980). Third world women's lower education levels and (as I shall presently show) their lesser media exposure may actually inhibit them from developing critical attitudes toward government. Indeed, questions directly tapping specific issues, such as government wastefulness, dishonesty, incompetence, and unfairness, generally reveal statistically insignificant sex differences in developed and developing nations alike.

The variations in sex differences in internal and external efficacy may result from different cultural traditions across the first world nations. Table 2.3 presents evidence of varying traditions among the six countries for which data are available. It gives the proportion of respondents holding that politics is an appropriate concern for women. Although attitudes have become more egalitarian everywhere in the last decade, distinctive cross-national variations still remain. Americans and British are most egalitarian, and Germans least so. There are some discrepancies, for example, in the rankings over time (the Netherlands) and also between egalitarian attitudes and sex differences in efficacy (France). Additional data may eliminate these discrepancies. Generally, however, nations with more egalitarian cultures show smaller sex differences in both internal political efficacy (confidence in one's ability to understand politics) and external efficacy (confidence in leaders' responsiveness to one's demands).

If cross-national variations in efficacy are indeed influenced by cultural traditions, three corollaries follow. First, economic development has relatively little impact on cultural traditions compared to events far in the past, such as the Reformation, for one.

Table 2.3
Cross-National Variations in Political Egalitarianism

	United States[a]	Great Britain[b]	France[b]	Netherlands[b]	Italy[b]	Germany[b]
Proportion High in Political Egalitarianism						
1972-75	79% (2662)	73% (944)	68% (1087)	59% (968)	63% (947)	51% (960)
1983		83% (1241)	78% (941)	78% (928)	74% (966)	58% (935)

Notes:

[a]Disagree with the statement "women should stay out of politics."

[b]Disagree (a little or a lot) with the statement "politics should be left to men."

Sources: For the United States, the "American National Election Study, 1972." For the remaining nations, the "Euro-Barometer 3: European Men and Women, May, 1975" and "Eurobarometer 19: Gender Roles in the European Community, April, 1983." The number of cases are in parentheses.

Second, the time of women's enfranchisement imperfectly reflects these traditions. In fact, the decision to enfranchise women was also influenced by contemporary events—such as Germany's new constitution at the end of World War I facilitating women's enfranchisement or the political stalemate of France's Third Republic delaying enfranchisement for several decades. Third, traditional attitudes that persist even in the most economically developed and politically egalitarian nations cause sex differences everywhere to be larger for internal political efficacy than external efficacy. Because tradition decrees that politics is men's affair, confessing to not understanding politics is easier for women than men. However, tradition does not encourage women to blame political elites for unresponsiveness to their concerns. Although sex differences in external political efficacy are in fact largest in traditional cultures, egalitarian women there may feel least politically efficacious.

Sex differences in partisanship are significantly larger in the less-developed nations of this sample, but the relationship weakens considerably among first world nations. This suggests that other factors influence differences in partisanship, factors such as the time of women's enfranchisement, characteristics of particular political systems, and cultural traditions.

The length of time women have been voting apparently has a stronger effect on sex differences in partisanship than on the other attitudes. Partisanship tends to increase in extent and depth over one's lifetime, partly because it is reinforced by the actual experience of voting. Women's late enfranchisement thus can delay the development of partisan attachments. Besides the two third world nations, four of the first world nations delayed enfranchising women until after World War II. In two of these, Switzerland and Japan, sex differences in partisanship are as large as those in Nigeria. In fact, since developing nations generally enfranchised women later than developed nations, development may not actually affect partisanship at all. The positive correlation may simply signal the diffusion of Western democratic and individualistic egalitarian customs to non-Western countries. Across the entire sample sex differences in partisanship correlate nearly as strongly with the proportion of pre-franchise generation women as with economic development. Moreover, the relative weakness of the development model among first world nations may be further evidence of how little development has to do with sex differences in partisanship.

However, neither development nor the proportion of pre-franchise women sufficiently explains the cross-national variations in partisanship. Another influence may be the length of time men have been voting, and thus developing their own partisan attachments. Political and cultural traditions also exert their influence. The relatively small sex differences in late-enfranchising France and Italy may reflect the presence of influential Catholic parties and women's politicization by the Catholic Church. Indeed, sex differences in partisanship in Italy became small two decades after women's enfranchisement (Christy 1980, p. 397). In India families and extended consanguineous groups such as castes vote as blocs, following their male leaders' advice. Indian women may be particularly reluctant to voice a party affiliation in an interview because they consider it more properly the decision of male family heads. The literature frequently mentions the influence of male recommendations on women's opinions and vote decision (Devon 1980, p. 128; Luthra 1976; Muni 1979). Like India, Nigeria has deep communal divisions, but women apparently operate more independently. They are as least as active as men in tribal unions (Mackintosh 1966, pp. 294, 354), and they are also quite active in women's auxiliaries of the ethnically based political parties (Mba 1982, chap. 8; P. Baker 1974, pp. 223–43). These female activists are described as fiercely loyal to their party (Bretton 1966, p. 61), even more loyal than men (Mba 1982, p. 279). The major constraint to women's partisanship, apparently, is their lesser awareness of political parties (Mackintosh 1966, pp. 303, 350).[3]

Finally, sex differences in political interest do correlate fairly well with economic development, the correlation weakening only slightly among first world nations. Assuming that development does reduce differences in political interest, it may do so in third world countries through two processes: the diminution in sex differences in education and in media exposure. Both of these give women the skills to understand politics and the awareness of how politics affects their lives. However, this still leaves unexplained the question of why the sex differences are smaller in the most-developed of the first world nations.

There are, however, some discrepancies with the development model. For example, sex differences in Nigeria are similar to those in Italy and Japan. And the differences are not as large in India and Yugoslavia as the development model would predict. Again, cultural norms certainly have some effect; women who believe that politics is not properly their concern are more likely to declare themselves uninterested in politics. There is also apparently some connection between partisanship and political interest. An earlier study found that sex differences are everywhere smallest in partisanship, larger in election concern, still larger in campaign interest, and largest of all in political interest. The study hypothesized that partisanship most stimulates interest in the outcome of the election campaign, then interest in the campaign itself, and finally perhaps some interest in the abstract realm of politics in general (Christy 1984).

In sum, both economic factors and noneconomic factors influence sex differences in participatory attitudes. Particular factors affect particular attitudes in varying degrees. Thus the development model's predictions are only partially correct, while those of the generational model are even less accurate.

Political Participation

Communications Activities

Following and discussing politics does not require an institutional base, so these communications activities are most clearly tied to individuals' political interest. The connection works both ways: following politics stimulates interest as well as reflects it. Therefore, cross-national variations in sex differences in communications activity should parallel variations in political interest, and should be likewise affected by both economic and noneconomic factors.

Figures 2.2 and 2.3 present the cross-national data for various types of communications activities. Some results strongly support the development model; for instance, development particularly narrows sex differences in access to the mass media and in opportunities to discuss politics outside the family. However, as is the case with political interest, the variations among the first world nations are more influenced by noneconomic factors. None of the results support the generational model.

The Mass Media. In the third world countries women's access to the media is quite restricted. Most striking are the much larger sex differences in attention to the broadcast media (radio in the third world nations and television in the others). Only 12 percent of Indian households and 14 percent of Nigerian respondents own radios. In India sex differences in radio ownership are negligible, and differences in radio listening in homes with radios are also miniscule. However, among households without radios men listen much more frequently than women, which indicates that they have better access outside the home, through friends or public settings. The radio listening clubs being formed for Indian women (Government of India, *Towards Equality*, 1974, p. 349) apparently have had little effect at the time of the survey. The Nigerian situation is similar, but not identical. As in India, sex differences are very large among those who do not own radios. However, although access in households may be more equal, fewer Nigerian women than men own radios, and even among owners sex differences in listening still remain.

In striking contrast, among first world nations women's exposure to television is nearly equal to or even greater than men's. Once ownership becomes nearly universal, women can actually have better access than men, because listening to the radio and watching television is compatible with domestic work.

The large sex differences in newspaper readership in India and Nigeria may stem from the fact that so many more women than men are illiterate in these countries. But differences in newspaper readership are almost as large in Japan, so obviously there are other factors besides literacy involved. Women working at home may have difficulty buying or finding opportunities to read newspapers. Moreover, even if women do have access to newspapers, their political content may be uninteresting or incomprehensible to less politically involved women. In short, although development reduces sex differences in newspaper readership, other factors can maintain a relatively large gap even in developed nations.

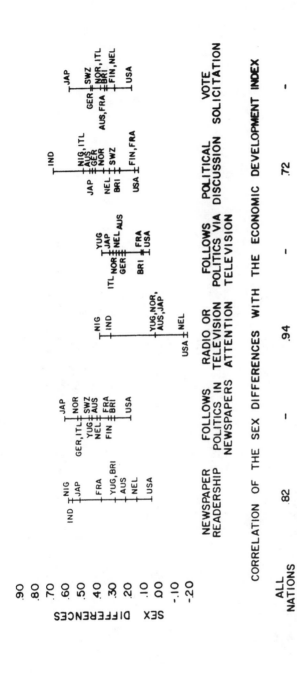

Figure 2.2

Sex Differences in Communications Activity, by Nation

Note: Figure 2.1 explains the statistics

49

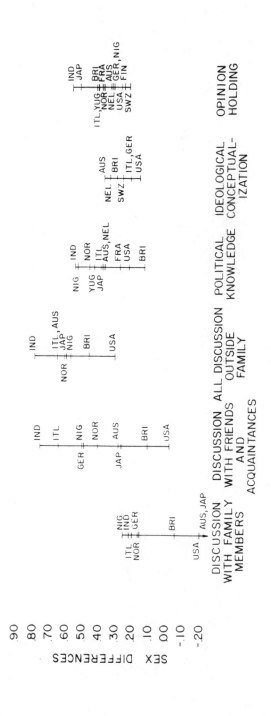

Figure 2.3
**Sex Differences in Political Discussion Channels
and Political Knowledge, by Nation**

	DISCUSSION WITH FAMILY MEMBERS	DISCUSSION WITH FRIENDS AND ACQUAINTANCES	ALL DISCUSSION OUTSIDE FAMILY	POLITICAL KNOWLEDGE	IDEOLOGICAL CONCEPTUAL-IZATION	OPINION HOLDING
CORRELATION OF THE SEX DIFFERENCES WITH THE ECONOMIC DEVELOPMENT INDEX						
ALL NATIONS	(.56)	.75	.71	.80	–	.50
FIRST WORLD NATIONS	(.19)	.73	.95	(.56)	(.46)	(.48)

Note: Figure 2.1 explains the statistics

50

Following politics in the media requires both access and interest. Sex differences in following politics in the media, like differences in interest, correlate more weakly with development than do the differences in access. Once development gives women more equal access to the media, women's lower political interest becomes the more important constraint on their attention to politics.

Note that sex differences in following politics on television everywhere are smaller than those in following politics in newspapers. This reflects women's easier access to television and the greater likelihood of being accidentally exposed to political information on television than in print. Thus, women's information about politics is more likely than men's to be derived from the broadcast media as opposed to newspapers. When survey respondents are directly asked where they obtain political information, sex differences are smaller for the broadcast media than the print media, and this holds true for third and first world nations alike.

In sum, these data suggest that the expansion of literacy and radio ownership in third world countries could accelerate women's exposure to political information, and thereby stimulate their interest in politics. However, cultural norms dictating that politics is a male preserve can still prevent women from following politics as closely as men.

Interpersonal Communications. Interpersonal communication does not require literacy or possessions, yet sex differences in political discussion and vote solicitation still tend to diminish with development. These cross-national variations coincide with those of political interest and probably reflect the influence of the same underlying economic and noneconomic factors. Moreover, as with interest, sex differences in discussion correlate more weakly with development among the first world nations. Once again, noneconomic factors such as cultural norms become more important among developed countries.

Some surveys provide information on the persons with whom discussion takes place. These data show that, regardless of development level, sex differences are larger for discussing politics outside the family circle than inside. In particular, women are much less likely to discuss politics in the work place, in voluntary associations, and with local notables. Women obviously have fewer opportunities for political discussion in such formal settings. Sex differences in work force participation are large, and although sex differences in voluntary association activity are sometimes very small, women everywhere are less likely to be active in those voluntary associations where politics are discussed. More surprising, however, is the finding that sex differences are usually quite large even for discussing politics in informal settings, with friends, neighbors, and acquaintances. When women are less interested in politics, they naturally talk about politics less often, but the measure of the variable discussed here excludes frequency. Rather, certain factors limit women's opportunities to talk about politics even with friends and neighbors. Women are more likely to feel inhibited about publicly expressing their political views; this phenomenon, evident in the 1959 Almond and Verba study, still exists according to a 1980 German survey. Perhaps most startling, an Italian survey finds that women are more likely than men to claim having no friends and acquaintances. Thus, even in the absence of obvious constraints like purdah, women still can be more confined to families for social interactions than men.

Intriguingly, development stimulates women's discussion outside the family, but not inside. This is because economic development affects family discussion in contradictory ways. For one, the high proportion of single-adult female-headed households in developed nations limits women's opportunity for discussing politics with other family members. In the Italian and Norwegian surveys, when those reporting no family with whom to discuss politics are eliminated, sex differences disappear. Among less-developed countries cultural norms sometimes inhibit women from talking politics within the family. The traditional Indian family follows elaborate rules governing interactions within the household by age and sex. For example, women are expected to remain silent in the presence of senior male family members (B. Miller 1982; Government of India, Towards Equality 1974, pp. 407–15). Not surprisingly, these women are more likely to discuss politics with other women than even with their husbands (Devon 1980, p. 130). Sex differences in Nigeria may reflect similar traditions, although other Nigerian data show women more likely than men to report discussing politics with family members (Mackintosh 1966, pp. 293, 340).

When women are more likely than men to discuss politics within the family, the reasons vary by nation. Japanese men rarely report talking about politics with their wives, but women mention their husbands immediately. Both discuss politics with other family members at an equal rate. On the other hand, British and U.S. husbands and wives equally report discussing politics with each other, but women are more likely than men to talk with other family members. Thus, even in highly developed countries women may still specialize in family relationships, counteracting the tendency for more women to live alone.

Discussion outside the family is also influenced by both economic and noneconomic factors. Again, cultural traditions are important. Because Nigerian women have long been active in the work force and voluntary associations, sex differences in that country are smaller than in some first world countries. There are also fewer cultural constraints against women discussing politics in informal settings in Nigeria than in Italy and India. Nevertheless, economic development does apparently narrow sex differences in discussion outside the family, the correlation being similar to that between development and organizational activity. The fragmentation of the family in industrialized societies may influence both findings. That is, women with fewer family members may compensate by increasing interactions with friends, neighbors, and acquaintances and by voluntary association activity.

Political Knowledge and Opinion Holding. Because women are less exposed to political communications than men are, women demonstrate less knowledge of politics and have less-developed opinions on political issues. Moreover, even when women have formed opinions, social norms can inhibit them from voicing those opinions. Because economic development narrows sex differences in communications activities, it also reduces differences in political knowledge. However, the impact of development on knowledge weakens among first world nations. Development also does a poorer job of explaining sex differences in opinion holding, both among first world countries and among the entire sample.

Early on, development can increase women's knowledge of politics by more equitably distributing both education and access to the mass media. At later stages of development, however, economic factors no longer have as much effect on sex differences in education and media exposure, so the impact of development on political knowledge weakens as well. Development also has little effect on sex differences in opinion holding when women are traditionally discouraged from voicing opinions—for example, in first world Japan (Cole and Nakanishi n.d.). Thus sex differences in opinion holding (or more accurately, opinion stating) are unusually large in Japan, particularly in view of the relatively moderate sex differences in political knowledge.

The measures of both opinion holding and political knowledge are somewhat problematic, causing large variations in sex differences according to the subject matter of the question. For opinion holding, differences are usually smaller on questions about domestic issues than about foreign or military affairs (particularly the more technical or obscure foreign affairs issues). Even with domestic issues there is marked variation by subject matter. Sex differences are smallest when the topic is closest to women (e.g. abortion, divorce, schools, general welfare policies), and largest on more abstract issues (evaluating the actions or power of business or unions, nationalization, the government's role in the economy). The opinion-holding scales presented here combine opinions on as many topics as possible. However, only opinions on domestic issues are solicited in the Barnes and Kaase studies and, with the exception of the Netherlands and Austria, the Verba, Nie, and Kim studies. Sex differences thus tend to be smaller in these studies than in the election studies, which tap opinions on a broader range of issues.

Sex differences in political knowledge also vary with the type of knowledge being tested. Subject matter apart, however, there are still other factors affecting the findings for both knowledge and opinion holding. Sex differences increase with the difficulty of the tests. (Exceptions exist, however, as a German survey attests. The 5 percent of Germans who could not name both parties' candidates for chancellor were disproportionately female; the sex differences were a large .54.) Another distortion occurs because men are more likely than women to guess, and the probability of guessing correctly affects the results. For example, in the U.S. election studies respondents had a fifty-fifty chance of correctly guessing which party controlled the House before and after the election; sex differences turned out to be relatively large because so many men guessed correctly. In fact, differences were largest when the newly elected House and president were both from the same party, for those who guess tend to confuse the two (Christy 1980, pp. 419–20).

For many reasons, then, cross-national variations in knowledge and opinion holding deviate from the variations in communications activities. Even identical or nearly identical questions still produce discrepancies. For example, the Barnes and Kaase seven-nation test of knowledge and use of ideological concepts reveals unusually small and somewhat discrepant cross-national variations. Another example is that, although sex differences in media attention are smallest in the United States and largest in Italy, differences in the ability to name the candidates running for office in one's own district are .10 in Great Britain, .22 in Italy and the United States, and .29 in France.

Because of problems in developing cross-nationally equivalent measures of political knowledge and opinion holding, the nations cannot be reliably ranked according to sex differences. Without solid data, the impact of economic development on these types of behavior also cannot be precisely determined.

Other Types of Participation

In contrast to communications activities, voting, campaigning, communal, unconventional, and certain types of contacting activities take place in organized social settings, and so are influenced by particular political and institutional factors. Such activities do not simply reflect individuals' political interest.

These political and institutional factors also affect the sex differences and thus reduce the models' explanatory power. Figures 2.4 and 2.5 illustrate the cross-national variations in sex differences. Differences in contacting, communal, and campaign activities narrow with economic development, while those in voting and unconventional activity do not. The generational model best explains variations in sex differences in voter turnout, but it has little relevance for the other types of participation.

Voting. Voting is more easily mobilized than other types of political participation. The same political and institutional factors that are responsible for voter turnout also affect sex differences in voting, so much so that the effect of economic development is negligible. Among first world nations there is no connection at all between development and differences in voter turnout. Furthermore, the positive relationship over the entire sample is largely a result of women's later enfranchisement in less-developed nations.

More often than not, recently enfranchised women have particularly low voter turnout rates. In time, however, women develop the habit of voting and are joined by new generations of women for whom voting is the norm. Among the countries of this sample, the proportion of pre-franchise generation women correlates most strongly (.74) with sex differences in voter turnout. With the exceptions of Italy and Japan, those countries that enfranchised women after World War II have distinctly larger sex differences than those countries where women have been voting longer. Differences in turnout are as large or larger in affluent Switzerland than in Nigeria and India. Clearly, economic development is not a satisfactory explanation.

Because voting is easily mobilized, differences in political systems can also have a strong impact on sex differences in turnout. Differences in Italy have been negligible as long as women have been voting (Ferrari-Occhionero 1978), because of the quasi-mandatory voting requirements and the Catholic Church's mobilization of women. Differences in Japan were initially large, but declined fairly rapidly; men's turnout fell more than women's as the traditional obligation to vote lost its hold, particularly on young, urban, and better-educated men (Christy 1980, pp. 378–80).

Figure 2.4

Sex Differences in Voting and Campaign Activity, by Nation

Note: Figure 2.1 explains the statistics

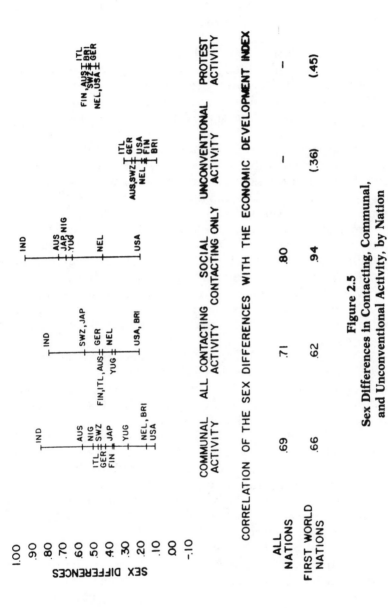

Figure 2.5

Sex Differences in Contacting, Communal, and Unconventional Activity, by Nation

Note: Figure 2.1 explains the statistics

57

These data only weakly support Tingsten's law, (that is, that sex differences in turnout are smaller when men's turnout is higher). The correlation between men's turnout rate and the sex differences, −.38,[4] is not particularly strong and certainly less important than other factors such as the time of women's enfranchisement and unique political forces. Moreover, because in my data male turnout is completely unrelated to economic development, the mild effect of male turnout on the sex differences further weakens the impact of development.

In sum, a number of factors unrelated or accidentally related to development are responsible for the cross-national variations in voter turnout. Sex differences are everywhere relatively small, indicating that women are less constrained from voting than from participating in other kinds of activity. And since the variations in turnout are most discrepant with those of other activities, the factors affecting sex differences in turnout are probably most unique.

Campaign Activity. Sex differences in campaign activity are clearly smaller in more economically developed nations. The correlation with development is stronger for campaign work and meeting attendance than for party membership. Sex differences in all three activities are also influenced by such noneconomic factors as party organizations and campaign procedures.

Political parties draw their members from specific social groups, and these recruitment channels can either facilitate or hinder women's representation. Close ties between labor unions and certain political parties reduce the proportion of female party members. In Great Britain union members affiliate with the Labour Party directly through the union; since men are more likely to be employed and thus belong to unions, this arrangement especially advantages men. (See also R. Ross 1976, p. 169.) When union-affiliated Labour Party members are no longer classified as members in the surveys, sex differences in party membership are more than halved. Similar connections between party and union no doubt affect sex differences in other countries as well.

Political parties may also be tied to other kinds of economic interest groups. In Japan, for example, parties maintain alliances with agricultural, business, and professional groups as well as with labor unions. The parties that recruit from these groups have large sex differences (Foster 1982; Robins-Mowry 1983, p. 246; Hargadine 1981) because women are underrepresented in all types of economic interest groups.

In contrast, separate women's auxiliaries in political parties can stimulate women's membership, as they do in India (Dubey and

Trikha 1979; Devon 1980, p. 124). The fact that sex differences in party membership are as large in Japan as in India (especially surprising considering India's large sex differences in other types of political participation) may reflect the influence of their very different recruitment channels. Although campaign activity data are unavailable for Nigeria, the women's auxiliaries of political parties may also have facilitated female party membership (Mackintosh 1966, pp. 302, 349).[5]

Since campaign workers are often drawn from party rolls, the same factors affecting women's party membership also indirectly affect their campaign work. However, sex differences in campaign work do not precisely mirror those in party membership. In Great Britain and Japan differences in campaign work are smaller than those in party membership. British survey data show that male party members are less likely to be active in party affairs as well; presumably the British union connection and like factors facilitating men's membership also produce more perfunctory members. In contrast, Japanese males remain heavily over-represented among party activists, but not as extensively among campaign workers, because Japanese women are often recruited for campaign work in extra-party, neighborhood-based candidate support organizations (Robins-Mowry 1983, p. 246). Sex differences increase slightly for campaigning in India; parties sometimes hire female canvassers to approach female voters, but their effectiveness is limited due to the tradition of male family heads making the family choices and to suspicions of female campaigners (Dubey and Trikha 1979; Government of India, *Towards Equality* 1974, p. 299).

Sex differences in meeting attendance also vary with particular institutional practices. For example, Japan's sex differences in meeting attendance are remarkably small compared to other types of political participation. This is partly because campaign meeting attendance is not entirely voluntary but rather a duty, especially in rural areas (Richardson 1974, p. 143). Women are no freer from this obligation than men. In other countries sex differences may be affected by such factors as whether campaign rallies are traditionally held at workplaces or elsewhere.

These data do not support Duverger's observation that sex differences increase as political activities become more elitist. For example, campaign work is considered elitist, engaging fewer citizens than party membership or meeting attendance. Yet sex differences are just as likely to be smallest for campaign work. I have not systematically tested Duverger's law because of difficulties in obtaining cross-nationally equivalent data on activity rates. However, the examples for Japan, Great Britain, and India demonstrate how the features of particular political systems affect sex differences in campaign work and thus call into question the precise accuracy of Duverger's thesis.

In sum, sex differences in campaign activity are powerfully affected by unique political conditions, and so the cross-national variations do not perfectly match those for other kinds of political participation. The sex differences are, however, still significantly smaller in developed countries. The correlation is somewhat weaker for party membership than for the other two measures because party membership is most sensitive to institutional influences. These findings parallel those for sex differences in organizational membership and organizational activity, suggesting that economic development makes it easier for women to translate organizational and party membership into organizational and campaign activity. In both cases, the fragmentation of the family that accompanies economic development in this sample apparently stimulates women's activity outside the home.

Communal Activity. The cross-national variations for communal activity coincide with those for organizational activity—not surprisingly, since communal activity takes place in groups (the survey questions specifically ask about "working with others on community problems"). The Verba, Nie, and Kim surveys measure activity in organizations dealing with community problems, and these findings match even more closely with communal activity. The obvious conclusion is that the same factors explain variations in sex differences in both organizational and communal activity. Development narrows the sex differences, again perhaps because of family fragmentation, but noneconomic factors can also be crucial. Nigerian women have traditionally been active in organizations, and this may be why sex differences in communal activity are as small in Nigeria as in some first world nations. Just as there are almost no Indian women active in organizations, so there are virtually none among communal activists. Indian parties' efforts to recruit and activate female members do not extend to the nonpartisan realm of communal politics. Women are almost never seen on traditional caste or village councils, except when they occupy seats reserved for women in government-sponsored councils (Jacobson 1977).

Besides cultural traditions, political institutions can affect communal activity. For example, Yugoslavia's differences are relatively small, although the differences in organizational activity are somewhat larger. This reflects that country's well-developed local self-government institutions and its encouragement of communal activity. Women are particularly active in self-management councils dealing with their traditional concerns, such as housing and schools (Jancar 1978, pp. 29, 98). In general, nations with strong local institutions handling women's traditional concerns (such as the United States) may also have smaller sex differences in communal activity.

Note that sex differences are not any smaller for communal activities than for other types of political participation. Other data confirm that compared to men, women are not necessarily more involved in politics at the local than at the national level. Sex differences in political efficacy, interest, discussion, and knowledge are no smaller on the average when the topic is local rather than national politics. Nor are sex differences in voting and contacting activity necessarily smaller in local elections or with local officials. The Yugoslavian and U.S. pattern is not universal; traditional women's concerns are not always more closely addressed by local rather than national institutions. Moreover, the Indian example shows how the absence of parties and national ties may actually reduce women's access.

Contacting Activity. Regardless of development, sex differences in contacting activity vary with the issue prompting the contact. Verba, Nie, and Kim data show that everywhere sex differences in particularized contacting (concerns affecting individuals or their families) are smaller than those in social contacting (concerns affecting social groups, the community, or nation). Figure 2.5 includes two types of cross-national variations: in social contacting (from Verba, Nie, and Kim studies) and in all contacting (from all the studies).

Sex differences in both measures of contacting do narrow with economic development. Two processes may be involved. Since development correlates with smaller sex differences in political interest and knowledge, it gives women the awareness of broader political concerns necessary for social contacting. Also, the fragmentation of the family accompanying development leaves more women with no convenient male intermediary. This increases the proportion of women who have no choice but to contact decision makers directly, and this narrows sex differences in both particularized and social contacting.

Again, however, development is not a sufficient explanation; note that sex differences in contacting are as small in Yugoslavia and Nigeria as in some first world countries. Promoted by elaborate patron-client relationships, contacting activity can be quite extensive in less developed rural areas and nations (Huntington and Nelson

1976). In these cases, men's and women's lesser involvement and awareness may not inhibit their contacting activity. Other relevant factors are the family structure and the organization of patronage relationships. For example, the Indian family structure is predominantly patrilocal (with wives residing with or near husbands' kin), and the patronage system is organized around kinship ties. Patrilocal family structures weaken women's ties to kin, and thus, in the Indian example, their ties to the patronage system through kin groups as well (Dixon 1982). Perhaps the greater incidence of matrilocal family structures in Nigeria promotes relatively smaller sex differences in contacting activity.

Unconventional Activity. Sex differences in unconventional political participation do not narrow significantly with economic development. In fact, the cross-national variations are very small. However, quite large variations occur *within* each nation depending on the exact type of activity. Sex differences are everywhere relatively small for signing petitions, boycotting, and rent and tax strikes, but larger for participating in legal demonstrations, wildcat strikes, and more disruptive or violent protests. Figure 2.5 illustrates the result of dividing these activities into two categories: unconventional activity (those with small sex differences) and protest activity (those with large sex differences). Unconventional activities are generally performed alone, are not immediately disruptive, and do not involve taking physical risks. Protest activities, on the other hand, tend to be performed in groups, to be more disruptive, and also to incite violent response by the opposition.

Data on these activities are only available for first world nations, but the argument of the previous chapter suggests that sex differences in unconventional and protest activities are probably not any larger in developing than in developed nations. These kinds of activities do not require as much knowledge, interest, or sometimes even organizational resources as do many other political activities, so the large sex differences in education and media access in third world countries would not limit women's participation as much.

There are several reasons why women in first world countries would be constrained from protest activities, and why women everywhere would be drawn to unconventional activities. The Barnes and Kaase data examined here reveal that, among those who never participated in protest activity, women are more likely than men to say that they would never do so.[6] The cross-national variations in negative attitudes towards protesting are mild and unrelated to development, just like the differences in protest activity. However, the sex differences in negative attitudes average only .23, about half that for protest activity, so there must be other factors at work. Because the differences are so large and unvarying, it is tempting to consider biological explanations. Even legal demonstrations involve some risk, and women may be less willing to take that risk because they feel more physically vulnerable. However, because of their demonstrated potential for misuse, biological explanations are suspect and require very careful documentation.

Some unconventional activities, on the other hand, are quite compatible with traditional female roles. For instance, women's role as consumers makes them essential to the success of any consumer boycott. Other activities, like signing petitions, may be so easy as to undercut any constraint on women's participation. These data support the literature's observation that sex differences in unconventional activity are small, but only when unconventional activity is defined to exclude the more disruptive and violent types of behavior.

Summary and Conclusion

The data confirm that sex differences in both political participation and participatory attitudes and resources are often smaller in more-developed countries. However, the development model requires elaboration and revision. For some types of political participation, notably unconventional and protest activity, the sex differences correlate weakly or not at all with development. Also, developed nations do not have a more equitable distribution of certain participatory attitudes and resources, namely, income, employment, and political efficacy. Finally, the impact of development sometimes weakens considerably among first world nations.

When economic development does reduce sex differences, two processes appear to be relevant. First, in the early stages of development the introduction of universal primary schooling and the broadening ownership of radios particularly stimulates women's political interest, knowledge, and communications activity. Second, the fragmentation of the family with economic development apparently encourages women's social interaction outside the family, including campaigning, contacting, and communal activity. Chapters 3 and 4 will test these two explanations with other kinds of data.

Sex differences in voter turnout and partisanship are best explained by the generational model, for differences tend to be smallest in those countries which enfranchised women earliest and have the fewest remaining pre-franchise generation women. As might be expected, women's enfranchisement has the greatest effect on these attitudes and behaviors most directly related to the voting act.

Other factors that can have a strong impact on the sex differences include cultural norms defining the political role of women and particular political institutions and practices. Institutional and political factors become even more important at elite levels. The powerful effects of the electoral system on women's representation in legislatures has been widely documented (Jensen 1983, among many others). In fact, political and institutional factors are so important that sex differences in mass-level political participation correlate only weakly with women's representation among political elites. India clearly illustrates this point; despite the example of Indhira Gandhi and a fairly average proportion of women in the national legislature, sex differences in political participation are very large (Desai and Bhagwati 1975; Katzenstein 1981; C. Mukhopadhyay 1982; Nuss 1982; Shaul 1982).

In short, the cross-national variations cannot be accounted for by the universal application of any combination of factors, much less by any single neat explanation. Interpretation of the data is further complicated by the fact that the independent and intervening variables are interrelated.

Tables 2.4 and 2.5 summarize these interrelationships and compare the effects of these factors on sex differences in five types of political participation. The problem of missing data is minimized in two ways. The two nations with a great deal of missing information, France and Norway, are eliminated from the analysis. And when data on certain forms of political participation are missing, sex differences are estimated on the basis of other information. (Appendix C explains this procedure.)

Tables 2.4 and 2.5 show that economic development does correlate with smaller sex differences in all five types of political participation. But the correlation is in every case weaker than that with one or more of the other independent or intervening variables. For instance: (1) Communications and contacting activities, which need not take place through institutional channels, correlate best with political interest. (2) Sex differences in campaign activity most closely reflect the differences in both political interest and organizational activity. (3) Communal activity, less overtly political than campaign activity, is tied more closely to organizational activity than to political interest. (4) Sex differences in voter turnout coincide best with the proportion of pre-franchise generation

Table 2.4
Intercorrelation of the Independent and Intervening Variables,
Twelve Nations

	GEN	PI	EDU	INC	EMP	ORG
Economic development index (ECDEV)...	(.48)	.77	.69	(.33)	(−.12)	.68
Pre-franchise generation (GEN)............		.63	(.47)	(.00)	(.24)	(.41)
Sex Differences in political interest (PI)......			.81	(.02)	(.30)	.85
Sex differences in education (EDU).................				(.42)	(.17)	.70
Sex differences in income (INC)........................					(−.27)	(−.02)
Sex differences in employment (EMP).............................						(.43)
Sex differences in organizational activity (ORG)						

Notes: Based on data in Tables 2.1 and 2.2. The correlation coefficients are Pearson's *r*, and parentheses indicate the relationship is not statistically significant at the .05 level. Norway and France are excluded from these calculations.

Table 2.5
Correlation of the Independent and Intervening Variables
with the Dependent Variables, Twelve Nations

	ECDEV	GEN	PI	EDU	INC	EMP	ORG
Communications activity index.	.85	.57	.96	.85	(.22)	(.25)	.81
Campaign activity index[a]......	.79	.54	.95	.82	(−.03)	.56	.92
Contacting activity..........	.68	.58	.73	.65	(.26)	(.40)	.69
Communal activity............	.69	(.41)	.71	.73	(.41)	(.31)	.82
Voting.......................	.61	.77	(.14)	.52	(.33)	(−.19)	(.23)

Notes: See Table 2.4 for the key to the abbreviations. Appendix C explains how the indices are constructed and how data missing from certain nations are estimated.
[a]Eleven nations only because data are missing for Nigeria.

women. Note that in all cases the correlations are strongest with communications activity and weakest with voting. Weaker correlations indicate the increased importance of variables not measured in this study, such as the unique cultural and political forces that mobilize voters.

Partial and multiple correlations and multiple regression analysis support the general findings presented in these tables. In fact, economic development is more likely to wash out when the other variables are controlled than the other way around. However, the correlation is quite strong between development and certain intervening variables, such as sex differences in political interest and organizational activity. Therefore, tracing the causal relationships between these variables in other types of data is vital.

Taken alone, cross-national variations in sex differences are an insufficient test of the three models. The positive correlation between development and smaller sex differences may be unique to this group of nations, or it may be spurious, reflecting some underlying cause. For example, in Europe Protestantism may have once spurred both economic development and more egalitarian gender roles, but development in itself may not have increased sexual equality. In Chapter 3 the models will be tested further by comparing groups within nations.

Notes

1. The precise measures of the indicators and procedures for constructing the index are discussed in Appendix C.

2. Living costs, of course, are lower in smaller households. More women than men live alone, but also more women head households with children. Thus it cannot be said that women as a group need less money than men because their households are smaller.

3. Incidentally, this Nigerian example contradicts one hypothesis presented in Chapter 1, namely, that communally based politics maintain the subordination of women because the harmony of communal groups depends on traditional gender roles.

4. Pearsons's r. Appendix C details the methodology.

5. Note, however, that sex segregation in parties may lessen women's influence on party policy (Aviel 1981).

6. Lovenduski reports that a recent survey of the European Economic Community (EEC) nations found women slightly more willing to engage in public demonstrations (1986, p. 127). Perhaps the term "public demonstration" has less negative connotations to women than the various types of protest activities examined here.

3

Within-Nation Variations

The development and generational models predict that sex differences in political participation will also vary within nations. The development model expects sex differences to be smaller among more educated, affluent, urban, and nonfarm groups. The generational model assumes that differences will be smaller among the younger post-franchise generation (women never barred from voting along with their male contemporaries). The strength of these relationships within nations, the models further imply, will vary across nations.

However, the generational and development models are less well supported by these within-nation data than by the cross-national data. This chapter examines the shortcomings of these two models and the reasons for discrepancies between within-nation and cross-national data.

The Independent Variables

The development model is tested by variations in sex differences according to respondent's education, family income, place of residence, and the occupation of the head of household. Generational effects are inferred from variations in sex differences by age. Appendix C further discusses the measures of these five independent variables, and Appendix D presents the complete survey results. Here we are concerned with only the more significant findings. Also, except for Table 3.1, the tables and figures in this chapter present only the reduction in sex differences, that is, the amount of change in sex differences in participation across the two categories of each independent

Table 3.1
Interrelationships between the Independent Variables, by Nation

	Place of Residence (urban/rural)			Occupation (nonfarm/farm)		Education (high/low)		Income (high/low)		Age (under 35/over 49)			
	EDU[a]	INC[a]	AGR[b]	EDU[a]	INC[a]	INC[a]	AGR[b]	EDU[a]	AGR[b]	EDU[a]	INC[a]	AGR[b]	GEN[b]
The United States	.20	.25	11%	.41	.25	.44	4%	.48	4%	.47	.21	6%	17%
West Germany	.22	.02	12	.42	.18	.46	4	.46	2	.44	.46	2	8
Great Britain	-.02	.08	14	.16	.30	.44	2	.45	3	.70	.41	2	14
The Netherlands	.14	.04	16	.36	.46	.42	8	.40	6	.58	.36	8	17
Switzerland	···	···	···	.54	.56	.42	12	.48	11	.37	.33	6	43
Austria	.55	.35	26	.68	.54	.50	19	.56	14	.40	.36	2	0
Finland	···	···	···	.51	.50	.38	14	.49	22	.66	.62	19	0
Norway	.31	.42	30	.33	.61	.38	8	.41	24	.58	.24	14	6
Japan	.28	.25	30	.51	.28	.40	20	.39	10	.66	.10	18	100
France	.39	.40	25	.56	.60	.60	12	.62	13	.36	.47	7	59
Italy	.30	-.08	18	.59	.28	.48	20	.48	12	.62	.34	12	95
Yugoslavia	.19	.17	20	.77	.60	.60	50	.62	20	.60	.30	40	100
Nigeria	.67	.65[c]	53	.53	.57[c]	.73[c]	29	.71[c]	31[c]	.67	.21[c]	19	96
India	.64	.43	68	.40	.04	.49	19	.57	1	.29	.01	6	100
Correlation with the Economic Development Index[d]	.71	.61	.87	(.28)	(.00)	.65	.65	.68	(.38)	(-.03)	-.46	(.40)	.73

Note: Appendix C describes the measures of these independent variables, and Appendix A the surveys.

[a] Correlations (gamma) of years of schooling (EDU) and family income (INC) with the independent variables, a positive sign indicating that education and income is higher among urban, nonfarm, more-educated, higher-income, or younger respondents.

[b] The proportion of those in farming (AGR) or in the pre-franchise generation (GEN) among urban, higher status, and younger respondents subtracted from the proportion of the same among rural, lower status, and older respondents.

[c] Respondent's income, not family income.

[d] Pearson's r, a positive sign denoting that the gamma correlation or percentage difference is larger in less economically developed nations. Relationships not statistically significant at the .05 level are in parentheses.

variable. A positive sign indicates that the data support the model(s), that sex differences are indeed smaller among better-educated, more affluent, urban, nonfarm, and younger groups.

These variables are all closely related, and Table 3.1 presents the cross-national variations in the strength of the interrelationships. When these coincide with cross-national variations in economic development, this coincidence allows a further refinement of the development model. That correlation—between these cross-national variations and the economic development index discussed in the previous chapter—appears at the bottom of the table. A positive sign indicates that in less-developed countries the categories of the independent variables differ most strongly according to the other indicators of development.

Quite distinctive cross-national variations occur for place of residence. Urban-rural differences in income, education, and—of course—occupation are greater in less-developed nations. (Exceptions to this rule, such as Yugoslavia, result from less appropriate measures of place of residence.) It follows that if the development model is correct, sex differences in political participation will diminish more strongly with urban residence in less-developed countries. In the most-developed countries urban-rural differences in income, education, and occupation are slight and may cause only mild reductions in sex differences in political participation.

These data suggest additional corollaries to the development model. Development not only decreases urban-rural distinctions, but also apparently diffuses the attributes of social status. That is, education and income are less closely related in more-developed countries. However, development does *not* reduce education and income differences between farm and nonfarm families, or between younger and older respondents. In this case the cross-national variations reflect differences in the rates that years of schooling have increased and the primary sector has shrunk. Apparently these rates have not been more rapid in less-developed nations. The correlation of income with age reflects life cycle effects, which are lessened by the extended family system's softening the drop in income accompanying retirement and widowhood. Because the less-developed nations of this sample also have more extended families (as well as fewer able to retire), family income tends to drop less severely in those countries. So the development model would predict that sex differences in political participation should narrow more strongly in less-developed nations with increased income and education, but not with nonfarm occupations or youth.

The figures and tables in the rest of the chapter will present the correlation between cross-national variations in economic development and the reduction in sex differences within nations. Two different measures of development are given. The economic development (ECONDEV) index is that used in Chapter 2 and Table 3.1; it measures development processes across entire countries. The economic distinctiveness (ECONDIST) index derives from the relationships presented in Table 3.1 and is simply an additive index of them; it measures the effect of the distribution within nations of the attributes of economic development (income, education, and so on—Appendix C details these indices).

The generational model also predicts cross-national variations in the reduction of sex differences with youth, according to the "generational distinctiveness" of the age categories. Table 3.1 shows this distinctiveness, which is measured by subtracting the proportion of pre-franchise generation women in the younger age group from that in the older. The age groups are least generationally distinctive in Finland and Austria, where no pre-franchise generation women remain, and most distinctive in India, Yugoslavia, and Japan, where all older women belong to the pre-franchise generation and none of the younger women do. Presumably, the more generationally distinctive the age groups, the stronger the reduction in sex differences with youth.

Note that while age is a substitute for generation, it also reflects the impact of development. Thus both the development and the generational models expect sex differences in political participation to diminish with youth. The development model expects this diminution because the young have higher education and income levels and are less likely to work in the primary sector. The generational model predicts this reduction because pre-franchise generation women were socialized into more restricted views of women's roles.

Participatory Resources and Attitudes

Participatory Resources

Sex differences in participatory resources are as likely to widen as to narrow with increased education, affluence, urban residence, and nonfarm occupation. Table 3.2 shows that these results vary only slightly with the type of resource. Sex differences diminish as

Table 3.2
Within Nation Reduction in Sex Differences in Participatory Resources, by Nation

	Place of Residence				Occupation				Education			Income			Age			
	Edu[a]	Inc[a]	Emp[a]	(Org)[a]	Edu[b]	Inc	Emp	Org	Inc	Emp	Org	Edu	Emp	Org	Edu	Inc	Emp	Org
United States	-.06	-.01	-.03	-.01	-.24	-.12	.00	-.24	-.02	-.10	.01	-.11	-.40	.02	-.24	.13	-.26	-.19
West Germany	.12	.00	.14	-.12	.04	.02	.06	.01	.04	.16	.00	.08	-.01	-.05	.17	.22	-.05	.08
Great Britain	-.05	-.21	.03	...	-.24	-.22	.15	.21	.12	-.18	-.03	.04	-.29	-.11	-.10	.24	-.22	-.13
The Netherlands	-.08	-.05	.04	-.06	-.26	-.24	-.07	-.16	-.05	.10	-.08	-.12	-.09	-.10	-.10	.12	.08	-.20
Switzerland	...	...	...	...	.10	-.55	.05	-.06	-.09	-.03	-.02	-.15	-.16	.05	.10	.17	-.14	-.33
Austria	.19	.05	.03	.19	.08	.08	.02	.08	.08	.10	.22	.07	-.06	.22	.18	.14	-.20	.00
Finland	...	...	...	...	-.16	-.04	.10	-.08	-.06	.04	.08	-.17	-.09	-.14	.00	.17	-.09	-.26
Norway	-.09	-.11	.06	...	-.15	-.15	.09	...	.06	-.03	...	-.08	-.18	...	-.21	.11	-.09	...
Japan	.04	.02	-.02	-.03	-.08	-.09	-.12	-.05	.10	-.02	.11	.02	-.08	.21	.23	.16	-.12	.08
France	-.04	-.04	.01	.01	.07	.06	-.06	...	-.01	.07	...	-.17	-.14	...	.10	.42	-.39	...
Italy	.03	-.08	.02	.37	-.07	.08	-.04	.30	.08	.26	.12	-.02	.02	.16	.06	.12	.09	-.01
Yugoslavia	.01	.02	-.14	-.08	.00	.10	...	.09	.23	.18	.16	.21	.07	.11	.18	.22	-.41	.12
Nigeria	.07	-.24	.30	.02	.08	.19	.52	.11	.12	.49	.06	.20	.23	-.13	.08	.30	-.02	.18
India	.18	.07	.03	.14	.10	-.17	.03	.07	.24	-.02	.07	.23	-.02	.10	.24	-.05	-.07	.03
	Correlation with the Economic Development Indices[b]																	
Econdev Index	.50	(-.01)	(.48)	(.27)	.37	(.32)	(.14)	(.03)	.58	.70	.56	(.32)	.62	(-.10)	(-.20)	(.44)	(-.04)	
Econdist Index	(.46)	(-.09)	(.29)	(.22)	.56	.36	.50	(.46)	.69	.55	(.35)	.71	.76	(.07)	.51	(.10)	(.11)	.61

Notes: The reduction in sex differences is measured by subtracting differences (gamma) in participatory resources among urban, nonfarm, higher status, and younger respondents from differences among rural, farm, lower status, and older respondents. A positive sign supports the development or generational models. Appendix A describes the surveys.

[a] The participatory resources are education (Edu), family income (Inc), employment (Emp), and organizational activity (Org) and are described in Appendix B.

[b] Pearson's r, a positive sign denoting that the reduction is greater in less economically developed nations (econdev index) or more economically distinctive sectors or groups (econdist index). Relationships not statistically significant at the .05 level are in parentheses.

expected in only 45, 48, 51, and 55 percent of the cases for income, education, organizational activity, and employment, respectively. These data thus provide no support for the assumption that urbanization, industrialization, increased education, and affluence more equitably distribute participatory resources. The development model may still be relevant, however, for a limited range of cases, depending on the stage of economic development and type of participatory resource.

These data show that, as the interpretation of Chapter 2 would predict, sex differences in family income are least likely to diminish with economic development. In first world nations, sex differences in family income are often *smallest* among rural residents and farm families, where fewer women are responsible for supporting themselves. Rural traditionalism and the special difficulties of solitary women and men pursuing farm occupations both operate to distribute income more equitably in these shrinking segments of society. In the third world nations the data are mixed, and interpretation is complicated by the somewhat anomalous measure of income for Nigeria. For India, at least, several forces can be identified. As in richer countries, sex differences in family income are smallest among farming households, where extended families are more prevalent. However, the exigencies of poverty disrupt extended families (Mandelbaum 1970, pp. 35-52), and so sex differences in income are largest among less-educated and rural residents. Thus industrialization and increased affluence may actually have contradictory effects on future sex differences in family income in India.

Nor are sex differences in employment likely to diminish with development; the within-nation variations are best explained by noneconomic factors. Life cycle factors have the strongest impact in first world nations. Sex differences in employment are usually smaller among older individuals because of men's retirement, and they can be smaller among less-educated and lower income individuals because they also tend to be older. The effects of life cycle factors on women's work force participation varies from one nation to another. For example, Italian women traditionally work only before marriage, while many British women return to the work force as their children grow up (Christy 1983). Because younger women are better educated than older women, sex differences in employment are smaller among the more educated in Italy and the less educated in Great Britain.

In third world nations poverty and primary sector occupations allow few people to retire, and so, all other factors being equal, sex differences in employment are more likely than in first world nations to narrow with increased income and education. However, noneconomic factors are often crucial. India's and Nigeria's very different traditions on women's work cause sex differences to diminish more strongly in Nigeria than in India with increased education, income, urban residence, and nonfarm occupation. Both countries have a high rate of employment among educated professional women, but their numbers are small. The typical working woman is a rural farm laborer in India and an urban trader in Nigeria (Khanna and Varghese 1978; Jain 1975, pp. 169–70; Njoku 1980; Awosika 1981). In neither of these occupations are job opportunities likely to expand in the future. In short, these data support Chapter 2's conclusion that economic development has a complex and sometimes contradictory impact on sex differences in work force participation.

The data on sex differences in education are also consistent with the argument of the previous chapter: sex differences narrow with development only in the early stages. In nearly half the first world nations sex differences are larger among the young, suggesting that they have been *widening* in recent decades. Moreover, whenever these differences increase with youth, they invariably also widen with increased income, urban residence, and nonfarm occupation, groups who tend to be younger. Conversely, in third world nations sex differences in education are consistently smaller in urban, nonfarm, and higher income households, as well as among the young. These more affluent groups can better afford to educate girls along with boys, and they may be more tolerant about the value of educating women (as noted in Narain 1967). Indeed, families in India (as elsewhere) may educate their girls simply to increase their value as mates for educated males (Mandelbaum 1970, pp. 108–9; Silver 1977; Pharr 1977).

Latent traditional gender roles and changes in vocational training can increase sex differences in education in first world nations. Wherever sex differences increase with youth, they were previously relatively small, at least partly because vocational training programs were not well developed in the public school system. The explanation for this relationship in the United States may apply to other nations as well. In the past U.S. vocational programs were weak, and boys were more likely than girls to drop out of high school to work or receive private vocational training. As vocational training moved into the public schools and as academic training became more important for employment, boys no longer left school earlier than girls (Christy 1980, pp. 187, 190). This, along with the widening sex differences in college attendance in the 1950s (due to the GI Bill of Rights and high birth rates), increased sex differences in years of schooling.

The most critical discrepancy between the cross-national and within-nation data occurs for sex differences in organizational activity. The within-nation data do not support either the development model or the supplementary explanations of Chapter 2. Sex differences within nations are *not* smaller where families are more fragmented (as indicated by increased proportions of female-headed households). Differences in organizational activity are as likely as not to be largest in urban and nonfarming households. And although women living alone fall quite disproportionately in the lower income category, sex differences are not related to income either. Life cycle factors affect these relationships. For instance, men's retirement disrupts their membership and activity in occupationally related organizations, making the sex differences sometimes smallest among older respondents and those demographic groups which contain more older respondents, such as lower income, less-educated, and farming households.

Nor does the development model work better for third world nations. Sex differences do tend to diminish in urban and nonfarming households, but anomalies remain. The data thoroughly contradict the proposition presented in Chapter 1 that women in farming households are most socially isolated. No Indian rural or farm women reported being organizationally active, but neither did most of their urban, nonfarm sisters. Conversely, one-third of Nigerian rural and farm women are active in organizations, and rural women are slightly more active than urban women. Affluence does not necessarily widen women's social interactions either. For example, in India purdah tended to be more widely practiced among upper status castes, which could afford the loss of women's labor outside the home (Mandelbaum 1970, p. 38; Bhatty 1976, p. 110-11). Countervailing influences today are education and the existence of organized groups for middle class women (Khanna and Varghese 1978, pp. 67–68; Devon 1980, p. 140). Thus purdah varies little by caste or place of residence (Government of India, *Towards Equality* 1974, pp. 407–15).

These relationships are actually as much affected by variations in men's activity as women's. For instance, in Italy the much smaller sex differences among urban residents and nonfarm families is primarily due to rural and farm men's much higher rates of organizational activity; few Italian women in either sector are active. In general, a variety of social and cultural factors cause certain demographic groups to be better organized than others and affect the sex differences.

In sum, the development model apparently holds only for sex differences in education in third world nations. The model's failure to explain differences in income and employment is consistent with the argument of Chapter 2. However, the results for sex differences in organizational activity are not explained by the development model, and are discrepant with the cross-national data and their interpretation presented in Chapter 2.

Participatory Attitudes

Sex differences in participatory attitudes decrease among higher status, urban, and nonfarm groups in half the cases, a rate similar to that of participatory resources. Sex differences also fail to diminish with youth in similar proportions. Overall these results do not support the development and generational models; however, they do support these models better for certain types of participatory attitudes. Intriguingly, the development model works better for sex differences in psychological involvement, while the generational model, at first glance, better explains sex differences in efficacy. Furthermore, the cross-national variations in the relationships sometimes suggest refinements of the development model according to the stage of economic development.

As the interpretations of Chapter 2 would predict, the development model is best supported by sex differences in political interest. Although the within-nations variations are often weak, in more than three-quarters of the cases sex differences narrow among urban, nonfarm, and better-educated people. Moreover, as Figure 3.1 shows, the sex differences generally narrow most strongly in the two third world countries. If the development model indeed works best for developing nations, it may be because sex differences in education and (as I will show later) in exposure to political communications both narrow in the early stages of development. At the later stages, however, the impact of development weakens and may even disappear.

For political interest, income and occupation most frequently fail to support the development model. British and American farm households have relatively small sex differences not only in these participatory attitudes, but also in participatory resources and many types of political participation. Whether this is due to economic or to cultural reasons, it indicates that shrinking primary sectors in these two nations will not narrow their sex differences. Lower income individuals are older, and income reflects the effects of age more strongly than the other independent variables. Because sex differences in political interest often widen with youth, they also often fail to diminish with increased income. Predicting the effects of increased affluence thus partly depends on understanding the effects of age.

Figure 3.1
Within Nation Variations in Sex Differences in Political Interest, by Nation

CORRELATION OF THE REDUCTION IN SEX DIFFERENCES WITH THE ECONOMIC DEVELOPMENT INDICES †

	PLACE OF RESIDENCE	OCCUPATION	EDUCATION	INCOME	AGE
ECONDEV INDEX	.55	(.33)	(.24)	.56	(.38)
ECONDIST INDEX	.65	.22	.62	.72	(.17)

*Sex differences (gamma) among urban, nonfarm, higher status and younger groups subtracted from sex differences among their opposite counterparts.

†Pearson's r, a positive sign denoting that the reduction in sex differences is stronger in less economically developed nations (econdev index) or more economically distinctive sectors or groups (econdist index).

Sex differences in partisanship tend to support the development model, but not as well as differences in political interest. Differences in interest and partisanship diminish as the model expects in roughly similar proportions; but for partisanship the cross-national variations do not correlate with [either of the economic] development indices. Political practices affect within-nation variations in partisanship and thus the sex differences. For example, while differences in political interest in Italy are largest among rural and farm families, differences in partisanship are smallest. This may be because rural women attend church more and so are more easily politicized by Catholic organizations.

Lastly, within-nation variations in sex differences in efficacy fail to support the development model, as was true with the cross-national data. Sex differences even *increase* among urban, nonfarm, and higher status groups in 60 and 70 percent of the cases for external and internal efficacy respectively. Sex differences in the Verba, Nie, and Kim efficacy index do usually diminish with development; however, contrary to the model's expectations, they diminish more strongly in more-developed nations. Several competing processes may be at work here. First, although urban, better-educated women are usually more egalitarian in their beliefs about women's political roles, Holter (1970) has thoroughly documented how latent traditional attitudes persist among these groups in very subtle ways. Such persistence may be responsible for the larger sex differences in internal efficacy at the higher status and urban center. Second, alienation may increase most among urban, higher status women. Egalitarian women may be most aware of the discrepancies between democratic ideals and reality. In the rural sector, on the other hand, women's perceptions of their powerlessness may be mitigated by less fragmented families. Third, urban, higher status men may feel especially alienated; perhaps because of their greater awareness and exposure to cynical views spread by the media, such men are sometimes most likely to see themselves as powerless and represented by unresponsive leaders. When men's efficacy falls with education and urban residence, women's efficacy is often still rising, and then sex differences diminish strongly. In short, just as the processes associated with development do not make citizens feel more politically efficacious, so those processes also do not necessarily narrow sex differences in efficacy.

The generational model fares no better than the development model in these data. Sex differences in all types of political efficacy do diminish with youth in roughly 80 percent of the cases. However, sex differences in partisanship diminish in only half the cases, and for political interest only one-third of the time. Unspecifiable life cycle factors may be crucial here. Moreover, the cross-national variations do not coincide with generational distinctiveness for any of the participatory attitudes. In the cross-national data of the previous chapter partisanship reflected generational influences; but here the age variations in sex differences correlate with the generational distinctiveness measure only by a very weak .20. In Italy, Nigeria, and Switzerland differences in partisanship actually decrease with age despite the fact that those older women invariably belong to the pre-franchise generation. Once again, political factors in particular countries may weaken the generational model's power to explain sex differences in partisanship. In Italy, for example, women's church attendance increases with age; older women are thus most exposed to the Church's politicizing influence, and this in turn causes sex differences in partisanship to narrow with age.

Finally, these data do not support the diffusion model either. The diffusion model predicts that center/periphery and age differences will diminish over time, as egalitarian attitudes spread to the rural, lower status periphery and among the old. However, in those surveys administered longest after women's enfranchisement the sex differences do *not* narrow less at the urban, higher status center and among the young.

In sum, only the development model is even partially supported by these data. But development notably narrows sex differences only in the case of political interest and only at the early stages of development.

Political Participation

The Overall Results

Within nation variations in sex differences in political participation do not precisely mirror those in participatory attitudes and resources. As Table 3.3 shows, sex differences in participation are in fact slightly smaller among urban, nonfarm, and higher status groups. The proportion of cases supporting the development model varies according to the indicator of development, ranging from 57 percent for income to 70 percent for education. How strongly these results support the development model, however, is open to argument. On the one hand, the stronger relationships (a change of .10 or more) are especially likely to narrow with development. On the other hand, the mean reduction in sex differences is quite mild, ranging

Table 3.3
Change in Sex Differences in Political Participation within Nations

	Place of Residence	Occupation	Education	Income	Age
Amount of change by category					
.10 or more	35%	33%	41%	27%	40%
.01 to .09	34%	25%	29%	30%	28%
.00 to -.09	22%	19%	18%	32%	22%
-.10 or less	9%	22%	12%	11%	10%
Total	100%	99%	100%	100%	100%
Mean reduction	.05	.02	.06	.03	.07
N of cases[a]	136	165	165	161	165

Notes: The amount of change is calculated by subtracting sex differences (gamma) in political participation among urban, nonfarm, higher status, and younger respondents from sex differences among rural, farm, lower status, and older respondents. A positive sign supports the development or generational models. Appendix A describes the surveys.

[a]All types of political participation in fourteen nations. Measures of place of residence and income are unavailable in some surveys.

from .02 to .06. The mean sex differences for the maximum fourteen types of political participation in all fourteen nations is .39. Thus, urban residence, nonfarm occupations, and above average education and affluence narrow sex differences by only 5 to 15 percent.

Chapter 2 found the development model most relevant for certain types of political participation. The within nation data also show variation by type of political activity, but the results do not parallel those from the cross-national data. Figure 3.2, which presents the within nation reduction by type of political participation,[1] shows somewhat inconsistent results across the four indicators of economic development. (The results are even less consistent for each nation taken separately.) The types of political participation correlating best with the economic development index across nations are often different from those that diminish most strongly within nations. For instance, sex differences in political knowledge and in following politics in newspapers tend to be smaller in more-developed countries, but these sex differences change little across

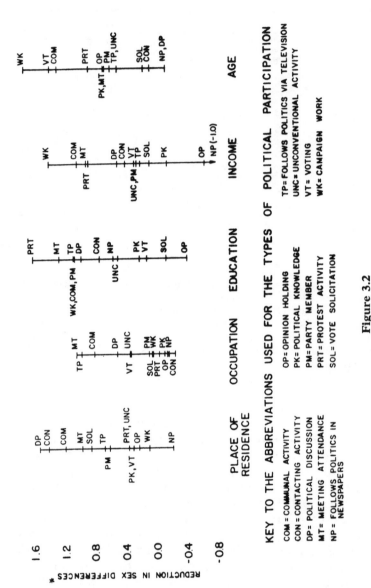

Figure 3.2
Within Nation Variations in Sex Differences
by Type of Political Participation

*Index based on the direction and the amount of change as categorized in Table 3.3. A positive sign denotes that sex differences are smaller among urban, nonfarm, higher status, and younger groups.

groups within countries. Here and there in the rest of this chapter I shall offer tentative explanations for some of these results.

The development model has often been most relevant to the early stages of development. However, in the cross-national variations in Figure 3.3 this is not the case, at least when the types of political participation are averaged together. These cross-national variations do not correlate well with either of the economic development indices. Nor do the third world nations show any especially strong diminutions in sex differences. The cross-national variations change with each indicator of economic development, which complicates any analysis. I shall discuss below those types of participation which do correlate with the development indices and thus better support the development model.

The other models fare even worse than development by these condensed results. First the generational model: Figure 3.3 illustrates that sex differences do not diminish more strongly with youth in late-enfranchising nations, nor do the cross-national variations correlate with the generational distinctiveness measure. Moreover, data not presented here show no more reduction in sex differences when the pre- and post-franchise generations are compared directly. For both age and generation sex differences narrow as expected in roughly two-thirds of the cases. Figure 3.2 does show differences in voter turnout diminishing strongly with youth. Is the generational impact of women's enfranchisement limited to voter turnout, the behavior most directly affected by enfranchisement? I will discuss this question later.

These data also fail to support certain corollaries of the diffusion model. First, sex differences do not diminish least at the urban, higher status center and among the young in those surveys administered longest after women began voting. So if diffusion occurs, it is not closer to completion in early-enfranchising countries. Also the magnitude of the sex differences in the entire nation is unrelated to the extent that differences diminish at the center and among the young. That is, nations with smaller sex differences do *not* have weaker within-nation variations, as would be the case if diffusion had run its course. I will say more about how surveys of a single nation can show quite varied results at different times, and how these variations may partly reflect diffusion effects. For now, however, note that these data suggest that diffusion has not occurred with any cross-national consistency in rate or manner.

Not even the models' intervening variables can satisfactorily explain these cross-national variations. As the preceding chapter noted,

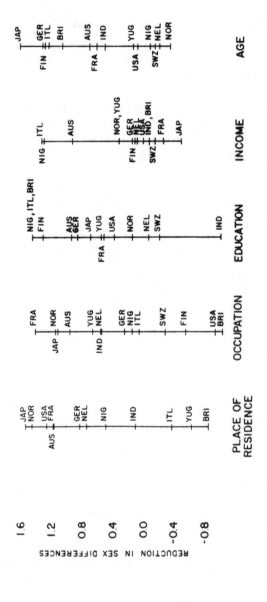

Figure 3.3
Within Nation Variations in Sex Differences, by Nation

82

the effects of differences in participatory resources and attitudes depend on the type of political participation, and these condensed results mask those effects. There is one exception: cross-national variations by age correlate fairly well (.76) with variations in sex differences in political interest. In Chapter 2 political interest often correlated best with the cross-national variations, but it remains to be explained why it predicts variations within nation by age but not by the four indicators of economic development.

Before moving on to explanations for each type of political participation, let me say a few words about survey error. Comparing surveys of a single country administered at different times is a good way to test the reliability of these data. Generally the sex differences in the nations as a whole change very little, at least over short periods. But there are sometimes quite striking discrepancies between surveys in the relationships within nations. A comparison of the 1976 and 1980 U.S. election studies is typical: in one-third of the comparisons the within-nation variations differed by .20 or more; in another third from .10 to .19; and the remaining third showed only mild discrepancies.

Sampling error is only partially responsible for such discrepancies. Error is certainly present, and its probability increases as the sample is broken down into smaller groups. For instance, discrepancies are greatest when comparing farm and nonfarm respondents in nations with small primary sectors, or types of political participation with a small proportion either active or inactive. Yet other factors are also at work. Some discrepancies occur between two elections held only a few years apart and suggest that factors specific to campaigns particularly involve one sex. Long-term changes are reflected in surveys taken further apart. For example, in a 1959 Italian survey sex differences diminish strikingly with youth, but a decade later the diminution is .25 points weaker, even among birth cohorts. The reverse also occurs, as when sex differences diminish more strongly with youth in the 1967 French election study than in the 1958 survey. It is impossible to know exactly how much the discrepancies are due to error and how much to election influences, diffusion, or other social changes. But it is important to recognize that these results are all time bound.

Communications Activity

Economic development very subtly alters the communications channels through which each sex acquires political information. For instance, it has different effects on access to the print media as compared to the broadcast media, and on discussion inside versus outside the family. Moreover, the effects of economic growth sometimes change at different levels of development. Sex differences in the frequency of discussing and following politics mirror such variations in access.

Development may narrow sex differences in newspaper readership at early stages, but not later. As Figure 3.4 shows, differences in readership diminish most strongly with increased status and urban residence in less-developed countries. As argued earlier, the key factor may be literacy; as sex differences in literacy shrink most strongly among urban, more affluent groups in developing countries, so do differences in readership. But when literacy becomes universal, sex differences in newspaper readership no longer diminish as expected within nations. In the first world nations of this sample sex differences in following politics in newspapers tend to *widen* with urban residence, nonfarm occupations, and increased income. Only with education do the differences narrow slightly, in weak reflection of the obvious skills that education provides in third world countries.

At all levels of development sex differences in access to the broadcast media tend to diminish among more affluent, urban, and nonfarm groups. (See Figure 3.5.) Sex differences in following politics via television also shrink relatively strongly at the urban, higher status center. One reason for this finding is that even in rich nations fewer women own televisions, especially in less affluent and rural groups. Another possibility is that women's accidental exposure to television broadcasts is greater at the urban, higher status center. This may be a function of more frequent television watching at the center combined with the likelihood that accidental viewing of political programs occurs at home. Both explanations imply that sex differences in following politics via television will stop decreasing with development when ownership becomes universal or when families at the periphery are fully integrated into the broadcast media infrastructure.

Figure 3.6 illustrates striking cross-national variations in sex differences in discussing politics within the family. Economic development strongly reduces these sex differences in less developed countries. In India and Nigeria the relationships actually reverse; in less-developed segments men discuss more with family members, while in more-developed segments women take the lead in discussions within the family.[2] However, in more-developed countries as more women live alone, sex differences in family discussion widen.

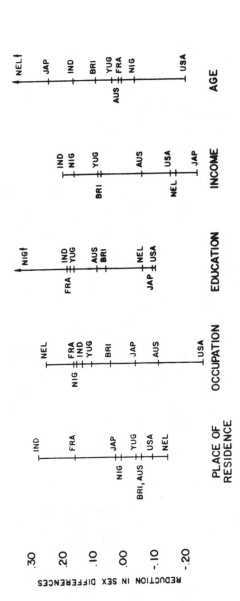

CORRELATION OF THE REDUCTION IN SEX DIFFERENCES WITH THE ECONOMIC DEVELOPMENT INDICES

	PLACE OF RESIDENCE	OCCUPATION	EDUCATION	INCOME	AGE
ECONDEV INDEX	.66	(.13)	.76	(.58)	(.04)
ECONDIST INDEX	.62	(.56)	.83	.77	(.08)

Figure 3.4
Within Nation Variations in Sex Differences
in Newspaper Readership, by Nation

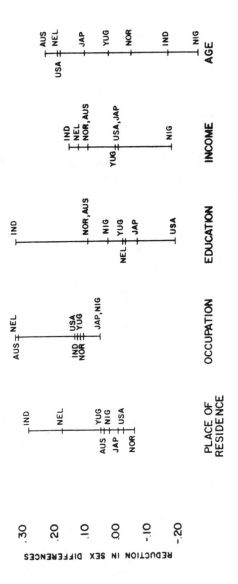

Figure 3.5
Within Nation Variations in Sex Differences
in Radio or Television Attention, by Nation

Here the within-nation variations mirror the distribution of female-headed households, which are most prevalent among older, non-farm, and less-educated and affluent groups.

At odds with the previous chapter's interpretation, in these data economic development does not appreciably narrow sex differences in discussing politics outside the family. (See Figure 3.7.) As was shown in Table 3.2, urban, higher status men often have greater opportunities to discuss politics in formal settings—the workplace and organizations. Although sex differences in informal discussion with friends and neighbors are frequently smallest in urban, high status groups, this does not sufficiently offset the greater sex differences in discussion in formal settings. This interpretation holds true for both developed and developing countries. Thus, while development apparently revolutionizes women's political role inside Nigerian and Indian families, that change does not extend outside the family.

Sex differences in frequency of political discussion are a function of differences in both political interest and opportunities for discussion. Differences in discussion tend to diminish most strongly in less-developed countries, as do sex differences in political interest and discussing politics in the family. But even in first world nations sex differences in discussion narrow relatively well among higher status, nonfarm, and (especially) urban groups. Presumably, even in developed countries women in more traditional groups are still reluctant to publicly demonstrate their political involvement by discussing politics (or soliciting votes).

One unexpected finding is that although development most reduces sex differences in following and discussing politics in third world countries, nowhere does it significantly diminish sex differences in political knowledge or opinion holding. On the average these differences change very little within nations. Perhaps the information communicated through the broadcast media and discussion is not as detailed or comprehensive as that conveyed by newspapers, and thus the reduction in sex differences in discussion and television viewing does not narrow differences in political knowledge. Also, as I suggested earlier, traditional attitudes may constrain women, even in developed nations and at the higher status center, from feeling confident in their political understanding, voicing their opinion, and showing their knowledge. At any rate, increased education slightly equalizes political knowledge, and urban residence mildly reduces the constraints upon women's expressing their opinions and showing political knowledge. In general, however, these changes are considerably weaker than those suggested by the cross-national data.

Figure 3.6

Within Nation Variations in Sex Differences in Political
Discussion within the Family, by Nation

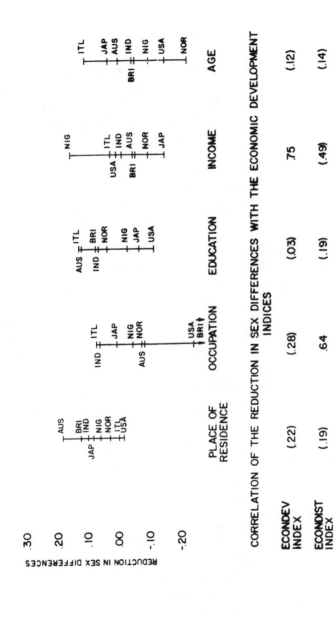

Figure 3.7
Within Nation Variations in Sex Differences in Political
Discussion outside the Family, by Nation

	PLACE OF RESIDENCE	OCCUPATION	EDUCATION	INCOME	AGE
ECONDEV INDEX	(.22)	(.28)	(.03)	.75	(.12)
ECONDIST INDEX	(.19)	.64	(.19)	(.49)	(.14)

CORRELATION OF THE REDUCTION IN SEX DIFFERENCES WITH THE ECONOMIC DEVELOPMENT INDICES

REDUCTION IN SEX DIFFERENCES

.30 .20 .10 .00 -.10 -.20

89

Other Types of Activity

Campaigning, communal, and contacting activities are most easily mobilized. Mobilization within nations occurs when rural, lower status groups are activated despite their lesser awareness of and interest in politics. For example, social pressures and traditional norms stimulate high rates of voting, meeting attendance, and campaign work in rural Japan. India's Congress Party concentrates its recruiting in the primary sector, and European working-class parties recruit and activate those low in social status. Communal and contacting activities have also been mobilized among these groups, even in third world nations. In these data the sex differences have been affected by the forces mobilizing certain social groups. Thus the within-nation variations in sex differences are not explained by development or even by the intervening variables, nor can future trends be predicted from economic factors.

The following examples illustrate the complex relationship between the within nation variations and temporal variations. Sometimes sex differences in party membership and campaign activity diminish strongly with increased social status, due to working-class parties' comparatively greater mobilization of blue collar men. One reason for this mobilization is that such parties are closely tied to unions, which overrepresent men. Changes in sex differences in campaign activities may depend on changes in these parties' mobilization rates; if they become less successful, sex differences can narrow over time while concurrently diminishing less strongly with increased social status. Another frequently mentioned example is the Italian Catholic Church's mobilization of rural women, not simply their voter turnout but also their party membership and campaign activity. Secularization can weaken the Church's mobilizing potential, thus increasing sex differences overall and ensuring that in the future sex differences *will* diminish with urban residence. Identifying how such mobilizing forces affect the sex differences is clearly essential for predicting future trends.

These mobilizing forces make sex differences in such types of activity vary within nations differently from those in communications activity. For instance, in India increased education invariably narrows differences in communications activity, political knowledge, and all participatory attitudes and resources except employment. Yet sex differences in all other activities but voting *increase* with education.[3] For some reason education stimulates men's contacting, campaign, and communal activity more than women's.

Homogeneous social environments facilitate the mobilization of political interests. Social interaction occurs more with those of similar class and residence than those of similar age and sex; so political mobilization also occurs more by class and geography than by age and sex—at least this has been so in the past. When such mobilizing influences are weak, as with age, variations in sex differences in political interest better predict the variations in these political activities.

The connection between sex differences and age is also affected by life cycle factors, as can be seen in the variations by type of political activity. Sex differences in voter turnout diminish strongly with youth almost everywhere, even in nations with no remaining pre-franchise generation women. Life cycle factors like widowhood apparently depress the turnout of older women.[4] In general, although life cycle effects often promote smaller sex differences in employment, organizational membership, and perhaps even political interest among older people, these effects do not extend to narrowing differences in campaigning, communal, or contacting activity. Whatever the reasons, future trends in sex differences in these activities may be more a function of changes in these life cycle influences than generational turnover. Trend data are best for sorting out these various causes.

Conclusion

Why do these within-nation variations only weakly support the development and generational models? The statistics are not at fault. The models' weaknesses were documented by two types of statistics: the high proportion of cases where sex differences fail to diminish as expected, and the small mean reductions. There are several possible explanations for the former, including, of course, survey error. Most significantly, mobilization and life cycle factors affect within-nation relationships more than the cross-national ones because their influence is usually concentrated in certain demographic groups. However, this does not explain the weak mean reduction in sex differences. Theoretically, survey error is randomly distributed and thus is equally likely to cause sex differences to diminish *more* strongly than they actually do. And the effects of mobilization and life cycle factors probably average out to be randomly distributed as well. In fact, diffusion effects may even bias the data toward the development and generational models, if in fact diffusion causes smaller sex differences at the center of society and among the young. (The trend data to be presented next can best identify diffusion effects.)

I do not want to exaggerate the discrepancies between the cross-national and within-nation data. The former include a much broader range of economic development levels than the latter. For example, countries in which adults average twelve years of schooling are compared to those in which they average two, but the difference in the means between those in the high and low education categories is not nearly as great. Also, economic development typically explains less than half of the cross-national variance (r^2), even for strong relationships such as communal, contacting, and campaign activity. Finally, the within-nation data do match one of the patterns discerned in the cross-national data for nations in the early stages of development: sex differences in education, media attention, and political interest *are* narrowed with development. In a new twist, at early stages development also appears to weaken the constraints against women's discussing politics with family members. However, in contrast to the cross-national data, these processes within nations do not have a corresponding strong effect on sex differences in political knowledge.

The greatest discrepancy between the cross-national and within-nation data concerns the hypothesis that development broadens women's social interactions. Within nations, sex differences do not diminish strongly with development for activity outside the home, in organizations, campaigns, community affairs, or contacting. The mean sex differences in discussion with nonfamily members diminishes only slightly and only with urban residence and education.

This discrepancy indicates that different processes are operating at different levels of analysis. The negative results for the within-nation data may partly occur because life cycle effects cause female-headed households (hypothesized as the main impetus behind women's broadening social interaction) to be *less* prevalent in more-affluent and educated groups. Because economic development tends to increase the proportions of women living alone, it may also narrow sex differences more than the within-nation data suggest. However, other factors may counteract any such tendency. Specifically, agricultural occupations can socially isolate men as much as women, and thus industrialization can actually increase the gap between the sexes' employment rates and organizational memberships. It is even possible that the cross-national variations are mostly a product of cultural differences, so that their correlation with development is spurious. For example the more-developed nations are also more Protestant, and Protestantism places less emphasis on women's unique role within the family. Moreover, the remarkable contrasts between Indian and Nigerian women's activity outside the home illustrates the important role of culture in third world nations.

As does the within-nation data, trend data controls for cultural differences between nations and thus can clarify the discrepancies between the two types of data.

Notes

1. The index used in Figures 3.2 and 3.3 summarizes the extent and strength of the reduction in sex differences. For each relationship, a strong reduction (.10 or more) is 2 points, a weak reduction 1 point, a weak increase −1 points, and a strong increase (.10 or more) −2 points. The index is the mean of these relationships.

2. Two explanations for this reversal come to mind. One is because development alters the sexes' social relationships with other family members and kin, partly due to increases in neo-local family structures and modern egalitarian views about women's role. Another is because development increases women's exposure to political communications, and, barring their increased activity outside the home, the family becomes the natural forum for discussions.

3. Other Indian survey data show sex differences in both voting *and* contacting to diminish with increased education (Goel 1975, pp. 94–97).

4. Women are more likely to be widowed than men, and Mossuz-Lavau and Sineau (1978) find, for instance, that turnout falls off for elderly widows but not elderly nuns.

4

Temporal Variations

Each of the three models predicts distinct trends in sex differences in political participation. According to the development and generational models, sex differences should diminish steadily, because economic development and generational turnover proceed at a regular pace. Moreover, controlling for the economic and demographic changes should eliminate temporal variations. The diffusion model accommodates more irregular changes, which vary by group. Since the young, better-educated, and urban are more receptive to change than older, lower status and rural people, the diffusion model predicts that differences between these groups will widen initially, then narrow.

However, the two preceding chapters have suggested that changes over time are more complex, depending, for instance, on the type of political participation and the level of development. In this chapter trend data will be used to test the hypothesized refinements. Data are available for only two nations (the United States and the Federal Republic of Germany) and two types of political participation (communications and electoral activities). (The appendices describe the surveys and measures of the variables.) However, fragmentary information from other nations (Christy 1980) indicates that the trends presented here are fairly representative of first world nations.

This chapter revises and updates my article published in *Comparative Political Studies* (April, 1985). Thanks to Sage Publications for permission to reproduce the figures presented in the article.

The Independent Variables

According to the survey data, the U.S. and German economies grew regularly and at roughly similar rates since the early 1950s. Table 4.1 shows that the proportion of household heads engaged in agriculture fell from 14 to 2–4 percent. The proportion of women with advanced education rose from 13 to 26 in Germany and from 13 to 33 in the United States. In both nations rural and small town

Table 4.1
Trends in the Independent Variables

Year of Survey								
USA	1952	1956	1960	1964	1968	1972	1976	1980
FRG	1953		1961	1965	1969	1972	1976	1980
Indicators of Economic Development								
Occupation (% farming)[a]								
USA	14	12	10	8	6	5	3	2
FRG	14		11	7	6	5	4	4
Education (% high)[b]								
USA (some college +)	13	16	23	21	23	24	30	33
FRG (some secondary +)	13		13	19	22	22	31	26
Place of residence (%)								
USA - belt code; central city	...	29	28	30	26	27	28	27
suburbia	...	...	26	31	30	37	35	39
adjacent/outlying	...	...	46	39	44	36	37	33
FRG - town size								
100,000 +	26		28	33	27	34	33	36
5,000 - 99,999	27		33	34	35	33	41	48
under 5,000	47		39	33	38	33	26	16
Generation (%)[c]								
USA (12 year groupings)								
pre-franchise	29	20	19	14	10	7	4	2
post-franchise	24	21	22	18	17	14	13	10
depression and war	29	30	27	24	23	19	18	17
early post-war	18	26	28	26	26	22	18	17
later post-war		2	5	18	23	25	22	21
women's liberation					2	13	24	30
FRG (15 year groupings)								
pre-franchise	20		16	14	8	3		
post-franchise	30		28	22	19	19	13	8
Nazi	29		26	26	25	24	24	23
early post-war	21		30	30	30	29	32	29
later post-war				8	17	25	28	28
women's liberation							3	11

Notes: See Appendix C for further information on the measures and Appendix A for a description of the survey.

[a]Occupation of the head of household.

[b]Women only. Some college or more in the United States and continuation beyond primary school (excluding apprenticeship training) in Germany.

[c]Women only. Because age was collapsed in early German surveys, the measure is not perfectly identical across the early surveys and differs from that used for the United States.

residency diminished and urban residency increased, especially suburbia in the United States and middle-sized cities in Germany. (Different measures of place of residence prevent more precise comparison of the rates of change.) A nonsurvey measure of economic development, per capita gross domestic product (GDP), indicates that growth was more rapid in Germany.[1]

The pace of generational turnover was the same in both countries. In the early 1950s roughly one quarter of the female electorate belonged to the pre-franchise generation, but this percentage decreased steadily until the 1970s, when it became negligible. If events other than enfranchisement had a generational impact, however, the trends in the two nations could differ. If, for instance, the Nazi regime socialized younger women into more traditional gender role attitudes, then any reduction in sex differences would be delayed until the 1980s, when the Nazi generation begins to shrink appreciably. However, the literature disagrees on whether the Nazi regime did have such a generational effect (Christy 1980, pp. 147–49).

The pace of economic development and generational turnover in other first world nations is similar to that for the United States and Germany, with two minor differences: (1) countries with a larger primary sector show a larger initial drop in the proportion of farming households; and (2) the decrease in the proportion of pre-franchise generation women tends to be greatest immediately after enfranchisement (Christy 1980, p. 351). In all cases the relevant economic and demographic changes since World War II are extensive enough that sex differences in participatory resources, attitudes, and behavior should diminish if the models are correct.

Participatory Resources and Attitudes

Resources

Economic development has not in fact distributed participatory resources more equitably over time in either the United States or Germany. Table 4.2 shows that in both countries sex differences in education and family income increased slightly, and differences in organizational membership remained the same. Sex differences in employment did narrow in the United States, but not in Germany.

Development clearly has not spurred women's activity outside the home, either in the work force or organizations. (Cross-national and within-nation data already suggested that development does not narrow sex differences in employment.) In Germany the diminution of the agricultural sector, where women were widely employed as family workers, actually increased sex differences in work force participation. (This increase does not show up in Table 4.2 because the measure of work force participation excludes farm and family workers.) Moreover, with the lessening severity of the postwar shortage of male workers, the demand for female workers has been decreasing. Nor is Germany an exception: in three of the nine other first world nations, sex differences in employment have not diminished during the last several decades (United Nations 1980, p. 20; Darling 1975, p. 18). As for third world countries, women's decreasing economic participation is so common that it has earned the name "Boserup's dilemma" (Osmond 1981).

There are not much data available on trends in sex differences in organizational membership and activity, but what there are indicate that, at least in first world countries, differences do not always diminish with development. Of course, sex differences in the United States were negligible in the first place. But the large differences in Germany have changed little over twenty years. Changes in women's work and family roles may alter the types of groups women join more than their overall activity rates.

The development model also errs in predicting trends in sex differences in education and family income. The previous chapters observed several times that increases in female-headed households also increase sex differences in family income. Female-headed households nearly doubled in the United States over the last 30 years, but they apparently grew more slowly in Germany. (Germany's trend may reflect either unknown measurement discrepancies or the slight increase in marriage rates that accompanied the lessening shortage of males.) Sex differences in family income widened only mildly in both nations, indicating the influence of a complex array of factors beside female-headed households.

As already discussed, the widening sex differences in education in the United States mainly stem from changing vocational requirements and the G.I. Bill of Rights. I have found no explanation for the increase in Germany. However, these sex differences will probably narrow in the future. U.S. and German universities have enrolled a rising proportion of female students during the last decade, and German vocational schools have increased their enrollment of women as well, apparently since the 1950s (Merkl 1976 and 1986; Sullerot 1971; Pross 1967). (The measure for Germany in Table 4.2 does not tap vocational training, however.) Moreover, except for Great Britain, the proportion of women in universities has also risen in other first world nations (Wolchik 1978, p. 45; see also Lupri 1983, p. 19). Nevertheless, it remains clear that greater equality in education comes not from economic growth but from changing values.

Table 4.2
Trends in Participatory Resources

Year of Survey								
USA	1952	1956	1960	1964	1968	1972	1976	1980
FRG	1953		1961	1965	1969	1972	1976	1980
Sex differences - education[a]								
USA	-.08	.03	-.12	.07	.10	.14	.11	.10
FRG	.09		.14	.14	.17	.18	.23	.22
Sex differences - employment[b]								
USA	.90	.88	.80	.84	.69	.70	.55	.49
FRG	.78		.84	.86	.85	.84	.83	.80
Sex differences - organizational membership								
USA	.16					.14	.17[c]	
FRG	.66			.67	.67		.61[c]	
Sex differences - organizational participation								
USA	-.06					.11	-.03[c]	
Sex differences - family income[d]								
USA	.16	.16	.14	.17	.19	.15	.21	.20
FRG	.17		.18	.20	.25	.23	.25	
Percent female in single adult households								
USA	19	16	20	23	28	28	35	31
FRG	16		16		25	29	19	22
Percent female married								
USA		75	72	67	62	63	58	58
FRG	59		68	69	66	67	73	68

Note: See Appendix B for further information on the measures and Appendix A for a description of the surveys. Sex differences are measured by gamma, a positive sign indicating that men have more of the resource than women.

[a]Trichotomized for the United States and dichotomized for Germany. The actual categories are shown in Figure 4.4.

[b]For Germany the employed category excludes family workers in 1953 and for comparison purposes, farm workers in subsequent surveys.

[c]From the Barnes and Kaase studies.

[d]Income of household head for the German studies of 1953 and 1965.

Attitudes

Trends in participatory attitudes vary with the type of attitude. Attitudes toward women's political roles have become more egalitarian, apparently in the irregular pattern predicted by the diffusion model. The strongest support for this model comes from the best and most thoroughly studied trend data, that on willingness to vote for a woman as president of the United States. Women's willingness changed little during the 1950s and 1960s, then rocketed 26 percentage points between 1969 and 1975, and subsequently stabilized again. Group trends also support the diffusion model: age and education differences were negligible in the 1950s and 1960s but appeared during the early 1970s (Smith 1976; Schreiber 1978), presumably because younger and better educated women were initially more receptive to feminist messages. The diffusion model cannot explain, however, why the diffusion process has been interrupted; age and educational differences remained during the late 1970s while attitudes did not change further (Welch and Sigelman 1982). Trends in other attitudes about women's political role also complicate the issue. Although the questions were posed infrequently, they suggest that attitudes grew more egalitarian prior to the onset of the feminist movement, and have continued to do so throughout the late 1970s (Klein 1984, chaps. 5,9; McGlen and O'Connor 1983, pp. 83–87).

German trend data on egalitarian attitudes are too scanty to provide a good test of the models of change. The Allensbach Institute's series show quite remarkable changes in general attitudes about gender roles over the last 30 years. However, similarly worded questions about women's political role have been repeated only since 1966. Disagreement with the statement that "politics is man's business" leaped 14 percentage points among women between 1966 and 1974 (Noelle-Neumann 1981, p. 151). According to the Eurobarometer studies of the Commission of the European Economic Communities, disagreement with the statement "women should stay out of politics" rose an additional 5 percentage points among women between 1976 and 1983. (In both cases the increase was even greater among men.) Better-educated and younger women have been more egalitarian at least since 1975, when such data were first available. However, the lack of information from before the feminist movement makes it impossible to determine if the movement actually caused these group differences.

Although cultural norms are certainly more egalitarian today, sex differences in participatory attitudes have not invariably narrowed. Figure 4.1 shows that in the United States differences diminished slightly for partisanship, election concern, and external political efficacy, but not at all for campaign interest and internal political efficacy. Intriguingly, the least diminution occurred when the sex differences were initially largest. Thus there is no evidence of a floor effect, where sex differences are so small that they fail to diminish further. In Germany the trend is irregular: differences in these attitudes narrowed rapidly in the 1950s and 1960s, but the diminution slowed or even stopped during the 1970s.[2] Whether this

Figure 4.1
Trends in Sex Differences in Psychological
Involvement and Political Efficacy

irregular diminution in Germany reflects diffusion effects, and why so little change occurred in the United States, will be considered later, when trends among groups are examined. However, clearly these trends in participatory attitudes do not simply reflect trends in either the independent variables, the participatory resources, or egalitarian political norms.

Political Participation

The Trends

No single factor explains trends in sex differences in political participation. Figures 4.2 and 4.3 show that the trends vary by nation and type of political activity. In the United States differences in communications activity diminished only weakly, while those in campaign activity shrunk dramatically, if irregularly. Germany, on the other hand, shows the opposite pattern: sex differences in communications activity narrowed extensively, but differences in party membership actually increased until 1970. Moreover, sex differences in voter turnout decreased moderately in both nations.

The trends in communications activity mirror those in attitudes of involvement and efficacy—the same coincidence revealed by cross-national data in Chapter 2. Communications activities are conducted independently of political organizations, and so depend mainly on individual motivation. In contrast, political and institutional factors do strongly affect trends in sex differences in voter turnout, party membership, campaign work, and, to a lesser extent, campaign meeting attendance. (Since campaign meetings attract persons from outside the circle of party members and campaign workers, it makes sense that individual motivation would become more important, and factors relating to political organization less important.)

What are the relevant political and institutional factors? The widening sex differences in German party membership until 1970 run counter to all other participatory trends. Social Democratic Party statistics show that this enlargement occurred primarily because new party members were increasingly male (Fulles 1969, pp. 27–42). Why the recruitment channels favored men during this period remains elusive; perhaps there was more recruiting through labor unions. At any rate, since 1970 feminist demands for more equal representation in the two major parties (Hall 1981) probably underlies the shrinking sex differences in party membership.

In the United States the dramatic if irregular decrease in sex differences in party membership and especially campaign work has been caused by political factors. Women were most stimulated to work in campaigns during the elections of 1972 and 1980, when

Figure 4.2
Trends in Sex Differences in Communications Activity

McGovern and Reagan took unusually distinct stands on women's reproductive, economic, and legal rights. The irregular fluctuations over time appear to stem from the relatively loose and open

Figure 4.3
Trends in Sex Differences in Campaign Activity,
Party Membership, and Voter Turnout

organization of U.S. political parties, in which interest groups' campaign activity varies across elections according to candidates' platforms. The more structured German parties fluctuate less, and the decline in sex differences has been less rapid than in the United

State. Thus, while women in both nations were organizing into distinctive interests during the 1970s, U.S. party and campaign organizations were more easily penetrated by these newly organizing interests, particularly in 1972.[3]

In the case of voter turnout, German trends support Tingsten's law: sex differences diminished as men's turnout rose. However, the U.S. trends imperfectly mirror the fluctuations in men's turnout rate. Intriguingly, the election variations tend to parallel those in communications activity and campaign interest, but this coincidence may simply reflect minor sampling variations. Government statistics beginning in 1964 show a more regular diminution, with sex differences disappearing by 1980 (Christy 1980, p. 376; U.S. Department of Commerce 1982, pp. 4–5).

In short, the three models are irrelevant for these electoral activities, because trends are so strongly influenced by political and institutional factors. Controlling for changes in the independent variables is thus unnecessary. In fact, for these types of participation I have found quite marked variations over time in the relationships within nations, suggesting that particular groups are activated into different campaigns (Christy 1980, chap. 6). The next section will thus discuss the models' relevance to only those attitudes and activities which are fairly independent of political and institutional influences.

The Impact of Development

The developmental model definitely can not explain trends in sex differences in participatory attitudes or communications activities. Figures 4.4 and 4.5 show that urbanization and rising education levels have had little effect on the trends in psychological involvement and political efficacy.[4] Other data (not presented here) show the same negative results when the diminution of the agricultural sector is controlled and when the dependent variable is sex differences in communications activity.[5] In general, the trends in the nations as a whole are replicated in each demographic group, and sex differences still diminish more extensively in Germany than in the United States.

The development model fails to explain the trends because, as Chapter 3 demonstrated, sex differences never were appreciably smaller among nonfarm families, urban residents, or (since the late 1960s) more-educated persons. In the case of third world nations, however, development may still have an effect.

The impact of education, in particular, changes over time. In Germany sex differences narrowed more with increased education

Figure 4.4
Trends in Mean Sex Differences in Psychological Involvement
and Political Efficacy, by Education

in the 1950s than in the 1970s. In the United States differences
decreased strongly and regularly with more education only in the
elections of 1956 and 1960. In 1952 and since 1964, sex differences
have been either the same or smaller among high school graduates

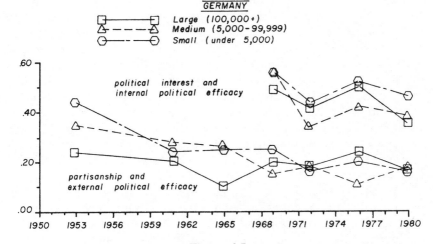

Figure 4.5
**Trends in Mean Sex Differences in Psychological Involvement
and Political Efficacy, by Place of Residence**

than among the college educated. Trends in sex differences in political conceptualization (a measure of political knowledge) show the
same pattern when education is controlled (Wassenberg et al. 1983).

These temporal variations may indicate changes in the types of
women seeking higher education, or in the nature of the educational
experience. For instance, as advanced education becomes more
common, women enrolling in universities and German *gymnasiums*

may be less pioneering and less distinctively egalitarian in their gender attitudes. Or perhaps these later generations of women come from lower status families, where egalitarian norms are presumably less widespread. This interpretation is flawed, however. It fails to explain why sex differences did not narrow with increased education in the 1952 U.S. election study. Moreover, because U.S. and German sex differences in education widened until the mid-1970s, women with advanced training remained exceptional compared to other women, and were even more likely than their male counterparts to come from higher status backgrounds.

The German trends may indicate diffusion effects. The demise of the Nazi regime was followed by sweeping cultural transformations in Germany. Democratic participatory attitudes increased; traditional gender norms and authority relationships within the family faded (Baker, Dalton, and Hildebrandt 1981; Noelle and Neumann, passim). Following the diffusion model, better-educated, urban, and younger Germans may have changed first. In the 1953 survey sex differences in psychological involvement were clearly smallest among these groups. Subsequently, differences narrowed somewhat more rapidly among less-educated, rural, and older generations, suggesting the diffusion of these new attitudes to the remainder of the population. The slowing reduction in sex differences in the 1970s may thus represent the culmination of this diffusion process. In the United States, however, there is no evidence of similar diffusion by age or place of residence, and the diffusion model offers no explanation for the widening differences between education groups in 1956 and 1960.

Surprisingly, there is no evidence that the women's liberation movement initiated a new wave of diffusion in the 1970s. In neither country did differences between demographic groups widen for psychological involvement, political efficacy, and communications activity. The abstract egalitarian principles spreading out among the populace at this time apparently had no effect on more specific participatory attitudes and behaviors. The feminist movement made itself felt most strongly at elite levels, among party members and campaign workers.

Generational Turnover

The generational model also fails to explain trends in sex differences. Figure 4.6 shows no significant cohort variations for involvement and efficacy in the United States and Germany. There are some minor variations among cohorts, however. In Germany sex

Figure 4.6
Trends in Mean Sex Differences in Psychological Involvement and Political Efficacy, by Cohort

differences narrowed more rapidly among the older cohorts during the 1950s, suggesting diffusion effects. The Nazi regime had no distinctive generational impact on these sex differences. In the

United States three cohorts average slightly smaller sex differences: women reaching adulthood immediately after women's enfranchisement, coming of voting age in the early postwar period, and growing up during the women's liberation movement. These variations are nevertheless too small to have had any effect on the trends. Nor are life cycle effects discernible in either nation.[6]

Trends in Other Nations

The U.S. and German trends are generally typical of those in other countries. In certain other nations women's representation in parties has been altered by changes in membership recruitment channels. For example, in Italy urbanization (Ergas 1982) and secularization (Weber 1981) have weakened women's ties to Catholic political organizations. The increased success of left wing parties in establishing units at the workplace (as in France—Wilson 1979) can lower women's representation, unless met with an increase in women's employment rate. On the other hand, at higher levels of party organizations feminist demands for greater representation of women have been effective in the United States (Jennings and Farah 1981), France (Mossuz-Lavau and Sineau 1982), and Scandinavia (Haavio-Mannila et al. 1985, pp. 42–44). It may be that the feminist movement's politicization of issues relevant to women has narrowed differences in party membership, but unfortunately the trend data are fragmentary and permit only rough estimates. Even in Scandinavia, where data are generally good, scholars report an increase in women's party membership over the last decades with the preface "as far as we know" (Haavio-Mannila et al. 1985, p. 42).

In socialist nations statistics on party membership are more readily available. These trends vary by nation, and sex differences decreased in all but two Eastern European nations (Wolchik 1978, pp. 115–18). In this case also the development, generational, and diffusion models are irrelevant, because women's representation is strongly influenced by political decisions about who deserves party membership.

At more elite levels, institutional and political factors become even more important. Institutional reforms have remarkably altered women's representation in legislatures, decreasing it in France in 1958 and increasing it in Yugoslavia in 1974 (Flanz 1982, pp. 285–87; Buric 1983; Rener 1985; but see also Denitch 1981 and Springer 1986). Moreover, Norwegian women effected a massive increase in their proportions in local office by making use of an obscure balloting feature (Albrektsen 1978; Skard 1983).

Nor can the three models explain trends in sex differences in voter turnout. Certainly sex differences have either diminished—as in Scandinavia, Japan, India—or were small to begin with—as in Italy and Yugoslavia (Christy 1980, pp. 365–86; Jain 1975, p. 182; Wolchik 1978, p. 113). But the pace of change reflects many diverse influences. Tingsten's law is relevant for short-term changes: when men's turnout falls sex differences have temporarily widened in such different countries as Norway and India. Short-term political forces also can temporarily narrow the differences: in the French presidential elections of 1969 men were more responsive than women to left wing parties' call for abstention, and more women actually voted than men (Charzat 1972, p. 22). In the long run, however, sex differences become quite small everywhere because the vote is easily mobilized and because groups beside women (e.g. the family, certain parties, and, in socialist countries, the state) benefit by women's turnout.

As for partisanship, the generational model may be more relevant immediately after women's enfranchisement than later. Generational turnover and diffusion have narrowed sex differences in Japan, and generational effects are evident in U.S. and British survey respondents' recall of their parents' partisanship. However, again political factors affect the rate of change, speeding up the process in Italy and slowing it down in France (Christy 1980, pp. 391–407). In general, as with voter turnout, partisanship has relatively small sex differences even immediately after enfranchisement, in part because partisanship can be reinforced by other family members (Claggett 1982; Niemi et al. 1985). And as early as a few decades after women's enfranchisement, generational effects may become trivial in comparison to political factors. For example, in the United States the mild diminution in sex differences in partisanship since 1964 occurred primarily because men became independents more rapidly than women. Perhaps the depoliticizing forces beginning in the mid-1960s had a slightly greater impact on men because of their marginally greater attention to politics. Or the factors underlying the emergence of the gender gap may be relevant here; for example, women's changing family and work roles may have strengthened their attachment to the Democratic Party, thus counteracting the depoliticizing influences.

Trend data on sex differences in political interest and communications activity are very scarce. It appears, however, that the strong diminution in Germany also occurred in France, Norway, and Sweden, while the weak diminution in the United States may *possibly* have been replicated in Japan, Canada, and Great Britain

(Christy 1980, pp. 407–15; see also Bashevkin (1984) and Lovenduski (1986, p. 121) for France, and Christy (1986a and 1986b) for Norway, Sweden, and Canada). Only more extensive data that include trends among groups can precisely determine and explain these cross-national variations in the rate of change.

Conclusion

None of the three models of change satisfactorily explain trends in sex differences in political participation in first world nations. Adequate interpretations must be worked out individually for each type of political participation. Trends in voting and campaign activity, for instance, are almost entirely shaped by institutional and political factors. German trends in participatory attitudes and communications activity do support the diffusion model, but the corresponding U.S. trends do not. And in neither country do these trends support either the development or the generational models: the pace of change is too irregular (Germany) or weak (United States), and the controls have no effect. The period of time covered by the surveys witnessed striking changes in egalitarian norms and sometimes also family organization. However, these changes often did *not* translate into greater equality in participatory resources, nor sometimes in participatory attitudes and behavior as well.

In the last chapter I will address the broader implications of these findings.

Notes

1. Published information on economic development rates, including changes in the per capita GDP, are presented in Christy (1980). This information shows that the diminution of the primary sector in Germany has been more extensive than the survey data indicate, but that education, measured by years of schooling, has risen more extensively in the United States. Discrepancies between this information and the survey data are partly due to survey variations in the measure of head of household, treatment of the retired, and the coding of farm workers. However, both survey and published data concur that economic development was more rapid in Germany by some indicators but not others.

2. Here and for communications activities the German election studies show a curvilinear trend, but the Allensbach data indicate a more linear diminution. The small number of data points in the Allensbach data may mask the curvilinearity of the trends. Or certain elections may particularly stimulate the participation of one sex. Perhaps the 1980 results were affected by the discussion of an election boycott by women to protest the

inadequate alternatives offered by parties (Merkl 1986). Other data not collected during election campaigns show no change in sex differences in political discussion between 1973 and 1978 (M. Inglehart 1981, p. 305), thus confirming the general interpretations given here.

3. The increasing activism of employed women over this period, shown by Andersen (1975) and McDonagh (1982), may reflect the increased relevance of candidates' stands and government policies to employed women's interests. In a more general vein, Beck and Jennings (1984) interpret changes over time in the association of campaign activity with age and political ideology as also due to candidate evaluation.

4. The dependent variable is the mean of the five measures of involvement and efficacy in the United States and the two measures of the same in Germany. In two German elections, data are missing for one of the measures, and the sex differences were estimated by extrapolating from the preceding and following elections. The results summarized by the mean are mirrored by each of the measures in the United States, but not so clearly in Germany.

5. Again, after controls the results represented by the mean sex differences in communications activity are more clearly evident for each of the measures in the United States than in Germany. However, in both nations after controls the trend in mean communications activity coincides fairly closely with the trend in mean involvement and efficacy. There are two minor discrepancies: (1) in the United States sex differences in communications activity decrease regularly with increased education for the election of 1964 as well as those of 1956 and 1960; (2) in Germany differences in communications activity remain largest among rural residents throughout this period.

6. The trends in communications activity also show no distinctive generational or life cycle effects. These trends are somewhat more erratic across the cohorts than those of involvement and efficacy.

5

Conclusion

Although data are limited, sex differences in political participation have usually decreased. However, this trend is not well explained by the development, generational, and diffusion models. These models also poorly explain variations across and within nations.

Only a complex equation with many interrelated variables can adequately account for the changes that have taken place and predict those of the future. Economic development, generational turnover, and post-franchise diffusion processes have only small weights in this equation. Nor would it assume, as the three models I have tested do, that sex differences must diminish in the future. The evidence suggests that future trends will likely depend more on human choice and action than on abstract, mechanical forces.

Where are the three models I have looked at most relevant, and how could they be improved? The diffusion model as originally presented is too limited; it identifies only one event, women's enfranchisement, as commencing the diffusion process, and presumes that sex differences will only narrow, not widen. Sometimes in these data smaller differences in participatory attitudes and communications activities did diffuse from center to periphery and from young to old. But many kinds of social movements and general cultural changes set off waves of diffusion, which may be in the direction of *less* egalitarian gender attitudes. A satisfactory model of the diffusion process would have to take more events into account and avoid making assumptions about the direction of change.

Some of the questions a more sophisticated diffusion model would have to address include: precisely why do cultural norms about gender roles change? The feminist movement clearly made itself felt in the early 1970s, but exactly when and why did attitudes change prior to that time? Also, how are abstract cultural norms about women's proper political involvement translated into participatory attitudes? Why, for instance, was this translation so weak during the 1970s? Perhaps we can learn from studies of why people fail to apply egalitarian principles to their own situation (e.g. Holter 1970). Until these questions are answered, the significance of the diffusion model for explaining change cannot be further specified.

The generational model works best for sex differences in voter turnout and partisanship during the first few decades after women's enfranchisement. Even then , however, political and institutional forces strongly influence sex differences, as they also affect partisanship and voting rates in general. Women's enfranchisement has had no important generational effect on any of those attitudes and behavior unconnected with the act of voting. Nor have other historical events, such as the Nazi and feminist movements, had any significant generational impact. Generational turnover simply plays a very small part in explaining change, and after several decades its part will shrink further when the pre-franchise generation no longer remains in the electorates of most nations.

Although data from third world nations are scarce, the evidence suggests that the development model is more appropriate for these countries. Apparently, three processes combine to decrease sex differences in psychological involvement and communications activities. First, sex differences in education narrow with affluence and increased government support of universal and compulsory primary schooling. (Strictly speaking, the latter is simply a common correlate of development.) The literacy acquired with primary school allows access to political information in newspapers, magazines, and pamphlets. Second, sex differences in access to the broadcast media diminish with wider ownership of radios and televisions. Women can follow broadcasts while working at home, and thereby be exposed, even accidentally, to political information. Finally, urban, higher status women are much less constrained from discussing politics with other family members. In short, the early stages of development promote more equal exposure to political communications.

However, the impact of development is weaker outside the home, in activities aimed toward influencing decision makers. All sorts of political, cultural, and social forces affect sex differences in voting, campaigning, contacting, communal, and unconventional activities. The early stages of development may still indirectly decrease sex differences in these, by narrowing differences in psychological involvement. But any such influence would be small, because some of these activities, especially voting, can be mobilized without high levels of involvement, and others can be essentially closed even to highly motivated women. Moreover, sex differences in involvement depend on more than just development in the first place. The obvious contrasts between India and Nigeria indicate the important role of culture in determining women's activity outside the home, not only in politics, but at work and in voluntary associations as well.

More information from third world nations is needed; but modernization theory's blithe expectation of progress is clearly unwarranted. Economic development is largely unrelated to women's potential for political power, as indicated by sex differences in political activities conducted outside the home. Other measures of political influence, such as women's representation among political elites, support this finding. Moreover, change in women's status is not linear; history reveals many instances where women's influence has diminished, as with the advent of colonial rule in West Africa. Also, political events not directly connected to economic development, such as the institution of military rule, can greatly reduce women's influence. In many military oligarchies (and even the more autocratic one-party states) women are particularly excluded from elite political positions and independent women's organizations are suppressed (Howard 1985).

Among first world nations the power of the development model weakens even further. With near universal literacy and access to radios or televisions, the constraints on women's communications activities become more subtle—such as, for instance, the belief that being interested in politics is unfeminine. These attitudes nevertheless can be quite powerful (even when unvoiced), so that sex differences in involvement and communications activities are nearly as large in some highly developed nations as in certain developing ones. To be sure, when first world countries are compared, development correlates with more egalitarian gender norms and smaller sex differences in most political activities. However, within nation and trend data indicate that this positive correlation is largely spurious. As in third world nations, women's political participation, particularly in activities outside the home, depends on a variety of cultural, social, and political factors.

If these models are of minor import, then why *have* sex differences usually narrowed? And what is the prognosis for future trends? These questions cannot be definitively answered with only the survey data currently available. Many of the factors mentioned in the explanations are not even measured in surveys. Perhaps future surveys of political participation will include some important additional variables, such as cultural attitudes about the relevance of politics to women's concerns and the appropriateness of women's active participation in politics. Also relevant would be a detailed record of the daily activities and social interactions of the sexes along the lines of time-use studies. Other factors are better documented by nonsurvey data or surveys with specialized samples—for instance, the recruitment practices of particular political parties. The descriptive case studies discussed here suggest many factors relevant to specific types of political participation that need to be measured and studied more systematically and comparatively.

In fact, easy availability of data partly explains why the three models have been so popular. Surveys almost always include such sociodemographic variables as age and education. Because these variables strongly correlate with citizens' political participation, it is tempting to apply them to discussions of sex differences as well. This book simply examines these variables more systematically and comprehensively. In doing so, it pushes this kind of analysis to its limits and uncovers fundamental weaknesses in the explanatory power of these variables. Moreover, the surveys themselves are found to have serious limitations, particularly their lack of variables directly measuring the politically relevent aspects of gender roles. These limitations are only just beginning to be corrected by current research.

Although empirical documentation is currently unavailable, some general reasons for the trends can be proposed. The most significant finding is that sex differences in participatory attitudes and political activity have tended to decrease even when the distribution of participatory resources did not improve. Moreover, as far as we know, rarely have differences in political participation *widened* over time, nor have attitudes toward women's political role become *less* egalitarian. Apparently certain broad social and cultural forces are narrowing differences in the political domain, while concurrently other indicators of women's status fail to show definitive progress.

What factors may be promoting greater male-female equality in political activity? Perhaps one explanation is the widening acceptance of democratic, egalitarian values and their application to gender roles. Although this trend is not specifically tied to economic development, some argue that these cultural changes generally accompany broad economic ones. For example, Whyte proposes that the movement toward more complex industrial societies gives rise to a new "participatory and egalitarian ethos," where "new forms of participatory politics emerge, and traditional norms that certain groups are destined by nature to rule over others give way to the expansion of citizenship rights . . . " (1978, p. 182). Such an egalitarian ethos may be changing power relationships within the family as well; in many nations authoritarian family traditions are declining and decision-making power inside the household is increasingly being shared by husband and wife (Lupri 1983; Scanzoni and Fox 1980).

Political and social forces can accelerate or slow this trend. For example, after World War II the rapid growth of a democratic participatory culture in Germany apparently hastened the reduction in sex differences in political participation. Perhaps the institution of a socialist government in Yugoslavia had a similar effect, particularly for those activities most responsive to egalitarian directives from the leadership. On the other hand, political elites can also block the forces for equality and undermine women's progress, as frequently happens during military rule. Moreover, social movements can either increase women's representation among political activists, as did the women's liberation movement in Western countries, or decrease it, as when Moslem fundamentalists gained ascendency in some Middle Eastern countries.

A second factor narrowing sex differences may be the entry of the state into areas formerly reserved to women or the family, which increases the relevance of politics to women's lives. For example, the polity is now making decisions, such as those concerning reproduction and the socialization of children, once made by cultural, religious, or familial institutions. The state is also replacing the family as the provider of economic security. And with more women living alone, more are becoming entirely dependent upon government policies for their economic well-being. Note that this second explanation does not require more egalitarian gender roles. Rather, it simply expands the definition of the political to include traditionally defined women's interests and concerns.

Again, political and social forces can affect the pace of change. For example, when the women's liberation movement broadened the definition of the political to include what were once considered private concerns, new issues were added to the political agenda. Ironically, sometimes these issues also successfully activated anti-feminist women, who could justify their political activity, however untraditional, by reference to their traditional aims. Even if the increasing relevance of politics to women's lives is spurred by broad economic trends, such as the declining economic role of the family and the growth of the welfare state, these trends are not irreversible, nor do they uniformly increase the government's impact on women's lives. For instance, Nigerian market women have been very politically active in defense of their interests, because market activities are regulated by the state (P. Baker 1974; Mba 1982). But as large-scale (and predominantly male) retail firms take over market women's business, there will be fewer women with as much at stake in the political process.

These two factors—growing egalitarianism and the widening scope of government activities—are controversial political issues. They engender battles between parties and other groups, and the outcomes of these conflicts ultimately affect sex differences in political participation. Thus, in the final analysis, collective political action has a much greater impact on trends in sex differences than deterministic economic forces. But that leaves unexplained why the forces for increased egalitarianism and government involvement have tended to win over the long run, at least in Western political experience.

A third force, cultural and institutional inertia, slows the pace of change. The very striking cross-national variations uncovered here reflect quite diverse cultural views about the appropriateness of political activity for women. Whatever the initial reasons for these cultural differences, such attitudes change very slowly in ordinary situations. Also changing very slowly are attitudes about the division of labor in the family. Because such attitudes tend to leave women with less leisure time than men, women will continue to be constrained in the more time-intensive types of political activity. Moreover, political party organizations tend to become rigid and bureaucratized and thus insulated from the forces for change (except when confronted by well-organized groups). Such was the case in early postwar Germany, where sex differences in party membership even widened for several decades.

What might the future hold? In general, sex differences in participatory attitudes and behavior should continue to diminish slowly, as egalitarian norms spread and the scope of government activities widens. At more elite levels of political participation, however, the pace and direction of change is less predictable. There well-organized groups can more easily mobilize others and even alter the institutional procedures that recruit activists, such that change may occur quite rapidly. Conversely, change may not occur for very long periods if the institutions are insulated from the relevant social forces. Projected trends for third world countries will also be tentative, for their situation is quite different from that of the developed nations from which most of the data came.

Whether sex differences will ultimately disappear is another issue entirely. For some types of activity in certain nations, equality has already been achieved. In particular, sex differences in voting and partisanship are close to disappearing almost everywhere. Yet in other instances female activists are very rare, and even among male and female political activists gender differences in behavior persist in subtle ways (Holter 1971, chap. 5; Margolis 1979; Fowlkes, Perkins, and Rinehart 1979). Some even argue that women's political style is so different from men's that real equality requires a radical restructuring of social and political institutions (Buric 1983).

Whether or not real political equality will eventually come about, more equality is definitely needed now. Social changes have been such that women's underrepresentation in politics can no longer be ignored. In the past, such inequality was somewhat counter-balanced by women's influence inside the family. Even today some cultures (such as India) highly respect women in their domestic roles (Madan 1976). However, this traditional sexual division of labor has become outmoded with the fragmentation and scattering of families and the increasing numbers of women who head their own households. If women want real control of their lives in the era of the welfare state, they must have political influence. And such influence is only possible through political participation.

Appendix A

The Surveys

The Inter-university Consortium for Political and Social Research (ICPSR) of Ann Arbor, Michigan provided for surveys used in this study. Its *Guide to Resources and Services* describes these surveys and lists the principal investigators. The ICPSR also publishes codebooks for each survey which detail the sampling methodology and question wording. Incidentally, neither the original collectors of the data nor the consortium bear any responsibility for the analyses or interpretations presented here. The main body presents only the combined results from different surveys of a single nation. Appendix D presents the results broken down by survey.

1. Election Studies

United States. "American National Election Study, 1976" (weighted N=1204 men, 1657 women)

"American National Election Study, 1980" (N=694 men, 919 women)

Great Britain. "Political Change in Britain, 1963–1970" Data from the 1963–1964 waves only. (weighted N=813 men, 970 women)

"British Election Studies: October 1974, Cross Section" (N=1177 men, 1188 women)

Germany. "German Election Panel Study, 1976" (weighted N=947 men, 1128 women)

"German Election Panel Study, 1972" (weighted N=916 men, 1102 women)

Norway. "Norwegian Election Study, 1965" (N=885 men, 864 women)

France. "French Election Study, 1958" Results from the two elections were combined. (weighted N=871 men, 998 women)

"French National Election Study, 1967" (N=935 men, 1034 women)

Italy. "Italian Mass Election Survey, 1972" (N=884 men, 952 women)

"Italian Mass Election Survey, 1968" (N=1228 men, 1251 women)

Japan. "Japanese National Election Study, 1967" Those under twenty were excluded. Results replicated in both waves were combined. (weighted N=849 men, 923 women)

The two election studies were combined into one large SPSS file for the United States, Great Britain, Germany, France, and Italy. The large number of cases in the resulting files lowers the probability of sampling error. However, some variables were only available in one survey.

2. Barnes and Kaase Studies

"Political Action: An Eight Nation Study; 1973–1976"
Those under eighteen were omitted from the analysis.

Great Britain (N=642 men, 782 women)
Germany (N=1031 men, 1219 women)
The Netherlands (N=573 men, 582 women)
Austria (N=631 men, 915 women)
United States (N=704 men, 930 women)
Italy (N=857 men, 949 women)
Switzerland (N=636 men, 648 women)
Finland (N=582 men, 582 women)

3. Verba, Nie, and Kim Studies

"Political Participation and Equality in Seven Nations, 1966–71"

Austria (N=835 men, 934 women)
Japan (N=1300 men, 1357 women)
The Netherlands (weighted N=949 men, 797 women)
United States (weighted N=1496 men, 1599 women)
Yugoslavia (weighted N=1548 men, 1414 women). Those under twenty were excluded.
India (weighted N=1376 men, 1262 women, but actual N=2098 men, 540 women)
Nigeria (weighted N=682 men and 830 women, but actual N=875 men and 584 women). Those under eighteen and those from the Northern Region were excluded.

The surveys of Yugoslavia, India, and Nigeria are not nationally representative samples. The four states sampled in India (Andhra Pradesh, Kujarat, Uttar Pradesh, and West Bengal) are geographically and economically diverse, and their average sex differences in voter turnout are representative of the all-India average. The four provinces in Yugoslavia sampled (Croatia, Serbia, Slovenia and Macedonia) include nearly 80 percent of Yugoslavia's population. Thus, the survey results for India and Yugoslavia are probably not very discrepant from what would be found in the entire nation. However, as the main text notes, the exclusion of Northern Nigeria from the sample (where no women were interviewed) almost certainly has caused sex differences in Nigeria to appear smaller than they are in fact. The Nigerian survey is actually more representative of non-Moslem Western African cultures than of the state of Nigeria. Note that the deliberate undersampling of women in Nigeria and India has increased the probability of sampling error. (In other surveys the weighted N is quite similar to the actual N.)

4. Trend Studies

The United States
"American National Election Study, 1980" (N=658 men, 872 women)
"American National Election Study, 1976" (weighted N=1152 men, 1582 women)
"American National Election Study, 1972" (N=1107 men, 1453 women)
"American National Election Study, 1968"(N=684 men, 873 women)
"American National Election Study, 1964" (N=703 men, 868 women)
"American National Election Study, 1960" (weighted N=881 men, 1073 women)
"American National Election Study, 1956" (N=787 men, 975 women)
"American National Election Study, 1952" (N=821 men, 978 women)

Germany
"German Election Panel Study, 1980" (N size varies, ranging from 449 men and 550 women for internal political efficacy to 5202 men and 6295 women for partisanship.)
"German Election Panel Study, 1976" (weighted N=902 men, 1054 women)
"German Election Panel Study, 1972" (weighted N=876 men, 1047 women)
"German Pre- and Post-Election Study, 1969" (weighted N=535 men, 623 women) and "German Election Study, August–September 1969" (weighted N=854 men, 1038 women). Results from identical measures were merged for the tables.
"German Election Study, September 1965" (weighted N=622 men, 786 women) and "German Election Study, October 1965" (N=586 men, 728 women). Results from identical measures were merged for the tables.
"German Election Study, July 1961" (weighted N=645 men, 810 women) and "German Election Study, November 1961" (weighted N=674 men, 827 women). Results from identical measures were merged for the tables.
"Social Bases of West German Politics, 1953" (weighted N=1430 men, 1976 women).

To make the samples more equivalent, I excluded those voters aged eighteen to twenty, included in the later surveys of the United States and Germany due to the lowering of the voting age. Also omitted were all those ineligible to vote in the German surveys due to youth or residence in West Berlin.

5. Published Information on Trends

Allensbach Institute Data
There are seven volumes in the German language series and two volumes

in the English language summary. (See Bibliography under Noelle for the citations.) Although the question wording does not vary over time, the sampling frames sometimes vary slightly. The gammas are calculated on the basis of the percentages. The publications describe these sampling frames and present the percentages. The location of these data is presented by the temporal order of the surveys, from earliest to latest. The letters in parentheses signify either the German language (G) or English language (E) publications.

> Political Discussion: vol. 2(G), p. 46; vol. 3(G), p. 241; vol. 5(G), p. 215
> Newspaper Attention: vol. 1(E), p. 90; vol. 5(G), p. 187; vol. 7(G), p. 263
> Political Interest: vol. 1(G), p. 51; vol. 3(G), p. 239; vol. 1(E), p. 209; vol. 5(G), p. 214; vol. 6(G), p. 62; vol. 7(G), p. 62

German Official Turnout Statistics

The Statistisches Bundesamt of the German Federal Republic publishes yearly the *Statistiches Jahrbuch für die Bundesrepublik Deutschland.* These yearbooks present the turnout statistics broken down by sex and age. The 1976 edition (p. 143) has the information for the 1972 and 1969 elections, and the 1981 edition (p. 86) has the 1976 and 1980 election data. Data for the earlier elections come from Margarete Heinz's book (1971, p. 21) cited in the Bibliography.

German Party Statistics

Trends in the proportion of party members who are female are available in two books. Mechtild Fulles' book (1969) covers the earlier years (pp. 24–42), and Jane Hall's article (1981) updates this information (pp. 160–64). These trend data were converted to gamma first by calculating the number of male and female party members and, second, by calculating the number of male and female adults residing in West Germany. Slight changes in sex ratio over the postwar period were thus controlled.

6. Inglehart and Rabier Studies

"Euro-barometer 3: European Men and Women, May 1975."

"Euro-barometer 19: Gender Roles in the European Community, April 1983."

The N sizes are presented in Table 2.3. Those under eighteen were excluded from the analysis.

Appendix B

The Intervening and Dependent Variables

The typical wording of the questions used to make measure participatory attitudes and behavior is given below. Deviations in question wording that might affect the results in some unknown manner are also presented. Those who fail to answer the survey question are usually excluded from the calculation, the exceptions being partisanships, opinion holding, and political knowledge, where a "don't know" response is meaningful. I have looked at the results from other coding procedures and related questions on participation, and as far as I can tell the measures used here have not affected the substance of this analysis.

1. Participatory Attitudes
   a. Psychological Involvement
      i. Typical wording
         Interest in Politics. Would you say that generally speaking you are very interested in politics, somewhat interested in politics, or not very interested in politics?
         Interest in the Campaign. How much interest did you have in the campaign—a good deal, some, or not very much?
         Concern about the Election Outcome. Generally speaking, would you say that you personally care a good deal which party wins the presidential election this fall or that you don't care very much which party wins?
         Partisanship. To which party do you habitually feel closest? Do you feel you are very close to this party, fairly close, or not very close? Those replying don't know to the initial question are coded as independents.
      ii. Deviations
         France—Partisanship. Measure in the 1958 election study excludes strength of identification.
         Nigeria—Partisanship. Asks whether respondent was a strong party

supporter. (Parties were abolished at the time of the survey.)

Germany—Partisanship Trend. 1972/1976/1980—Many people in the Federal Republic lean towards a particular party for a long time, although they may occasionally vote for a different party. How about you: do you in general lean towards a particular party? If so, which one? How strongly or weakly do you lean towards this party—very strongly, fairly strongly, moderately to weak?

1969—Generally speaking, do you think of yourself as a supporter of a particular party, or don't you feel particularly committed to any party? Do you think yourself a convinced supporter of _____ or not?

1961—Would you please tell me which political party you like best? Would you say you are a convinced supporter of . . . or would you rather say you favor . . . because it seems best suited to you, given the present conditions?

1953—Which party is comparatively the best? Which is, so to speak, the least of all evils?

b. Political Efficacy
   i. Typical wording
   External Political Efficacy. People like me don't have any say about what the government does. (agree or disagree) I don't think officials care much what people like me think. (agree or disagree) The responses to the two questions were combined for the analysis.
   Internal Political Efficacy. Sometimes politics and government seem so complicated that a person like me can't really understand what's going on.
   Verba, Nie, and Kim Efficacy Index. In relation to the nation as a whole, where would you place yourself on this ladder in terms of power? How much effect do you think people like you have on what the government does—a great deal, some, or none? Responses combined.

   ii. Deviations
   Britain—External Political Efficacy. 1963—Over the years, how much do you feel the government pays attention to what the people think?
   1974—How much attention do you think MPs and local councillors generally pay to local organizations or groups of citizens?
   Netherlands, Austria, Yugoslavia, United States—Verba, Nie and Kim Index. One question only, the first for the United States and the second for the other countries. Also wording variations for the second question.
   *Germany—External Political Efficacy Trend—*1969/1972/1976/1980— Typical Wording.
   1961—Do you think that it is worthwhile for the individual to concern himself with politics and thus to influence political decisions, or is your opinion that it is not worthwhile for the individual to concern himself with politics since he cannot influence decisions?

1953—There are always matters on which one is not satisfied with the government. If you and your acquaintances did not like something, what would you do against that—possibly not right away but maybe in the long run? (Those who replied that they would do something were coded as efficacious, and those who replied that there was nothing one could do were coded as not efficacious.)

2. Participatory Resources

Education. Sex differences in years of formal schooling. Often estimated on the basis of the average years of schooling acquired upon completing a certain level of education (e.g. high school, university, etc.) Appendix C1 describes how this estimation was made.

Income. Sex differences in family income. The Nigerian survey only measures respondent's income, a less than ideal measure because of possibly large numbers of unemployed respondents who still have those participatory resources provided by affluent lifestyles. Ownership of various consumer goods was also examined and rejected as an alternative to income in third world nations.

Work Force Participation. Whether or not respondent is currently employed. Measure includes family workers or part-time workers whenever categorized separately. However, some surveys do not indicate how such workers were classified. Even official statistics vary by nation in their treatment of these types of workers.

Organizational Participation. One or more organizations. Usually measured from a list of organizations read or handed to respondents. Sometimes certain organizations are not mentioned and this can affect the sex differences. For example, union membership is not available for the Barnes and Kaase survey of Austria. The surveys often distinguish between membership and activity in an organization.

3. Participatory Behavior
   a. Electoral Activity
      i. Typical wording
         Meeting Attendance. How often do you attend a political meeting or rally?
         Campaign Work. How often do you spend time working for a political party or candidate?
         Party Membership. Are you a member of a political party?
         Voter Turnout. In talking to people about elections, we often find that a lot of people weren't able to vote because they weren't registered, or they were sick, or they just didn't have time. How about you—did you vote in the elections this fall?
      ii. Deviations
         Verba, Nie, and Kim—Voter Turnout. Frequency of voting
         Yugoslavia—Party Membership, Meeting Attendance, Campaign Work.

Are you a member of the League of Communists? Do you attend voter's meetings when candidates for election are discussed? Do you attend other voter's meetings?

Have you ever been a member of a committee or a group that nominated a list of candidates for the elections of the commune, republic, or federal assembly? Have you ever proposed a candidate at a voter's meeting?

United States—Party Membership Trend. 1972—Here is a list of some kinds of organizations to which people may belong. Just tell me on the card of any type of organization that you belong to . . . political clubs or organizations.

Other—Do you belong to any political clubs or organizations?

Germany—Meeting Attendance Trend. 1972/1976—Did you attend any campaign meetings or similar events before the election?

1965—Before the election—did you visit any campaign meeting of the parties or public discussions with politicians?

1953—Have you ever attended a party meeting or an election campaign rally (since 1945)?

  b. Communications Activity
    i. Typical wording
      Follows politics in newspaper. How often do you read about politics in the newspapers? (The campaign for election studies).
      Follows politics on television. Did you watch any programs about the campaign on television? How many . . . ? (politics for nonelection studies).
      Political discussion. How often do you discuss politics with other people? (the campaign for election studies).
      Vote solicitation. How often do you try to convince friends to vote the same as you?
      Related Variables:
      Newspaper readership. How often do you read newspapers?
      Television attention. How often do you watch television? (Radio for India and Nigeria, either for Yugoslavia).
      Discussion channels. Whom do you discuss politics/the campaign with? (Relatives, spouse/friends, neighbors/work colleagues, political activists, others).
      Political knowledge. Questions tap knowledge of political leaders (e.g. representative's name), current events (e.g. outcome of the election), and government characteristics (e.g. number of regions, voting age). Cumulative index. Questions vary widely among surveys.
      Opinion holding. Opinions on a wide variety of current domestic and international issues. Cumulative index.
      Ideological conceptualization. Understanding and active use of ideological modes of thought, based on responses to several open-ended questions about "right" and "left," and about parties (Barnes and Kaase study).

   ii. Deviations
      There are many but probably insignificant variations in the question wording, such as simply whether or not the respondent engages in an activity rather than the frequency of the activity.
      In some election studies, attention to specific campaign broadcasts (e.g. party debates, special election programs) is measured instead of general broadcasts.

c. *Unconventional Activity.* Signed petition or participated in a boycott or rent strike (did one or more).

d. *Protest Activity.* Participated in a lawful demonstration, wildcat strike, occupying buildings, blocking traffic, painting slogans, damaging property, or personal violence (did one or more).

e. *Contacting Activity.* How often do you contact public officials or politicians? Sometimes constructed from a series of questions about contacts with various local and national officials about some need or problem, and those contacting one or more officials are compared to the remainder.

   The Verba, Nie, and Kim studies also ask the subject of the contact. Particularized contacting involves only family or friends. Social contacting involves broader groups. The Nigerian survey asks only about contacts regarding a *community* need or problem.

f. *Communal Activity.* How often do you work with other people in this community to try to solve some local problems?

Appendix C

The Independent Variables

1. Cross-National Data
   a. The Economic Development Index
   Three variables are standardized and summed: proportion in nonfarm households (NAG), mean years of schooling (EDY), and per capita gross domestic product (GDP). The actual formula is:

$$ECONDEV = (NAG-78.4)/19.4 + (EDY-77.7)/27.7 + (GDP-215.5)/134.65$$

The signs are reversed for ease in presenting the correlation coefficients. The measure of each variable is as follows:
   i. Nonfarm Households
Ideally, this term excludes any primary sector occupation (i.e. farming, forestry, fishing), defines occupation by that of the head of the household, and classifies the retired by their former occupation. Survey coding schemes do not always permit the full realization of these objectives. Sometimes the surveys do not indicate where those in forestry and fishing are classified, although this is not so in nations with a sizable group employed in these areas. Also, sometimes there is a great deal of missing data because the survey failed to indicate retired individuals' former occupations or the occupations of housewives' husbands. These shortcomings cause only minor discrepancies between these results and published data. In a few cases the survey data do indicate significantly fewer in the primary sector than do other data. However, these discrepancies apparently result not from poor measures but rather from undersampling the primary sector. Since the measure accurately reflects this undersampling, it is most appropriate for testing the development model.
   ii. Years of Formal Schooling
The surveys usually indicate the type or grade of school the respondent attended last. In a few nations, such as the United States, the years of schooling are easily derived from these data. In many other nations, more information

133

on educational systems is needed. This matter can be quite complex when educational reforms have altered the number of years of schooling required for various levels. The Barnes and Kaase study converts type of school to years of schooling, and I have followed their guidelines whenever possible. The *World Survey of Education* by UNESCO and more specialized books give detailed information on educational systems. And some surveys indicate the age of leaving school, which easily converts into years of schooling once the normal age for beginning school is known. Comparison of these results with published information suggests that some surveys have oversampled better-educated people, but again such oversampling does not invalidate the test of the development model.

    iii. Per Capita Gross Domestic Product

This measure is in U.S. dollars, and its value changes over time. To control for these changes, I first obtained the 1970 GDP for each nation and then extrapolated to the year of the survey from statistics on the percentage change in per capita GDP before and after 1970. This information comes from the United Nations *Statistical Yearbook* of 1979–1980 (Tables 155 and 163) and 1977 (Table 185). The OECD's economic surveys of Yugoslavia for 1973 and 1974 provide the data on Yugoslavia's GDP. I realize that I.B. Kravis and others have developed more precise measures of cross-national variations in standards of living, but their data are not available for all the nations of this sample and their results do not deviate that much from those of the per capita GDP in the first place.

    b. Pre- and Post-Franchise Generation

The post-franchise generation includes those who came of voting age during or after the first year women voted in national elections. These women were thus never barred from voting with their male contemporaries. The partial enfranchisement of women—for example, on the basis of income or region—is discounted when less than the majority of women became eligible to vote.

The post-franchise generation begins in each nation as follows:

Finland: 24 in 1907	France: 21 in 1945
Norway: 25 in 1915	Yugoslavia: 21 in 1945
Great Britain: 21 in 1918	Japan: 20 in 1946
Germany: 20 in 1919	Italy: 21 in 1946
Austria: 20 in 1919	India: 21 in 1952
United States: 21 in 1920	Nigeria: 21 in 1954
The Netherlands: 24 in 1922	Switzerland: 21 in 1971

Note that this cutoff point may vary by several years for surveys which group age into categories.

    c. Twelve Nation Summary Data

After eliminating Norway and France from the analysis, I still had missing data for certain types of political participation. The values of these variables are estimated from the values of other closely associated variables. For example, sex differences in attention to politics in newspapers average 11 and 6 points higher than sex differences in newspaper readership and political interest respectively. On this basis, Indian and Nigerian data on newspaper readership and political interest each allow an estimate for the following politics in newspapers, and the two estimates are then simply averaged. In a similar fashion, political interest and radio listening are the basis for estimates on following politics in the broadcast media (Nigeria and India), and political interest alone for both political discussion (Yugoslavia) and attention to politics on television (Switzerland and Finland). Estimates of campaign work come from party membership (France) and general contacting activity from social contacting (Nigeria). The indices of communications activity and campaign activity represent the mean of the three indicators of each (vote solicitation not being included in the index). These methods of estimating missing data and constructing indices do not produce results substantively different from those when cases with missing data are excluded from the calculations. However, estimating is necessary when interpreting the results from multivariate analysis.

   d. Voter Turnout Levels

The correlation of men's turnout level with sex differences in voting is based only on ten nations. Four nations do not have cross-nationally equivalent measures of men's turnout level (Austria, Netherlands, Yugoslavia, and Nigeria). As much as possible, official election statistics on both turnout rates and sex differences are used in lieu of the survey data. Some survey respondents report having voted when they actually did not, and sometimes men tend to overreport voting more than do women (Katosh and Traugott 1981; Christy 1980, pp. 254–58). Thus this test of Tingsten's law is only a rough one.

2. Within Nation Data
   a. The Five Independent Variables
      i. Place of Residence

The measurement of urban/rural residence varies by survey, ranging from the population size of the geographic unit to more elaborate and generally more appropriate classifications by the economic base or proximity to urban centers. Three criteria decide the cutoff for this dichotomous variable: division into two equally sized groups; compatibility with the cutoff points of other surveys of the same nation; and natural breaks in the continuum according to the proportion engaged in farming. Sometimes there are only two or three values for the variable in the first place. In India and Nigeria the distribution is unavoidably skewed, with only 20 percent of the population classified as urban. For the remaining nations, the groups are more evenly divided, and usually more than 30 percent of the sample are in one category. For Yugoslavia, place of residence is missing in the single nation data set and is derived from the cross-national data set by respondent ID.

      ii. Occupation (primary/nonprimary)

Same measure as described in section 1a (i)

iii. Education

The most educated third to half of the population is compared to the remainder. Education is measured by years of formal schooling, and the actual cutoff varies by nation. It ranges from over twelve years for the United States to any schooling or simply literacy for India and Nigeria.

iv. Income

Family income is always presented except in Nigeria, where only the respondent's income is available. Because so many in India and Nigeria earn so little cash in the first place, this measure has problems. However, an alternative measure of affluence based on ownership of consumer goods is not any better, at least judged by its correlation with other indicators of social status. In all nations, the more affluent half of the population is compared to their less affluent counterparts.

v. Age

Those under 35 are compared to those over 49 except for France, where the grouping of age in the 1958 study was such that those under 45 had to be compared to those over 54. Other studies that group age deviate only slightly from these cutoff points. Removing the middle age category from the analysis generates more missing data than usual, but this procedure better highlights possible generational and life cycle effects specific to women.

b. Other Measures

i. The Economic Distinctiveness Index

Derived by adding EDU, INC and AGR in Table 3.1. EDU and INC denote the correlation (gamma) of years of schooling and family income respectively, and AGR represents the proportion of farming households at the center subtracted from those at the periphery. All three are converted into raw numbers before addition. As an example, for place of residence the economic distinctiveness index in the United States is 56 (20 + 25 + 11) and in India is 175 (64 + 43 + 68). Thus urban-rural differences are more distinctive in terms of economic development in India than in the United States.

ii. The Generational Distinctiveness Index

The proportion of pre-franchise generation women in the younger age group subtracted from the proportion of the same in the older age group. The larger the number, the more the women in the two groups had distinctive enfranchisement experiences.

iii. Post-Franchise Diffusion Years

The year women first began voting in national elections (presented in section 1b) subtracted from the year the survey was administered. The larger the number the more time for the diffusion of modern egalitarian norms.

3. The Trend Data

Table 4.1 describes the measures of the three indicators of economic development. The measurement problems discussed in section 2a also sometimes occur in the trend data, particularly for farming occupation in earlier surveys. Also, place of residence in the 1972 U.S. study was derived from the 1976 election study according to the primary sampling unit.

The measure of generation is more refined than in the within-nation data. The cohorts represent those who became 21 during a range of twelve years in the United States and fifteen years in Germany. For example, the post-franchise generation represents those becoming 21 between 1920 and 1931 in the United States and between 1915 and 1929 in Germany. From this information the range of years for subsequent cohorts can be calculated. Because the early German surveys grouped age, the range of years differs from that in the United States. Also, the labels for the cohorts in Germany are somewhat misleading; the post-franchise generation includes some who came of voting age before women's enfranchisement, and the women's liberation generation begins with those becoming 21 in 1974, although this movement actually appeared several years before this date. Finally, the cutoff points in Germany sometimes differ by several years in the early surveys.

Appendix D

Sex Differences in Political Participation

Throughout this analysis, sex differences are measured by gamma. Gamma has rather unique properties in comparison to other common ordinal level measures of association such as Tau b and c. Specifically, gamma is relatively insensitive to skewed marginals (for example, when a large proportion of the sample clusters at either end of a scale). Many types of political participation are highly skewed; that is, few individuals engage in campaign, contacting, and protest activities. In such cases, gamma remains large while other measures of association commonly shrink. Conventional conceptions of inequality center on the representation of women among political activists. Gamma best taps this conception because it continues to show sex differences to be large in elitist activities where a small proportion of activists are female.

There are some drawbacks to gamma. Even when the marginals are not skewed, sex differences measured by gamma run nearly twice as large as for other common measures of association. (See Christy 1980, pp. 534–38.) Also, gamma is especially vulnerable to sampling error when the marginals are skewed and in fact is not even accompanied by a test of statistical significance in the SPSS version. However, the seriousness of these problems is mitigated by the large number of cases, the frequent replications across different surveys of the same nation, and the general objective of *comparing* sex differences rather than discussing their absolute level. (In fact, because of this general objective, tests of the statistical significance of the sex differences are meaningless. More appropriate would be a test of the statistical significance of the variations in sex differences, but such a test is not easily available.) Nevertheless, the reader should interpret the results cautiously and realize that the sex differences are exaggerated.

Pearson's r is used to measure the cross-national and within-nation variations in sex differences. The statistic is standard for multivariate analysis and is easily understood because of its widespread use. However, note that the test of statistical significance is mainly an interpretive aid; the sample of nations is not random and the sex differences themselves can be widely off base because of sampling error.

The tables and figures in the main text simply average the results of several surveys of the same nation. The following tables present the complete results. They also explain the data bases of these statistics. However, the actual number of cases is at times somewhat less because of missing values in the intervening and dependent variables.

**Economic Development, Generation, and Sex Differences
in Participatory Resources and Attitudes, by Survey**

NAT	TYP	NAG	EDY	GDP	GEN	SDE	SDI	EMP	ORG	ORA	PI	IDM	IE	EE	PEV
USA	4	96%	11.9	$5560	4%	.08	.21	.51	.	.	.	-.12	.34	.03	.
USA	3	95	11.9	5220	4	.08	.18	.60	.17	-.03	.13	-.01	.28	.10	.
USA	2	91	10.7	4600	10	-.04	-.01	.58	.17	.00	.17	-.06	.	.	.02
BRI	4	96	9.8	2180	10	.00	.24	.70	.	.	.34	-.02	.	.01	.
BRI	3	96	10.0	2400	5	-.01	.18	.70	.45	.23	.11	-.01	.31	.10	.
GER	4	96	8.8	3370	6	.34	.23	.73	.	.	.37	.08	.45	.25	.
GER	3	94	9.3	3370	3	.25	.22	.71	.61	.38	.37	.08	.46	.32	.
ITL	4	77	6.0	1730	50	.26	.12	.78	.	.	.53	.06	.40	.19	.
ITL	3	84	7.5	1900	28	.23	.05	.66	.60	.64	.45	.11	.36	.21	.
AUS	3	83	9.4	2360	0	.46	.25	.72	.51	.63	.32	-.03	.40	.17	.
AUS	2	87	9.5	1880	0	.46	.16	.74	.58	.60	.55	.08	.	.	.04
NEL	3	91	9.8	2820	2	.08	.05	.67	.51	.23	.31	.10	.38	.18	.
NEL	2	89	9.2	2500	5	.21	.01	.90	.33	.30	.34	.14	.	.	.04
JAP	4	82	10.4	1490	52	.21	.15	.90	.	.	.54	.26	.58	.30	.
JAP	2	76	10.2	1490	53	.18	.09	.87	.17	.34	.48	.24	.	.	.12
FRA	4	88	7.0	1840	71	.20	.	.77	.	.	.30	.12	.	.	.
NOR	4	82	8.4	2420	3	.05	.09	.87	.41	.	.42	.07	.	.	.
SWZ	3	90	7.9	3350	86	.30	.13	.84	.54	.42	.41	.30	.40	.27	.
FIN	3	82	8.3	2760	0	-.14	.15	.42	.32	.18	.20	.02	.28	.09	.
YUG	2	62	6.4	720	42	.28	.00	.51	.50	.62	.55	.	.	.	.09
NIG	2	40	2.1	120	50	.56	.	.30	.39	.35	.50	.31	.	.	.05
IND	2	35	2.2	90	50	.53	.20	.96	.90	.96	.61	.61	.	.	.08

Notes: TYP=Type of survey (4=election study, 3=Barnes and Kaase, 2=Verba, Nie, & Kim); NAG=nonfarm household heads; EDY=mean years of schooling; GDP=per capita gross domestic product; GEN=pre-franchise generation.

The remaining columns measure sex differences in the following resources and attitudes: years of schooling (SDE); family income (SDI); employment (EMP); organizational membership (ORG); organizational activity (ORA); political interest (PI); partisanship (IDM); internal efficacy (IE); external efficacy (EE); and the Verba, Nie, and Kim efficacy index (PEV).

The sex differences are measured by gamma, a positive sign indicating men have more participatory resources and attitudes than women. Appendix A describes these surveys and gives the sample sizes (male and female) of each.

Table D.2
Economic Distinctiveness and the Change in Sex Differences in Participatory Resources and Attitudes with Urban Residence, by Survey

NAT	TYP	EDY	INC	AGR	SDE	SDI	EMP	ORG	ORA	PI	IDM	IE	EE	PEV
USA	4	.20	.18	9	-.13	-.06	-.10	.	.	.	.12	-.02	-.09	.
USA	3	.25	.29	9	-.01	-.01	.01	-.17	-.03	.12	-.04	-.03	.09	.
USA	2	.14	.29	15	-.03	.02	.01	-.06	.01	-.05	.10	.	.	.14
BRI	4	-.02	.08	14	-.05	-.21	.03	.	.	.01	.05	.	-.11	.
GER	4	.22	.01	9	.12	.04	.12	.	.	.04	-.02	-.07	-.04	.
GER	3	.23	.02	14	.11	-.04	.17	-.03	-.12	-.01	.01	.05	.01	.
ITL	4	.28	.18	18	.07	-.03	-.04	.	.	.21	-.01	-.02	.13	.
ITL	3	.32	-.02	18	-.01	-.12	.08	.20	.37	.16	-.02	-.05	-.07	.
AUS	3	.54	.27	29	.21	.09	.10	.16	.06	-.04	-.05	-.16	-.03	.
AUS	2	.56	.43	22	.17	.01	.07	.14	.32	.05	.01	.	.	.17
NEL	3	.09	.05	15	-.09	-.08	.00	-.09	-.10	.06	.06	-.07	-.10	.
NEL	2	.18	.04	16	-.06	-.02	.08	-.09	-.03	.11	.06	.	.	.13
JAP	4	.29	.23	30	-.02	.05	-.04	.	.	.08	-.01	-.01	.14	.
JAP	2	.27	.27	29	.11	-.01	.00	-.03	-.03	.04	.05	.	.	.07
FRA	4	.39	.40	25	-.04	-.04	.01	.	.	.08	.22	-.01	.06	.
NOR	4	.31	.42	30	-.09	-.11	.06	-.41	.	-.05	.11	.	.09	.
YUG	2	.19	.17	20	.01	.02	-.14	-.01	-.08	.01	.	.	.	.04
NIG	2	.67	.65	53	.07	-.24	.30	.11	.02	.11	-.01	.	.	.00
IND	2	.64	.43	68	.18	.07	.03	.11	.14	.30	.14	.	.	.01

Notes: TYP=Type of survey (4=election study, 3=Barnes and Kaase, 2=Verba, Nie, and Kim); EDY=years of schooling and INC=family income (the stronger the correlation—gamma—the greater the increase with urban residence); AGR=% in farm households (the larger the number the greater the reduction with urban residence).

The remaining columns show the change in sex differences (gamma) in participatory resources and attitudes with urban residence (the larger the number, the greater the decrease (positive sign) or increase (negative sign)). The note in Table D.1 explains these column headings.

Table D.13 presents the number of cases in the urban and rural categories for each survey.

Table D.3
Economic Distinctiveness and the Change in Sex Difference in Participatory Resources and Attitudes with Nonfarm Occupations, by Survey

NAT	TYP	EDY	INC	SDE	SDI	EMP	ORG	ORA	PI	IDM	IE	EE	PEV
USA	4	.44	.23	-.39	-.29	-.11	.	.	.	.17	-.34	-.08	.
USA	3	.37	.23	-.19	.00	.10	-.32	-.10	-.14	.22	.16	.03	.
USA	2	.41	.28	-.15	-.08	.02	-.23	-.38	-.10	.20	.	.	.23
BRI	4	.18	.36	-.23	-.20	.07	.	.	-.06	.14	.	.01	.
BRI	3	.14	.23	-.24	-.24	.23	-.27	.21	-.12	.09	-.01	-.14	.
GER	4	.44	.01	.06	.01	-.01	.	.	.02	-.10	-.63	-.34	.
GER	3	.40	.36	.01	.04	.13	.11	.01	-.09	-.03	-.01	-.01	.
ITL	4	.66	.51	.04	.06	-.04	.	.	.16	-.04	.01	-.03	.
ITL	3	.52	.06	-.18	.09	-.05	.10	.30	.09	-.28	-.32	-.02	.
AUS	3	.70	.47	.07	.09	.06	.18	.05	.12	.00	-.37	.04	.
AUS	2	.66	.60	.09	.07	-.02	.15	.11	.01	.00	.	.	.04
NEL	3	.36	.60	-.16	-.27	-.05	-.16	-.04	.22	.15	-.37	-.36	.
NEL	2	.36	.33	-.35	-.21	-.09	-.41	-.28	.13	-.04	.	.	.15
JAP	4	.54	.27	-.10	-.08	-.14	.	.	.06	-.12	.15	.27	.
JAP	2	.48	.30	-.07	-.10	-.11	-.06	-.05	.03	.12	.	.	.02
FRA	4	.56	.60	.07	.06	-.06	.	.	.02	.22	-.12	-.05	.
NOR	4	.33	.61	-.15	-.15	.09	-.75	.	.02	.13	.	-.19	.
SWZ	3	.54	.56	.10	-.55	.05	-.09	-.06	.12	-.01	.08	-.06	.
FIN	3	.51	.50	-.16	-.04	.10	-.06	-.08	.01	-.09	-.06	.03	.
YUG	2	.77	.60	.00	.10	.	-.16	.09	-.04	.	.	.	.06
NIG	2	.53	.57	.08	.19	.52	.28	.11	.08	.09	.	.	-.09
IND	2	.40	.04	.10	-.17	.03	.03	.07	.01	.04	.	.	.07

Note: Same as Table D.2, except that years of schooling (EDY) and family income (INC) now correlate with the occupation of the household head (nonfarm=1, farm=2), and the remaining columns show the change in sex differences with nonfarm households (a positive sign indicates a decrease). See Table D.13 for the number of cases.

**Economic Distinctiveness and the Change in Sex Differences in
Participatory Resources and Attitudes with Increased Education, by Survey**

NAT	TYP	INC	AGR	SDI	EMP	ORG	ORA	PI	IDM	IE	EE	PEV
USA	4	.44	3	.04	-.10	.	.	.	.11	-.15	.07	.
USA	3	.41	4	-.04	-.08	-.16	-.11	.05	.08	-.12	.03	.
USA	9	.48	5	-.05	-.13	.14	.13	.05	.24	.	.	.10
BRI	4	.40	2	.12	-.14	.	.	.08	.10	.	.01	.
BRI	3	.47	1	.13	-.23	.06	-.03	-.03	-.01	-.01	.06	.
GER	4	.48	4	.04	.12	.	.	.02	-.03	-.08	.01	.
GER	3	.43	5	.04	.19	-.01	.00	-.08	-.06	-.13	.02	.
ITL	4	.68	24	.06	.15	.	.	.13	.04	.09	.07	.
ITL	3	.27	16	.09	.36	.13	.12	.08	.01	.19	.06	.
AUS	3	.49	21	.13	.15	.25	.16	-.05	.03	.60	.00	.
AUS	2	.50	17	.03	.06	.10	.27	.11	.00	.	.	.12
NEL	3	.41	6	-.10	.12	-.02	-.02	.10	-.12	-.03	.08	.
NEL	2	.42	10	.00	.07	-.08	-.14	.02	.02	.	.	.11
JAP	4	.37	19	.15	.00	.	.	-.01	-.06	.06	-.10	.
JAP	2	.43	22	.05	-.04	.03	.11	-.08	.15	.	.	.09
FRA	4	.60	12	-.01	.07	.	.	.06	.06	.01	-.04	.
NOR	4	.38	8	.06	-.03	-.13	.	.01	.05	.	-.26	.
SWZ	3	.42	12	-.09	-.03	-.17	-.02	-.20	.09	-.02	.07	.
FIN	3	.38	14	-.06	.04	.04	.08	.10	.13	.46	.14	.
YUG	2	.60	50	.23	.18	.05	.16	.02	.	.	.	.02
NIG	2	.73	29	.12	.49	.40	.06	.12	.06	.	.	.05
IND	2	.49	19	.24	-.02	.18	.07	.33	.04	.	.	.21

Note: Same as Table D.2, except that increased family income (INC) now correlates
with increased education, AGR indicates the percentage reduction in farming
households with high education, and the remainder show the change in sex differences with high education, a positive sign denoting a decrease.

Table D.5
Economic Distinctiveness and the Change in Sex Differences in Participatory Resources and Attitudes with Increased Income, by Survey

NAT	TYP	AGR	EDY	SDE	EMP	ORG	ORA	PI	IDM	IE	EE	PEV
USA	4	2	.46	-.06	-.41	.	.	.	.10	-.14	.02	.
USA	3	3	.46	-.15	-.39	-.20	-.03	.05	.06	-.11	-.16	.
USA	2	6	.52	-.12	-.41	-.10	.08	-.03	.21	.	.	.04
BRI	4	4	.49	.07	-.30	.	.	-.06	.06	.	-.04	.
BRI	3	2	.41	.00	-.28	-.24	-.11	-.16	-.12	.04	.00	.
GER	4	0	.47	.14	-.02	.	.	-.01	.10	.05	.12	.
GER	3	4	.45	.01	.00	-.07	-.05	-.17	.05	.14	-.10	.
ITL	4	22	.68	.03	-.05	.	.	.05	.03	-.02	-.02	.
ITL	3	2	.28	-.08	.09	-.02	.16	.03	-.11	-.04	-.05	.
AUS	3	14	.56	.15	-.03	.28	.31	.13	.14	.06	.06	.
AUS	2	15	.56	-.01	-.10	-.02	.14	-.08	.13	.	.	-.14
NEL	3	5	.45	-.16	-.04	-.06	.01	.14	-.03	-.12	-.15	.
NEL	2	7	.36	-.08	-.14	-.14	-.21	-.15	-.15	.	.	.11
JAP	4	10	.37	.09	-.10	.	.	-.14	-.05	-.14	-.14	.
JAP	2	11	.41	-.04	-.06	-.11	.2	-.15	.07	.	.	.00
FRA	4	13	.62	-.17	-.14	.	.	.02	.07	-.10	-.02	.
NOR	4	24	.41	-.08	-.18	-.53	.	.00	.13	.	-.11	.
SWZ	3	11	.48	-.15	-.16	-.15	.05	-.15	.17	-.12	-.01	.
FIN	3	22	.49	-.17	-.09	.00	-.14	-.12	-.02	.12	.12	.
YUG	2	20	.62	.21	.07	.20	.11	-.02	.	.	.	.11
NIG	2	31	.71	.20	.23	.42	-.13	.24	.06	.	.	-.35
IND	2	1	.57	.23	-.02	.01	.10	.16	-.07	.	.	.07

Note: Same as Table D.2, except that increased years of schooling (EDY) now correlates with increased income, AGR indicates the percentage reduction in farming households with high income, and the remainder show the change in sex differences with high income, a positive sign denoting a decrease.

Table D.6

Economic and Generational Distinctiveness and the Change in Sex Differences in Participatory Resources and Attitudes with Youth, by Survey

NAT	TYP	EDY	INC	AGR	GEN	SDE	SDI	EMP	ORG	ORA	PI	IDM	IE	EE	PEV
USA	4	.48	.22	4	8	-.19	.17	-.07	.	.	.	.09	.10	.06	.
USA	3	.42	.16	4	12	-.25	.17	-.21	-.22	-.21	-.21	.07	.00	-.03	.
USA	2	.51	.24	9	30	-.27	.05	-.50	-.04	-.17	-.05	.12	.	.	.11
BRI	4	.70	.36	2	20	-.16	.30	-.24	.	.	-.07	-.07	.	-.06	.
BRI	3	.70	.46	1	7	-.03	.17	-.20	-.09	-.13	.04	.12	.02	.02	.
GER	4	.42	.45	1	11	.13	.23	-.01	.04	.08	-.05	.03	-.01	.04	.
GER	3	.45	.47	4	6	.21	.22	-.09	.	.08	-.07	-.04	.06	.11	.
ITL	4	.55	.43	14	100	.19	.17	-.05	.	.	.04	-.08	.01	.13	.
ITL	3	.68	.26	9	90	-.07	.08	.23	-.07	-.01	.03	-.03	-.01	-.10	.
AUS	3	.44	.36	6	0	.16	.01	-.19	-.01	-.03	.05	.14	.13	.03	.
AUS	2	.36	.35	- 3	0	.19	.28	-.22	-.07	.03	.12	.13	.	.	-.17
NEL	3	.62	.25	2	6	-.16	.05	.33	-.06	-.08	-.12	.02	-.03	.36	.
NEL	2	.54	.46	13	28	-.03	.20	-.16	-.20	-.32	-.18	-.16	.	.	.20
JAP	4	.71	.14	18	100	.25	.21	-.08	.	.	.17	.03	.07	.20	.
JAP	2	.62	.07	18	100	.21	.11	-.16	-.05	.08	.21	.29	.	.	.21
FRA	4	.36	.47	7	59	.10	.42	-.39	.	.	-.01	.14	.21	.12	.
NOR	4	.58	.24	14	6	-.21	.11	-.09	-.44	.	-.27	-.06	.	-.07	.
SWZ	3	.37	.33	6	43	.10	.17	-.14	-.23	-.33	-.15	-.10	.29	.18	.
FIN	3	.66	.62	19	0	.00	.17	-.09	.05	-.26	.21	.11	.52	.32	.
YUG	2	.60	.30	40	100	.18	.22	-.41	.11	.12	-.05	.	.	.	.00
NIG	2	.67	.21	19	96	.08	.30	-.02	.18	.18	.05	-.02	.	.	.03
IND	2	.29	.01	6	100	.24	-.05	-.07	.07	.03	-.07	.23	.	.	.21

Note: Same as Table D.2, except that increased education (EDY) and income (INC) now correlate with youth, AGR shows the percentage reduction in farming households with youth, GEN the percentage reduction in pre-franchise generation women with youth, and the remainder indicate the change in sex differences with youth, a positive sign denoting a decrease.

Table D.7
Sex Differences in Political Participation, by Survey

NAT	TYP	NEW	NP	TV	TP	DP	SOL	DF	DA	DO	OPI	PK	PM	MT	WK	VT	CON	CNN	COM	PRP	PRV
USA	4	.15	.19	.	.08	.10	.21	.02	.11	.29	.32	.28	.09	-.02	-.07	.17	.	.	.	.	.
USA	3	.	.21	.	.	.19	.23	.	.	.	.34	.18	.17	.21	.21	.	.27	.	.19	.21	.48
USA	2	-.03	.	-.16	.	.17	.14	-.40	-.10	.35	.23	.19	.07	.05	.10	.	.19	.22	.05	.	.
BRI	4	.30	.25	.	.12	.29	.	.	.	.	.51	.14	.35	.	.	.06	.	.	.	.	.
BRI	3	.	.34	.	.	.25	.41	.	.	.	.37	.32	.19	.31	-.06	.01	.23	.	.18	.11	.54
GER	4	.	.54	.	.23	.40	.45	.18	.51	.	.39	.	.69	.53	.41	.32	.46	.	.46	.	.
GER	3	.	.50	.	.	.43	.44	.	.	.	.30	.23	.72	.53	.48	.09	.51	.	.42	.27	.50
ITL	4	.	.61	.	.31	.55	.39	.21	.67	.67	.50	.41	.58	.73	.52	-.01	.	.	.	.	.
ITL	3	.	.43	.	.	.44	.39	.	.	.	.36	.23	.77	.63	.58	-.11	.46	.	.49	.32	.59
AUS	3	.	.41	.	.	.30	.30	.	.	.	.34	.40	.59	.45	.56	-.12	.55	.	.53	.25	.56
AUS	2	.23	.42	.04	.25	.61	.42	-.28	.30	.67	.39	.39	.61	.67	.69	.00	.36	.74	.66	.	.
NEL	3	.	.42	.	.	.28	.20	.	.	.	.23	.36	.24	.43	.39	-.13	.42	.	.24	.19	.48
NEL	2	.16	.39	-.14	.27	.39	.40	.	.	.	.47	.39	.36	.61	.51	.16	.38	.45	.11	.	.
JAP	4	.53	.62	-.01	.33	.53	.58	-.47	.	.76	.60	.40	.	.48	.62	.04	.	.	.	.	.44
JAP	2	.53	.	.08	.	.35	.	-.36	.28	.50	.47	.40	.75	.38	.43	.04	.57	.69	.40	.	.
FRA	4	.	.	.	.13	.	.36	.	.	.	.41	.	.	.	.	.18	.	.	.	.	.
NOR	4	.	.54	.04	.29	.37	.39	.17	.42	.62	.40	.48	.38	.47	.46	.08	.	.	.	.	.
SWZ	3	.	.47	.	.	.30	.45	.	.	.	.25	.28	.70	.51	.44	.36	.57	.	.47	.25	.53
FIN	3	.	.32	.	.	.17	.30	.	.	.	.28	.	.31	.32	.38	.03	.46	.	.39	.18	.56
YUG	2	.30	.45	.04	.38	.	.	.	.	.	.43	.45	.60	.60	.62	.21	.38	.65	.30	.	.
NIG	2	.60	.	.40	.	.50	.	.27	.52	.59	.34	.55	.	.	.	.40	.	.69	.52	.	.
IND	2	.57	.	.33	.	.69	.	.23	.78	.81	.59	.57	.75	.87	.79	.23	.81	.96	.86	.	.

Notes: TYP = Type of survey (4 = election study, 3 = Barnes and Kaase, 2 = Verba, Nie, and Kim). The remaining columns show the sex differences, which are measured by gamma with a positive sign indicating men participate more than women.

The types of participation are as follows: NEW = newspaper readership; NP = follows politics in newspaper; TV = television viewing; TP = follows politics on television; DP = political discussion; SOL = vote solicitation; DF = discuss politics in family; DA = discuss politics with friends and neighbors; DO = discuss politics outside family; OPI = opinion holding; PK = political knowledge; PM = party member; MT = meeting attendance; WK = campaign work; VT = vote; CON = contacting activity; CNN = social contacting; COM = communal activity; PRP = unconventional activity; PRV = protest activity.

Appendix A gives the sample sizes.

Change in Sex Differences in Political Participation with Urban Residence, by Survey

NAT	TYP	NEW	NP	TV	TP	DP	SOL	DF	DA	DO	OPI	PK	PH1	MT	WK	VT	CON	COM	PRP	PRV
USA	4	-.06	-.05	.	-.07	-.03	.01	-.06	.04	-.09	-.05	.09	.36	-.03	-.17	-.03	.	.	.	.
USA	3	.	.08	.	.	.15	.00	.	.	.	.07	.00	-.23	.17	.29	-.11	.18	.14	.11	.13
USA	2	-.11	.	-.02	.18	.04	.10	.08	.23	.07	.03	.07	.13	.18	.17	-.02	.08	.22	.	.
BRI	4	-.05	-.14	.	-.08	.13	-.30	.10	.15	.13	.00	.04	-.01	-.04	-.34	-.08	.	.	.	.
GER	4	.	.06	.	.06	.05	.14	-.18	.03	.	.10	-.06	.07	.07	.00	.27	.11	.00	.	.
GER	3	.	-.05	.	.	.10	.05	.	.	.	.35	-.13	.03	.21	.22	-.20	.14	.22	.17	-.22
ITL	4	.	.08	.	-.05	-.03	-.24	-.12	.02	.05	-.02	-.02	-.03	-.13	-.34	-.27	.00	.	.	.
ITL	3	.	.10	.	.	.11	.07	.	.	.	-.14	-.02	.02	.05	.14	.05	.12	.14	-.15	.01
AUS	3	.	-.10	.	.	.03	.08	.	.	.	.30	.	.26	.14	.11	.17	.00	.10	.02	.10
AUS	2	-.05	-.09	.05	.04	.19	.17	-.15	.41	.19	.15	.10	.17	.25	.35	-.05	-.06	.28	.	.
NEL	3	.	-.09	.	.	.03	.00	.	.	.	.14	-.03	-.15	.01	-.02	.	.07	.14	.00	-.04
NEL	2	-.14	.12	.18	.16	.14	.10	.	.	.	.01	.05	.19	.18	-.27	.	.14	.18	.	.
JAP	4	-.14	.03	-.02	.23	.12	.21	.17	.03	.06	.03	.22	.	-.05	.05	-.05	.	.	.	.
JAP	2	.10	.	.03	.	.11	.	.10	.22	.12	.10	.10	.13	.13	.10	.12	.13	.10	.	.
FRA	4	.17	.06	.	.14	.11	.10	.	.	.	-.15	.04	.52	.31	.	.09	.	.	.	.
NOR	4	.	-.03	-.05	.06	.12	.24	.11	.17	.04	.10	.09	.12	.36	.27	.35	.	.	.	.
YUG	2	-.03	-.04	.06	-.07	.	.	.	.	.	-.05	-.02	-.08	-.05	-.07	-.07	.01	.03	.	.
NIG	2	.01	.	.03	.	.05	.	.60	.08	.07	.04	-.06	.	.	.	.04	.12	-.03	.	.
IND	2	.28	.	.29	.	.28	.	.69	.12	.11	-.11	.09	-.08	.06	.00	.09	-.06	-.04	.	.

Note: The notes in Table D.7 explain the column headings. The change in sex differences is measured by gamma, a positive sign indicating that they are smaller among urban residents than among their rural counterparts. Table D.13 presents the number of urban and rural residents for each survey.

NAT	TYP	NEW	NP	TV	TP	DP	SOL	DF	DA	DO	OPI	PK	PM	MT	WK	VT	CON	COM	PRP	PRV
USA	4	-.38	-.34	.	-.07	-.48	-.45	-.43	-.10	-.32	-.28	-.14	.85	-.23	-.69	-.17	.	.	.	.
USA	3	.	-.16	.	.	-.13	-.01	.	.	.	.20	.05	-.43	.31	-.21	-.11	-.12	.03	.01	-.10
USA	2	-.17	.	.14	.25	-.13	.03	-.02	.45	-.15	.06	.07	-.35	.10	-.05	-.05	.10	.00	.	.
BRI	4	.05	-.20	.	-.12	-.17	-.20	-.29	-.13	-.34	-.19	.05	-.43	-.38	-.83	-.19	.	.	.	.
BRI	3	.	-.30	.	.	-.14	-.33	.	.	.	-.51	-.18	.75	-.01	-.66	.35	-.59	-.11	.03	.44
GER	4	.	.11	.	.15	.02	-.27	-.20	-.30	.	.08	.	.33	-.06	-.53	.41	-.39	-.22	.	.
GER	3	.	-.18	.	.	.02	-.04	.	.	.	.21	-.20	-.20	.23	-.03	-.38	.01	.28	.29	.12
ITL	4	.	.10	.	.09	.09	.15	.04	.08	.08	.02	.00	.06	.06	-.05	.04	.	.	.	.
ITL	3	.	.00	.	.	-.05	.07	.	.	.	-.06	-.12	-.37	.00	-.10	-.11	-.09	.23	.13	-.22
AUS	3	.	.01	.	.	.04	.33	.	.	.	.24	.10	.30	.30	.34	.57	.18	.25	.	.
AUS	2	-.11	-.29	.32	.11	-.01	.24	-.11	.30	-.08	.13	-.01	-.14	.15	.08	-.10	.03	.37	-.01	-.11
NEL	3	.	.03	.	.	.08	-.22	.	.	.	.10	.21	-.28	.27	-.46	.01	.13	.33	.	.
NEL	2	.26	.09	.33	.12	.19	-.27	.	.	.	-.29	-.07	-.06	.10	.13	-.08	.16	.03	.20	.21
JAP	4	-.14	-.05	-.04	-.05	.10	.46	.33	.	.01	-.12	.05	.	.02	.00	.07	.	.	.	.
JAP	2	.08	.	.17	.	.21	.	.12	.37	.04	.12	.12	.10	.17	.12	.07	.18	.39	.	.
FRA	4	.17	.16	.	.20	.35	.34	.	.	.	-.15	.02	.50	.14	.	.21	.	.	.	.
NOR	4	.	.15	.11	.25	-.02	.14	-.13	.15	-.07	.12	.15	.03	.23	.27	-.14	.	.	.	.
SWZ	3	.	-.01	.	.	.00	.04	.	.	.	.42	-.05	-.12	-.02	.05	.04	-.07	-.04	-.11	.16
FIN	3	.	.00	.	.	.04	-.11	.	.	.	-.14	.	.05	.14	.05	-.25	-.09	.05	-.17	-.79
YUG	2	.11	.10	.12	.06	.	.	.	.	.	-.01	-.03	-.01	.03	.02	.01	.11	.10	.	.
NIG	2	.16	.	.06	.	.03	.	.45	.01	-.03	.24	-.06	.	.	.	.16	-.10	-.02	.	.
IND	2	.14	.	.13	.	.19	.	.36	.06	.07	-.03	.04	-.18	.06	.30	.18	-.03	.02	.	.

Note: Same as Table D.8, except that a positive sign indicates that sex differences are smaller among nonfarm households.

Table D.10
Change in Sex Differences in Political Participation with
Increased Education, by Survey

NAT	TYP	NEW	NP	TV	TP	DP	SQL	DF	DA	DO	OPI	PK	PM	MT	WK	VT	CON	COM	PRP	PRV
USA	4	-.20	-.06	.	.03	-.19	-.01	-.06	-.08	-.18	-.01	.05	.55	.06	.22	.03	.	.	.	.
USA	3	.	-.15	.	.	-.08	-.05	.	.	.	-.02	.09	.03	-.08	-.02	-.10	-.07	.15	-.06	.16
USA	2	.01	.	-.18	-.06	.03	.00	.13	.17	-.02	-.05	.03	.23	.31	.15	.25	.19	.17	.	.
BRI	4	.06	.06	.	.11	.10	.17	.01	.07	.08	.11	.06	.24	.09	.02	.14	.	.	.	.
BRI	3	.	.06	.	.	.07	-.05	.	.	.	.17	.02	-.05	.21	.27	-.09	.08	.21	.08	.26
GER	4	.	-.01	.	.10	.06	.03	-.04	-.01	.	.03	-.18	.26	.21	.05	.77	.06	.17	.	.
GER	3	.	.06	.	.	.06	-.08	.	.	.	-.05	-.09	.10	.08	.11	-.08	.09	.05	.09	.48
ITL	4	.	.04	.	.13	.16	.02	.18	.13	.14	.00	.11	.19	.01	-.13	.19	.	.	.	.
ITL	3	.	.06	.	.	.16	.05	.	.	.	-.09	.04	.17	.21	.40	.18	.16	.20	.07	.22
AUS	3	.	.00	.	.	.03	.04	.	.	.	-.03	.19	.06	.02	.20	-.45	.03	.17	.17	.13
AUS	2	.09	.05	.10	-.02	.12	.04	-.06	.23	.13	.14	.01	.14	.16	.09	-.40	.15	-.03	.	.
NEL	3	.	.01	.	.	.11	.14	.	.	.	-.02	.00	-.13	.23	.06	-.15	.02	.06	-.06	-.08
NEL	2	-.06	-.01	-.03	.11	.18	-.03	.	.	.	-.08	-.04	.12	.20	.07	-.10	-.08	.05	.	.
JAP	4	-.11	-.12	-.11	.28	.00	-.20	.12	.	-.10	-.03	.24	.	-.09	.08	-.03	.	.	.	.
JAP	2	-.07	.	.00	.	.11	.	.12	.13	.00	.19	.04	.12	.20	.16	.02	.10	.09	.	.
FRA	4	.18	.16	.	.12	.04	-.03	.	.	.	-.09	-.01	-.02	.19	.	.13	.	.	.	.
NOR	4	.	.13	.10	.16	.15	-.13	.05	.03	.05	.09	-.19	.07	.00	-.10	.03	.	.	.	.
SWZ	3	.	-.06	.	.	-.15	.09	.	.	.	-.42	.01	.07	.15	.03	-.13	-.01	-.06	-.03	.23
FIN	3	.	.23	.	.	.11	.04	.	.	.	-.32	.	.24	.17	.22	-.03	.12	.26	.19	.16
YUG	2	.17	.15	-.02	-.05	.	.	.	.	.	-.04	-.04	.22	.18	.18	-.19	.10	.07	.	.
NIG	2	.39	.	.03	.	.05	.	.06	.00	-.02	.69	.03	.	.	.	.32	.03	.23	.	.
IND	2	.19	.	.33	.	.17	.	.64	.12	.07	-.20	.07	-.14	-.13	-.24	.01	-.21	-.11	.	.

Note: Same as Table D.8, except that a positive sign indicates that sex differences are smaller among those high in education.

Table D.11
Change in Sex Differences in Political Participation with Increased Income, by Survey

NAT	TYP	NEW	NP	TV	TP	DP	SOL	DF	DA	DO	OPI	PK	PM	MT	WK	VT	CON	COM	PRP	PRV
USA	4	-.12	.02	.	.08	.10	-.04	.23	.14	-.02	.03	.05	.39	.21	.20	.04	.	.	.	.
USA	3	.	-.09	.	.	-.08	.06	.	.	.	-.08	-.06	.29	-.15	.17	-.23	-.04	.09	-.01	-.09
USA	2	-.18	.	.00	-.01	-.11	-.05	.39	.33	.05	-.06	-.07	.37	.20	.15	.09	.13	.21	.	.
BRI	4	.06	-.08	.	.06	-.01	.18	.11	.01	-.04	.01	.03	-.03	.09	.32	.16	.	.	.	.
BRI	3	.	-.17	.	.	-.11	.00	.	.	.	-.14	-.13	-.29	.04	.05	-.19	.03	.09	.10	-.07
GER	4	.	.11	.	.07	.13	.02	.28	-.06	.	.16	.33	.38	-.08	.06	-.09	.11	.14	.	.
GER	3	.	-.13	.	.	-.05	-.06	.	.	.	-.21	-.17	.06	.07	.01	.08	-.02	-.03	-.03	.05
ITL	4	.	-.05	.	.04	.04	-.09	.03	.04	.04	.06	.01	-.04	.03	-.16	.06	.	.	.	.
ITL	3	.	.11	.	.	.11	.22	.	.	.	.04	.07	.50	.24	.25	.15	.16	.05	.14	.03
AUS	3	.	.09	.	.	.08	.19	.	.	.	-.21	.31	.12	.27	.27	.44	.14	.19	.	,
AUS	2	-.06	-.20	.10	-.05	-.02	.09	.09	.20	-.03	.09	-.20	.13	.05	-.02	.03	-.09	.03	-.08	.46
NEL	3	.	-.03	.	.	.13	-.13	.	.	.	-.25	-.11	.08	.10	-.06	.10	.14	.15	.01	.40
NEL	2	-.17	-.13	.13	-.03	-.11	-.24	.	.	.	-.19	-.17	.09	.11	.47	.07	-.30	-.03	,	.
JAP	4	-.17	-.06	.04	.08	-.08	-.16	.15	.	-.15	-.07	-.05	.	-.07	-.14	-.46	.	.	.	.
JAP	2	-.35	.	-.05	.	-.07	.	.04	-.07	-.12	-.05	.00	.09	.08	.07	-.03	.04	.33	.	.
FRA	4	.	.	.	-.06	.	.09	.	.	.	-.09	.04	.	.	.	-.01	.	.	.	.
NOR	4	.	-.07	.10	.15	.11	.17	.32	.15	-.08	-.01	-.07	-.05	-.18	.30	.63	.	.	.	.
SWZ	3	.	-.26	.	.	-.09	-.02	.	.	.	-.44	-.07	-.23	.20	.06	.16	.02	.03	-.17	.36
FIN	3	.	.00	.	.	.09	.03	.	.	.	-.24	.	-.15	.16	.20	-.10	-.08	.04	.28	.01
YUG	2	.07	-.01	.01	-.11	.	.	.	.	.	.15	-.03	.24	.10	.09	.18	-.17	.09	.	.
NIG	2	.16	.	-.17	.	.13	.	.38	.23	.17	.18	-.03	.	.	.	.17	.16	.01	.	.
IND	2	.20	.	.16	.	.09	.	.34	.00	.00	-.05	.12	-.35	.01	.13	-.05	-.09	-.09	.	.

Note: Same as Table D.8, except that a positive sign indicates that sex differences are smaller among those high in income.

Table D.12
Change in Sex Differences in Political Participation with Youth, by Survey

NAT	TYP	NEW	NP	TV	TP	DP	SOL	DF	DA	DO	OPI	PK	PM	MT	WK	VT	CON	COM	PRP	PRV
USA	4	-.11	-.05	.	-.08	.04	.02	.41	-.01	-.03	.05	.03	.	-.12	.40	.26	.	.	.	.
USA	3	.	.00	.	.	-.05	.05	.	.	.39	.10	-.04	.04	-.04	-.05	-.02	.00	.	.	
USA	2	-.29	.	.19	-.05	-.06	.02	.21	.27	-.26	.08	.02	-.26	-.17	.08	.09	-.13	.15	-.12	.05
BRI	4	.09	.04	.	.05	.02	-.20	.23	.17	-.04	.07	.05	-.37	-.21	.14	.23	.	.	.	.
BRI	3	.	.14	.	.	.10	.24	.	.	.	.20	.08	.01	.36	.75	-.07	.19	.30	.03	.13
GER	4	.	-.02	.	.17	.02	-.12	.17	.12	.	.17	.07	.24	.04	-.01	.40	.11	.17	.	.
GER	3	.	.01	.	.	.06	.06	.	.	.	.08	.02	.03	.13	.22	.30	.16	.15	.18	.43
ITL	4	.	-.04	.	.07	.09	-.09	.26	.10	.13	-.02	.03	.09	-.01	.07	.58	.	.	.	.
ITL	3	.	.10	.	.	.16	.10	.	.	.	.23	-.80	.24	.20	.30	.28	.19	.25	.06	.06
AUS	3	.	.16	.	.	-.04	.02	.	.	.	-.17	.07	-.01	.04	.13	.04	.04	.09	.05	-.03
AUS	2	.01	.02	.24	.08	.09	.09	.21	.16	.01	.11	.20	.16	-.06	.18	.13	.11	.18	.	.
NEL	3	.	-.01	.	.	-.07	-.07	.	.	.	.09	-.04	-.07	.16	.17	-.06	-.01	.04	-.03	.10
NEL	2	.39	-.01	.20	-.17	-.05	.01	.	.	.	.05	.02	-.09	.12	.27	.04	-.23	.22	.	.
JAP	4	.18	.16	.14	.39	.11	.11	.28	.	.04	.14	.27	.	-.08	.20	.25	.	.	.	.
JAP	2	.29	.	.08	.	.15	.	.27	.22	.06	.18	.30	.13	.09	.08	.28	.06	.29	.	.
FRA	4	.00	-.15	.	.06	-.01	-.06	.	.	.	.10	.10	.51	.11	.	.04	.	.	.	.
NOR	4	.	.00	-.04	.05	-.13	-.52	.15	-.13	-.21	.07	.07	-.21	-.26	.35	.01	.	.	.	.
SWZ	3	.	-.04	.	.	-.16	.05	.	.	.	-.51	.00	-.09	.06	.03	.21	-.03	.03	-.03	.56
FIN	3	.	.36	.	.	.21	.21	.	.	.	.00	.	.23	.28	.16	.28	.18	.19	.07	-.11
YUG	2	.03	-.04	.03	-.06	.	.	.	.	.	-.07	.02	.12	.02	.07	.09	-.14	.08	.	.
NIG	2	-.04	.	-.25	.	-.11	.	-.14	-.03	-.08	.19	-.07	.	.	.	.30	-.26	.01	.	.
IND	2	.16	.	-.16	.	-.01	.	.33	-.01	-.03	-.07	.12	.20	.16	.27	.11	-.08	-.11	.	.

Note: Same as Table D.8, except that a positive sign indicates that sex differences are smaller among the young.

Table D.13
The Number of Cases in the Independent Variable Categories for the Within Nation Data, by Survey

		Place of Residence		Occupation		Education		Income		Age	
		Urban	Rural	Non-Farm	Farm	High	Low	High	Low	Under 35	Over 49
USA	4	2517	1392	3571	158	1356	2537	1704	1840	1482	1553
USA	3	1048	604	1494	77	561	1083	656	686	607	653
USA	2	1988	1107	2671	261	683	2410	1258	1641	932	1279
BRI	4	1460	368	4369	205	2317	2359	1766	2403	1358	2029
BRI	3			1278	55	721	676	456	682	410	685
GER	4	2841	1259	3652	164	1263	2789	1900	1886	1214	1695
GER	3	1584	659	1871	115	657	1567	953	1012	642	949
ITL	4	2030	2309	3061	936	1168	3162	1669	1977	1172	1795
ITL	3	1109	600	1367	265	765	943	451	608	634	560
AUS	3	775	770	1144	231	743	801	442	547	455	625
AUS	2	823	946	1455	218	976	792	780	896	495	687
NEL	3	877	278	996	93	571	578	427	487	492	386
NEL	2	947	798	1364	172	692	1045	660	675	562	355
JAP	4	1220	632	1422	321	791	1023	789	934	688	557
JAP	2	1851	806	1833	577	1018	1563	1130	1005	891	894
FRA	4	2126	1551	3044	435	1136	2497	645	1017	1135	1539
NOR	4	837	914	1419	300	751	977	872	796	434	744
SWZ	3			1086	124	818	432	488	485	436	535
FIN	3			795	174	490	656	488	533	426	418
YUG	2	1780	1182	1586	978	974	1982	919	1290	836	901
NIG	2	341	1171	588	858	423	1054	226	957	674	297
IND	2	476	2162	754	1405	921	1701	963	1369	1264	498

153

Table D.14
Trends in Sex Differences in Political Participation

Year of Survey USA FRG	1952 1953	1956	1960 1961	1964 1965	1968 1969	1972 1972	1976 1976	1980 1980
WEST GERMANY								
political interest					.46	.34	.40	.43
partisanship	.27		.12		.14	.07	.08	.14
internal efficacy					.60	.43	.49	.34
external efficacy	.50			.29	.25	.26	.23	.20
political discussion	.55		.44	.41	.37		.48	
discussion with friends	.73				.58	.39	.51	.30
follows politics-television				.26	.35			.39
follows politics-radio	.66			.31				
meeting attendance	.71			.67		..57	.52	
THE UNITED STATES								
campaign interest	.11	.18	.20	.07	.14	.20	.10	.10
election concern	.09	.09	.09	-.01	.05	.00	.04	-.01
partisanship	.00	-.05	-.11	-.02	-.05	-.08	-.16	-.07
internal efficacy	.36	.27	.25	.25	.35	.29	.34	.38
external efficacy	.12	.08	.06	.03	.07	.06	.03	.02
follows campaign-newspapers	.21	.31	.21	.11	.18	.12	.21	.18
follows campaign-television	.08	.10	.03	-.03	.07	.08	.11	.04
vote solicitation	.26	.32	.22	.23	.29	.23	.27	.15
meeting attendance	.09	.21	.15	.13	.05	.08	-.11	.08
party member	.06	.32	.00	-.03	.02	-.32		.06
campaign work	.28	.06	.26	.05	-.07	-.14	-.01	-.18
vote	.27	.30	.28	.14	.11	.16	.23	.10

References and Bibliography

Albrektsen, Beatrice Halsaa. 1978. "Women's Political Activity." *International Journal of Sociology.* 8 (Fall): 112–137.

Almond, Gabriel A. and Sidney Verba. 1963. *The Civic Culture: Political Attitudes and Democracy in Five Nations.* Princeton NJ: Princeton University Press.

Andersen, Kristi. 1975. "Working Women and Political Participation, 1952–1972." *American Journal of Political Science* 19 (August): 439–453.

Andersen, Kristi and Elizabeth A. Cook. 1985. "Women, Work, and Political Attitudes." *American Journal of Political Science* 29 (August): 606–625.

Annuario Statistico Italiano. 1982. Rome: Institute Centrale di Statistica.

Atkinson, Jane Monnig. 1982. "Review Essay: Anthropology." *Signs: Journal of Women in Culture and Society* 8 (Winter): 236–258.

Aviel, JoAnn Fagot. 1981. "Political Participation of Women in Latin America." *Western Political Quarterly* 34 (March): 156–171.

Awe, Bolanle. 1977. "The Iyalode in the Traditional Yoruba Political System," pp. 144–160 in Alice Schlegel (ed.) *Sexual Stratification: A Cross-Cultural View.* New York: Columbia University Press.

Awosika, Keziah. 1981. "Women's Education and Participation in the Labour Force: The Case of Nigeria," pp. 81–93 in Margherita Rendel (ed.) *Women, Power and Political Systems.* London: Croom Helm.

Azmon, Yael. 1981. "Sex, Power and Authority." *British Journal of Sociology* 32 (December): 547–559.

Babchuk, Nicholas and Alan Booth. 1969. "Voluntary Association Membership: A Longitudinal Analysis." *American Sociological Review* 34 (February): 31–45.

Baker, Kendall L. 1973. "Political Participation, Political Efficacy, and Socialization in Germany." *Comparative Politics* 6 (October): 73–98.

Baker, Kendall L.; Russell J. Dalton; and Kai Hildebrandt. 1981. *Germany Transformed: Political Culture and the New Politics.* Cambridge, MA: Harvard University Press.

Baker, Pauline H. 1974. *Urbanization and Political Change: The Politics of Lagos, 1917–1967.* Berkeley, CA: University of California Press.

Barnes, Samuel H. 1974. "Italy: Religion and Class in Electoral Behavior," pp. 171–225 in Richard Rose (ed.) *Electoral Behavior: A Comparative Handbook.* New York: The Free Press.

———. 1977. *Representation in Italy: Institutionalized Tradition and Electoral Choice.* Chicago: University of Chicago Press.

155

Barnes, Samuel H.; Max Kaase, et al. (eds.) 1979. *Political Action: Mass Participation in Five Western Democracies*. Beverly Hills: Sage.

Bashevkin, Sylvia B. 1984. "Changing Patterns of Politicization and Partisanship Among Women in France." *British Journal of Political Science* 15 (no. 1): 75–96.

Basu, Aparna. 1976. "The Role of Women in the Indian Struggle for Freedom." pp. 16–40 in B.R. Nanda (ed.) *Indian Woman: From Purdah to Modernity*. New Delhi: Vikas Publishing House.

Baxter, Sandra and Marjorie Lansing. 1983. *Women and Politics: The Visible Majority*. Revised ed. Ann Arbor: The University of Michigan Press.

Beck, Paul Allen and M. Kent Jennings. 1984. "Communications: Updating Political Periods and Political Participation." *American Political Science Courses* 78 (March): 198–201.

Beckwith, Karen. 1980. "The Cross-Cultural Study of Women and Politics: Methodological Problems." *Women & Politics* 1 (Summer): 7–28.

Benson, Mike; Mariah Evans; and Rita Simon. 1982. "Women as Political Terrorists." *Research in Law, Deviance and Social Control* 4: 121–130.

Bertelsen, Judy. 1974. "Political Interest, Influence and Efficacy: Difference Between the Sexes and Among Marital Status Groups." *American Politics Quarterly* 2 (October): 412–26.

Beteille, André. 1975. "The Position of Women in Indian Society." pp. 59–68 in Devaki Jain (ed.) *Indian Women*. New Delhi: Publications Division, Ministry of Information and Broadcasting, Govt. of India.

Bhatty, Zarina. 1976. "Status of Muslim Women and Social Change." pp. 99–112 in B.R. Nanda (ed.) *Indian Women: From Purdah to Modernity*. New Delhi: Vikas Publishing House.

Biles, Robert E. 1983. "Women and Political Participation in Latin America: Urban Uruguay and Columbia." Working Paper #25, June. Michigan State University Working Papers on Women in International Development, East Lansing.

Blumberg, Rae Lesser. 1978. *Stratification: Socioeconomic and Sexual Inequality*. Dubuque, IA: Wm. C. Brown Co.

Booth, Alan. 1972. "Sex and Social Participation." *American Sociological Review* 37 (April): 183–192.

Bose, Ashish. 1975. "A Demographic Profile of Indian Women." pp. 125–184. In Devaki Jain (ed.) *Indian Women*. New Delhi: Publication Division, Ministry of Information and Broadcasting, Government of India.

Bose, Christine E.; Philip L. Bereano; and Mary Malloy. 1984. "Household Technology and the Social Construction of Housework." *Technology and Culture* 25 (no. 1): 53–82.

Boserup, Ester. 1970. *Woman's Role in Economic Development*. London: George Allen and Unwin.

Boulding, Elise; Shirley A. Nuss; Dorothy Lee Carson; and Michael A. Greenstein. 1976. *Handbook of International Data on Women*. New York: John Wiley, Halsted Press.

Bourque, Susan C. and Jean Grossholtz. 1974. "Politics as an Unnatural Practice: Political Science Looks at Female Participation." *Politics and Society* 4 (Winter): 225–266.

Brass, Paul R. 1984. "National Power and Local Politics in India: A Twenty-Year Perspective." *Modern Asian Studies* 18 (February): 89–118.

Bremme, Gabriele. 1956. *Die Politische Rolle der Frau in Deutschland.* Göttingen: Vandenhoeck & Ruprecht.

Bretton, Henry J. 1966. "Political Influence in Southern Nigeria." pp. 49–84 in Herbert J. Spiro (ed.) *Africa: The Primacy of Politics.* New York: Random House.

Brody, Richard A. 1978. "The Puzzle of Political Participation in America," pp. 287–324 in Anthony King (ed.) *The New American Political System.* Washington, DC: American Enterprise Institute for Public Policy Research.

Brown, L. A. and E. G. Moore. 1969. "Diffusion Research in Geography: A Perspective," vol. 1, pp. 119–157 in Christopher Board, et al. *Progress in Geography.* New York: St. Martin's Press.

Buric, Olivera. 1983. "Change in the System of Social Power: Conditions for the Social Equality of Women in Yugoslavia." pp. 311–327 in Eugen Lupri (ed.) *The Changing Position of Women in Family and Society: A Cross-National Comparison.* Leiden (Netherlands): E. J. Brill.

Butler, David and Donald Stokes. 1969. *Political Change in Britain: Forces Shaping Electoral Choice.* New York: St. Martin's Press.

Cahalan, Don. 1968–1969. "Correlates of Respondent Accuracy in the Denver Validity Survey." *Public Opinion Survey* 32 (Winter): 607–621.

Campbell, Angus; Philip E. Converse; Warren E. Miller; and Donald E. Stokes. 1960. *The American Voter.* New York: John Wiley.

Carlbert, Eileen. 1976. "Women in the Political System," pp. 233–253 in Joyce Lebra, Joy Paulson, Elizabeth Powers (eds.) *Women in Changing Japan.* Boulder, CO: Westview Press.

Carroll, Berenice A. 1980. "Political Science, Part II: International Politics, Comparative Politics, and Feminist Radicals." *Signs: Journal of Women in Culture and Society* 5 (Spring): 449–458.

Cavalli, Alessandro. 1983. "The Changing Role of Women: The Case of Italy." pp. 179–189 in Eugen Lupri (ed.) *The Changing Position of Women in Family and Society: A Cross-National Comparison.* Leiden (Netherlands): E. J. Brill.

Chafetz, Janet Saltzman. 1980. "Toward a Macro-Level Theory of Sexual Stratification and Gender Differentiation." pp. 103–125 in Scott G. McNall and Gary N. Howe (eds.) *Current Perspectives in Social Theory,* Vol 1. Greenwich, CT: JAI Press.

Charzat, Gisele. 1972. *Les françaises sont-elles des citoyennes?* Paris: Denoël/Gonthier.

Cherlin, Andrew and Pamela Barnhouse Walters. 1981. "Trends in United States Men's and Women's Sex-Role Attitudes: 1972 to 1978." *American Sociological Review* 46 (August): 453–460.

Christy, Carol A. 1980. "Must Sex Difference in Political Participation Diminish? A Test of the Modernization and Diffusion Theories in Seven Nations." Unpublished Ph.D. dissertation. The Ohio State University.

_____. 1983. "Gender, Employment, and Political Participation in Eleven

Nations." Paper presented at the Annual Meeting of the American Political Science Association.

———. 1984. "Economic Development and Sex Differences in Political Participation." *Women & Politics* 4 (Spring): 7–34.

———. 1985. "American and German Trends in Sex Differences in Political Participation." *Comparative Political Studies* 18 (April): 81–103.

———. 1986a. "Trends in Sex Differences in Political Participation: Results from the Norwegian and Swedish Election Studies." Paper presented at the Annual Meeting of the American Political Science Association.

———. 1986b. "Canadian Trends in Sex Differences in Political Participation: 1945–1984." Paper presented at the Annual Meeting of the Southern Political Science Association.

Claggett, William. 1982. "Life Cycle Model of Partisanship Development: An Analysis of Aggregate Electoral Instability Following the Enfranchisement of Women." *American Politics Quarterly* 10 (April): 219–220.

Clausen, Aage R. 1968–69. "Response Validity: Vote Report." *Public Opinion Quarterly* 32 (Winter): 588–606.

Cole, Allan B. and Naomichi Nakanishi. n.d. *Japanese Opinion Polls with Socio-Political Significance, 1947–1957.* Medford, MA: Fletcher School of Law and Diplomacy, Tufts University and Williamstown, Mass.: Roper Opinion Poll Research Center, Williams College.

Commission of the European Communities. 1975. *Men and Women of Europe: Comparative Attitudes to a Number of Problems of Our Society.* Brussels.

Converse, Philip E. 1969. "Of Time and Partisan Stability." *Comparative Political Studies* 2 (July): 139–171.

Converse, Philip E. and Georges Dupeux. 1962. "Politicization of the Electorate in France and the United States." *Public Opinion Quarterly* 26 (Spring): 1–23.

Craig, Stephen C. and Michael A. Maggiotto. 1982. "Measuring Political Efficacy." *Political Methodology* 8 (No. 3): 85–109.

Currell, Melville E. 1974. *Political Woman.* London: Croom Helm.

Curtis, Gerald. 1971. *Election Campaigning Japanese Style.* New York: Columbia University Press.

Curtis, James. 1971. "Voluntary Association Joining: A Cross-National Comparative Note." *American Sociological Review* 36 (October): 872–880.

Cutler, Stephen J. 1976. "Age Differences in Voluntary Association Memberships." *Social Forces* 55 (September): 43–58.

Danforth, Sandra. 1982. "Women, Development and Public Policy: A Selected Bibliography." *Women & Politics* 2 (Winter): 107–128.

Darling, Martha. 1975. *The Role of Women in the Economy.* Paris: Organization for Economic Co-operation and Development.

Das, Veena. 1976. "Indian Women: Work, Power, and Status." pp. 129–145. B.R. Nanda (ed.) *Indian Women: From Purdah to Modernity.* New Delhi: Vikas Publishing House.

Denich, Bette. 1977. "Women, Work, and Power in Modern Yugoslavia." pp. 215–244 in Alice Schlegel (ed.) *Sexual Stratification: A Cross-Cultural View*. New York: Columbia University Press.

Denitch, Bogdan. 1981. "Women and Political Power in a Revolutionary Society: The Yugoslav Case." pp. 115–123 in Cynthia Fuchs Epstein and Rose Laub Coser (eds.) *Access to Power: Cross National Studies of Women and Elites*. London: George Allen and Unwin.

Desai, Padma and Jagdish N. Bhagwati. 1975. "Women in Indian Politics." pp. 165–199 in Myron Weiner and John Osgood Field (eds.) *Studies in Electoral Politics in the Indian States*. Vol. II: Three Disadvantaged Sectors. Boston, MA: Massachusetts Institute of Technology.

Devon, Tonia K. 1980. "Up from the Harem? The Effects of Class and Sex on Political Life in Northern India." pp. 123–142 in Beverly Lindsay (ed.) *Comparative Perspectives of Third World Women: The Impact of Race, Sex, Class*. New York: Praeger.

Di Palma, Giuseppi. 1970. *Apathy and Participation: Mass Politics in Western Society*. New York: The Free Press.

Dixon, Ruth B. 1982. "Mobilizing Women for Rural Employment in South Asia: Issues of Class, Caste, and Patronage." *Economic Development and Cultural Change* 30 (January): 373–390.

Dogan, Mattei. 1959. Le comportement politique des italiens." *Revue française de science politique* 9 (June): 383–409.

_____. 1967. "Political Cleavage and Social Stratification in France and Italy," pp. 129–195 in Seymour M. Lipset and Stein Rokkan (eds.) - *Party Systems and Voter Alignments: Cross-National Perspectives*. New York: The Free Press.

Dogan, Mattei and Jacques Narbonne. 1954. "L'abstentionnisme electoral en France." *Revue française de science politique* 4 (Jan-Mar and April-June): 5–26, 301–325.

_____. 1955. *Les françaises face à la politique: comportement politique et condition sociale*. Paris: Armand Colin.

D'Souza, Nella and Ramani Natarajan. 1986. "Women in India: The Reality." pp. 359–380 in Lynne B. Iglitzin and Ruth Ross (eds.) *Women in the World, 1975–1985: The Women's Decade*. 2nd, revised ed. Santa Barbara, CA: American Bibliographical Center, Clio.

Dubey, Swaroop Rani and S. Trikha. 1979. "Indian Women as Seen in Election Studies." pp. 67–76 in Vina Mazumdar (ed.) *Symbols of Power: Studies on the Political Status of Women in India*. Bombay: Allied Publishers Private Limited.

Dupeux, Georges. 1960. "Citizen Participation in Political Life: France." *International Social Science Journal* 12: 40–52

Duverger, Maurice. 1955. *The Political Role of Women*. Paris: UNESCO.

Eisenstein, Zillah. 1979. "Developing a Theory of Capitalist Patriarchy and Socialist Feminism." pp. 5–40 in Zillah R. Eisenstein (ed.) *Capitalist Patriarchy and the Case for Socialist Feminism*. New York: Monthly Review Press.

Ergas, Yasmine. 1982. "1968–79—Feminism and the Italian Party System:

Women's Politics in a Decade of Turmoil." *Comparative Politics* 14 (April): 253–279.

Erskine, Hazel G. 1971. "The Polls: Women's Role." *Public Opinion Quarterly* 35 (Summer): 275–290.

Everett, Jana Matson. 1979. *Women and Social Change in India*. New York: St. Martin's Press.

Ferrari-Occhionero, Marisa. 1978. "Women in Italian Political Life." *International Journal of Sociology* 8 (Fall): 12–37.

Ferree, Myra Mary. 1974. "A Woman for President? Changing Responses: 1958–1972." *Public Opinion Quarterly* 38 (Fall): 390–399.

Ferriss, Abbott L. 1971. *Indicators of Trends in the Status of American Women*. New York: Russell Sage Foundation.

Finland, Central Statistical Office. 1976. *Statistical Yearbook of Finland 1975*. Helsinki.

Finn, Jeremy D.; Loretta Dulberg; and Janet Reis. 1979. "Sex Differences in Educational Attainment: A Cross-National Perspective." *Harvard Educational Review* 49 (November): 477–503.

Flammang, Janet A. 1983. "Feminist Theory: The Question of Power." *Current Perspectives in Social Theory* (vol. 4). Greenwich, CT: JAI Press.

Flammang, Robert A. 1979. "Economic Growth and Economic Development: Counterparts or Competitors." *Economic Development and Cultural Change* 28 (October): 47–61.

Flanagan, Scott C. 1978. "The Genesis of Variant Political Cultures: Contemporary Citizen Orientations in Japan, America, Britain and Italy." pp. 129–63 in Sydney Verba and Lucian W. Pye (eds.) *The Citizen and Politics: A Comparative Perspective*. Stamford, CT: Greylock.

Flanagan, Scott C. and Bradley M. Richardson. 1980. "Political Disaffection and Political Stability: A Comparison of Japanese and Western Findings." *Comparative Social Research* 3: 3–44.

Flanz, Gisbert H. 1982. *Comparative Women's Rights and Political Participation in Europe*. Dobbs Ferry, NY: Transnational Publishers, Inc.

Flora, Cornelia Butler. 1977. "Working-Class Women's Political Participation: Its Potential in Developed Countries," pp. 75–95 in Marianne Githens and Jewel L. Prestage (eds.) *A Portrait of Marginality: The Political Behavior of the American Woman*. New York: David McKay.

Flora, Cornelia B. and Naomi B. Lynn. 1974. "Women and Political Socialization: Considerations of the Impact of Motherhood," pp. 37–53 in Jane S. Jaquette (ed.) *Women in Politics*. New York: John Wiley.

Foster, James J. 1982. "Ghost-Hunting: Local Party Organization in Japan." *Asian Survey* 22 (September): 843–857.

Fowlkes, Diane L; Jerry Perkins; and Sue Tolleson Rinehart. 1979. "Gender Roles and Party Roles." *American Political Science Review* 73 (September): 772–780.

Frieze, Irene H.; Jacquelynn E. Parsons; Paula B. Johnson; Diane N. Ruble; Gail L. Zellman. 1978. *Women and Sex Roles: A Social Psychological Perspective*. New York: W.W. Norton.

Fujita, Taki. 1968. "Women and Politics in Japan." *Annals of the American Academy of Political and Social Science* 375 (January): 91–95.

Fulles, Mechtild. 1969. *Frauen in Partei und Parlament*, Cologne: Verlag Wissenschaft und Politik.

Galli, Giorgio and Alfonso Prandi. 1970. *Patterns of Political Participation in Italy*. New Haven, CT: Yale University Press.

German Federal Republic, Statistisches Bundesamt. 1976. *Statistisches Jahrbuch für die Bundesrepublik Deutschland 1976*. Wiesbaden.

———. 1979. *Statisches Jahrbuch für die Bundesrepublik Deutschland 1979*. Wiesbaden.

Ghosh, Chitra. 1985. "The Political Potential of Women's Movements and Women Politicians in India." Paper presented at the World Congress of the International Political Science Association.

Giele, Janet Zollinger. 1977a. "Introduction: Comparative Perspectives on Women," pp. 1–31 in Janet Zollinger Giele and Audrey Chapman Smock (eds.) *Women: Roles and Status in Eight Countries*. New York: John Wiley.

———. 1977b. "United States: A Prolonged Search for Equal Rights," pp. 301–345 in Janet Zollinger Giele and Audrey Chapman Smock (eds.) *Women: Roles and Status in Eight Countries*. New York: John Wiley.

———. 1978. *Women and the Future: Changing Sex Roles in Modern America*. New York: The Free Press.

Glenn, Norval D. n.d. "Trend Studies with Available Survey Data: Opportunities and Pitfalls," pp. I–6 to I–50 in Philip K. Hastings (gen. ed.) *Survey Data for Trend Analysis: An Index to Repeated Questions in U.S. National Surveys Held by the Roper Public Opinion Research Center*. Williamstown, MA: The Roper Public Opinion Research Center in cooperation with the Social Science Research Council.

Goel, Madan Lal. 1975. *Political Participation in a Developing Nation: India*. New York: Asia Publishing House.

Goode, William J. 1963. *World Revolution and Family Patterns*. New York: The Free Press.

Goot, Murray and Elizabeth Reid. 1975. *Women and Voting Studies: Mindless Matrons or Sexist Scientism?* Beverly Hills, CA: Sage Professional Papers in Contemporary Political Sociology, nos. 06–008.

Gray, Paul S. 1976. "Voluntary Organizations in Ghana." *Journal of Voluntary Action Research* 5 (July-October): 221–230.

Gronseth, Erik. 1955. "The Political Role of Women in Norway," pp. 194–221 in Maurice Duverger *The Political Role of Women*. Paris: UNESCO.

Guha, Smt. Phulrena. 1978. "Socio-Political Status of Women." pp. 19–23 in Seminar of Women Legislators, *Women's Development: Some Critical Issues*. Seminar sponsored by Ghandi Peace Foundation in collaboration with the Indian Council of Social Science Research, Department of Social Welfare, Government of India, and UNICEF. New Delhi: Marwah Publications.

Gustafson, Kathleen; Alan Booth; and David Johnson. 1979. "The Effect of

Labor Force Participation on Gender Differences in Voluntary Association Affiliation: A Cross-National Study." *Journal of Voluntary Action Research* 8 (July-October): 51–56.

Haavio-Mannila, Elina. 1969. "The Position of Finnish Women: Regional and Cross-National Comparison." *Journal of Marriage and the Family* 31 (May): 339–347.

_____. 1970. "Sex Roles in Politics." *Scandinavian Political Studies* 5: 209–239.

_____. 1971. "Convergence between East and West: Tradition and Modernity in Sex Roles in Sweden, Finland and the Soviet Union." *Acta Sociologica* 14, no. 1–2: 114–125.

_____. 1972. "Sex-Role Attitudes in Finland, 1966–1970." *Journal of Social Issues* 28, no. 2: 93–110.

_____. 1978. "Changes in Sex Roles in Politics as an Indicator of Structural Change in Society." *International Journal of Sociology* 8 (Fall): 56–85.

_____. 1983. "Economic and Family Roles of Men and Women in Northern Europe." pp. 243–260 in Eugen Lupri (ed.) *The Changing Position of Women in Family and Society: A Cross-National Comparison.* Leiden (Netherlands): E. J. Brill.

Haavio-Mannila, Elina, et al. 1985. *Unfinished Democracy: Women in Nordic Politics.* Oxford: Pergamon Press.

Hall, Jane. 1981. "West Germany," pp. 153–181 in Joni Lovenduski and Jill Hills (eds.) *The Politics of the Second Electorate: Women and Public Participation.* London: Routledge & Kegan Paul.

Hamilton, Richard F. 1967. *Affluence and the French Worker in the Fourth Republic.* Princeton, NJ: Princeton University Press.

Hansen, Susan B.; Linda Franz; and Margaret Netemeyer-Mays. 1976. "Women's Political Participation and Policy Preferences." *Social Science Quarterly* 56 (March): 576–590.

Harasymiw, Bohdan. 1980. "Have Women's Chances for Political Recruitment in the USSR Really Improved?" pp. 140–184 in Tova Yedlin (ed.) *Women in Eastern Europe and the Soviet Union.* New York: Praeger.

Hargadine, Eileen. 1981. "Japan." pp. 299–319 in Joni Lovenduski and Jill Hills (eds.) *The Politics of the Second Electorate: Women and Public Participation.* London: Routledge & Kegan Paul.

Heinz, Margarete. 1971. *Über das politische Bewusstsein von Frauen in der Bundesrepublik.* Munich: Wilhelm Goldmann Verlag.

Hernes, Helga Maria. 1980. "Research Note: Predicting Support for the Women's Movement: A Diffusion Model." *Scandinavian Political Studies* 3 (New Series No. 3): 265–273.

Hernes, Helga Maria and Kirsten Voje. 1980. "Women in the Corporate Channel: A Process of Natural Exclusion?" *Scandinavian Political Studies* 3 (New Series, No. 2): 163–186.

Hettne, Björn. 1983. "The Development of Development Theory." *Acta Sociologica* 26 (Nos. 3/4): 247–266.

Holter, Harriet. 1967. "Scandinavia." pp. 437–462 in Raphael Patai (ed.) *Women in the Modern World*. New York: The Free Press.

_____. 1970. *Sex Roles and Social Structure*. Oslo: Universitetsforlaget.

_____. 1971. "Sex Roles and Social Change." *Acta Sociologica* 14, no. 1–2: 2–12.

Howard, Rhoda E. 1985. "Women and the Crisis in Commonwealth Africa." *International Political Science Review* 6 (No. 3): 237–296.

Hughes, John A. 1971. "Girls, Boys and Politics." *British Journal of Sociology* 22 (March): 53–67.

Huntington, Samuel P. and Joan M. Nelson. 1976. *No Easy Choice: Political Participation in Developing Countries*. Cambridge, MA: Harvard University Press.

Iglitzin, Lynne B. and Ruth Ross (eds.). 1976. *Women in the World: A Comparative Study*. Santa Barbara, CA: American Bibliographical Center, Clio Press.

Ike, Nobutaka. 1973. "Economic Growth and Intergenerational Changes in Japan." *American Political Science Review* 67 (December): 1194–1203.

_____. 1978. *A Theory of Japanese Democracy*. Boulder, Colorado: Westview Press.

Illich, Ivan. 1982. "Vernacular Gender." *Alternatives* 8 (Winter): 381–448.

India, Government of, Department of Social Welfare. 1974. *Towards Equality: Report of the Committee on the Status of Women in India*. New Delhi: Department of Social Welfare.

Inglehart, Margaret. 1979. "Sex Role, Historical Heritage, and Political Participation in Switzerland." pp. 137–160 in Howard R. Penniman, (ed.) *Switzerland at the Polls: The National Elections of 1979*. Washington, DC: American Enterprise Institute for Public Policy Research.

_____. 1981. "Political Interest in West European Women: An Historical and Empirical Comparative Analysis." *Comparative Political Studies* 14 (October): 299–326.

Inglehart, Ronald. 1977. *The Silent Revolution: Changing Values and Political Styles Among Western Publics*. Princeton, NJ: Princeton University Press.

Jacobson, Doranne. 1977. "The Women of North and Central India: Goddesses and Wives." pp. 17–111 in Doranne Jacobson and Susan S. Wadley (eds.) *Women in India: Two Perspectives*. Columbia, MO: South Asia Books.

Jain, Devaki (ed.) 1975. *Indian Women*. New Delhi: Publications Division, Ministry of Information and Broadcasting, Govt. of India.

Jancar, Barbara Wolfe. 1978. *Women under Communism*. Baltimore: Johns Hopkins University Press.

Japan, Bureau of Statistics, Office of the Prime Minister. 1978. *Japan Statistical Yearbook 1978*. 28th issue. Tokyo.

Japan, Ministry of Labor, Women's and Minors' Bureau. 1968. "The Status of Women in Japan, 1968." Tokyo.

Jaquette, Jane S. 1982. "Women and Modernization Theory: A Decade of Feminist Criticism." *World Politics* 34 (January): 267–284.

_____. 1984. "Female Political Participation in Latin America: Raising Feminist Issues." Paper presented at the Annual Meeting of the American Political Science Association.

Jarlov, Carsten and Lise Togeby. 1979. "Political Involvement and the Development of Political Attitudes." *Scandinavian Political Studies* 2 (New Series, No. 2): 121–140.

Jennings, M. Kent. 1979. "Another Look at the Life Cycle and Political Participation." *American Journal of Political Science* 23 (November): 755–771.

_____. 1983. "Gender Roles and Inequalities in Political Participation: Results from an Eight-Nation Study." *The Western Political Quarterly* 36 (September): 364–385.

Jennings, M. Kent and Barbara G. Farah. 1980. "Ideology, Gender and Political Action: A Cross-National Survey." *British Journal of Political Science* 10 (April): 219–240.

_____. 1981. "Social Roles and Political Resources: An Over-Time Study of Men and Women in Party Elites." *American Journal of Political Science* 25 (August): 462–482.

Jennings, M. Kent and Richard G. Niemi. 1981. *Generations and Politics: A Panel Study of Young Adults and Their Parents.* Princeton, NJ: Princeton University Press.

Jensen, Ulla Skovgaard. 1983. "Political and Economic Gender Inequalities in Capitalist Polyarchies." *European Journal of Political Research* 11 (September): 265–282.

Johnson, Cheryl. 1982. "Grass Roots Organizing: Women in Anticolonial Activity in Southwestern Nigeria." *African Studies Review* 25 (June/September): 137–157.

Jones, H. J. 1975. "Japanese Women in the Politics of the Seventies." *Asian Survey* 15, no. 8: 708–723.

_____. 1976. "Japanese Women and Party Politics." *Pacific Affairs* 49 (Summer): 213–234.

Juillard, Joelle Rutherford. 1976. "Women in France." pp. 115–28 in Lynne B. Iglitzin and Ruth Ross (eds.) *Women in the World: A Comparative Study.* Santa Barbara, CA: American Bibliographical Center, Clio Press.

Kaplan, Temma. 1974. "A Marxist Analysis of Women and Capitalism." pp. 257–266 in Jane S. Jaquette (ed.) *Women in Politics.* New York: Wiley.

Katosh, John P. and Michael W. Traugott. 1981. "The Consequences of Validated and Self-Reported Voting Measures." *Public Opinion Quarterly* 45 (Winter): 519–535.

Katzenstein, Mary Fainsod. 1981. "Toward Equality? Cause and Consequence of the Political Prominence of Women in India." pp. 286–303 in Gail Minault (ed.) *The Extended Family: Women and Political Participation in India and Pakistan.* New Delhi: Chanakya Publications.

Kay, Barry J.; Ronald D. Lambert; Steven D. Brown; and James E. Curtis. 1986. "An Examination of Canadian Women's Political Activity: Evidence from the 1984 National Election Study." Paper presented at the Annual Meeting of the Midwest Political Science Association.

Kelly, Rita Mae and Mary Boutilier. 1978. *The Making of Political Women*: *A Study of Socialization and Role Conflict*. Chicago: Nelson-Hall.

Kendrigan, Mary Lou. 1984. *Political Equality in a Democratic Society*: *Women in the United States*. Westport, CT: Greenwood Press.

Khanna, Girija and Mariamma A. Varghese. 1978. *Indian Women Today*. New Delhi: Vikas Publishing House.

Kim, Jae-On; Norman Nie; and Sidney Verba. 1974. "The Amount and Concentration of Political Participation." *Political Methodology* 1 (Spring): 105–132.

Kirkpatrick, Maurine A. 1975. "Consumerism and Japan's New Citizen Politics." *Asian Survey* 15 (March): 234–246.

Klein, Ethel. 1984. *Gender Politics*: *From Consciousness to Mass Politics*. Cambridge, MA: Harvard University Press.

Klein, Viola. 1967. "Great Britain." pp. 463–488 in Raphael Patai (ed.) *Women in the Modern World*. New York: The Free Press.

Köckeis-Stangl, Eva. 1983. "The Position of Austrian Women in the Family." pp. 148–178 in Eugen Lupri (ed.) *The Changing Position of Women in Family and Society*: *A Cross-National Comparison*. Leiden (Netherlands): E. J. Brill.

Koyama, Takashi. 1961. *The Changing Social Position of Women in Japan*. Geneva: UNESCO.

Koyama, Takashi; Hachiro Nakamura; and Masako Hiramatsu. 1967. "Japan." pp. 290–314 in Raphael Patai (ed.) *Women in the Modern World*. New York: The Free Press.

Koygoku, Junichi and Nobutaka Ike. 1960. "Urban-Rural Differences in Voting Behavior in Postwar Japan." *Economic Development and Cultural Change* 9 (October): 167–185.

Kravis, Irving B.; Alan W. Heston; and Robert Summers. 1978. "Real GDP per Capita for More Than One Hundred Countries." *The Economic Journal* 88 (June): 215–242.

Lafferty, William M. 1978. "Social Development and Political Participation: Class, Organizations and Sex." *Scandinavian Political Studies* 1 (New Series, No. 4): 233–254.

———. 1980. "Sex and Political Participation: An Exploratory Analysis of the 'Female Culture'." *European Journal of Political Research* 8 (September): 323–347.

Lancelot, Alain. 1968. *L'abstentionnisme electoral en France*. Paris: Armand Colin.

Lane, Robert E. 1965. *Political Life*: *Why and How People Get Involved in Politics*. Paperback edition. New York: The Free Press.

Lansing, Marjorie. 1970. *Sex Differences in Political Participation*. Unpublished Ph.D. dissertation, University of Michigan.

_____ . 1974. "The American Women: Voter and Activist." pp. 5–24 in Jane S. Jaquette (ed.) *Women in Politics*. New York: Wiley.

Lapidus, Gail Warshofsky. 1974. "Modernization Theory and Sex Roles in Critical Perspective: The Case of the Soviet Union." pp. 243–256 in Jane S. Jaquette (ed.) *Women in Politics*. New York: Wiley.

Lateef, Shahida. 1981. "The Indian Women's Movement and National Development: An Overview." pp. 195–216 in Gail Minault (ed.) *The Extended Family: Women and Political Participation in India and Pakistan*. New Delhi: Chanakya Publications.

Leghorn, Lisa and Katherine Parker. 1981. *Woman's Worth: Sexual Economics and the World of Women*. London: Routledge and Kegan Paul.

Lehmann, Andree. 1967. "France," pp. 229–246 in Raphael Patai (ed.) *Women in the Modern World*. New York: The Free Press.

Lehr, Ursula and Hellgard Rauh. 1970. "Male and Female in the German Federal Republic." pp. 220–239 in Georgene H. Seward and Robert C. Williamson (eds.) *Sex Roles in Changing Society*. New York: Random House.

Leith-Ross, Sylvia. 1965. *African Women: A Study of the Ibo of Nigeria*. New York: Praeger.

Lindsay, Beverly. 1980. "Perspectives of Third World Women: An Introduction." pp. 1–22 in Beverly Lindsay (eds). *Comparative Perspectives of Third World Women: The Impact of Race, Sex, and Class*. New York: Praeger.

Lipset, Seymour Martin. 1963. *Political Man: The Social Basis of Politics*. Garden City, NY: Anchor Books.

Listhaug, Ola and Ola Kindseth. 1979. "Sex, Resources, and Political Participation: Direct and Indirect Effects." *Scandinavian Political Studies* 2 (New Series, No. 4): 373–383.

Lovenduski, Joni. 1986. *Women and European Politics: Contemporary Feminism and Public Policy*. Amherst, MA: The University of Massachusetts Press.

Lovenduski, Joni and Jill Hills (eds.). 1981. *The Politics of the Second Electorate: Women and Public Participation*. London: Routledge & Kegan Paul.

Lupri, Eugen (ed.). 1983. *The Changing Position of Women in Family and Society: A Cross-National Comparison*. Leiden (Netherlands): E.J. Brill.

Luthra, Bimla. 1967. "Techniques of Election Campaign in Delhi." *The Indian Political Science Review* 1 (April-September): 251–272.

_____ . 1976. "Nehru and the Place of Women in Indian Society." pp. 1–15 in B.R. Nanda (ed.) *Indian Women: From Purdah to Modernity*. New Delhi: Vikas Publishing House.

Lynn, Naomi B. and Cornelia B. Flora. 1973. "Motherhood and Political Participation: The Changing Sense of Self." *Journal of Political and Military Sociology* 1, no. 1: 91–103.

McDonagh, Eileen L. 1982. "To Work or Not to Work: The Differential Impact of Achieved and Derived Status upon the Political Participation of Women, 1956–1976." *American Journal of Political Science* 26 (May): 280–297.

McGlen, Nancy E. 1980. "The Impact of Parenthood on Political Participation." *Western Political Quarterly* 33 (September): 297–313.

McGlen, Nancy E. and Karen O'Connor. 1983. *Women's Rights: The Struggle for Equality in the Nineteenth and Twentieth Centuries.* New York: Praeger.

Mackintosh, John P. 1966. *Nigerian Government and Politics.* London: George Allen and Unwin.

McPherson, J. Miller and Lynn Smith-Lovin. 1982. "Women and Weak Ties: Differences by Sex in the Size of Voluntary Organizations." *American Journal of Sociology* 87 (no. 4): 883–904.

Madan, T. N. 1976. "The Hindu Woman at Home." pp. 67–86 in B. R. Nanda (ed.) *Indian Women: From Purdah to Modernity.* New Delhi: Vikas Publishing House.

Mahajan, Vijay and Robert A. Peterson. 1985. "Models for Innovation Diffusion." Sage University Paper Series on Quantitative Applications in the Social Sciences. Beverly Hills: Sage.

Mandelbaum, David G. 1970. *Society in India.* Vol I: Continuity and Change. Berkeley: University of California Press.

Margolis, Diane Rothbard. 1979. "The Invisible Hands: Sex Roles and the Division of Labor in Two Local Political Parties." *Social Problems* 26 (February): 314–324.

Marshall, Susan E. 1984. "Politics and Female Status in North Africa: A Reconsideration of Development Theory." *Economic Development and Cultural Change* 32 (April): 499–524.

Martinussen, Willy. 1971. "Political Awareness and the Distribution of Other Social Resources: The Case of Norway." *Scandinavian Political Studies* 6: 153–170.

———. 1977. *The Distant Democracy: Social Inequality. Political Resources and Political Influence in Norway.* New York: John Wiley.

Mason, Karen Oppenheim; John L. Czajka; and Sara Arber. 1976. "Change in U.S. Women's Sex Roles Attitudes, 1964–1976." *American Sociological Review* 41 (August): 573–596.

Masters, Roger D. 1983. "Explaining 'Male Chauvinism' and 'Feminism': Cultural Differences in Male and Female Reproductive Strategies." *Women & Politics* 3 (Summer/Fall): 165–210.

Mazumdar, Vina. 1979. "Editor's Note." pp. ix–xxiii in Vina Mazumdar (ed.) *Symbols of Power: Studies on the Political Status of Women in India.* Bombay: Allied Publishers Private Limited.

Mba, Nina Emma. 1982. *Nigerian Women Mobilized: Women's Political Activity in Southern Nigeria, 1900–1965.* Research series no. 48. Berkeley, CA: Institute of International Studies, University of California, Berkeley.

Means, Ingunn Norderval. 1976. "Scandinavian Women." pp. 375–390 in Lynne B. Iglitzin and Ruth Ross (eds.) *Women in the World: A Comparative Study*. Santa Barbara, CA: American Bibliographical Center, Clio Press.

Meguro, Yoriko and Kiyomi Morioka. 1983. "The Changing Status or Role of Women in Japan." pp. 207–221 in Eugen Lupri (ed.) *The Changing Position of Women in Family and Society: A Cross-National Comparison*. Leiden (Netherlands): E. J. Brill.

Merkl, Peter H. 1976. "The Politics of Sex: West Germany." pp. 129–47 in Lynne B. Iglitzin and Ruth Ross (eds.) *Women in the World: A Comparative Study*. Santa Barbara, CA: American Bibliographical Center, Clio Press.

_____. 1986. "West German Women: A Long Way from 'Kinder, Kuche, Kirche.'" pp. 27–52 in Lynne B. Iglitzin and Ruth Ross (eds.) *Women in the World, 1975–1985: The Women's Decade*. 2nd, revised ed. Santa Barbara, CA: American Bibliographical Center, Clio.

Michel, Andree. 1977. "Projected Future Employment and Leadership Needs and Areas." pp. 138–163 in the Rockefeller Foundation (working papers) *Changing Roles of Women in Industrial Societies*.

Milbrath, Lester W. and M. L. Goel. 1977. *Political Participation: How and Why Do People Get Involved in Politics?* 2d ed. Chicago: Rand McNally.

Miller, Arthur H.; Patricia Gurin; Gerald Gurin; and Oksana Malanchuk. 1981. "Group Consciousness and Political Participation." *American Journal of Political Science* 25 (August): 494–511.

Miller, Barbara D. 1982. "Female Labor Participation and Female Seclusion in Rural India: A Regional View." *Economic Development and Cultural Change* 30 (July): 777–794.

Minault, Gail. 1981. "Introduction: The Extended Family as Metaphor and the Expansion of Women's Realm." pp. 3–18 in Gail Minault (ed.) *The Extended Family: Women and Political Participation in India and Pakistan*. New Delhi: Chanakya Publications.

Morgan, S. Philip and Kiyosi Hirosima. 1983. "The Persistence of Extended Family Residence in Japan: Anachronism or Alternative Strategy?" *American Sociological Review* 48 (April): 269–281.

Mossuz-Lavau, Janine and Mariette Sineau. 1978. "Sociologie de l'abstention dans huit bureaux de vote parisiens." *Revue française de science politique* 28 (February): 73–101.

_____. 1981. "France." pp. 112–133 in Joni Lovenduski and Jill Hills (eds.) *The Politics of the Second Electorate: Women and Public Participation*. London: Routledge and Kegan Paul.

_____. 1982. "Women and Politics in France Today." pp. 151–166 in Gisbert H. Flanz *Comparative Women's Rights and Political Participation in Europe*. Dobbs Ferry, NY: Transnational Publishers, Inc.

_____. 1983. *Enquête sur les femmes et la politique en France*. Paris: Presses Universitares de France.

Mukhopadhyay, Carol Chapnick. 1982. "Sati or Shakti: Women, Culture and Politics in India." in Jean F. O'Barr (ed.) *Perspectives on Power: Women in Africa, Asia, and Latin America.* Durham, NC: Duke University, Center for International Studies.

Mukhopadhyay, Maitrayee. 1984. *Silver Shackles: Women and Development in India.* Oxford (England): OXFAM.

Muller, Edward N. 1979. *Aggressive Political Participation.* Princeton, NJ: Princeton University Press.

Muni, S.D. 1979. "Women in the Electoral Process." pp. 24–50 in Vina Mazumdar (ed.) *Symbols of Power: Studies on the Political Status of Women in India.* Bombay: Allied Publishers Private Limited.

Nachmias, David. 1977. "On the Calculus of Time and Political Participation." *Political Methodology* 4 (No. 4): 451–459.

Nagel, Joane. 1981. "Politics and the Organization of Collective Action: The Case of Nigeria, 1960–1975." *Political Behavior* 3 (No. 2): 87–116.

Narain, Vatsala. 1967. "India." pp. 21–42 in Raphael Patai (ed.) *Women in the Modern World.* New York: The Free Press.

Nie, Norman H.; Bingham G. Powell, Jr.; and Kenneth Prewitt. 1969. "Social Structure and Political Participation. Parts 1 and 2." *American Political Science Review* 63 (June & September): 361–388, 808–832.

Nie, Norman; Sidney Verba; and Jae-On Kim. 1974. "Participation and the Life-Cycle." *Comparative Politics* 6 (April): 319–340.

Niemi, Richard G.; G. Bingham Powell, Jr.; Harold W. Stanley; C. Lawrence Evans. 1985. "Testing the Converse Partisanship Model with New Electorates." *Comparative Political Studies* 18 (October): 300–322.

Njoku, John E. Eberegbulam. 1980. *The World of the African Woman.* Metuchen, NJ and London: The Scarecrow Press. Inc.

Noelle, Elisabeth and Erich Peter Neumann (eds.). 1956. *Jahrbuch der öffentlichen Meinung,* vol. 1: 1947–1955. Allensbach and Bonn: Verlag für Demoskopie.

––––––. 1957. *Jahrbuch der öffentlichen Meinung,* vol. 2: 1957. Allensbach and Bonn: Verlag für Demoskopie.

––––––. 1965. *Jahrbuch der öffentlichen Meinung,* vol. 3: 1958–1964. Allensbach and Bonn: Verlag für Demoskopie.

––––––. 1967. *Jahrbuch der öffentlichen Meinung,* vol. 4: 1956–1967. Allensbach and Bonn: Verlag für Demoskopie.

––––––. 1967. *The Germans: Public Opinion Polls 1947–1966.* Allensbach and Bonn: Verlag für Demoskopie.

––––––. 1974. *Jahrbuch der öffentlichen Meinung,* vol 5: 1968–1973, Allensbach and Bonn: Verlag für Demoskopie.

Noelle-Neumann, Elisabeth (ed.). 1976. *Allensbacher Jahrbuch der Demoskopie,* vol. 6: 1974–76. Vienna: Verlag Fritz Molden, Institut für Demoskopie Allensbach.

––––––. 1977. *Allensbacher Jahrbuch der Demoskopie,* vol. 7: 1976–1977. Vienna: Verlag Fritz Molden, Institut für Demoskopie Allensbach.

––––––. 1981. *The Germans: Public Opinion Polls, 1967–1980.* Westport, CT: Greenwood Press.

Norpoth, Helmut, 1978. "Party Identification in West Germany: Tracing an Elusive Concept." *Comparative Political Studies* 11 (April): 36–61.

Norway, Central Bureau of Statistics. 1969. *Historical Statistics 1968.* Oslo.

———. 1978. *Statistical Yearbook of Norway 1978.* 97th issue. Oslo.

Nuss, Shirley A. 1980. "The Position of Women in Socialist and Capitalist Countries: A Comparative Study." *International Journal of Sociology of the Family* 10 (Jan-June): 1–13.

———. 1981. "The Commitment of Fathers to Equality in the Performance of Family Maintenance Activities: A Comparison of Developed Market-Oriented and Centrally-Planned Countries." *International Journal of Sociology of the Family* 11 (Jan-June): 1–14.

———. 1982. "Women in Political Life: Global Trends." *International Journal of Sociology of the Family* 12 (Spring): 1–10.

Nuss, Shirley and Lorraine Majka. 1983. "The Economic Integration of Women: A Cross-National Investigation." *Work and Occupations* 10 (February): 29–48.

O'Barr, Jean F. (ed.). 1982. *Perspectives on Power: Women in Africa, Asia, and Latin America.* Durham, NC: Duke University, Center for International Studies.

Okonjo, Kamene. 1976. "The Dual-Sex Political System in Operation: Igbo Women and Community Politics in Midwestern Nigeria." pp. 45–58 in Nancy J. Hafkin and Edna G. Bay (eds.) *Women in Africa: Studies in Social and Economic Change.* Stanford, CA: Stanford University Press.

Oppong, Christine. 1983. "Women's Roles and Conjugal Family Systems in Ghana," pp. 331–343 in Eugen Lupri (ed.) *The Changing Position of Women in Family and Society: A Cross-National Comparison.* Leiden (Netherlands): E. J. Brill.

Organization for Economic Cooperation and Development. 1973. *OECD Economic Surveys: Yugoslavia.* Paris: OECD Publications.

———. 1974. *OECD Economic Surveys: Yugoslavia.* Paris: OECD Publications.

Orum, Anthony M.; Roberta S. Cohen; Sherri Grasmuck; and Amy W. Orum. 1974. "Sex, Socialization and Politics." *American Sociological Review* 39 (April): 197–209.

Osmond, Marie Withers. 1981. "Comparative Marriage and the Family." *International Journal of Comparative Sociology* 22 (3–4): 169–196.

Parry, Geraint. 1980. "Orderly and Disorderly Conduct: Some Recent Work on Political Participation." *Government and Opposition* 15 (Spring): 223–234.

Passin, Herbert. 1965. "Japan," pp. 272–312 in James S. Coleman (ed.) *Education and Political Development.* Princeton, NJ: Princeton University Press.

Patai, Raphael. 1967. "Introduction." pp. 1–18 in Raphael Patai (ed.) *Women in the Modern World.* New York: The Free Press.

Pesonen, Pertti. 1968. *An Election in Finland: Party Activities and Voter Reactions.* New Haven, CT: Yale University Press.

Peterson, Abby. 1984. "The Gender-Sex Dimension in Swedish Politics." *Acta Sociologica* 27 (No. 1): 3–17.

Pharr, Susan J. 1977. "Japan: Historical and Contemporary Perspectives." pp. 217–55 in Janet Zolliger Giele and Audrey Chapman Smock (eds.) *Women: Roles and Status in Eight Countries*. New York: John Wiley.

———. 1981. *Political Women in Japan*. Berkeley: University of California Press.

Pickles, Dorothy. 1953. "The Political Role of Women." *International Social Science Bulletin* 5:75–104.

Pollock, Philip H. III. 1982. "Organizations as Agents of Mobilization." *American Journal of Political Science* 26 (August): 485–503.

———. 1983. "The Participatory Consequences of Internal and External Political Efficacy: A Research Note." *The Western Political Quarterly* 36 (September): 400–409.

Pomper, Gerald M. 1975. *Voters' Choice: Varieties of American Electoral Behavior*. New York: Dodd, Mead & Co.

Poole, Keith T. and L. Harmon Zeigler. 1981. "The Diffusion of Feminist Ideology." *Political Behavior* 3 (No. 3): 229–256.

Porter, Mary Cornelia and Corey Venning. 1976. "Catholicism and Women's Role in Italy and Ireland." pp. 81–103 in Lynne B. Iglitzin and Ruth Ross (eds.) *Women in the World: A Comparative Study*. Santa Barbara, CA: American Bibliographical Center, Clio Press.

Pross, Helge. 1967. "West Germany." pp. 247–66 in Raphael Patai (ed.) *Women in the Modern World*. New York: The Free Press.

Rabier, Jacques-Rene. 1979. *European Men and Women in 1978*. Brussels: Commission of the European Communities.

Randall, Vicky. 1982. *Women and Politics*. London and Basingstoke: Macmillan.

Rapoport, Ronald B. 1981. "The Sex Gap in Political Persuading: Where the 'Structuring Principle' Works." *American Journal of Political Science* 25 (February): 32–48.

———. 1982. "Sex Differences in Attitude Expression: A Generational Explanation." *Public Opinion Quarterly* 46 (Spring): 86–96.

Reid, Ivan and Eileen Wormald. 1982. *Sex Differences in Britain*. London: Grant McIntyre.

Remy, Dorothy. 1975. "Underdevelopment and the Experience of Women: A Nigerian Case Study." pp. 358–371 in Rayna R. Reiter, *Toward an Anthropology of Women*. New York: Monthly Review Press.

Rendel, Margherita. 1981. "Women, Power and Political Systems." pp. 15–49 in Margherita Rendel (ed.) *Women, Power and Political Systems*. London: Croom Helm.

Rener, Tanja. 1985. "Yugoslav Women in Politics: Selected Issues." *International Political Science Review* 6 (No. 3): 397–354.

Richardson, Bradley M. 1974. *The Political Culture of Japan*. Berkeley, CA: University of California Press.

Robins-Mowry, Dorothy. 1983. *The Hidden Sun: Women of Modern Japan*. Boulder, CO: Westview Press.

Rochon, Thomas R. 1983. "Political Change in Ordered Societies: The Rise of Citizens' Movements." *Comparative Policy* 15 (April): 351–373.

Rogers, Barbara. 1979. *The Domestication of Women: Discrimination in Developing Societies*. New York: St. Martin's Press.

Rogers, Everett. 1983. *Diffusion of Innovation*. 3rd ed. New York: The Free Press.

Rokkan, Stein. 1970. *Citizens, Elections, Parties: Approaches to the Comparison Study of the Processes of Development*. New York: David McKay.

Rosaldo, Michelle Zimbalist. 1974. "Women, Culture, and Society: A Theoretical Overview." pp. 17–42 in Michelle Zimbalist Rosaldo and Louise Lamphere (eds.) *Women, Culture, and Society*. Stanford, CA: Stanford University Press.

_____. 1980. "The Use and Abuse of Anthropology: Reflections on Feminism and Cross-Cultural Understanding." *Signs: Journal of Women in Culture and Society* 5 (Spring): 389–417.

Rosenstone, Steven J. and Raymond E. Wolfinger. 1978. "The Effect of Registration Laws on Voter Turnout." *American Political Science Review* 72 (March): 22–45.

Ross, Mark Howard. 1983. "Female Political Participation: Towards a Cross-Cultural Explanation." Paper presented at the Annual Meeting of the American Political Science Association.

Ross, Mark Howard and Veena Thadani. 1980. "Participation, Sex, and Social Class: Some Unexpected Results from an African City." *Comparative Politics* 12 (April): 323–334.

Ross, Ruth. 1976. "Tradition and the Role of Women in Great Britain." pp. 163–174 in Lynne B. Iglitzin and Ruth Ross (eds.) *Women in the World: A Comparative Study*. Santa Barbara, CA: American Bibliographical Center, Clio Press.

Rowbotham, Sheila. 1972. *Women, Resistance and Revolution: A History of Women and Revolution in the Modern World*. New York: Pantheon Books.

Rubin, Gayle. 1975. "The Traffic in Women: Notes on the 'Political Economy' of Sex." pp. 157–210 in Rayna R. Reiter (ed.) *Toward An Anthropology of Women*. New York: Monthly Review Press.

Sacks, Karen. 1975. "Engels Revisited: Women, the Organization of Production, and Private Property." pp. 211–234 in Rayna R. Reiter (ed.) *Toward An Anthropology of Women*. New York: Monthly Review Press.

_____. 1982. "An Overview of Women and Power in Africa." pp. 1–9 in Jean O'Barr (ed.) *Perspectives on Power: Women in Africa, Asia and Latin America*. Durham, NC: Duke University Center for International Studies.

Safilios-Rotshchild, Constatina. 1971. "A Cross-Cultural Examination of Women's Marital, Educational and Occupational Options." *Acta Sociologica* 14, nos. 1–2: 96–113.

Sanday, Peggy R. 1974. "Female Status in the Public Domain." pp. 189–206 in Michelle Zimbalist Rosaldo and Louise Lamphere (eds.) *Women, Culture, and Society*. Stanford, CA: Stanford University Press.

_____ . 1981. *Female Power and Male Dominance: On the Origins of Sexual Inequality.* Cambridge (England): Cambridge University Press.

Sani, Giacomo. 1977. "The Italian Electorate in the Mid 1970's: Beyond Tradition?" pp. 81–122 in Howard R. Penniman (ed.) *Italy at the Poles: The Parliamentary Election of 1976.* Washington, DC: American Enterprise Institute for Public Policy Research.

Sapiro, Virginia. 1980. "News from the Front: Intersex and Intergenerational Conflict over the Status of Women." *The Western Political Quarterly* 33 (June): 260–277.

_____ . 1983. *The Political Integration of Women: Roles, Socialization, and Politics.* Urbana, IL: University of Illinois Press.

Scanzoni, John and Greer Litton Fox. 1980. "Sex Roles, Family and Society: The Seventies and Beyond." *Journal of Marriage and the Family* 42 (November): 743–756.

Schlegel, Alice, 1977. "Toward a Theory of Sexual Stratification." pp. 1–40 in Alice Schlegel (ed.) *Sexual Stratification: A Cross-Cultural View.* New York: Columbia University Press.

Schreiber, E.M. 1978. "Education and Change in American Opinions on a Woman for President." *Public Opinion Quarterly* 42 (Summer): 171–182.

Scott, Hilda. 1978. "Introduction: Women in Politics." *International Journal of Sociology* 8 (Fall): 3–11.

Shaul, Marnie S. 1982. "The Status of Women in Local Governments: An International Assessment." *Public Administration Review* (November/December): 491–500.

Shrivastava, Rashmi. 1982. "The Role of Women in Indian Politics." *Political Science Review* 21 (No. 4): 351–358.

Siemienska, Renata. 1983. "Women's Political Participation in Poland." Paper presented at the Annual Meeting of the American Political Science Association.

_____ . 1985. "Women's Political Participation and the 1980 Crisis in Poland." *International Political Science Review* 6 (No. 3): 332–346.

Sigel, Roberta S. and John V. Reynolds. 1979–1980. "Generational Differences and the Women's Movement." *Political Science Quarterly* 94 (Winter): 635–648.

Silver, Catherine Bodard. 1977. "France: Contrasts in Familial and Societal Roles." pp. 257–299 in Janet Zollinger Giele and Audrey Chapman Smock (ed.) *Women: Roles and Status in Eight Countries.* New York: John Wiley.

Skard, Torild. 1983. "Women in the Political Life of the Nordic Countries." *International Social Science Journal* 35 (No. 98): 639–657.

Sklar, Richard L. 1963. *Nigerian Political Parties: Power in an Emergent African Nation.* Princeton, NJ: Princeton University Press.

Smith, Tom W. 1976. "A Study of Trends in the Political Role of Women, 1936–1974," vol. 2, pp. 215–253 in James A. Davis (ed.) *Studies of Social Change since 1948.* Chicago: National Opinion Research Center, University of Chicago.

Smock, Audrey Chapman. 1977a. "Conclusion: Determinants of Women's Roles and Status." pp. 383–421 in Janet Zollinger Giele and Audrey Chapman Smock (eds.) *Women: Roles and Status in Eight Countries.* New York: John Wiley.

———. 1977b. "The Impact of Modernization on Women's Position in the Family in Ghana." pp. 192–214 in Alice Schlegel (ed.) *Sexual Stratification: A Cross-Cultural View.* New York: Columbia University Press.

Sondages: Revue française de l'opinion publique. 1954. "La psychologie politiques des femmes." Vol. 16, nos. 2 & 3: 3–87, 3–62.

Spitze, Glenna and John Huber. 1980. "Changing Attitudes Toward Women's Nonfamily Roles: 1938 to 1978." *Sociology of Work and Occupations* 7 (August): 317–335.

Springer, Beverly. 1976. "Yugoslav Women." pp. 291–302 in Lynne B. Iglitzin, and Ruth Ross (eds.) *Women in the World: A Comparative Study.* Santa Barbara, CA: American Bibliographical Center, Clio Press.

———. 1986. "Yugoslav Women." pp. 415–438 in Lynne B. Iglitzin and Ruth Ross (eds.) *Women in the World, 1975–1985: The Women's Decade.* 2nd, revised ed. Santa Barbara, CA: American Bibliographical Center, Clio.

St. Erlich, Vera. 1966. *Family in Transition: A Study of 300 Yugoslav Villages.* Princeton, NJ: Princeton University Press.

Stacey, Margaret and Marion Price. 1981. *Women, Power, and Politics.* London: Tavistock Publications.

Staudt, Kathleen A. 1982. "Sex, Ethnic, and Class Consciousness in Western Kenya." *Comparative Politics* 14 (January): 149–167.

Staudt, Kathleen A. 1984. "Public Women, Private Policies, and Development: A Review Essay." *Women & Politics* 4 (Spring): 55–67.

Stolte-Heiskanen, Veronica. 1971. "Sex Roles, Social Class and Political Consciousness." *Acta Sociologica* 14, no. 1–2: 83–95.

———. 1975. "Family Needs and Societal Institutions: Potential Empirical Linkage Mechanism." *Journal of Marriage and the Family* 37 (November): 903–916.

Stucker, John J. 1977. "Women as Voters: Their Maturation as Political Persons in American Society." pp. 264–83 in Marianne Githens and Jewel L. Prestage (eds.) *A Portrait of Marginality: The Political Behavior of the American Woman.* New York: David McKay.

Sullerot, Evelyne. 1971. *Women, Society and Change.* New York: McGraw-Hill.

Tentori, Tullio. 1967. "Italy." pp. 153–175 in Raphael Patai (ed.) *Women in the Modern World.* New York: The Free Press.

Thomson, Aisla and Margrit Eichler. 1985. "The Impact of Labor Force Attachment on Political Participation: A Reconsideration." *International Political Science Review* 6 (No. 3): 367–381.

Thornton, Arland and Deborah Freedman. 1979. "Changes in the Sex Role Attitudes of Women, 1962–1977: Evidence from a Panel Study." *American Sociological Review* 44 (October): 831–842.

Tiffany, Sharon W. 1979. "Women, Power, and the Anthropology of Politics: A Review." *International Journal of Women's Studies* 2 (Sept.-Oct.): 430–439.

Tingsten, Herbert. 1937. *Political Behavior: Studies in Election Statistics.* London: P. S. King & Son.

Tinker, Irene; Michele Bo Bramsen; and Magra Buvinic (eds.). 1976. *Women and World Development: With an Annotated Bibliography.* New York: Praeger, in cooperation with the Overseas Development Council.

Tomsic, Vida. 1980. *Women in the Development of Socialist Self-Managing Yugoslavia.* Belgrade (Yugoslavia): Stvarnost Newspaper and Publishing House.

Ullrich, Helen E. 1977. "Caste Differences Between Brahmin and Non-Brahmin Women in a South Indian Village." pp. 94–108 in Alice Schlegel (ed.) *Sexual Stratification: A Cross-Cultural View.* New York: Columbia University Press.

United Nations. 1980. *The Economic Role of Women in the ECE Region.* New York: United Nations.

United Nations, Department of Economic and Social Affairs, Statistical Office. 1951–74. *Demographic Yearbook.* New York.

United Nations, Department of Economic and Social Affairs, Statistical Office. 1967–1978. *Statistical Yearbook.* New York.

United Nations, Educational, Scientific, and Cultural Organization. 1968. *Compendium of Social Statistics: 1967.* New York: UNESCO.

United Nations, Educational, Scientific, and Cultural Organization. 1971. *World Survey of Education Educational Policy, Legislation and Administration,* Vol. V. Paris: UNESCO.

Urwin, Derek W. 1974. "Germany: Continuity and Change in Electoral Politics." pp. 108–70 in Richard Rose (ed.) *Electoral Behavior: A Comparative Handbook.* New York: The Free Press.

U.S. Department of Commerce, Bureau of the Census. 1965. *Current Population Reports,* Population Series P–20, no. 143 (October 25).

_____. 1969. *Current Population Reports,* Population Series P–20, no. 192 (December 2).

_____. 1972. *Current Population Reports,* Population Series P–20, no. 244 (December).

_____. 1975. *Historical Statistics of the United States: Colonial Times to 1970, Bicentennial Edition, Part 2.*

_____. 1976. *Current Population Reports,* Population Series P–20, no. 304 (December).

_____. 1982. *Current Population Reports,* Population Series P–20, no. 370 (April).

Van Allen, Judith. 1974. " 'Memsahib, Militante, Femme Libre': Political and Apolitical Styles of Modern African Women." pp. 304–321 in Jane S. Jaquette (ed.) *Women in Politics.* New York: Wiley.

_____. 1976a. " 'Aba Riots' or Igbo 'Women's War'? Ideology, Stratification, and the Invisibility of Women." pp. 59–85 in Nancy J. Hafkin and Edna G. Bay (eds.) *Women in Africa: Studies in Social and Economic Change.* Stanford, CA: Stanford University Press.

————. 1976b. "African Women. 'Modernization,' and National Liberation." pp. 25–54 in Lynne B. Iglitzin and Ruth Ross (eds.) *Women in the World: A Comparative Study.* Santa Barbara, CA: American Bibliographical Center, Clio Press.

Veld-Langeveld, H. M. In't; I. J. Schoonenboom; L. In't Veld. 1983. "The Position of Women in the Netherlands: Marginal Change." pp. 120–135 in Eugen Lupri (ed) *The Changing Position of Women in Family and Society: A Cross-National Comparison.* Leiden (Netherlands): E. J. Brill.

Verba, Sidney. 1965. "Germany: The Remaking of Political Culture." pp. 130–170 in Lucian W. Pye and Sidney Verba (eds.) *Political Culture and Political Development.* Princeton, NJ: Princeton University Press.

Verba, Sidney and Norman H. Nie. 1972. *Participation in America: Political Democracy and Social Equality.* New York: Harper & Row.

Verba, Sidney; Norman H. Nie; and Jae-On Kim. 1971. *The Modes of Democratic Participation: A Cross-National Analysis.* Beverly Hills, CA: Sage Professional Papers in Comparative Politics 2, no. 01–013.

————. 1978. *Political Participation and Political Equality: A Seven-Nation Comparison.* Cambridge (England): Cambridge University Press.

Wassenberg, Pinky S.; Kay G. Wolsborn; Paul R. Hagner; John C. Pierce. 1983. "Gender Differences in Political Conceptualization, 1956–1980." *American Politics Quarterly* 11 (April): 181–203.

Watanuki, Joji. 1973. "Social Structure and Political Participation in Japan." Institute of International Relations Research Paper Series A-9.

————. 1975. "Japan." pp. 119–55 in Michael Crozier, Samuel P. Huntington, and Joji Watanuki (eds.) *The Crisis of Democracy: Report on the Governability of Democracies to the Trilateral Commission.* New York: New York University Press.

Weber, Maria. 1981. "La partecipazione politica femminile in Italia: Evoluzione, determinanti, caratteristiche." *Rivista Italiana di Scienza Politica* 11 (August): 281–311.

Welch, Michael R. 1983. "Women and Political Leadership Roles: A Cross-Cultural Study." *International Journal of Sociology of the Family* 13 (Spring): 57–77.

Welch, Susan. 1977. "Women as Political Animals? A Test of Some Explanations for Male-Female Political Participation Differences." *American Journal of Political Science* 21 (November): 711–730.

————. 1980. "Sex Differences in Political Activity in Britain." *Women & Politics* 1 (Summer): 29–46.

Welch, Susan and Lee Sigelman. 1982. "Changes in Public Attitudes Toward Women in Politics." *Social Science Quarterly* 63 (June): 312–322.

Welch, Susan and Philip Secret. 1980. "Sex, Race and Political Participation." *Western Political Quarterly* 34 (March): 5–16.

Wertman, Douglas. 1977. "The Italian Electoral Process: The Election of June 1976." pp. 41–79 in Howard R. Penniman (ed.) *Italy at the Polls: The Parliamentary Elections of 1976.* Washington, DC: American Enterprise Institute for Public Policy Research.

Wheeler, Elizabeth Hunting. 1967. "Sub-Saharan Africa." pp. 317–345 in Raphael Patai (ed.) *Women in the Modern World.* New York: The Free Press.

Whyte, Martin King. 1978. *The Status of Women in Preindustrial Societies.* Princeton, NJ: Princeton University Press.

Wiarda, Howard J. 1983. "Toward a Nonethnocentric Theory of Development: Alternative Conceptions from the Third World." *The Journal of Developing Areas* 17 (July): 433–452.

Wilson, Frank L. 1979. "The Revitalization of French Parties." *Comparative Political Studies* 12 (April): 82–103.

Wipper, Audrey. 1982. "Riots and Rebellion Among African Women: Three Examples of Women's Political Clout." pp. 50–72 in Jean O'Barr (ed.) *Perspectives on Power: Women in Africa, Asia, and Latin America.* Durham, NC: Duke University, Center for International Studies.

Wolchik, Sharon Lee. 1978. "Politics, Ideology, and Equality: The Status of Women in Eastern Europe." Unpublished Ph.D. dissertation, The University of Michigan.

_____. 1981. "Ideology and Equality: The Status of Women in Eastern and Western Europe." *Comparative Political Studies* 13 (January): 445–476.

Zipp, John F., Richard Landerman, Paul Luebke. 1982. "Political Parties and Political Participation: A Reexamination of the Standard Socioeconomic Model." *Social Forces* 60 (June): 1140–1153.

Zipp, John F. and Joel Smith. 1979. "The Structure of Electoral Political Participation." *American Journal of Sociology* 85 (July): 167–177.

Index

179

About the Author

CAROL A. CHRISTY is Associate Professor of Political Science at Ohio University–Lancaster, Lancaster, Ohio, and has taught there since 1970.

Dr. Christy has published in *Women & Politics* and *Comparative Studies.* She is currently President of the Midwest Women's Caucus for Political Science.

Dr. Christy holds a B.A. from Duke University and an M.A. and Ph.D. from The Ohio State University, Columbus, Ohio.

Series Editors' Sketches

RITA MAE KELLY is a Professor at the School of Public Affairs, Arizona State University, Tempe, Arizona. She holds a Ph.D. in political science from Indiana University, has served on numerous editorial boards, including *Evaluation Quarterly, Journal of Women and Politics, Policy Studies Review*, and was issue editor for *The Journal of Social Issues* symposium, "Productivity Satisfaction in the Public Sector: A Socio-Psychological Perspective" (Fall, 1980, 36, 4). She has written several books, including: *Community Control of Economic Development* (Praeger, 1977) and *The Making of Political Women* (with Mary Boutilier; Nelson-Hall, 1978). She currently is editor of the Praeger Series on Women and Politics (with Ruth B. Mandel) and is editor of the *Policy Studies Review* Special Symposium "Productivity, Public Policy, and Societal Well-Being" (February 1985) and the anthology *Promoting Productivity in the Public Sector: Problems, Strategies, and Prospects*. She is also editor of the *Journal of Women and Politics* special symposium on Political Socialization.

RUTH B. MANDEL, Associate Professor at Rutgers University's Eagleton Institute of Politics, is Director of Eagleton's Center for the American Woman and Politics (CAWP). Established in 1971 as a research, education, and public service center, CAWP studies women's participation in American public life, with special emphasis on candidates, officeholders, and women seeking political leadership roles. Mandel is the author of *In the Running: The New Woman Candidate* (Boston: Beacon Press, 1983).

TARGET SWITZERLAND

TARGET
SWITZERLAND

◈

Swiss Armed Neutrality
in World War II

By
STEPHEN P. HALBROOK

DA CAPO
A Member of the Perseus Books Group

Cataloging-in-Publication data for this book is available from the Library of Congress.

First Da Capo Press edition 2003
Originally published by Sarpedon, an imprint of Combined Publishing, in 1998
ISBN 0-306-81325-4

Published by Da Capo Press
A Member of the Perseus Books Group
http://www.dacapopress.com

Da Capo Press books are available at special discounts for bulk purchases in the U.S.
by corporations, institutions, and other organizations. For more information, please
contact the Special Markets Department at the Perseus Books Group, 11 Cambridge
Center, Cambridge, MA 02142, or call (800) 255–1514 or (617) 252–5298,
or e-mail j.mccrary@perseusbooks.com.

1 2 3 4 5 6 7 8 9—07 06 05 04 03

Contents

One of several plans for an invasion of Switzerland submitted to the
German Army High Command (OKH) after the fall of France.
(Adapted from Kurz, *Operationsplanung Schweiz*, 41.)

Preface

Even the most casual student of World War II is familiar with the "white spot" that appears in the center of maps depicting the conquests of the Third Reich. This territory, of course, was Switzerland: the one nation on the European continent from the Iberian peninsula to the Volga River that never succumbed to German occupation or submitted to Nazi threats. Over half a century since the end of the war, the story of how this small democracy maintained its independence while completely encircled by aggressive, totalitarian powers seems to have been forgotten. It was a time when Switzerland's existence as a democratic nation was imperiled and a time when Switzerland, alone among the nations of central Europe, successfully deterred Germany from invading and occupying her territory.

Switzerland "has one tenth of its population under arms; more than any other country in the world. . . . They're ready to fight to defend their way of life," wrote William L. Shirer, the eminent war correspondent, in 1939, just after Hitler launched World War II.[1] In 1940, only weeks before the Wehrmacht would topple most of the nations of Western Europe, Shirer predicted that "the Dutch will be easy pickings for the Germans. Their army is miserable. Switzerland will be a tougher nut to crack, and I doubt if the Germans will try."[2] While the Swiss would put closer to a fifth of their population under arms during the war, rather than a tenth, the key to why Switzerland escaped Nazi occupation while others succumbed is revealed in these observations.

What was Switzerland's secret? Why did a state with a German-speaking majority choose to reject the siren songs of Nazism and the

pan-European fascist movement which proved enticing to large portions of the populations of neighboring countries? Where did a small
nation find the resolve and strength—military and spiritual—to resist
against overwhelmingly larger and more powerful foes?

One answer lies in two words which describe Switzerland's
national military doctrine: armed neutrality. Yet that alone is not sufficient, for an equal—perhaps greater—part of the story is that
Switzerland's long tradition of democracy, together with the racial,
religious, ethnic and linguistic tolerance inherent in her decentralized
federal state, gave the Swiss a fierce determination to resist any threats
to their independence, particularly in the form of ideologies wholly
foreign to the Swiss experience. Other European nations were characterized by centralized governments often headed by elites with the
power to surrender their sovereignty to Hitler, either with a short
(even token) resistance or no fight at all. By contrast, in Switzerland,
sovereignty began with the individual, not the central authorities. And
every man kept a rifle for the defense of his home, his family, his canton and, finally, Switzerland herself.

This book describes how Switzerland's war-time mobilization
and armament—rooted in the centuries-old policy of active, armed
neutrality—effectively deterred invasion by the most powerful and
aggressive totalitarian state in modern European history. As such, it
fills a void on a subject not covered in English-language publications
and contributes to the understanding of the military history of the
period before and during World War II. Memories dimmed by the passage of over half a century, certain revisionists today denigrate Switzerland's military preparedness as mythical. They are wrong. As the
sources utilized for much of this book demonstrate, during the war
many Americans and Britons saw Switzerland as a heroic island of
democracy in a sea of Axis tyranny.

The book begins with a brief account of Switzerland from its
founding in 1291, including her medieval warrior tradition, and continues through the modern era, from Napoleonic times to the period
following World War I. It discusses the Swiss institutions of federalism
and a citizens army that deeply influenced the development of similar
American institutions.

Our primary focus, however, is on Switzerland's political and military efforts to defend her independence during the period 1933–45. Switzerland was immediately threatened when Hitler came to power in 1933. The threat did not abate until the final defeat of the German Wehrmacht in 1945. This is the first publication in English to give a year-by-year account of Switzerland's preparations to resist a direct Nazi attack and to combat fifth column subversion. This is also the story of the Nazi abhorrence of Swiss democracy and the reciprocal hatred—by most Swiss—of Nazism. It is the story of Swiss determination to avoid being swallowed up in the German Reich—a fate which would have meant the extinction of Swiss identity and culture, the extermination of large numbers of political dissidents who had fled to Switzerland, and the almost certain death of 50,000 Jews, both natives and refugees, who lived in Switzerland during the war. (This fact attains added meaning when one considers that within Germany and Austria only 28,000 Jews survived the war.)

Switzerland was the only country in Europe that had no single political leader with the authority to surrender the people to the Nazis. On Swiss soil there were no Jewish victims, no Gestapo jurisdiction and no slave labor for the German war machine. Every man in Switzerland had a rifle in his home. Switzerland was the only European country which proclaimed that, in the event of invasion, any announcement of surrender was to be regarded as enemy propaganda, and that *every* soldier must fight to the last cartridge and then with the bayonet.

The Swiss, by their timely and prudent decision to mobilize in anticipation of conflict, deterred invasion and occupation. As a consequence, Switzerland was, for the duration of the war, a strategic stumbling block in the heart of Europe, complicating significantly Axis, and in particular, German, movements on land and in the air. By contrast, most of the other countries of Europe failed to forestall invasion and long-term occupation, thereby vastly increasing the cost of the war in lives and treasure. Many of these countries surrendered to Hitler without armed resistance or after brief fights, following which the standing armies were ordered to lay down their arms. One consequence of this widespread collapse was the ceding to Germany of naval and air bases along the Atlantic, Mediterranean and North Sea coasts—providing a significantly expanded scope of operation for German naval and air power.

Much has been made in recent years of what are described as Swiss accommodations to Germany during World War II, particularly in banking practices. These accommodations—a direct, if regrettable, consequence of encirclement—merit serious and detailed treatment. The media focus on international banking transactions, however, has resulted in a distortion of the historical record that misrepresents the true Swiss experience during the war. The extraordinary and courageous efforts of the Swiss military to prevent invasion and preserve a haven in which individual rights were protected, and in which thousands of refugees and escaped prisoners of war found respite in the midst of the savagery of World War II and the Holocaust, have been ignored or forgotten.

The Swiss, with a long and vigorous tradition of academic and press freedom, have not run from their historical demons, as readers of the Swiss press and current historical scholarship know. It is important that others who judge Switzerland not run from the reality of Switzerland's dogged, successful resistance to tyranny during a time in which every surrounding country failed the first test of sovereignty. Even when completely encircled by Nazi Germany and its allies, the Swiss remained defiant of the New Order in Europe, their citizens army inspired by the simple two-word concept: "no surrender." This book is an effort to render justice to Switzerland's heroic resistance to Hitler during World War II. It would be difficult to find a more enduring democracy in the world than Switzerland, or one that has faced greater challenges to its continued existence.

*   *   *

The author would like to acknowledge the assistance of several persons who graciously gave of their time and effort in providing information for this book. However, the opinions expressed herein and any inaccuracies are solely those of the author.

A number of current and retired members of the Swiss Military Department provided extensive information about Swiss defenses during World War II as well as today. Special thanks are due to Lt. General Arthur Liener, Chief of Staff of the Swiss Armed Forces; Dr. Hans Senn, Lt. General (Ret.) and former Chief of Staff of the Swiss

Armed Forces; and Ernst C. Wyler, Lt. General (Ret.) and former Commander-in-Chief of the Swiss Air Force.

Ambassador August R. Lindt provided valuable insights into the events that took place in Switzerland during and immediately after the war, in light of hisr own fascinating experiences. Prof. Ernst Leisi also provided unique insights from the perspective of a young soldier of the time.

Several historians with special expertise in the German invasion plans and the Swiss will to resist assisted me by providing guidance through the voluminous literature on the subject in German. They included Dr. Willi Gautschi, Dr. Hans Rudolf Fuhrer, Prof. Klaus Urner and Dr. Oskar F. Fritschi. Thanks also goes to Dr. and Mrs. Robert Vögeli for their scholarly tour of the Reuenthal fortification.

Dr. Jürg Stüssi-Lauterburg, Dr. Josef Inauen and the staff at the Federal Military Library in Bern have provided the author with research over several years on Swiss military history. Bruno Suter, a doctoral candidate, has worked tirelessly to assist with archival material. Additional thanks go to Dr. Daniel Bourgeois, H. von Rütte and the staff of the Federal Archives in Bern, particularly for making available their vast wartime photographic library.

Major Peter C. Stocker of the General Staff rendered invaluable assistance by providing current information on the Swiss military and by arranging tours of the Sargans fortifications, which Master Sergeant Malnati kindly guided. Lt. Colonel Daniel Lätsch gave an enlightening lecture tour of the defenses of the Linth Plain. For a tour of the Gotthard fortification, thanks go to Master Sergeant Beat Wandeler.

Special thanks go to Hermann Widmer for his review of archival material and to Ferdinand Piller for making these sources available at the Swiss Schützenmuseum in Bern. Friedrich E. Friedli kindly assisted in the location of archival sources from several cantons.

George Gyssler provided invaluable assistance by coordinating numerous interviews and by reviewing the manuscript. Mary Kehrli-Smyth assisted with bibliographical material. For their insights on Nazi policies for preventing Jewish armed resistance, I am indebted to Jay Simkin and David B. Kopel. Thanks go, too, to Donn Teal of Sarpedon Publishers for his scrupulous attention to detail while copyediting the manuscript, and to Karen Schmidt for lending her aesthetic talents to arranging the illustrations. Photographs used as illustrations were provided courtesy of the Schweizerisches Bundesarchiv and the Eidgenössisches Militärdepartement in Bern.

Over the years, a number of graduate students and law students have assisted in locating sources on Swiss history and Swiss influences on the American Constitution. Special thanks go to Heather Barry for her indefatigable efforts in locating both wartime sources and early American sources. Noreen Cary, Bob Nagel, and Dave Fischer also provided assistance. Gratitude for much hard work is also due to my paralegal and researcher, Lisa Halbrook-Stevenson. Thanks go to Russelle Rusczak for assisting in the manuscript preparation.

TARGET SWITZERLAND

Prologue
Companions of the Oath

IT IS JULY 25, 1940. GENERAL HENRI GUISAN, COMMANDER OF the Swiss Army, has summoned 600 of his highest officers to a jagged mountainside in central Switzerland near Lake Lucerne overshadowed by Alpine peaks—the Rütli Meadow.

During the preceding weeks, France, the Netherlands and Belgium have fallen to the forces of Nazi Germany, and the British Army has evacuated the continent, leaving its heavy equipment behind. Denmark and Norway had succumbed to German arms a few months before, Poland the preceding fall. Austria and Czechoslovakia were swallowed up by the Third Reich through bloodless coups, wrought by intimidation, during the previous two years. Fascist Italy threatens Switzerland's southern border.

Surrounded by totalitarian aggressors and occupied lands, the Swiss stand alone.

General Guisan faces his officers, who are arrayed in a semicircle before him. Urging them to prepare for total resistance to aggression that could come from any direction, he says:

> I decided to reunite you in this historic place, the symbolic ground of our independence, to explain the urgency of the situation, and to speak to you as a soldier to soldiers. We are at a turning point of our history. The survival of Switzerland is at stake.[1]

The General had chosen his site well to deliver this call to resistance. For history and tradition tell that in this spot, the Rütli

Meadow, the Swiss Confederation was formed on August 1, 1291. On that date, leaders of the three Alpine cantons of Uri, Schwyz and Unterwalden, who had successfully defended their democratically governed communities from foreign invasion, came together to form an alliance for mutual defense. They called themselves the *Eidgenossen*—Companions of the Oath—and vowed to help each other in fighting any enemy who threatened their independence.

The history of Switzerland's armed neutrality in the modern era, including the Swiss' valiant defense of their homeland in World War II, cannot be divorced from the record of her men-at-arms since that first meeting at the Rütli Meadow more than seven hundred years ago. For centuries, Swiss fighting men earned a reputation as the most ferocious in Europe, and their dominance of the battlefield, combined with their refusal to live under the rule of foreign kings, became a unique example in Europe of the successful defense of a nation's freedoms.

In the centuries after 1291, Switzerland would grow from the original 3 to 26 cantons and half-cantons. Switzerland today consists of an ethnic mix of 72 percent German speakers, 20 percent French, and 6 percent Italian—with 1 percent of Swiss, primarily in the mountainous southeast, speaking Romansh, a survival of ancient Latin combined with Italian and a trace of an ancient and once widespread Celtic tongue. Surrounded today by Italy, Austria, Germany, and France, Switzerland occupies a strategically important position in the heart of Europe. Nevertheless, with one brief interruption during the Napoleonic period at the turn of the nineteenth century, Switzerland has successfully maintained her integrity and defended her borders against foreign aggressors. At every stage of her military history, Switzerland would use her terrain to military advantage.

Switzerland is a landlocked, 41,293 square kilometer country, about the size of Maryland. The Alps in the south and east constitute 61 percent of the country, the Jura mountains in the northwest another 12 percent. Most of the remainder, the Swiss Mittelland (Plateau), is a flat area from Lake Geneva in the southwest to Lake Constance in the northeast. While the Plateau is the most vulnerable part of the country, it is dotted with natural barriers of rivers, lakes, and streams. The majority of the land—the mountains—constitutes a natural fortress, centering on the Alpine Redoubt, or *Réduit National.*

The first detailed account of the people who inhabited Switzerland in ancient times describes the Helvetii, a large Celtic tribe against whom Julius Caesar launched his 10-year Gallic War, known to generations of schoolchildren who learned Latin from reading Caesar's account of his campaigns in Gaul. (Today, multi-lingual Switzerland's stamps and coins are marked "Helvetia," and the country is known formally as the "Confederatio Helvetica," the Swiss Confederation.) The ancient Helvetic tribe Caesar described was at the time attempting to migrate to western Gaul (modern France) to escape Germans who were threatening their homeland. Caesar claimed to have killed three-quarters of the Helvetii before ordering the survivors back to their original land to serve as a buffer against the warlike German tribes living beyond the Rhine.[2]

The familiar legend of William Tell exemplifies Swiss resistance to foreign domination and cultivation of the martial spirit. Today, Tell is portrayed on the modern 5-franc piece and occupies a place as a Swiss folk hero similar to that of Robin Hood in English-speaking countries. Immortalized by Schiller in his 1804 play (written to encourage resistance to Napoleon's occupation of Europe), the feats of William Tell bear a striking resemblance to earlier tales from Scandinavian mythology (although archaeological evidence from Tell's time demonstrates that a number of castles in the area of Tell's exploits were burned or destroyed). Yet the reality behind the story illustrates both the fierce determination of Swiss to maintain their freedom and independence and their proud tradition of marksmanship.

Tell's story takes place just before the Alliance of 1291. According to an early American account, Governor Gessler of Uri, a puppet of the then-occupying Austrians, "placed a hat on a pole at Altdorf, and gave strict orders that every one should pay that hat the same honour as if he were present himself."[3] When Tell repeatedly passed by Gessler's hat without taking off his own, he was condemned to shoot an apple off the head of his six-year-old son at 120 paces; the alternative was death for both father and son. In a remarkable display of archery skill, Tell succeeded in hitting the apple and sparing the boy.

The less familiar remainder of the story equally illustrates Swiss virtues of independence and resistance to foreign invasions. After the shooting of the arrow, Gessler asked Tell why he had another arrow in his quiver. Tell responded that, had he injured the child, he would have sent the remaining arrow into the governor's heart.[4]

The governor condemned Tell to life imprisonment for his insolence, but Tell escaped while being transported across Lake Lucerne in a boat. After Gessler's own boat landed, "in the way to his castle he was waylaid by Tell in a narrow road, who placed the reserved arrow in his heart."[5] This instigated a rebellion in which the Austrian overseers were deposed, and the three cantons of Uri, Schwyz, and Unterwalden swore loyalty to each other—the very event recalled by General Guisan six and one-half centuries later in the face of the Nazi threat.

Tell's famous deeds have lived on in the hearts of those who love liberty, not least the founders of the American republic. John Adams, the second President of the United States, devoted a chapter to Switzerland in his *Defence of the Constitutions of the United States of America* of 1787. Noting that the arsenal at Zurich supposedly contained William Tell's bow and arrow, Adams quoted from a poem about Tell: "Who with the generous rustics fate, / On Uri's rock, in close divan, / And wing'd that arrow, sure as fate, / Which fixed the sacred rights of man."[6] Drawing an analogy to the American Revolution and the process of uniting thirteen states into one nation, Adams noted that the canton of Uri, birthplace of William Tell, "shook off the yoke of Austria in 1308, and, with Switz and Unterwald, laid the foundation of the perpetual alliance of the cantons, in 1315."[7]

That latter year was the date of one of Switzerland's most inspiring victories, the Battle of Morgarten, in which the Austrian invaders were routed and Swiss independence restored. One thousand four hundred Swiss peasants ambushed 20,000 Austrian knights and infantry in a narrow passage, showering them with rocks and driving them into a lake where many drowned. Hapsburg deaths numbered 2,000 to only 12 Swiss.[8]

The three cantons which had joined as "companions of the oath" then took their alliance a significant step further and established a permanent Swiss Confederation—the beginning of the nation of Switzerland. The original grouping of the three cantons grew over the course of the fourteenth century to include Lucerne, Zurich, Glarus, Zug and Bern, encompassing much of modern central and northern Switzerland.

Yet the foreign threat to Swiss independence—and bold Swiss resistance—continued. In 1339, feudal lords from southern Germany and Fribourg sent 12,000 soldiers against the Bernese, who fought back with 6,500 infantrymen. At the Battle of Laupen, the Bernese foot soldiers defeated the enemy's armored cavalry in open terrain, a first for Swiss warriors and a precedent for all of Europe. Until that time, the mounted knight had reigned supreme on the battlefield, and foot soldiers had been considered militarily—as well as socially—inferior to knights.[9]

At the Battle of Sempach in 1386, Duke Leopold III of Austria sent 4,000 armored knights against a 1,300-man Swiss peasant force armed only with halberds and pieces of wood on their arms to fend off blows.[10] Folklore has it that during the battle a Swiss fighter named Arnold Winkelried held onto a great number of enemy lances, which had been thrust into his body, long enough to allow his comrades to drive through the Austrian lines. The battle ended with half the Austrian force dead on the field (including the Duke himself) to 200 Swiss casualties.[11] Winkelried lives on in Swiss history as one of the Confederation's greatest heroes.

In 1388, the Austrians invaded again with a force of 15,000 men but were soundly defeated at the Battle of Näfels by about 650 Swiss, who rolled stones upon the invaders from the summit of a mountain and then "rushed down upon them with such fury, as forced them to retire with an immense loss."[12] The Austrians lost 1,700 men. The Swiss lost only 55—a ratio of almost 30 to 1.

The Swiss perfected the concept of a well-organized citizenry that could be called out for service at short notice. The ability of the Swiss militia to mobilize immediately would continue to be its distinguishing characteristic over the centuries, right up through World War II. The ruthlessness of the Swiss in battle and their courage was noted throughout Europe. Their fierceness and willingness to fight to the death in defense of their homeland deterred many potential aggressors.

In the Burgundian War, Switzerland defeated the most powerful army in Europe, led by Charles the Bold, Duke of Burgundy. In 1476,

Medieval Swiss Sites and Battlefields

1. Rütli (1291)
2. Altdorf (William Tell legend)
3. Morgarten (1315)
4. Laupen (1339)
5. Sempach (1386)
6. Näfels (Wesen) (1388)
7. Arbedo (1422)
8. Sankt Jakob an der Birs (1444)
9. Grandson (1476)
10. Morat (1476)

In the two centuries following the origins in 1291 of the "Companions of the Oath," Swiss warriors won victory after victory against overwhelming odds in conflicts with surrounding monarchies.

Charles led 20,000 soldiers across the Jura Mountains and persuaded Bernese troops in the Grandson castle to surrender. All 412 Bernese were then hanged or drowned.[13] The Swiss mobilized immediately and at the ensuing Battle of Grandson sent the Burgundian army into retreat with heavy losses.

Charles spent four months preparing an army of 23,000 men for revenge. The Swiss strengthened the defenses at the town of Morat (Murten), through which an invader would have to pass en route to Bern. When Charles laid siege to Morat, the Confederates mobilized an army of 25,000. The Swiss launched a surprise attack, killing 10,000 of the enemy and sustaining losses of only 410. The Swiss took no prisoners, but Charles the Bold managed to escape, only to be killed by a halberd-wielding Swiss the following year at the Battle of Nancy.[14] After Morat, the Swiss infantry was the most renowned in Europe.

Strong defense of the Swiss homeland and the position of Switzerland at the geopolitical crossroads of Europe led to another concept unique to the Swiss military tradition—neutrality. At the Diet of Stans in 1481, the Confederation accepted the advice of the politically influential Swiss monk Niklaus von Flüe (more commonly known as Brother Klaus) to remain neutral during foreign conflicts. Neutrality would deny potential aggressors a *casus belli*, a reason for war, against Switzerland and would thus itself serve to deter foreign aggression. Further, the Swiss came to see that neutrality was, indeed, necessary to maintain their independence and to ensure unity in a decentralized political society such as the Confederation. It would take another generation before the concept of Swiss neutrality would be truly realized. The threat from abroad, however, would recur throughout Swiss history, including in the twentieth century.

As Swiss freedom continued to be threatened, the Swiss developed new military tactics to deter foreign invasion. The Swiss pike square—thousands of men massed together with long pikes and halberds—ruled supreme on European battlefields. Cavalry could not penetrate it, and the pike square could outpush opposing infantry formations.

The attempt in 1495 by the Holy Roman Empire's Diet of Worms to impose a common penny tax on the Swiss and to subject them to the jurisdiction of an Imperial Chamber of Justice sparked a conflict that would complete the winning of Swiss independence from the Holy Roman Empire. To counter the Empire's heavy infantry, which threatened invasion from what is today southern Germany, the Swiss built fortifications all along the Rhine River and stayed at the ready for immediate mobilization—a tactic they would repeat in World War II. With the Empire's defeat at the Battle of Dornach, the Holy Roman Emperor Maximilian recognized the independence of the Swiss Confederation in 1501. Other cantons joined the Confederation, which by 1513 comprised a total of thirteen.[15]

The Swiss defeat at Marignano, near the Italian city of Milan, at the hands of the French in 1515, prompted Switzerland to adopt a policy of permanent armed neutrality, with no imperialist or territorial ambitions. The contemporary Florentine writer Niccolo Machiavelli, author of *The Prince* (1532) and a keen student of military affairs, described the battle thus: "if they [the Swiss] did not win the day as they had done at Novara [in 1513, when the Swiss beat the French], they fought valiantly for two days, and, though routed, got away with half their forces."[16] While the Swiss performed bravely, after the battle they finally adopted a foreign policy which allowed only for defensive wars.

Further, a policy of neutrality was the most logical course within a Confederation of disparate languages, ethnicity and traditions. The decentralized political system of the cantons, under which no leader from one canton was allowed to dominate the others, meant that aggressive wars could not easily be undertaken by the Confederation as a whole.

Neutrality, of course, could only be maintained by a well-armed citizenry. Machiavelli wrote that "the Swiss are well armed and enjoy great freedom."[17] On his travels through Switzerland, the Florentine observed her citizens army, which he found to be the worthy descendant of the militia of Republican Rome sixteen centuries earlier. As Machiavelli noted, the Swiss were "masters of modern warfare," but their armed citizenry made them superior only at defense, not aggression:

[W]hen states are strongly armed, as Rome was and as the Swiss are, the more difficult it is to overcome them the nearer they are to their homes: for such bodies [militias] can bring more forces together to resist attack than they can to attack others. . . . The Swiss are easy to beat when away from home, whither they cannot send more than thirty or forty thousand men; but to defeat them at home where they can muster a hundred thousand is very difficult.[18]

By the early 1500s the evolution of Swiss military doctrine, from reliance on the "irresistible" pike square in the open field to once more adopting a strategy of defense, had thus come full circle. This should not be surprising given the small size and limited resources of Switzerland in comparison to her neighbors. Consider Machiavelli's description of the tactics used by the Swiss and their ability to maintain their freedom despite their modest economic conditions:

since they are poor, yet anxious to defend their liberties against the ambitions of the German princes . . . the Swiss are obliged to engage an enemy on foot, and therefore find it necessary to continue their ancient manner of fighting in order to make headway against the fury of the enemy's cavalry.[19]

Though modern Switzerland is prosperous, the essential military situation has not changed: a small country in Europe facing potential foes far larger and more populous. As this book will discuss, the Swiss adopted a sophisticated defensive posture in World War II relying on the terrain of the country and the abilities of her well-trained shooters to repel foes. The reliance on a citizens army, rather than a standing army, required that ordinary Swiss constantly practice their marksmanship and military discipline, another tradition of long standing continued to this day.

A citizens army depends for its success on the cohesion of its units and the absolute devotion of each soldier. During World War II, the Swiss had no tolerance for soldiers convicted of espionage for the Nazis or sabotage. Death sentences were handed down for such activities. Machiavelli had written centuries earlier of the Swiss harshness toward soldiers who expressed fear or deserted from the ranks.

After their defeat at Marignano in 1515, the Swiss would no longer stray outside their borders, but would concentrate solely on the defense of Switzerland. In 1647, in the "Defensional of Wyl," the Swiss federal army took over defense of the borders from the cantons. The Treaty of Westphalia of 1648, which ended the European Thirty Years' War, recognized Switzerland's independence and confirmed her separation from the Holy Roman Empire.[20]

Following Switzerland's adoption of a national policy of armed neutrality, Swiss troops continued to enhance their reputation as fighters in the service of foreign monarchs, as mercenaries. It became a status symbol among European royalty to have their persons protected by Swiss Guards. When the Parisian mob came for Louis XVI at the Tuileries in 1792, no Frenchman came to his defense. His 600-man regiment of Swiss Guards, however, fought back against overwhelming odds, and nearly all were massacred. In 1848, the Swiss Constitution prohibited any new contracts for service in foreign armies, and in 1859, all mercenary service was prohibited.[21] Over the centuries, roughly one million Swiss had served as mercenaries. Today, as the last vestige of what was once a widespread practice, 90 Swiss soldiers continue to guard the Pope at the Vatican, their colorful uniforms a reminder of an even more colorful military tradition.

The Swiss example of a well-armed citizens army, instead of the standing armies typical of the European kingdoms, attracted the attention of English and American political observers in the eighteenth century, including many of the founders of the American republic. In 1771, the *Boston Gazette* drew a direct analogy to British rule in America using the example of the Austrian occupation of Switzerland and the patriotic resistance of William Tell. The newspaper's concluding remark and its application to the British was clear: "Was there not a cause, was it not high time to exterminate such instruments of cruelty?"[22]

In its *Appeal to the Inhabitants of Quebec* of October 26, 1774, the Continental Congress asked their northern neighbors not to let religious differences prevent them from pursuing unity. The *Appeal* stated:

The Swiss Cantons furnish a memorable proof of this truth. Their union is composed of Roman Catholic and Protestant

States, living in the utmost concord and peace with one another and thereby enabled, ever since they bravely vindicated their freedom, to defy and defeat every tyrant that has invaded them.[23]

In 1778, Johann R. Valltravers, a political leader from western Switzerland, wrote to Benjamin Franklin: "Let us be united, as two Sister-Republicks." He proposed a "lasting Foundation of Friendship, and of mutual good offices between the two Sisters, the 13 republican states of N[orth] America, and of Switzerland."[24] The term "Sister Republics" would stick and was frequently used in nineteenth-century America.

Once the American Revolution was won, the Swiss experience would figure prominently in the political debates that took place just before the Constitution was adopted. In his *A Defense of the Constitutions* (1787), a survey of ancient and modern republics and other political models, John Adams discussed the governance of the democratic Swiss cantons and noted two common institutions among them: the right to vote on laws and the right to bear arms. Thus in the canton of Bern, "every male of sixteen is enrolled in the militia, and obligated to provide himself an uniform, a musket, powder and ball; and no peasant is allowed to marry without producing his arms and uniform."[25]

George Mason, a delegate to the Constitutional Convention who was best known for his authorship of the Virginia Declaration of Rights, proposed that the office of President under the new constitution should consist of three persons rather than just one. He conceded that a single person as President had the advantages of unity and secrecy, especially during war. Yet that was also a principle of monarchies, which had been defeated when they invaded republics. Republics without a single leader had advantages too: "Every Husbandman will be quickly converted into a Soldier, when he knows & feels that he is to fight not in defense of the Rights of a particular Family, or a Prince; but for his own. . . . It is this which preserves the Freedom and Independence of the Swiss Cantons, in the midst of the most powerful Nations." This Swiss-like reliance on the individual soldier fighting to defend his home and liberties was also the secret of the success

of the Americans in the Revolution.[26] Ironically, Mason's proposal
was similar to the Swiss executive institution of the Federal Council,
which was adopted in 1848 and continues today.

Patrick Henry, whose Revolutionary-era speech with the words
"give me liberty or give me death" won him the reputation as
America's foremost orator, eloquently praised the 500-year history of
Switzerland, which "braved all the power of France and Germany,"
while retaining its "independence, republican simplicity and valour."[27]
He continued:

> Compare the peasants of Switzerland with those of any
> other mighty nation: You will find them far more happy—
> for one civil war among them, there have been five or six
> among other nations—Their attachment to their country,
> and to freedom—their resolute intrepidity in their defense;
> the consequent security and happiness which they have en-
> joyed, and the respect and awe which these things produced
> in their bordering nations, have signalized them republi-
> cans. ...Let us follow their example, and be equally happy.[28]

From its beginnings, the United States had a healthy regard for
the Swiss example of a decentralized federal state, guarded from invasion by a well-armed and well-trained citizens army. In 1789, in
response to the public debate over ratification of the U.S. Constitution, the first Congress proposed the Bill of Rights, which became
part of the Constitution in 1791. Two provisions of the Bill of Rights
bear the imprint of Swiss influence. The Second Amendment declares:
"A well-regulated militia, being necessary to the security of a free
state, the right of the people to keep and bear arms, shall not be
infringed."[29] The Tenth Amendment provides: "The powers not delegated to the United States by the Constitution, nor prohibited to it by
the States, are reserved to the States respectively, or to the people."
These declarations of popular sovereignty and federalism, inspired in
part by the Swiss model, remain part of the United States Constitution
today. History supported the position of those who argued that the
democratic and decentralized character of Switzerland made her
militarily stronger, rather than weaker.

Switzerland's history of standing unconquered by foreign aggressors since 1291 has not, however, remained unbroken. When the revolutionary energy of France, then Europe's most powerful nation state, became harnessed to the ambition of one of history's most charismatic leaders, the map of Europe was redrawn. The Swiss cantons found themselves forced to become a "protectorate of France." This unhappy experience with Napoleon would live long in Swiss hearts and minds and provide a backdrop both to the fierce Swiss determination to resist the Nazis and to the type of warfare the Nazis could have expected had they invaded the country.

It began in May 1797. After scouting out the country to plan an invasion, Napoleon demanded that the mountain passes be opened to French troops. The Swiss refused the demand. Napoleon decided to invade.[30]

Then—just as the Nazis would do a century and a half later—the French Directory (the Napoleonic government) launched propaganda barrages and promoted rumor-mongering against Switzerland as part of a campaign to reduce the Swiss will to resist. The clarion calls of "Liberty, Equality, Fraternity" emanating from Paris found receptive ears among some Swiss, particularly in the French-speaking cantons. The last vestiges of aristocracy and feudalism, argued Swiss radicals, should be swept into the dustbin of history. A revolutionary, Peter Ochs, accepted Napoleon's invitation to draft a new constitution for Switzerland. Before long, Geneva and parts of the Jura were occupied by French troops. Vaud was taken without a shot being fired. Lausanne fell on January 28, 1798, without resistance.[31]

The Swiss made a stand on March 5 in a field near the town of Fraubrunnen, where 400 years before they had defeated a horde of English mercenaries intent on abusing Swiss nuns in their convent. While the Swiss put up a brave fight against the French invaders, the rolling farmland was not defensible against Napoleon's infantry and artillery. Many Swiss who turned out for the fight were simply locals intent on defending their families and homesteads. Most of them were poorly equipped. Women, children and the elderly armed themselves with pitchforks and other farm implements to fight the French.[32]

The unique Swiss system of collective security for the cantons had operated successfully from the founding of the country until 1798.

In the face of the Napoleonic threat, however, the lack of a single command and superior French weapons and numbers led to Switzerland's defeat. (Remembering this failure, after 1815 the Swiss would expend great effort to improve both their weapons and their military tactics.) Equally important, massive revolutionary propaganda promising a new and better order in Europe permitted the French to sow disunity among the cantons and achieve their purpose to divide and conquer the country. As a result, in the 1930s and World War II, Switzerland would be vigilant against the threat of Nazi propaganda and subversive activities in the country and adopt a concept of "spiritual national defense."

After Napoleon's victory in 1798, those Swiss fighters who survived disappeared back into their villages and waited for a new opportunity to defeat the invader.[33] On April 12, after the French entered Bern—the first foreign army ever to do so—Peter Ochs proclaimed the Helvetic Republic. A new constitution replaced Swiss traditions of local democratic control with a highly centralized government and an executive dictatorship, the Directory of Five, headed by Ochs. Resistance movements that included thousands of Swiss citizens formed soon thereafter in several cantons, but were crushed by the French.[34] Sporadic guerilla warfare continued and thousands of Swiss were killed.[35]

After Austria and Britain made peace with France in 1802, French occupation troops withdrew from Switzerland. However, the country remained under Napoleon's heel. The second Helvetic Constitution, more centralist than the first, was promulgated even though the Swiss rejected it in a vote.[36] Though Switzerland remained in her degraded state, Swiss fighting men continued to uphold their high reputation for courage. Constantly placed in the forefront of battle, only 700 of the 9,000 Swiss troops forced into French service would return from Napoleon's disastrous 1812 Russian campaign. At the crossing of the Beresina during the retreat from Moscow, the Swiss bravely stood in the rearguard that allowed the bulk of Napoleon's fighting strength to escape the converging Russian armies.

In 1813, Switzerland became a battleground again and was overrun by Austrian and Russian troops—although the Swiss greeted them as liberators. It was not until Napoleon's final defeat at Waterloo in

1815 that the nightmare ended. Departing from neutrality, Switzerland joined the allies and participated in the last military actions against Napoleon.[37]

While in exile on St. Helena, Napoleon paid tribute to the courage and obstinacy of the Swiss: "The Swiss treated the French as their ancestors had treated the Austrians; but what could they do against the French cavalry and artillery? They hurled themselves upon the cannons like madmen, yielding only to numbers and tactics."[38] In his *Commentaires*, Napoleon warned against campaigns in mountainous areas and described the Alps as a place where one must "make supernatural efforts to cross inaccessible mountains and still find oneself amid precipes, defiles and rocks, with no prospect other than having the same obstacles to surmount."[39]

The period of Napoleonic domination was the last instance in which Switzerland's democracy and sovereignty were lost to a foreign invader. This occurred only because the Swiss themselves were disunited in the face of a pan-European revolutionary idea and because the small, poorly-armed Swiss forces were crushed by overwhelming French military superiority. After the Napoleonic experience, the Swiss were determined never to allow an invasion again and spent the next century and a quarter building a strong citizens army that anticipated new threats. They would be ready when a new, and far more sinister, military adventurer arose in the 1930s to launch another war against all of Europe.

According to the Swiss concept, the army was "the people in arms." Passed under the new 1815 Constitution, the general military regulation of August 20, 1817 organized the army of modern Switzerland. It required universal male service in the militia, which was subjected to uniform standards by, and came under the direction of, the Confederation as a whole.[40] In reaction to the Napoleonic invasion of Switzerland, patriotic shooting clubs sprang up. The Swiss Shooting Federation (in German, the *Schweizerischer Schützenverein,* or SSV) united the local groups in 1824. Article I of its constitution stated the organization's purpose:

> To draw another bond around the hearts of our citizens to increase the strength of the fatherland through unity and

closer connections and at the same time to contribute according to the capacity of each of our members, to the promotion and perfection of the art of sharpshooting, an art beautiful in itself and of the highest importance for the defense of the confederation.[41]

The SSV began to hold local, regional, and national shooting festivals, "Helvetic assemblies" designed to engender a stronger Swiss national feeling. The organization was heir to the centuries-old tradition of shooting festivals, about which records had been kept from the fourteenth century. It promoted a culture of marksmanship in the community and was an essential component of continued training for citizen soldiers.[42]

In the 1847 Sonderbund War, a separatist revolt in seven rural Catholic cantons was defeated by larger, more urbanized Protestant cantons. The war lasted only 25 days and took only 98 lives.[43] The victory against the Jesuit traditionalists horrified the old order in Europe and inspired those seeking a stronger centralized government. Reformists proceeded to draft a liberal constitution to replace the post-Napoleonic Pact of 1815. By a vote of almost seven to one, the citizenry adopted the proposed constitution.

During the years 1856–57, Kaiser Friedrich Wilhelm IV of Prussia prepared to mobilize as many as 150,000 soldiers to march on Switzerland over a border dispute. The Swiss Federal Council positioned 30,000 troops at the border, instructed reserves to stay in readiness, and fortified the Rhine against a possible attack. A German observer remarked: "No Swiss, but a stranger dare say it, that this militia was worth half a dozen standing armies." The possible war sparked an international crisis that was eventually resolved in Switzerland's favor through diplomacy.[44]

In 1866, Prussian Prime Minister Otto von Bismarck suggested to the Italian Ambassador that the French-speaking parts of Switzerland and Belgium could be given to France to compensate for territorial expansion by Prussia and Italy.[45] That same year, in a war using newly designed rifles, the Prussians soundly defeated Austria. Seeing a need during this period to design a rifle that would be superior to that of the Prussians, in 1866 the Swiss Federal Assembly approved funding to develop a repeating rifle. In response, Frederic Vetterli designed a repeating turn-bolt rifle with a tubular magazine holding 12 metallic cartridges that was in use from 1867 to 1889.[46] The Swiss adopted a new repeating rifle in 1889, using a straight-bolt system that allowed faster firing than the German Mauser rifles. The newer model carried 12 rounds of the Swiss-designed 7.5mm cartridge.[47]

For most of the nineteenth century, France would be seen as the greatest danger to Swiss independence and security. However, as time went on, Switzerland's neighbor to the north once again began to appear more threatening. Particularly after the Franco-Prussian War of 1870–71—during which Switzerland mobilized to prevent the Prussians from invading to pursue the fleeing French—the Swiss came to fear the new Second Reich in Germany. The enduring expression "hatred of the Germans" first appeared in Switzerland at this time.[48] The feeling of ill-will was reciprocated: one German writer of the time wrote that "for centuries, Switzerland has hung from our body like a paralyzed limb and sucks our juices without itself moving for them. To cut it off would be damaging to the limb and destructive to the body; it will again survive only through close association with the body."[49] Tensions between Germany and Switzerland increased in the late nineteenth century as German Social Democrats who had fled to Switzerland smuggled socialist newspapers back into Germany.

The perception of a new German threat convinced the Swiss to unify the armed forces in the federal system in 1874. The Federal Constitution provided that military instruction, armament, and equipment be in the federal, not cantonal, domains, and Article 18 stated that "Every Swiss is liable to military service." Rather than the citizen providing his own arms, as had traditionally been the case, the new constitution provided that "servicemen shall receive their first equipment, clothing, and arms without payment. The weapon shall remain in the hands of the soldier, subject to conditions to be determined by Federal legislation."[50]

During this period, in sharp contrast to the increasing centralization of power in other states in continental Europe, in Switzerland the federal government was becoming more responsive to the wishes of individual citizens. The 1874 Constitution introduced the referendum, under which a petition signed by 30,000 citizens would require a popular vote on an existing law. Under the 1891 amendment, the initiative was established, granting 50,000 signatories the power to demand a vote on new legislation they endorsed.[51]

After a series of reforms, by 1912 the Swiss Army included 281,000 men and could call on an additional 200,000 auxiliary troops. Kaiser Wilhelm II of Germany visited Switzerland that year. As the Kaiser observed Swiss army maneuvers, Swiss President Ludwig Forrer told his guest that "we have the resolute intention of protecting our independence against any attack on this [land], our dearest possession, and of upholding our neutrality against anyone who fails to respect it."[52] In a conversation depicted on a contemporary postcard, the Kaiser queried what the quarter of a million Swiss Army would do if faced with an invasion of half a million Germans. A Swiss militiaman replied, "Shoot twice."[53]

During the period just before the Great War, Americans were intensely interested in Swiss marksmanship culture. General George W. Wingate expressed the sentiment as follows:

> Switzerland has no regular army, but depends for her defense on her riflemen. Though poor, she spends annually large amounts in developing them, both in and out of the schools. Out of a population of but three million—less than that of the City of New York in 1904—she had 3,656 rifle clubs with a membership of 218,815, who shot twenty-one million cartridges with the army rifle.[54]

These words were uttered the year after the Swiss had developed two new infantry rifles to replace the model of 1889. The Schmidt-Rubin Infantry Rifle Model 1911 had a 6-round detachable magazine and used the more powerful Model 11 7.5mm cartridge. The Karabiner Model 1911, a handy carbine version, was also adopted. Both used the fast-acting straight-pull bolt. Over 300,000 Model 1911 rifles and carbines were manufactured and distributed to the populace.[55]

In 1911, American Colonel George Bell noted that Swiss soldiers marching in parades were not impressive to watch, but these soldiers had all the essential skills to defend their country. He wrote:

Any nation, however powerful, will pause before invading Switzerland, for, combined to this preparedness, there is a Spartan patriotism and valor, inherited from ancestors who had no fear of death, and a love of country unsurpassed by any known people, and this army, or nation in arms, before being killed or annihilated by sheer force of numbers, will inflict terrible losses, as, while the Swiss believes in peace, and desires it above all else, his good sense tells him this is best assured by preparedness at all times.[56]

When the "Great War" broke out, on August 1, 1914, with combatants on all borders of Switzerland, the Federal Council ordered mobilization of the entire army. Some 450,000 men answered the call. Switzerland's Parliament elected Lt. General Ulrich Wille, distinguished by his complete faith in the abilities of the citizen soldier, to the rank of general.[57] On August 4, the Federal Council reaffirmed that Switzerland would maintain "the strictest neutrality vis-a-vis the belligerent States"[58] in the widening conflict.

Known as the "occupation of frontiers," Swiss strategy during World War I was a strong border defense by three divisions, backed by a reserve of three more divisions, with four brigades in the southern mountains.[59] The border troops were concentrated at the northwest corner of the country to protect the frontier against *both* France and Germany.[60]

As they had in previous conflicts, the outnumbered Swiss placed great emphasis on superior military training and equipment. The army was supplied with Maxim machine guns and updated artillery. Both aviation and anti-aircraft defenses were introduced.[61] Although the Italians briefly contemplated a march through Switzerland,[62] both they and the Germans decided to respect Swiss neutrality. The French continued to fear the possibility of a German attack on France through Switzerland until the very end of the war and discussed the concept of a joint defense with the Swiss in the event of a German invasion. These talks, which took place during the last stages of the war in 1917–18, were the precursor of similar joint plans in 1939–40.[63]

The concept of armed neutrality served Switzerland well in World War I as it had for centuries. Despite her location in the center of the continental European powers fighting the war, Switzerland successfully preserved her strict neutrality and avoided becoming a battlefield.

Trade was vital to the existence of landlocked Switzerland. As a neutral she exercised her right under international law to trade with both groups of combatants, and she disregarded the objections of each military bloc against trade with the other. Surrounded by war for only the third time in her history, the nation could not afford to play favorites. Neutrality did not lead to prosperity during World War I— Switzerland faced shortages of food and other commodities.

At the outset of the war, many German-speaking Swiss sympathized with Germany, and French-speaking Swiss supported France. Over time, however—and especially prompted by Germany's invasion of neutral Belgium—the Central Powers were seen more and more to represent anti-democratic forces contrary to the Swiss tradition of individual liberty and democratic government.

In 1916, the U.S. Senate published a report entitled *The Military Law and Efficient Citizen Army of the Swiss.* Perhaps the most telling item in the report was the observation of American Attaché Eric Fisher Wood about French soldiers: "The only shooting that they had ever done was gallery shooting at a range of about 40 yards, and they were singularly poor even at this."[64] Further, the German soldiers "shoot poorly from an American standpoint, but do better than the French."[65] That same year, Julian Grande, in his book *A Citizens' Army: The Swiss System,* wrote that Switzerland had remained out of the Great War because "the Swiss Army, or part of it, is always mobilized, and its military value is well known to all the belligerents, none of whom are anxious to encounter the resistence of an army of 500,000 trained soldiers, all good marksmen."[66]

For a great power, or a country whose geographic position makes her unassailable, a declaration of neutrality is relatively cost-free. For a small country strategically located in the heart of Europe, however, the cost of neutrality was higher and needed to be earned by strength of arms and resolve to resist aggression. From the fall of Napoleon to the fall of the Kaiser, with every succeeding generation the Swiss renewed their commitment to the principles of local defense and democracy that had served the country well over the centuries.

Little could anyone have predicted, however, how well the model would serve Switzerland when she found herself surrounded not merely by combatants in a general European war, but by the forces of one of the most aggressive totalitarian states in history.

Chapter 1

FROM 1933 TO
THE EVE OF WAR

ADOLF HITLER WAS NAMED CHANCELLOR OF GERMANY ON January 30, 1933. Immediately, a reign of terror began. The Nazis attacked Social Democrats, Socialists and Communists. Their animosity toward Jews, Slavs, gypsies, homosexuals, the mentally ill and persons with birth defects or handicaps quickly became evident. The rights to assemble and to a free press were taken away.[1] As an essential component of preventing any armed resistance, the Nazis searched homes and seized firearms from private citizens on a wide scale.[2]

After the fire at the Reichstag (Parliament) in Berlin the following month, random massive searches and seizures were authorized; "serious disturbances of the peace" were punishable by death. Nazi thugs attacked members of the democratic parties and hauled them off.[3] By early March, Hitler was an absolute dictator. The Parliament had ceased to exist as a true legislature and the regional German states were taken over by the central authority.[4] The government became an instrument of terror.[5]

In neighboring Switzerland, the press reacted negatively against the new German regime with such articles as "The Dangers of the Hitlerite Dictatorship" in Geneva's leading newspaper, the *Journal de Genève*. The *Journal* began to run a regular column on the subject of Nazi Germany featuring snippets about police actions against political opponents, who seemed invariably to be described as "Communists."[6]

From early in the Nazi regime, the military threat to Switzerland was plain to see. Ewald Banse, a Nazi military theorist and geographer who advocated barbaric methods of warfare,[7] had published *Raum und Volk in Weltkriegen* (*Space and People in World War*) in late 1932. The Nazis appointed him Professor of Military Science in February 1933 and in July established the German Society for Military Policy, in part to promote Banse's ideas.[8]

Banse frankly asserted that a war against France, Germany's historic enemy, could be favorably waged only by attacking through the neutral nations of Belgium and the Netherlands in the north and through Switzerland in the south.[9] A key invasion path led through the Jura range and the Bellegarde (Geneva) Gap.[10] "Swiss neutrality, in fact, is of service only to the French, and not to us," Banse asserted.[11]

Banse rightly anticipated, however, that Switzerland would be a far harder nut for any foreign enemy to crack than the Netherlands. Topographically, the Jura contained lower mountains and valleys; even the central plateau, with its hills, streams and lakes, afforded "the chance of a stubborn defense against foreign invasion." As for the Alps, these were high mountains full of great rock masses, precipices and valleys—all watered by rushing torrents and topped by snowy pinnacles.[12] Such terrain would impede the movement of large forces.[13]

Despite its majority German-speaking population, Banse used Nazi racial theories to describe the Swiss as an inferior amalgamation: "Like Belgium and the United States of America, Switzerland has no people, but merely a population made up of different races."[14] There were Germans, French, Italians and Rhetians. As for the majority:

> The German Swiss imagine that in conjunction with the three other racial elements which speak foreign languages they constitute a single nationality, and they dig an artificial trench between them and ourselves, which is deeper and wider than Lake Constance [part of the German-Swiss border]. This conception, which they uphold with all the impartiality of the Eastern race, is the intellectual basis of the Confederation, which would otherwise have no reality, since the Latin elements have no such deep conviction.[15]

Banse expressed great resentment against the German-speaking Swiss for what he rightly perceived as their dislike of the kind of Nazi political ideology he espoused. He wrote:

From the military point of view, therefore, the character of the German Swiss is the decisive factor. . . . Its decisive features, however, are a calculating materialism, unlimited self-reliance and a tendency to criticism, not to say fault-finding. The latter tendency is directed mainly toward their German kinsfolk across the Rhine, and reminds us of the pelican which pecks its own breast. . . . This childish dislike needs to be taken very seriously indeed and is an important fact fraught with possible military consequences, being of itself equivalent to a strong army corps, and much more dangerous than the anti-German feeling of the Alsatians, since it is based upon the belief, doubtless justified in the Middle Ages but long since obsolete, that liberty and equality—those most sacred of human possessions—are at stake.[16]

While most of the world paid little attention to the disturbing nature of the new German regime, the Swiss were repelled by Nazism. On May 12, 1933, the Swiss Federal Council (the collective government of the country, from whose membership one Federal Councillor is selected to serve as Federal President each year) prohibited the wearing of "Hitlerite" uniforms and insignia and subjected violators to imprisonment or deportation.[17] On July 9, Federal Councillor Rudolf Minger, a farmer who headed the Military Department in the years from 1930 to 1940, declared in the ancient Roman amphitheater at Windisch in northern Switzerland:

Never will our people agree to weaken our democracy; it will defeat dictatorial ideas from whichever side they come. Never will our people accept a German-style *Gleichschaltung* [conformity]. In Swiss fashion we will hold in order our Swiss house. For this purpose we do not need extra shirts nor extra flags; the white cross in the red field will suffice. The Swiss will also defend the right to utter his opinion freely. . . . We will ever hold dear our federalist attitudes and be happy our people encompasses different languages and races. This is the best guarantee that our nation will, in times of war and of great international tensions, not be seduced by irresponsible political temptations.[18]

For the Swiss, the "armed" in armed neutrality was not merely a matter of maintaining a strong national defense force, but imposed responsibilities on the individual citizen. The 1933 edition of the manual issued with the rifle given to every Swiss male on reaching military service age stated:

> In combat, I have my rifle to overcome the enemy. It is the symbol of the independence and force of my fatherland, Switzerland, which I love and which I want to defend all the way to the last drop of my blood.[19]

The Swiss rifle "bible" went on to explain that a man must make it a pleasure to maintain his rifle. It was to be stored in a closet at home.[20] One was to practice constantly in both prone and kneeling positions and should be an active member of a shooting society. These voluntary shooting societies were considered an important element in the defense of the country.[21]

To fire accurately, the manual asserted that one should not shoot fast. Instead, one should pull the trigger slowly, using intelligence and judgment, and remember: "The conqueror always has another cartridge in his rifle."[22] The trigger was to be pulled only if the target would be hit. After each shot in combat, one should pause and observe. One had to shoot more accurately than the enemy and skillfully use the terrain.[23] Furthermore, each soldier was required to be engaged in marksmanship activities outside service until past age 40. This was a military duty one was obliged to fulfill each year with his own rifle and in a shooting society.[24]

The SSV, or Swiss Shooting Federation, was the backbone of the armed citizenry, which the *New York Times* termed in an August editorial "the army in civil life." The SSV's strong opposition to totalitarianism of both right and left was clear: "We want to think Swiss and to remain Swiss. Away with all foreign behavior. We need no brown, green or red uniforms or shirts; we marksmen know only one uniform and that is our field-gray, our honorary dress."[25]

While Swiss rifle shooting matches were conducted at the standard 300 meters, soldiers were trained in marksmanship at 50 to 300 meters and even shot at 400.[26] These were very long distances compared to the relatively short ones from which infantrymen typically fired at one another during the world wars. But the ability to snipe at such distances in mountain terrain would have given the Swiss a great advantage in combat with the Germans, who were only trained to shoot at 100 meters.

Hugh Wilson, American Ambassador to Switzerland from 1927 to 1937, described the Swiss citizen soldier: "The Swiss citizen retains his uniform and rifle at home, ready for instant mobilization; and he spends many of his Sundays qualifying for marksmanship awards with his friends in his community as men of other nationalities spend their leisure at golf, fishing, or other recreation."[27]

Hitler would in time be able to conquer most of Europe and much of Russia, but the armed Swiss population was an unappetizing potential conquest for the much larger German Army. In Switzerland, every man was trained with a rifle and was used to shooting accurately at 300 meters. No other European country offered this kind of disincentive to aggression.

On August 9, 1933, Nazi police trespassed on Swiss soil at Basel to search for Communist leaflets.[28] Nazi demonstrations near the border later that month were making the Swiss very uneasy. Large crowds gathered in support of Swiss democratic institutions and the army.[29] Nazi meetings, though well advertised in the German-speaking Swiss cantons, drew few enthusiasts. The *New York Times* observed the political climate in Switzerland:

> The decline of Hitlerism can be ascribed to two main causes. First, there has been a revival of Swiss patriotism as a consequence of psychological errors in the German Nazi propaganda. The Swiss also feel that the Nazi movement may at any moment threaten their independence.[30]

In its September 12 issue, the *Journal de Genève* reported Swiss sentiment as follows: "The attitude of Berlin toward Vienna proves to us that Hitlerism is an article of export. . . . Swiss independence counts for no more beyond the Rhine than does Austrian autonomy. No one need therefore be astonished if Swiss opinion remains agitated and anxious in the presence of the evolution of the Third Reich."[31]

The *Petit Parisien* published an article in September by the English journalist "Augur" (the pen name for M. Poliakoff) entitled "A Plan for the Invasion of Switzerland Preferred by the German General Staff."[32] It created a sensation in the international press and was, of course, carefully analyzed in the Swiss newspapers. Augur was described as a well-informed political commentator.[33]

The theme of the plan was "Geneva, Doorstep to France." It expressed a low opinion of the ability of the Swiss Army to resist, arguing that its soldiers were good but lacked training in modern armaments and equipment. Arms and munitions factories were located predominantly in the north, near Germany, and could be readily destroyed. To avoid a decisive defeat as early as the first day, therefore, the Swiss Army would withdraw to the mountains of central Switzerland, where it would be cut off from France. The wives and children of the battalions from the northern districts would remain in the hands of the Germans as hostages, which would undermine the troops' morale, for fear of reprisals.[34]

Without encountering any serious opposition in the northern Swiss plain, the German Army would then march right to the Jura. The German forces would rush to the south of Belfort, France, under its fortifications, and the main army would quickly march alongside the Jura, its right flank protected by the Lake of Neuchâtel. The initial goal to reach was the Léman Line, close to Geneva. Geneva was the gateway to France and particularly important for the seizure of Lyons, France, with its surrounding arms and munitions factories.[35]

Augur asserted that the precise information contained in the aforementioned German plan established its authenticity. The *Journal de Genève* commented, however, that even if the plan were real, it could be merely a technical study such as general staffs would routinely compose, as opposed to a plan intended for actual use.[36] The plan could also have been a fabrication intended to incite hostility against Germany and its rearmament or to create support in France for fortifying the region of Lyons.[37]

Two conclusions were in order, according to the *Journal*. First, the Swiss people had the right to know if this invasion plan, which threatened their security and independence, was real. The Federal Council was urged to investigate the subject thoroughly.[38] Second, the very fact that an eventual violation of Swiss neutrality was being publicly discussed showed the necessity of maintaining a strong national defense. In 1914, no army invaded Switzerland because her army was sufficient to deter every belligerent. In 1933, all precautions had to be taken so that the troops received modern equipment that inspired confidence in their capacity to resist.[39]

In Germany, Reich Defense Minister von Blomberg called the article by Augur "highly imaginative nonsense."[40] On September 26, at a League of Nations meeting in Geneva, Swiss Foreign Minister Giuseppe Motta "categorically explained to Nazi Propaganda Minister Goebbels that such an idea would be totally absurd. In Germany, no rational person would have in mind jeopardizing the existence of the Swiss Confederation."[41] Goebbels reassured him that Germany wanted nothing more from the Swiss than friendship.[42]

Despite Goebbels' lack of credibility, the French did have an interest in publicizing the supposed invasion plan, because their Maginot Line stopped near the Swiss border. Any improvement in Swiss defenses would in effect become an extension of the Maginot Line and further secure the French southern flank. Subsequent Swiss defensive preparations, combined with the rugged Swiss terrain, would, in 1940, encourage the Nazis to attack more vulnerable armies and easier terrain.[43] In fact, it could even be said that the Swiss in essence extended the Maginot Line eastward from its southern tip near the French-Swiss border all along the border with southern Germany to Austria. The fortifications and infantry positions essentially reached all the way from France to the Sargans fortress in eastern Switzerland, which pointed its guns toward Austria.[44]

On October 10, 1933, Swiss Defense Minister Rudolf Minger cited the reported German invasion plan to justify increased appropriations for armaments. The Parliament voted a credit of 15 million francs ($4.5 million) as the first installment of a multi-year budget of 100 million francs ($30 million).[45] This was a sharp upward turn. For years, following the horrors of the Great War, and with the

Socialist Party's opposition to militarism, military budgets had steadily declined.[46]

On October 14, Hitler announced that Germany intended to withdraw from the League of Nations and the Disarmament Conference. The *Journal de Genève* asserted: "The thunderbolts hurled on Saturday by Berlin have quite naturally provoked an explosion everywhere. It is an explosion of indignation, of inquietude . . . and of distrust toward Germany."[47]

On October 18, the Federal Council responded to Germany's withdrawal from the League by resolving that "there should be no doubt anywhere concerning the will of Switzerland to defend her neutrality and her capacity to do so."[48] The Council was expected to adopt Minger's proposal to increase appropriations to purchase arms for the infantry, as well as airplanes.[49] On November 16, the equivalent of $39 million was appropriated for new rifles, machine guns and artillery.

Swiss commanders planned increased defenses at the German border, just as Belgium was instituting along its own border with Germany.[50] In view of their military preparations, it was questioned whether the two countries were truly neutral; however, the more important question was whether Adolf Hitler would respect the international treaties under which their status was guaranteed. According to an article in the *New York Times,* the Germans would attack France through Switzerland, "crossing the Rhine upstream from Basel and penetrating to France along what tacticians call the Corridor of Belfort."[51] While the route through Belgium was easier, analysts observed, the Swiss route would offer a greater element of surprise.[52]

The issue of Swiss defense, said the *Times,* was "singularly acute since the advent of Hitlerism, and there are numerous Swiss nationals who are asking whether Switzerland's neutrality would be respected if her territory became strategic to another conflict." Fortifications were being constructed on the Rhine.[53] Federal President Edmund Schulthess stated, "Our people are schooled by the ages in democracy and do not allow themselves to be greatly influenced by propaganda."[54]

As the war scare continued, on December 14 the Federal Council approved 82 million francs in military spending.[55] Defense Minister Minger stated:

The 300,000 Swiss subject to mobilization will hold from valley to valley, from mountaintop to mountaintop, from river to river. . . . Whoever raises the slightest doubt about this fools himself badly. Any belligerent who tries to cross Switzerland will have to reckon with the entire Swiss Army.[56]

Besides Switzerland, there was another German-speaking nation in Europe: Austria. On the first page of *Mein Kampf*, Adolf Hitler had declared that "Common blood must belong to a common Reich" (*"Gleiches Blut gehört in ein gemeinsames Reich"*).[57] He referred to Austria and Germany as "two German states which we of the younger generation at least have made it our life work to reunite by every means at our disposal."[58] Hitler told the Reichstag on January 30, 1934, in a speech marking his first year in power, that what was happening in Germany "will not halt at the frontier posts of a land which is German not only in its people but in its history as well, and which was for many centuries an integral part of the German Empire."[59]

Switzerland would be Hitler's goal after he conquered Austria, argued G.E.W. Johnson in the June 1934 issue of *North American Review*. He wrote that a "slugging contest that is now being waged between the two Austrian-born Chancellors: Hitler, the 'little corporal' of Berlin, and Dollfuss, the 'Millimetternich' of Vienna, to decide whether or not Germany is to eat Austria for breakfast." The Swiss feared that if Austria were "served up for breakfast, it will be Switzerland's turn to furnish the lunch." After all, the Nazis claimed to "voice the aspirations not alone of the sixty-five million Germans who live in *Deutschland*, but of the eighty million 'Germans' who comprise *Deutschtum* [the greater German Empire]."[60]

Like a "restless swarm of termites," wrote Johnson, the Nazis "bored from within," to subvert regions with a German-speaking majority: Danzig, the Saar, Austria and Switzerland.[61] Their intentions, based on kinship of blood and speech, were to incorporate Switzerland within a Greater Germany by an appeal to the historic past.[62] During the Middle Ages, Switzerland had been part of the Holy Roman Empire, the "First Reich" in Nazi terminology, of which

Großdeutschland

"Greater
Germany,"
as typically
depicted in
Nazi propa-
ganda in
1935. Most
of Switzer-
land was to
be absorbed
into the
Third Reich
with smaller
portions
being swal-
lowed up by
Italy and
France.
(Adapted
from Rings,
*Schweiz im
Krieg*, 65.)

Hitler's was the Third. The Nazis now were proclaiming that they intended to "expand Germany's boundaries to the farthest limits of the old Holy Empire, and even beyond."[63] None other than Professor Ewald Banse, responding to Swiss criticism of his geographical textbook expounding German claims to Switzerland, stated:

> Quite naturally we count you Swiss as offshoots of the German nation (along with the Dutch, the Flemings, the Lorrainers, the Alsatians, the Austrians and the Bohemians). . . . Patience: one day we will group ourselves around a single banner, and whosoever shall wish to separate us, we will exterminate![64]

Sentiment in Switzerland held that "the moment that Austria succumbs to the Nazi boa constrictor, Switzerland is marked as the next victim to be strangled in the coils."[65]

In contrast with the beginning of the Great War, when many Swiss were divided along ethnic lines—French and Italian speakers leaning toward the Entente and German speakers sympathizing with the Central Powers—the Swiss were remarkably united from 1933 on in their distaste for the racist and anti-democratic bent of the Nazis. Switzerland proved that French-, German-, and Italian-speaking citizens could live together harmoniously. Almost alone among the European nations, Switzerland remained immune to what Johnson termed "the infective virus of Pan-This and Pan-That."[66] Zurich's leading newspaper, the *Neue Zürcher Zeitung,* admonished its readers that the National Socialist revolution in Germany demonstrated the need for "the spiritual defense of our country."[67]

At this time, the views of Nazi sympathizers could also be heard, if only from a tiny number of Swiss. Theodor Fischer, who headed the pro-German League of National Socialist Confederates, stigmatized Switzerland as a "vassal state of France under Jewish control."[68] That group called for abolition of the Swiss Parliament and cantons and a centralization of all power in the hands of the President.[69]

Jean Marie Musy, Swiss Minister of Finance, warned in a May 10, 1934 speech in Geneva that "Switzerland will either remain a democracy or cease to be Switzerland! . . . The racial ideal can never be the basis of Swiss nationality!"[70] Two days later, the Federal Council banned the wearing of uniforms by all political parties.[71]

As Hitler's rule continued, the Swiss became increasingly repelled not only by National Socialism's rhetoric but by its actions. "The Night of the Long Knives," on June 30, 1934, during which one Nazi paramilitary organization, the SS, assassinated the leadership of another, the SA, further revealed the regime's criminality. Hitler was consolidating his personal power through murder. The democratic Swiss, always wary of German strength, particularly abhorred what the swastika had come to represent. German-speaking Swiss, perhaps because they could more easily understand exactly what the Nazis were saying, became more vehemently anti-Nazi than the French Swiss,[72] and a war of words took place in Swiss and German newspapers. While the Swiss press criticized the Nazis and their domestic actions in Germany, the Nazi press attacked the Swiss, who, they claimed, were too inferior or self-absorbed to appreciate the benefits of the New Order.[73]

On July 25, 1934, Austrian Nazis murdered Austrian Chancellor Engelbert Dollfuss, leader of the clerical-fascist government. Supplied with arms and explosives from Germany, Nazis terrorized Austria and blew up buildings.[74] After the murder of Dollfuss, Italian troops moved into the northern Italian Alps near the Swiss border. Switzerland served notice that she would not tolerate violations of her neutrality.[75]

On July 26, at the Fribourg marksmanship competition, Federal President Marcel Pilet-Golaz reaffirmed that Switzerland was determined to defend her frontiers and that "the capacity of defense is the first condition of our security."[76] Defense Minister Minger told the competitors:

> Events abroad have reawoken Switzerland's old defiance and the feelings for justice and liberty have been renewed. The Swiss people will never allow themselves to be robbed of the right to freedom of expression and will never bow to a dictatorship, from whichever side it may come. In target shooting outside military service all marksmen strive

towards the same aim: the promotion of our defense in the interests of all the Swiss people. . . .[77]

It was reported on July 27 that the annual maneuvers of the First Division of the Swiss Army would be advanced due to the recent seizure of explosives being smuggled from Germany to Austria on Lake Constance.[78]

In mid-November 1934, four Swiss Nazis, members of the National Socialist Confederates, stood trial in Bern for promoting racial hatred. They had circulated the "Protocols of the Elders of Zion," a notoriously anti-Semitic document originally produced by Tsarist Russian intelligence, which the Swiss Federation of Jewish Communities, suing as a complainant in the action, noted was a complete fake and was subject to confiscation.[79] The trial strained relations between Switzerland and Germany. The testimony at trial and the trial court's decision confirmed the fraudulent character of the "Protocols."[80]

The largest German-speaking Nazi group in Switzerland was the National Front, which approved of Hitler's liquidating Socialist and Communist groups but distrusted what it believed to be the Third Reich's aggressive designs.[81] To oppose Nazism, Swiss socialists and left liberals organized a "Kampfbund" ("Fighting Group"). More broadly, in response to the influence of fascist ideas throughout Europe, a public debate was proceeding about whether federal power should be curtailed. Some Swiss believed the power of the executive, the Federal Council, should be extended; others wanted more influence vested in the voters' legislative meetings on the local level, like the centuries-old *Landsgemeinden*.[82]

Fear of the German Nazis soon prompted increased military preparations, including enhanced fortifications at the Rhine. Now even the Socialists were voting for military appropriations.[83] Also, Parliament extended the recruits' first year of basic military education by 23 days for infantrymen and 13 days for artillerymen. In a vote on February 23, 1935, the referendum against this bill initiated by the Communist Party was rejected by a majority. Along with other political parties, many Socialists favored the extended service as a necessity to defend democracy against the Nazi threat.[84] Rumors of German plans for sweeping through Switzerland near Basel to attack France south of her line of forts helped to defeat the referendum.

Even if the primary intention of a belligerent nation was only to "pass through" Switzerland to attack its enemy, the Swiss were under no illusion that such a move would be less dangerous than an actual occupation. According to the SSV marksmen's organization, what could have happened in the Great War served as a warning for the present: "If the Germans had come, we would not have been able to expel them from our country again. . . . Had a French invasion occurred, the Germans would have played the 'rescuer' of Switzerland. As a gesture of thanks they would have demanded that we become a part of the German Reich."[85] In just a few more years, Hitler would indeed "rescue" a number of small countries.

During this period, the small countries of Europe were making sharply varied expenditures for military purposes. This table sets forth average annual military expenditures in selected countries in the years 1934–35:

Military Expenditures, 1934–35[86]

Country	Expenditures (in millions of Swiss Francs)
Belgium	162
Denmark	53
Finland	92
The Netherlands	132
Norway	52
Austria	83
Switzerland	95

As these figures show, there would not necessarily be a direct relation between high expenditures in this period and the ability of the small neutrals to resist Nazi attack a half decade later. The figures for Denmark and Norway were the lowest, and predictably these countries would fall easily to the Nazis in 1940. But so would Belgium and the Netherlands, both of which spent more than Switzerland.

However, comparisons of the raw expenditures do not tell the full story. Spending on defenses modeled on World War I tactics would not help much in the 1940 blitzkrieg era. Moreover, expenditures for ordinary standing armies would be inherently higher per soldier than those for the Swiss-style citizens army because of the full-time pay to the soldiers, barracks and other costs. By contrast, because her army was primarily comprised of citizen soldiers receiving little or no pay and living at home, Switzerland's expenditure figure is deceptively low.

On March 16, 1935, Hitler renounced the Versailles Treaty and announced the rearming of Germany. On May 21, he gave a speech in which he promised peace; the borders of France and Poland would be considered inviolate, and Germany would never interfere in the internal affairs of Austria, much less undertake an *Anschluss*.[87]

During this period, Germany tripled its guards along the Swiss frontier and strictly controlled travelers and goods.[88] Giuseppe Motta and Johannes Baumann, members of the Federal Council, drafted additional measures to suppress Nazism in Switzerland for submission to the Federal Parliament at its upcoming June session.[89] Meanwhile, Switzerland began regular air raid drills.[90] Bern considered protesting to Berlin about violations of Swiss air space by Luftwaffe squadrons in training.[91]

On June 1–2, the Swiss voted against an initiative to adopt New Deal–type programs like those enacted in the United States. The measures were intended to fight the depression with governmental borrowing, spending and centralization.[92] Although Switzerland, along with the rest of Europe and America, had fallen into grave economic difficulty in the 1930s, the people voted overwhelmingly against the measures, agreeing with the Federal Council that they might lead to a socialist state.[93] The proposal had also been opposed as something that would transform grass-roots Swiss democracy into a parliamentary dictatorship.[94]

In 1935, a member of the National Front—Robert Tobler, from Zurich—was elected to Parliament for one year. He was the only Nazi elected to Parliament for the entire period of the Third Reich.[95] A country wary of the potential for a "dictatorship by a parliament" was not a fertile field for National Socialist ideals.

United States President Franklin Roosevelt reacted to the rise of Nazism with the policy preference, expressed at the beginning of 1936, of "a well-ordered neutrality to do naught to encourage the contest."[96] The Swiss had the same policy of neutrality but, unlike the Americans, were already doing everything possible to prepare for what they perceived as the coming onslaught.

During 1936, Defense Minister Minger continued to gain approval for major rearmament programs. Also, the Federal Council established the Federal Police to counter pro-German and Italian fifth column activity. Before that time, criminal enforcement had been a matter solely for the cantons.[97] Although fifth column activity in Switzerland was surprisingly small for a country with a majority Germanic population—less, in fact, than in any other country targeted by Nazi Germany—there was still a small number of Nazi sympathizers. (Switzerland also had a small Communist Party, which followed the Soviet line.) The pro-Nazis needed to be watched closely in the event that they attempted to facilitate espionage.

On February 4, 1936, Wilhelm Gustloff, the official leader of the German Nazi Party in Switzerland, was shot to death with a revolver by David Frankfurter, a Jewish medical student who wanted to "strike a blow at the régime of Adolf Hitler" and "avenge persecution of Jews in Germany."[98] Germany gave Gustloff a state funeral and demanded an investigation that would identify Frankfurter's possible co-conspirators.[99] The German Foreign Office found that "Switzerland is incapable of maintaining political order within her boundaries," and a semi-official German paper blamed the deed on "the anti-German baiting by the Swiss press."[100] Hitler's own newspaper in Berlin demanded the death penalty, but the Swiss Constitution prohibited execution for political crimes, and the canton of Grisons, in which the crime took place, had long since abolished the death penalty.[101] Frankfurter was sentenced to only 18 years imprisonment. He was pardoned after the war and emigrated to Israel.

On February 18, 1936, the Federal Council ordered the immediate suppression of all Nazi organizations in Switzerland.[102] This measure had great popular support. Hitler's organ in Berlin, the *Völkischer Beobachter* (*People's Observer*), reacted: "The government at Berne has struck at German-Swiss relations in a most painful fashion."[103] German Nazis blamed the Swiss law on Jews and leftists.[104] The German Foreign Minister lodged a formal protest, and the German embassy took over the task now banned by the Swiss: developing a network of agents.[105] The Swiss Parliament sought legislation to withdraw citizenship from naturalized foreigners who failed to sever political connections in their former countries.[106] The possibilities for fifth column activity in Switzerland would continue to be restricted by every legal means at the government's disposal.

Hitler had long been planning the reoccupation of the demilitarized Rhineland, along Germany's border with France. This took place on March 7, 1936.[107] In reaction to the remilitarization of the Rhineland, Switzerland began construction of a line of blockhouses on her northern border and readied for a surprise attack by a motorized force along the Rhine.[108] Swiss leaders anticipated that the coming war would involve new methods of aggression; for instance, the SSV marksmen's group advocated increased shooting skills so that as many paratroopers as possible could be shot and killed while still in the air.[109]

Meanwhile, Americans were caught in the dilemma of whether to stay out of Europe's troubles or recognize the unique nature of the Nazi threat. On July 9, addresses were delivered in Charlottesville, Virginia, by Brigadier General John Ross Delafield of New York and Hugo E. Prager of Zurich. General Delafield warned:

> It is fundamental in all fighting that he who strikes first wins, unless his opponent is prepared. Democracies seldom strike first. The case of dictatorships is very different. They can and do. They can plan and prepare for attack in secret, until the blow is about to be struck. The American people do not realize this distinction.[110]

Prager responded that Switzerland "realized the distinction only too well,"[111] noting that neither the Alps, "a great ally in the past," nor the traditional, "almost sacred" neutrality of his country could any longer be relied upon under conditions of modern warfare and the -

prevailing state of mind in Europe. "What counts," he said, "is the certainty that a possible aggressor will encounter real obstinate resistance."[112]

President Roosevelt, in remarks on August 14, urged that "we shun political commitment which might entangle us in foreign wars; we avoid connection with the League of Nations."[113] While the United States and Switzerland were co-neutrals, the critical difference was that the former was large and an ocean away from Germany; the latter was small and bordered Hitler's dictatorship.

Swiss Federal President Albert Meyer urged the public to purchase subscriptions to a national defense fund, noting that the country's neutrality and independence were more endangered now than in the Great War.[114] He added: "Our militia is the flower of our people, but armaments are necessary for our defense. As an example, Ethiopia speaks eloquently."[115] Italy had attacked and conquered poorly armed Ethiopia in 1935 to begin an occupation that would last until 1941. Mussolini's Fascist regime in the south, in addition to Nazi Germany to the north, threatened the Swiss democracy. In response to Meyer's call, the national defense fund was oversubscribed by more than 40 percent!

Switzerland's preparations for war were analyzed by *The Literary Digest* in early 1937. Seeking to avoid being overrun like Belgium in 1914, the " 'Isle of Peace' . . . is fortifying her frontiers to the tune of war rumbles," the article began.[116] When the inevitable war comes, "whoever moves the opening gambit will find Switzerland no easy checkmate." A Swiss general staff member was quoted, giving a frank analysis:

> When war comes, we will be unable to mobilize our entire Army. The Germans will probably destroy our strategic railroad centers, Aarau and Olten, within forty-eight hours. Hence, for our border defense, we shall have to rely strongly on the native population, and we are therefore preparing them for just such an emergency. It is utterly impossible for us to defend the city of Basel, because it is right under the guns of the new German fortress Isteiner Klotz. Our entire strategic problem boils down to this: Can we hold the line

for ten days? After that, the French will have moved up and closed the gap.[117]

Ironically, it would be the French who were defeated easily while the Swiss held out the entire war.

In March 1937 it was reported that Geneva would soon test its air raid defenses. The same newspapers which a few days before had printed Hitler's promise to respect Swiss neutrality were now filled with advertisements for items needed for the house and car during war.[118] A new Swiss law required that all buildings and autos be prepared by April 1 for a blackout, that roofs be made safer against incendiary bombs, including the removal of combustible materials from attics, and that cellars be readied with living and emergency supplies. The League of Nations palace and the world headquarters of the International Committee of the Red Cross (known as the ICRC) in Geneva were included in the preparations.[119]

An analysis of Europe's neutrals in the *Christian Science Monitor* in April noted:

> The more one gazes at contemporary Europe, with its diplomatic rivalries, embattled nationalisms, oppressed minorities, class struggles and militant dictatorships, the more one is constrained to render homage to the success of Swiss ideals. Here is a staunchly united land comprising not merely 22 self-governing units but also inhabited by a population of diverse racial origins, speaking four distinct languages and professing two traditionally antagonistic faiths.[120]

A Zeppelin airship flew over Swiss troops during maneuvers near Schaffhausen on the Rhine on April 28, 1937. The Swiss considered it an intentional provocation by the Germans.[121]

On June 13, the canton of Geneva voted to outlaw the Communist Party and authorized the government to outlaw other parties affiliated with foreign organizations.[122] Such laws would be applied to Nazis as well. A minister in Bern was quoted in August as stating: "The Germans are already treating Switzerland as if she were conquered territory. Switzerland is to come within the Nazi *Gleichschaltung* [forcing into line]. This is the Nazi aim, and by devious methods the Nazis are trying to familiarize the Swiss with the idea."[123] By then, there were allegedly some 500 Gestapo agents in Switzerland conducting espionage to obtain Swiss military secrets and spying on German refugees.

In 1935 a new rifle, the K31 carbine, was introduced into the Swiss army, even as the Germans were adopting a new design of their own, the Mauser 98k, which became their standard service rifle throughout the war. Not surprisingly for a nation in which marksmanship was (and is) the national sport, the Swiss design was far superior to the German in terms of accuracy, weight, handling and ease of loading. The advantages of the Swiss model became more evident at longer distances, and even the Swiss 7.5mm bullet had a better aerodynamic shape and weight combination than its German counterpart, giving it more accuracy and a greater range. Almost 350,000 units were produced by 1945, and the K31 remains in wide use today in target matches. Had the Germans attempted an invasion during World War II, they would themselves have been the targets of Swiss snipers armed with this superior rifle, firing from rugged mountain terrain.[124]

More important than material preparations was the cultivation of the Swiss national spirit, expressed with the term *geistige Landesverteidigung* (*défense nationale spirituelle* in French), meaning spiritual, ideological, or moral national defense. Federal Councillor Philipp Etter even authored a book with that title.[125] The primary attributes of this philosophy were "united community, the intrinsic value of democracy, and reverence for the dignity and freedom of the person."[126] National defense was seen as wholly dependent on the virtue and character of each citizen:

> The armed defense of the country is a primary and substantial task of the state. The mental defense of the country falls primarily not on the state but on the person, the citizen. No government and no battalions are able to protect right and freedom, where the citizen himself is not capable of stepping to the front door and seeing what is outside.[127]

The meaning of "spiritual national defense" evolved as the threat to Switzerland's existence grew. This concept of moral dedication to defense of the homeland and democratic ideals was Switzerland's answer to National Socialism, and the term applied to the distinctly Swiss military, economic, political, and cultural philosophy.[128]

Beginning in 1933, Switzerland expended large sums of money and human effort to arm herself and to have the capacity to resist a Nazi invasion. Though many Swiss spoke German, they had no desire to give up their unique Swiss liberty to join Hitler's increasingly menacing Reich.

Chapter 2

1938

Anschluss of Switzerland?

A KEYSTONE OF NAZI DOCTRINE WAS THE REUNIFICATION OF the German "Volk" into the Reich, regardless of existing national boundaries. Following World War I, the Austro-Hungarian Empire had been dissolved, and Austria had been established as a predominantly Germanic state. Some public sentiment both there and in Germany favored an *Anschluss* (Union) between the two countries, though this annexation was explicitly forbidden by the Treaty of Versailles. For Hitler, who had already renounced the World War I surrender agreement, *Anschluss* became a foreign policy imperative. The new Chancellor of Austria, Dr. Kurt von Schuschnigg, thought he could protect his country's sovereignty by appeasing Hitler. Nazi criminals in prisons were freed and Nazis were appointed to high office.[1] Not for the first time, appeasement failed and German plans to force an *Anschluss* progressed.

Franz von Papen, Nazi Minister to Austria, summoned Schuschnigg to a meeting with Hitler on February 12, 1938 at Berchtesgaden, the Führer's mountain retreat near the Austrian border. Hitler's harangue to Schuschnigg about Austria's shortcomings culminated in thinly veiled threats to overpower the smaller nation. After several hours, German Foreign Minister von Ribbentrop appeared with an ultimatum. Schuschnigg was told that the "agreement" must be signed without further discussion. All the top ministries would be given to Nazis, and the military forces and economies of the two countries would begin a merger process.[2] Hitler told Schuschnigg: "You will either sign it as it is and fulfill my demands within three days, or I will order the march into Austria." Schuschnigg finally signed and promised to persuade the Austrian President, the ultimate authority, to sign.

Schuschnigg arrived in Vienna the next morning and found President Wilhelm Miklas, who balked. The government was a single-party dictatorship, and free elections had not been held since 1933.[3] In the next few days, Schuschnigg maneuvered to avoid acceding to the Führer's demands, backed by growing military threats. However, the Chancellor was anxious to avoid violence and decided that the Army and the Militia of the Patriotic Front (the dictatorship's party) should not resist.[4] Despite his capitulation, Berlin also demanded that Schuschnigg resign. In a radio broadcast to the nation announcing his resignation, Schuschnigg declared: "President Miklas has asked me to tell the people of Austria that we have yielded to force since we are not prepared even in this terrible hour to shed blood. We have decided to order the troops to offer no resistance."[5] Field Marshal Hermann Goering and Austrian Nazi collaborator Arthur Seyss-Inquart meanwhile faked a telegram from the provisional Austrian government requesting the intervention of German troops to prevent bloodshed.[6] Hitler entered his native Austria on March 12 and was greeted by enthusiastic crowds.[7]

Thus Germany, with a population of sixty-six million, annexed Austria, a nation of seven million.[8] Not a shot was fired in the *Anschluss*.

Switzerland immediately reinforced her guards along the Austrian frontier. Now two-thirds of her borders—820 of 1,180 miles—were with the German and Italian dictatorships. Switzerland had only four million people, but she was committed to democracy and independence. Federal Cabinet members remained in Bern over the weekend. *The New York Times* commented:

> A grave view of the situation was taken here partly because of the methods Chancellor Hitler used, which are strongly condemned even by those who think Austria is a special case, and partly because of what these methods and Hitler's program for unifying the whole "German race" foreshadow not only for Czechoslovakia but for Switzerland.

The immediate effect of this, it is pointed out, is to make Switzerland a democratic peninsula in a politically autocratic and economically autarchic league. . . . The danger of a German attack on France via Switzerland is believed to be greatly increased thereby.[9]

On March 13, the total *Anschluss* law was proclaimed in Austria, complete with plans for a farcical plebiscite to be held in the future. The new President, Seyss-Inquart, announced: "Austria is a province of the German Reich." On the 14th, Hitler was in Vienna.[10]

The day Hitler paraded through the Austrian capital, there appeared in bookshops throughout the city maps which showed the territories "belonging" to the Reich. German-speaking Switzerland was included.[11]

That same day, however, the German ambassador in Bern assured the Swiss Minister of Foreign Affairs that the Führer had no ambitions regarding Switzerland. Just days later, though, the newspaper *Frankfurter Zeitung*, in a statement that would have required Propaganda Minister Goebbels' approval, asserted that "no branch of the German race has the right or the possibility of withdrawing from the common destiny of all the Germans." Another German publication chimed in: "Austria has had the experience of what can be called *Verschweizern* ["Swissing"], meaning the tragedy of a people which has been made to believe that they were a nation while in reality they were only part of a community of the same language."[12]

Simultaneously, Switzerland was flooded with a special, reduced-cost edition of the magazine *Berliner Illustrierte Zeitung*, filled with photographs showing the enthusiasm with which the German troops had been welcomed in Austria.[13] During the same period, Field Marshal Goering published a map of the Reich which included most of Switzerland. The Swiss frontier was called "the boundary of the internal separation of the German people," and German-speaking Swiss were called "exiled citizens of the German Reich." The materials were incorporated into a school text, and the Swiss filed a formal protest in Berlin.[14]

That year, German writer Christoph Steding published *The Reich and the Illness of European Culture*, a "scientific" work promoting racism and totalitarianism. He depicted Swiss neutrality and neutrality in general as a moral defect based on weakness of will. According to his theory, neutrality embodied rootlessness and the refusal to recognize destiny.[15]

Because of her weak political and military structure, Austria could be conquered without bloodshed in a few days as a result of one meeting lasting several hours between Hitler and Austria's Chancellor, a few telephone calls, some meetings within the Austrian ruling elite, and the announcement that the armed forces would not resist. A few leaders could surrender the country and guarantee that no armed resistance would occur.

In Switzerland, in contrast, no leaders had sufficient authority to surrender the nation. The Swiss Army was not subject to the commands of a political elite who might order it not to resist. Instead, both political and military power were decentralized and dispersed right down to the locality and the individual household. This system made capitulation much less likely and guaranteed that any invasion would be met with resistance at thousands of separate points. Nearly a million citizens, many in places where tanks could not go and the German air force could not be effective, would resist individually or in small groups, taking rifle shots at the invader.

The elimination of independent Austria led to a strengthened will to resist as well as additional defensive measures in Switzerland. The Swiss accelerated completion of their fortifications from Basel all the way to the Italian Tyrol. Mines were laid under bridges across the Rhine and on roads running to the frontiers.[16]

Meanwhile, Swiss fascists, a tiny minority of the population, advocated swallowing up cantonal power in a strong central government with a national Führer.[17] The call fell on deaf ears, especially in rural areas where the citizens had practiced pure democracy for centuries.[18]

Basel's *National Zeitung* newspaper described the fifth column activities and methods of subversion that had succeeded in Austria. It commented:

> The Nazi *coup* in Austria had hardly been carried out when the Austrian border patrols were provided with huge books

containing complete lists of former Austria's citizens, alphabetically arranged, in which "traitors" were distinguished from those who were to be permitted to pass the border. Why should we believe that we Swiss have been spied upon a lesser extent—that a blacklist of patriotic Swiss has not also been prepared? . . .

So it is imperative that we keep our eyes and ears open. Today every Swiss citizen must solemnly resolve to spot those agents of *Anschluss* and resignation, whether they are old citizens or new ones.[19]

In fact, Nazi agents were conducting espionage and planning fifth column activities. German intelligence operatives at a training center called the *Panoramaheim* (Panorama House) in Stuttgart taught the arts of subversion and bomb-making to those few treasonous Swiss saboteurs and fifth columnists they could identify. To counter these activities, the Swiss military organized the counter-spy SPAB (*Spionage-Abwehr*).[20]

When the Swiss Parliament opened its spring session on March 21, the following declaration was read on behalf of the Federal Council:

On March 13, the federal state of Austria, with which Switzerland maintained cordial relations of good neighborliness, ceased to exist as an independent state. This historical event, which took place before our eyes, is of immense importance. The wish to unite the peoples of Germany and Austria was not a new aspiration; it had already given rise to armed conflict in the last century; that wish has now been realized. . . .

None [such wish] threatens our democratic institutions, which are essential to the life of the Confederation and of its 22 cantons. It is Switzerland's secular mission in Europe to guard the passage over the Alps in the interests of all. It is the unanimous and unshakable will of the Swiss people to accomplish this mission and to assure the respect of its independence at the price of its blood. . . .

The Swiss people are united in the determination to

defend at any cost, to the last breath and against anyone, the incomparable country which is theirs by God's will.[21]

Every member of Parliament, except two Communists and the sole pro-Nazi, agreed with the following statement, which was read in German, French and Italian by deputies who represented the majority and also the Socialists:

> All the political groups of the two houses approve the declaration of the Federal Council. They solemnly affirm that the entire Swiss people—without regard to tongue, confession or party—are prepared to defend the inviolability of their territory against any aggressor to the last drop of their blood. . . .
> The Swiss people are prepared to consent to the sacrifices necessary for their national defense, but the military armament of the county would be useless if it did not rest on the spiritual and moral forces of the whole people.[22]

Before the Austrian *Anschluss*, Switzerland had feared attack from the northeast and had positioned her troops accordingly.[23] Now an attack could come from the east as well.

On April 29 the Federal Council, believing that membership was inconsistent with absolute neutrality, determined that changed circumstances required Switzerland to withdraw from the League of Nations. The Council declared:

> Swiss neutrality has a specific character which distinguishes it from any other neutrality. It is one of the essential conditions of the internal peace, of the union, and hence of the independence of a nation composed of elements which differ in language and culture. . . . The maintenance of this centuries-old institution is as precious for Europe as for Switzerland itself. It is neutrality which has held together for centuries peoples of different race, language and religion.[24]

The Council of the League of Nations acceded to Swiss requests that the Swiss no longer participate in League sanctions, declaring that: "The unique position of Switzerland has resulted in her perpetual neutrality founded on a secular tradition and the recognition of human rights."[25] Underlying Switzerland's withdrawal from the League, of course, was the combination of her growing appreciation of the German threat and her diminished view of the ability of the League to influence developments. Switzerland would instead rely on her own strength to defend her borders.

Accelerated defense preparations in Switzerland continued.[26] With talk of war ever present, many feared a German invasion of France through the region of the Jura, around Basel. While Basel, near the German border, would be hard to defend, the general staff noted that an invader would subsequently have the entire Swiss citizens army of probably 400,000 on its left flank. To repel German attack, according to the *New York Times*, the Swiss took the following measures:

1. Military service was extended. "There is no standing army in Switzerland, but every able-bodied man must serve for a time in the militia."
2. The Swiss negotiated with an American manufacturer to buy new fighter planes.
3. "The supply of tanks is being increased, although tanks are of little use in mountainous terrain," as the *Times* reported.
4. Swiss soldiers took home their guns and uniforms after their terms of duty each year. The frontier guards placed munitions caches in their villages, machine-gun emplacements, land mines, etc.
5. The large Swiss gold supplies were moved inland. Because of fear that Germany might make a bold grab for this gold, bullion was removed from the vaults of the national bank at Zurich to be stored in vaults near the Gotthard Pass in the Alps and near Bern.
6. The frontier was strengthened near Austria.
7. New pillbox fortresses were built along the Italian frontier.

The report further noted that the pro-Nazi National Front had essentially died out. It had held 10 of 120 seats on the Zurich Municipal Council, but lost them all in the election held after the German annexation of Austria. The *Times* article concluded: "Switzerland is the oldest republic in the world. It has a tradition of six centuries as the hub in a revolving wheel of war. Armies have been coming to grief in its mountains since the defeat of Charles the Bold at Murten."[27]

In 1938, the Swiss Army was organized into three army corps, including nine divisions (three of which were specially-trained mountain divisions), and three mountain brigades. Troops who resided near the borders would defend the frontier while the general army mobilized.[28]

"The purest democracy in Europe, if not in the world" was the subject of an August 1938 *New York Times* analysis, stating:

> Switzerland, an island of liberty and harmony in a sea of dictatorship and discord, has been a citadel of peace through stormy centuries. But it has not been a wholly passive peace. The Swiss are ready to fight, if need be. They demonstrated that last Spring when the Nazis seized Austria. Grimly the Swiss waited for the next move, in their calm, undramatic way—with loaded rifles and fixed bayonets.[29]

While Hitler and Mussolini ruled a combined 120 million people, the Swiss numbered but 4 million, a few more people than resided in the state of Missouri. Its land area was less than a third of New York State. Zurich, its largest city, numbered 300,000, about the same as Columbus, Ohio. "Yet," said the *New York Times*, "the merits of the Swiss Confederation among the world's democracies are far out of proportion to its size and population or the ranking of its cities. It is a land of hard work and frugal habits, of justice and cleanness and tolerance, of the very essence of live-and-let-live. There one finds no extremes of wealth or poverty, no billionaires, no paupers."[30]

On August 24, the Socialist Party in Basel obtained enough signatures for an initiative to ban the National Socialist Party and its propaganda. It obtained the highest number of signatures ever gained for an initiative.[31]

Contemporary Review reported that the German press had no success in frightening the Swiss people with Bolshevist conspiracy theories or in generating anti-Semitism. Swiss courts penalized authors of propaganda who asserted that various Swiss personalities were "being paid by Jews" and who argued that Switzerland was under the influence of "international Jewry."[32]

Although the Swiss people as a whole opposed the racist doctrines of National Socialism, the Swiss government was, regrettably, unwilling to grant unlimited asylum to political refugees or free emigration to German and Austrian Jews. The liberal entry policies which had existed since 1933 were curtailed in October 1938 by the Federal Police Department under Heinrich Rothmund, who accepted a suggestion by German officials that a "J" stamp be added to identify Jews on German passports. The police chief's role was not made public until 1954, at which time the Swiss public was outraged. On behalf of the nation, Federal President Villiger issued a public apology in 1995.[33]

Czechoslovakia, another country in the threatening shadow of Nazi Germany, resembled Switzerland in that her people consisted of an ethnic and linguistic mix. Despite promises made when the country was formed at the Paris Peace Conference of 1919, however, Czechoslovakia had not adopted a federal system of Swiss-like cantons. The Sudeten Germans—German-speakers in the western part of the country near the German border—had a number of grievances against the highly centralized government. They were thus ripe for Hitler's attention and would be handed over to the Nazis with only the signatures of a few Prague politicians on a scrap of paper.[34] In 1938, the perception grew that the British were willing to let the Sudetenland be ceded to Germany, even though it meant the complete loss of border fortifications for that part of the country which remained.[35] On September 15, British Prime Minister Neville Chamberlain promised Hitler to promote the cession.[36] Despite treaties protecting the territorial integrity of Czechoslovakia, Britain and France told Czechoslovakia's representatives that the country must accede to Hitler's wishes.[37]

By then Hitler was emboldened, and world crisis loomed. President Roosevelt announced that the United States would remain neutral in the event of war and would not participate in the ongoing negotiations regarding Czechoslovakia.[38] He nevertheless appealed to Hitler and Czech President Eduard Beneš not to break off talks and asked other governments to make similar appeals. The Swiss Federal Council, on September 28, urged Hitler and Beneš, "with deep emotion," to find a peaceful solution.[39]

After the Führer received another appeal from President Roosevelt, the German minister in Bern, Otto Carl Köcher, asked the Swiss Political Department whether Switzerland authorized Roosevelt to speak on her behalf and whether the Swiss felt threatened by Germany. The Federal Council answered the first question in the negative, but replied to the second that Switzerland relied for her independence on respect for her armed neutrality, which Germany had recognized. Berlin was displeased.[40]

Chamberlain and the French premier, Edouard Daladier, again acquiesced to Hitler, at Munich on September 29–30, 1938. Backed by Britain and France, under the Munich accord finalized on the 30th, Germany demanded that Czechoslovakia give up 11,000 square miles of her richest and most defensible territory along with 3.5 million citizens. The transformation was arranged after the Western powers dictated the terms. President Beneš conferred with his military and political leadership, concluded that resistance was futile and that surrender to the *Diktat* was his only alternative. What was left of the country then became known as "Czecho-Slovakia." A pro-German government was installed.[41]

Wilhelm Keitel, Chief of the German High Command, would later testify at Nuremberg that "we were extraordinarily happy that it had not come to a military operation because . . . our means of attack against the frontier fortifications of Czechoslovakia were insufficient. From a purely military point of view we lacked the means for an attack."[42] Similarly, Field Marshal Erich von Manstein admitted that "there is no doubt whatsoever that had Czechoslovakia defended herself, we would have been held up by her fortifications, for we did not have the means to break through." In fact, the German Army General Staff opposed a European war and was plotting to overthrow Hitler had they been ordered to attack Czechoslovakia at that time.[43]

Germany was not then prepared to go to war against a coalition of Czechoslovakia, Britain, and France; however, Hitler's ability to bluff foreign leaders had earned the Third Reich another bloodless victory.[44] Chamberlain gave the Führer what he wanted. The Western powers betrayed Czechoslovakia, the leaders of which then gave up without a fight.

The Swiss, however, were not demoralized. The decentralized Swiss state did not lend itself to the tactics Hitler had used on Czechoslovakia and Austria. Bluffs and intimidation against Switzerland's grass-roots democracy only made the Swiss more determined to preserve their independence and way of life.

While the world celebrated the Munich accord, with its promise of "peace in our time," and the Pope expressed joy that war had been avoided, Federal President Johannes Baumann said at the closing of the Swiss Parliament on that fateful September 30 that the accord "should not prevent us from executing and completing measures of a military, political, economic and spiritual order which our country needs to guard its independence and freedom."[45]

The Germans did, in fact, have further goals. On October 11, General (later, Field Marshal) Keitel telegraphed Hitler that Czechoslovakia could be finished off "in view of the present signs of weakness in Czech resistance."[46] This would be accomplished just a few months later.

Shortly after Munich, German newspapers began referring to Switzerland as a country that was detaining populations which did not belong to her.[47] On November 4, Federal President Baumann called a meeting of police chiefs to eliminate increasing Nazi activity in Switzerland.[48] On the 10th, seeking evidence of espionage, police squads raided the headquarters of the Swiss Socialist Workers Party and the Peoples League, which were small but active fascist groups.[49] Over 100 Nazi agitators were arrested. Baumann declared that evidence was found that the groups had maintained direct relations with Germany.[50]

The *Kristallnacht* (Night of the Broken Glass) pogroms of November 9–10 in Germany sent shockwaves through Switzerland.[51] The pretext for the attacks against Jews and Jewish property was revenge for the shooting of Ernst vom Rath, a Secretary of the German Embassy in Paris, by a Polish Jew. Berlin police announced the disarming of the Jews for what was called a new plot of the Jewish world conspiracy against National Socialism.[52] The Swiss press did not lose sight of the parallel with the 1936 shooting of Swiss Nazi Wilhelm Gustloff by a Jewish medical student and the manner in which the Nazis used the incident to condemn all Jews and spread anti-Semitism.[53]

Newspapers all over Germany published an article on November 9 declaring the need to disarm the Jews due to the Paris shooting. Yet this pretext was a sham: the confiscations of arms in Berlin had already been going on for several weeks, netting 2,589 swords, knives, and clubs, 1,702 firearms, and about 20,000 rounds of ammunition. A Berlin publication stated: "The provisional results clearly show what a large amount of weapons have been found with Berlin's Jews and are still to be found with them."[54] The names of Jews with firearm licenses were available to the police under the Nazi *Waffengesetz* (Weapons Law) signed by Hitler and SS Reichsführer (Interior Minister) Wilhelm Frick earlier that year and previous laws.[55] On November 10, newspapers in both Germany and Switzerland reported a document entitled "Weapons Ban for Jews" in which SS chief Heinrich Himmler decreed: "Persons who, according to the Nürnberg law are regarded as Jews, are forbidden to possess any weapons. Violators will be transferred to a concentration camp and imprisoned for a period of up to 20 years."[56]

The seizure of firearms from Jews gave the Nazis assurance that their attacks would not be resisted. The Nazis then proceeded to smash, loot and burn Jewish shops and temples.[57] Throughout Germany, thousands of Jewish men were taken from their homes and arrested.[58] The property destruction was carried out by wrecking crews under the protection of uniformed Nazis or police.[59] The Swiss press took note of the widespread disarming of the Jews and the anti-Semitic attacks.[60]

The Regulations Against Jews' Possession of Weapons (*Verordnung gegen den Waffenbesitz der Juden*) were promulgated by Interior Minister Frick on November 11, the day after *Kristallnacht*. The regulations stated that "Jews . . . are prohibited from acquiring, possessing, and carrying firearms and ammunition, as well as truncheons or stabbing weapons. Those now possessing weapons and ammunition are required at once to turn them over to the local police authority."[61]

The *Kristallnacht* rampages prompted Swiss cantonal and federal authorities to clamp down on Nazi hooligans, whose activities were banned.[62] The average Swiss, who kept a rifle at home for militia service and shooting matches, could not have lost sight of the significance of the Nazi seizures of firearms before attacking the Jews. Indeed, Switzerland was the only country in the world where every Jewish male, like every other citizen, was issued a rifle.

The *Völkischer Beobachter* (*People's Observer*), National Socialism's chief newspaper, warned Switzerland on December 2 to curb her press in its treatment of Germany.[63] The Berlin paper asserted: "If, therefore, small democratic States continue their indirect warfare against us they run the danger that of necessity we will one day legally consider them enemies, despite their neutral position, on the same basis as the world organizers of direct warfare."[64]

The next day, the Swiss responded. Giuseppe Motta, on behalf of the Federal Council, warned German Minister Köcher that Nazi agents in Switzerland must halt their activities. He also expressed "extreme displeasure" over remarks said to have been made repeatedly by Germans along the Swiss-German border that the two countries must become one.[65]

In addition, on December 5 the Federal Council prohibited the publication of misinformation that endangered the Confederation, ridiculed democratic principles, or excited hatred against any group based on race, religion, or nationality. It authorized imprisonment of anyone who attempted to overthrow the constitutional regime of the Confederation or of the cantons. The Council was also empowered to dissolve any group that violated these prohibitions. Not surprisingly, the prohibitions were criticized as contrary to the principle of a free press.[66]

Geneviève Tabouis, writing in the Parisian newspaper *L'Oeuvre* on December 8, substantiated beliefs widely held in Switzerland:

> It is reported that Herr von Bibra, counselor to the German Embassy at Berne, has recently received a secret order telling him particularly to encourage the National Socialist movement for the attachment of the German Swiss to the Reich. . . . By virtue of this order, Herr von Bibra has secretly received the title of "Special Commissar for the Attachment of Switzerland."[67]

As counselor to the German legation in Prague until late 1935, Bibra was instrumental in the spread of Nazi influence in Czechoslovakia. It was reported that Gestapo chief Himmler ordered Bibra to work toward the partition of Switzerland between Germany and Italy.[68] By the end of the year, the Swiss government instructed its Attorney General to prosecute members of Nazi organizations for attacks against the security and independence of the Swiss Confederation.[69]

In December, the obligation to serve in the Swiss militia was extended to age 60.[70] Further, the Swiss Parliament approved an increased armament program that was expected to cost 350 million Swiss francs.[71]

Hitler got a scare from a would-be William Tell in late 1938. A Swiss theology student, Maurice Bavaud, attempted to shoot Hitler on three occasions, actually getting very close to the dictator. Of all the assassination plots and attempts against Hitler during the entire Third Reich, Bavaud's was one of the few that almost succeeded. He was caught and executed in 1941. It was one more reason for the Führer to hate the Swiss.[72]

The Swiss concept of "spiritual national defense" was embodied in the December 1938 message of the Federal Council on national purpose. Authored by Federal Councillor Philipp Etter, the message noted the origins of Switzerland in the area around the St. Gotthard Pass in the Alps, the source of the Rhône, the Rhine, and the Ticino rivers. This mountain pass both separates and unites the three leading cultures of continental Europe—French, German and Italian—linking Switzerland to all three.[73] It continued:

> For the very reason that we reject the concept of race or common descent as the basis of a state and as the factor determining political frontiers, we gain the liberty and the strength to remain conscious of our cultural ties with the three great civilizations. The Swiss national idea is not based upon race or biological factors; it rests on a spiritual decision.[74]

The message added that Switzerland's federalism allows various cultures to live in harmony:

The Swiss federal state is an association of free republics: it does not swallow them, it federates them. The cantonal republics maintain their individuality, and thereby they are the sources and pillars of our intellectual wealth, the strongest bulwark against intellectual uniformity. Our Swiss democracy has been built up organically from the smaller units to the larger units, from the township to the canton, and from the canton to the federal state. Next to federalism and democracy, Switzerland is based upon respect for the dignity of the individual. The respect for the right and liberty of human personality is so deeply anchored in the Swiss idea that we can regard it as its basic concept and can proclaim its defense as an essential task of the nation.[75]

While this was a special message from the Federal Council, the concept of "spiritual national defense" was not mandated by law, in the way National Socialism imposed ideology from above, but rather expressed the historic tradition of the Swiss people. The concept was promoted not only by the government but by various social institutions and organizations.[76]

The Swiss Army is imbued with democratic principles. No generals exist other than as appointed by the Parliament in time of war and only a very small number of soldiers are full-time professionals.

In the 1930s, Henri Guisan was a full-time colonel from the French-speaking part of the country. He was bilingual and commanded a German-speaking army corps before commanding a French-speaking corps.

Colonel Guisan originally presented his *Our People and Its Army* as a lecture to the Federal Institute of Technology in Zurich on October 9.[77] When later published as a booklet, it was so well received that many people said that, should Switzerland ever need a general, this was the man.[78] Indeed, Guisan would later be elected commander-in-chief of the Swiss Army when the war came.

For Guisan, "a people defends itself in two ways: by its moral force, expressed by its patriotism, and by its material force, represented by its army." Switzerland, he pointed out, originated in a military alliance: "the treaty of August 1, 1291 is nothing other than an offensive and defensive pact against the exterior enemy."[79] On the slopes of Morgarten in 1315, "the young army of Confederates" routed the army of Leopold I, and "Swiss tactics had been born."[80] Then there was Sempach in 1386, where 1,500 mountain dwellers crushed the army of the Archduke Leopold III. After Marignano (1515), one of the few Swiss defeats, Francis I, of France, said: "I overcame those that only Caesar had been able to overcome!"[81]

The Swiss, said Guisan, had always been "united enough to withstand all the storms that shook Europe." Obligatory service was imposed for the defense of the people. "For a long time it was the only communal institution of the cantons, the expression of confederate solidarity. The army represents, therefore, national unity, the binding element, not only in theory but in reality."[82] Guisan reflected:

> What distinguishes the military tradition of Switzerland, is, above all, the persistence with which its essential principles maintained themselves in the course of its history. . . . In effect, the necessity "to be ready" at any instant required a mobilization and a quick concentration at the threatened points. Each citizen had his equipment, his arms, in his residence.[83]

Reflecting on Swiss history, Guisan emphasized some of the specific ancient martial customs. In Appenzell, a young man at his confirmation received a sword and could not marry unless he possessed a Bible and arms.[84] In Zurich, one was invited to a marriage by firing a pistol in front of the guest's house.[85] The day of recruitment was and remained a festival day, including processions with flags and music. "Today again," Guisan emphasized, "being capable of service is a physical certificate of health; our girls know it well!"[86]

In Geneva, since 1400, the military exercises of archers, crossbow shooters, arquebusiers, and elite bodies on which the state could rely embodied the very spirit of the city. All classes of the population were represented.[87] The best shooters won trophies and cash and led parades while carrying their arms.[88] At festivals, the ancient military influence was clear, and Guisan recounted colorful local traditions. Great battles had continued to be celebrated annually for over 500 years. The warrior spirit exhibited itself in the arts, literature, and architecture.[89]

For Guisan, the army was the incarnation of the federal republic. He wrote bluntly: "The people is the army, the army is the people." The people loved their army because they rediscovered themselves in it.[90] "Under the uniform, the social differences equalize themselves," he said, "the preconceived judgments disappear. Under the uniform, there is neither rich, nor poor, worker, employer, urbanite, or country person, there is only a soldier, a man who serves his country!"[91] The common experiences brought the people together. Beginning with recruit school and continuing regularly throughout life, the soldiers were united. The army was education for citizenship.[92]

In the army, one learned that there was "neither Swiss German, nor Swiss French, nor Swiss Italian, and that there was only one Switzerland, the one of our fathers, united, strong and vigilant." But this strength was based on diversity. "If federalism is the safeguard of the country, unification would be its loss!" The cantons therefore retained their particularism, and the army regiments their unique characteristics. Guisan insisted, "It would be as vain to want to unify Switzerland as to attempt to level her mountains!" The very differences in fact promote national cohesion.[93]

Guisan explained Switzerland's unique marksmanship culture:

While traversing Switzerland on Sundays, everywhere one hears gunfire, but a peaceful gunfire: this is the Swiss practicing their favorite sport, their national sport. They are doing their obligatory shooting, or practicing for the regional, cantonal or federal shooting festivals, as their ancestors did it with the musket, the arquebus, or the crossbow. Everywhere, one meets urbanites and country people, rifle to the shoulder, causing foreigners to exclaim: "You are having a revolution!"[94]

Guisan waxed religious, and even mystic, in describing military exercises in the Alps. Troops climbed to the summits in a form of "military worship"; at the top, the "rustic pulpit," rifles were stacked and the flag fluttered. "In this eternal, unchanging framework, in this sublimity of nature, one feels more than elsewhere the stability and continuity of the historic mission of our army."[95]

Men aged and died and governments changed, but the traditions and army endured. "Small army, yes, but made strong by the traditions that she has in her heart and in her blood." On the other hand, values which had to be jealously preserved had lately been confronted by spiritual confusion, uncertainties, foreign influences contrary to the national spirit, and the "various mystical racists"[96]—an obvious reference to German National Socialism.

Guisan recalled the army's readiness to defend Switzerland against the horrors of the Franco-Prussian War of 1870–71, the Great War of 1914–18, and the Moscow-inspired insurrectionist threat in 1918.[97] The Swiss Army thereafter withstood proponents of disarmament, pacifism and Bolshevism.[98]

When Guisan made those reflections, European tension was increasing: after the rise of the Nazis and Germany's rearmament had followed the occupation of the Rhineland, the plebiscite of the Saar (returning it to Germany), the civil war in Spain, the annexation of Austria and then, in September 1938, the annexation of Czechoslovakia, which brought "us within two fingers of war."[99] Anxiety was growing despite Switzerland's neutrality, which could only be maintained by an army capable of resisting attack.[100] The League of Nations had failed, and Hitler had bluntly declared that he recognized only rights that could be defended.[101]

According to Guisan, absolute neutrality and a strong army were inseparable. Switzerland was in a strategic position that those who sought to dominate the continent would envy. The nation would continue to exist only if it was strong enough to defend itself.[102]

The Swiss people understood defense needs and favored the modernization of armaments despite the great expense. The army was stronger than ever. The border troops were ready for a surprise attack. "The true Swiss defense," said Guisan, "is where the soldier, protected by fortifications and barricades, defends his cottage, his farm, his earth. He knows each rock, each tree, each path." He emphasized that the moral element predominates and that all citizens needed to participate.[103] "The army is like a factory of the nation in arms."[104] Guisan concluded that national defense rested not just on weapons but on reason and faith. The people had to be prepared to bear the trials of modern war and "to resist to the end." They needed to use the "greatest harshness against the fellow travelers in ideologies inconsistent with our democracy, against the agents of every foreign dictatorship."[105]

"The moral preparation of a people is as necessary as the material preparation, and means the mobilization of the spirit." Guisan insisted that "the oldest soldierly people in Europe must know neither defeatism nor fear; dignity forbids it!" What were dictatorships, with their mystical theories, compared with Swiss patriotism?[106] Responding to Guisan's challenge and the evocation of their ancient heritage, as the fateful year of 1939 approached, the Swiss continued to prepare for the military challenge they now believed was imminent.

Chapter 3

1939

Hitler Launches World War II

AT THE BEGINNING OF 1939, THE SWISS VIEWED THEIR GIANT neighbor to the north and east with a wary eye. Ominous signs indicated that their concern was fully justified.

Before unleashing the German Army to cross a neighbor's borders, the Nazis characteristically turned up the heat on their intended prey by launching a series of press attacks. Accordingly, the Swiss were distressed when, in early January, a spate of vehemently anti-Swiss articles suddenly appeared in the state-controlled German press. These articles asserted that criticism of the Nazis by Switzerland's (uncensored) press was incompatible with neutrality and warned the Swiss government to suppress the criticism. One of the leading Nazi organs, the *National-Sozialistische Monatshefte,* castigated Switzerland's policy of welcoming political refugees from Germany. The Swiss minister in Berlin, Hans Frölicher, was instructed to discuss the attacks with German authorities.[1]

On January 30, a few hours before the start of Hitler's annual Reichstag speech, this one marking the sixth anniversary of his coming to power, the apprehensive Swiss government announced an ordinance giving it the power to mobilize the militia without further notice. As it turned out, the Führer's speech did not single out Switzerland as the next target of the Reich; the bulk of his oration merely stressed the military might of Germany and Fascist Italy.[2] Nevertheless, during the winter of 1938–39, General Franz Halder, chief of the German General Staff, instructed Major General Eugen Müller to prepare a study on whether advantages would be gained by an incursion into Switzerland in the event of a French-German war. Weighing the factors of terrain and potential Swiss resistance, Müller recommended against a Swiss invasion at that time.[3]

Responding to the perceived threat, the Swiss shooting associations, among others, continued to encourage the strongest measures of preparedness. A rifleman from a mountain canton exhorted the people to resolve "to give our hearts and our blood" to defend the country against any attempted foreign takeover. He continued:

> We owe it to our ancestors, who always appreciated freedom and independence as the highest value. But we owe it also to those who will live after us, and to whom we wait to bestow our fatherland whole. . . . May the spirit of the Rütli especially beckon us riflemen, the spirit who goes through our history like a red line and which Schiller put in these words: "We must trust to God on high and never be intimidated by the power of man. It is better to die than to live in slavery!"

This parallel to the famous oration of Patrick Henry was characterized as "spiritual national defense" of the highest quality.[4]

Meanwhile, to the east, Nazi agents were stirring up the Slovaks against the Czechs. On March 11, General Keitel drafted an ultimatum for Hitler under which Germany would acquire Bohemia and Moravia, the western, Czech portion of the country (the modern Czech Republic). The Czechs were admonished not to resist the military occupation.[5] That same day, as the Slovak cabinet met, five German generals burst into the meeting and ordered them to declare Slovakia's independence at once. Slovak Premier Monsignor Tiso and Deputy Prime Minister Ferdinand Durcansky were summoned to Berlin. On March 13, the Führer dictated the terms.

Czechoslovak President Emil Hácha requested an audience with Hitler, however by the time he arrived in Berlin with his Foreign Minister, German troops had already occupied several Czech locations. Hitler informed Hácha that a full invasion was imminent and that "resistance would be folly." Hácha was instructed to warn the Czech people not to resist and was told the surrender must be signed immediately.[6] Hácha telephoned the Czech cabinet in Prague advising capitulation.

The meeting with Hitler had gone on only three-and-a-half hours before Hácha signed the prepared document placing the fate of the Czech people and country in the hands of the German Führer. Just two hours later—it was now 6:00 A.M. on March 15—German troops occupied Bohemia and Moravia. There was no resistance.[7] Meanwhile, Tiso had returned home, and on March 16 telegrammed Berlin asking for German protection and declaring independence.[8] The German occupation of Slovakia began.

Thus, Czechoslovakia ceased to exist. The population and armed forces offered no resistance. Britain and France had guaranteed the sovereignty of the country at Munich the previous autumn, but now did not lift a finger in response.[9]

Nazi occupation authorities immediately imposed repressive conditions on the former Czechoslovakia. The London *Times* announced: "All popular gatherings were forbidden; and weapons, munitions, and wireless sets were ordered to be surrendered immediately. Disobedience of these orders, the proclamation ended, would be severely punished under military law."[10] It is still remembered today, some sixty years later, that on the first day the Nazis occupied Czechoslovakia they put up posters in every town ordering inhabitants to surrender all firearms, including hunting guns.[11] The penalty for disobedience was death. Lists of potential dissidents and other suspects had already been prepared, and those persons disappeared immediately.[12]

The takeover of Czechoslovakia—a multi-ethnic state only a short distance away—was deplored in Switzerland, whose press called for preservation of national unity at all costs and the cessation of all internal differences and strife.[13] Federal Councillor Hermann Obrecht, in a speech on March 15 to the New Helvetic Society, reacted to the *Anschluss* of Austria and the dismemberment of Czechoslovakia with the warning: "Those who honor us and leave us in peace are our friends. Those, on the other hand, who seek to attack our independence and our political integrity will be met with war. It is not from Switzerland that one goes on pilgrimages to foreign lands"[14]—a reference to the "pilgrimages" to Hitler undertaken by national leaders who would then surrender their countries to the Führer.

In a broadcast to the Swiss people on March 18, Federal President Philipp Etter discussed the profound repercussions caused by the entry of German troops into Czechoslovakia and by its disappearance as an independent state. He said that "each citizen is resolved bravely to make all possible sacrifices to conserve for our country its independence and liberty in the midst of the danger of the present hour."[15]

Meeting on March 20, the Swiss Parliament reaffirmed its declaration of the previous March, when German troops occupied Austria, that the Swiss were ready to defend the nation's inviolability "to the last drop of blood." Federal President Etter told Parliament that Switzerland had nothing to add to this declaration since her determination to defend her neutrality and independence was well known to neighbor states.[16]

Finance Minister Wetter announced in Bern on March 22 that increased defense costs would triple the national debt, which would now amount to about 1,000 francs per capita. The citizens, though, would gladly bear the burden if they secured the right "to live in their immemorial liberty and in their modest but comfortable Swiss home."[17]

Military Department head Rudolf Minger told Parliament on the same day: "Today all preparations for war mobilization, with or without sudden attack, are in readiness. The arrangements for protecting the frontier will function automatically; there will be no need of waiting for a general's orders."[18] Minger's statement reflected the habit of the nearly invincible Swiss armies of the late medieval period to go into battle without an overall leader or general—the men themselves simply knew what to do. The centuries-old military practice of a well-armed citizens army could still effectively defend against a twentieth-century war of total aggression.

Preparing for an attack, the Swiss intensified work on fortifications along the Rhine and in the cantons bordering the former Austria. Heavy artillery, machine guns and ample stocks of munitions were concentrated in those areas. At Zurich, Schaffhausen, Basel, and other large industrial centers, anti-aircraft batteries were moved into position. Most households had gas masks. Mines under all bridges and roads leading into Switzerland were still in place from the Munich crisis, and there was now twenty-four-hour surveillance at all of these roads and bridges.[19]

On March 25, the frontier reserves were called out to guard the German border.[20] The next day, it was reported that large bodies of German troops—as many as 200,000—were being massed around and beyond Lake Constance. "Switzerland Puts Great Trust in Her Minute Men's Ability to Hold Border,"[21] read a caption in the *New York Times* on March 27. The newspaper reported that a general mobilization had not yet been ordered, explaining:

> the Swiss have a special defense force, which, like the Minute Men of American revolutionary days, is always ready for service. The purpose of this force is to delay an invader's advance for twenty-four hours to give the regular army time to assemble. All men in that corps keep their equipment, including arms and ammunition, at home and each knows where to go and what to do in an emergency. In a test in September the entire force reported within two hours after the alarm.[22]

Meanwhile, the Swiss Federal Government authorized the Military Department to call up in the course of the year all men aged 36 to 48 for six days of training.[23] Then, on April 4, the government instructed the population to stockpile at least two months of food.[24] It obtained large quantities of foodstuffs for army use, and, when invasion seemed imminent, moved these to fortified emplacements in the Alps.[25]

Not wanting the Führer to outdo him, the Italian Duce ended the independence of Albania in April.[26] To the Swiss it was clear that neither of their totalitarian neighbors—the Nazis in the north and east and the Fascists in the south—had any respect for the rights of small nations.

A letter printed in a leading Swiss newspaper expressed the common sentiment of militant resistance as follows:

> One must arm everybody who is capable of carrying arms and one should shoot everybody who wants to destroy our

country. It would be good to make these greedy people understand that the government of each canton has the right to call up troops itself. That means that if the entire Swiss Government were taken prisoner or surrendered, resistance would not yet be broken.[27]

Several letters in the women's section in the same newspaper concerned "the urgent desire of Swiss women to learn to shoot to get arms in order to defend themselves against invaders. Swiss women, it is pointed out, have fought and they sometimes decided the victory." One letter stated: "Some people ask that we shall be ready to go into the basement in order to be quietly buried. No. Everyone a rifle in her hand and shoot the bandits."[28]

A Swiss journalist from Geneva noted the democratic tradition of the local assemblies (*Landsgemeinde*), in which the citizens, each carrying a sword as a symbol of liberty, assemble and make the laws. He added:

Each man in Switzerland bound to do military service has his gun at home hanging on the wall to the great amazement of foreign visitors, who cannot understand that a free state allows free citizens to have their arms at home.

One thing is sure: The Swiss would use these guns; they would shoot and would not let their country fall into the hands of an enemy without defending their land with utmost readiness to give their lives for freedom. There would be few democrats in our country who would not repeat the famous words of the American hero, Patrick Henry.[29]

During 1939, the United States was, of course, neutral. On April 4, Secretary of State Cordell Hull denied that regulations were in force that dealt with German trade. American policy was based on equal treatment for all nations, and German participation in this policy had accordingly been invited.[30] In March, American exports to Germany were $6.5 million, and imports from Germany were $5 million, both increases from the previous month.[31]

As U.S. Congressional hearings at that time recognized, international law sanctioned free trade by neutrals during wartime. Contraband of war, including arms and munitions, exported from a neutral was subject to search and seizure on the high seas by a belligerent. However, a neutral government incurred no liability by permitting the manufacture and shipment of such articles. In other words, international law permitted private firms in a neutral country to make and export arms to a belligerent, but the arms could be seized by another belligerent after export.[32]

Anticipating a long war and wishing to obtain long-term agreements to secure food and raw materials from the United States, in April and May 1939 Swiss representatives met with Secretary of State Hull and State Department officials. The Americans thought war could be avoided and resisted the Swiss attempt to obtain binding contracts for a supply of American goods.[33] When the Swiss persisted, the Department responded that it could not make commitments until pending neutrality bills were decided in Congress.[34] Finally, the Swiss were successful in obtaining contract options, and when the war broke out in September they were able to obtain large amounts of food and raw materials to store for the coming emergencies.[35]

Later in the year, after the war began, President Roosevelt called for an end to legislation prohibiting the export of arms to belligerents. Arms were embargoed, but the raw materials of which they were made were not. Roosevelt urged that an end to the embargo would increase arms manufacture in the United States and thus would give employment to thousands of Americans as well as contribute to the national defense. Under "the normal practice under the age-old doctrines of international law," the President explained, in the event of a European war, "the United States would have sold to and bought from belligerent nations such goods and products of all kinds as the belligerent nations, with their existing facilities and geographical situations, were able to buy from us or sell to us."[36]

The June 1939 issue of *Travel* magazine included a feature article on the Swiss.[37] The Swiss militia, it said, "the best defensive force in Europe," was "an army of sharpshooters who have competed for marksmen's prizes from boyhood, trained to shoot downward from a terrain high up, able to dodge a massed air attack, too, as no troops could do whose home ground is less pitted and precipitous."[38] An official in Bern conveyed the idea that "the dictators who had just finished the erasure of a small democracy in the east of Europe—one whose army stood and did not fire—must not therefore conclude that a non-standing army in the west is likewise a non-firing one."[39]

Travel magazine reported that the citizens of the Swiss cantons were "so indifferent to national concerns that to the average man the name of the president of the Federation remains unknown, yet so cohesive in a crisis that only the great Napoleon violated, and in vain, the frontiers that have stood since the Dark Ages." There was a saying: "National liberty grew from individual liberty in Switzerland. Nothing lasted that was imposed from above."[40]

The national Shooting Festival (*Schützenfest*), which remains the largest rifle competition in the world, was held in Lucerne in June in conjunction with the world championships of the UIT, or International Shooting Union. Federal President Etter, author of the concept of "spiritual national defense," spoke at the event, stressing that something far more serious than sport was the purpose of their activity. His comments demonstrated the connection between national defense and the armed citizen:

> The Swiss always has his rifle at hand. It belongs to the furnishings of his home. . . . That corresponds to ancient Swiss tradition. As the citizen with his sword steps into the ring in the cantons which have the *Landsgemeinde*, so the Swiss soldier lives in constant companionship with his rifle. He knows what that means. With this rifle, he is liable every hour, if the country calls, to defend his hearth, his home, his family, his birthplace. The weapon is to him a pledge and sign of honor and freedom. The Swiss does not part with his rifle.[41]

Rudolf Minger, who had pushed through the country's immense defense buildup after Hitler came to power, also spoke. Noting the presence of the best rifle competitors from 19 foreign countries, Minger declared that the "foreign guests must see that the Swiss people are still martial and strong, and ready at any time to sacrifice everything for the maintenance of their freedom and independence."[42]

At that 1939 festival, Switzerland won the service rifle team competition for the world championship.[43] A Swiss also set a new world record in pistol. In the Free Rifle event, the Swiss team used rifles based on their standard army-issue carbine, the K31, and came in third, behind Estonia and Finland.[44] Count Hermann Keyserling, an apostle of Nietzsche, wrote at this time that in Germany "it is recognized that aristocracy has a higher value. But in Switzerland, plebianism is the ideal."[45] In a shooting war, the Swiss plebeian would have been quite a match for Nietzsche's *Übermensch*.

Secretary of State Cordell Hull, in a speech to the United States Senate on July 14, 1939, recalled the historic American avoidance of "entangling alliances" and insisted that "both sides agree that, in the event of foreign wars, this nation should maintain a status of strict neutrality."[46]

United States policy also strictly limited the immigration of refugees. In mid-May 1939, a boat of 930 German Jews tried to land in Cuba. The U.S. State Department attempted to facilitate their entry. Cuba refused. The State Department did not offer to allow the refugees to enter the United States, and they were thus forced to re-cross the Atlantic.[47]

Despite official Washington's standoffish attitude toward the whole subject of Europe, at least some politicians were willing to acknowledge Switzerland's evolving militance in the face of growing threats to her independence. On August 2, 15,000 people joined in celebrating Switzerland's 648th anniversary at the World's Fair in New York City. On that occasion, Mayor Fiorello LaGuardia described Switzerland as "a bulwark of democracy in Europe,"[48] adding:

> When people are suppressed in the different parts of Europe, when hope is gone in the Mediterranean, when the future is dim in the Balkans, when air raids threaten other sections, the people look to Switzerland as the hope of Europe. . . . We have so much in common. We have learned so much from the glorious history of your country. You were a free country before America was discovered.[49]

Returning from a visit to Switzerland, the Lord Mayor of London referred to Switzerland's army as "the oldest militia in

Europe. . . . The system is one which helps to ensure that the Swiss Army can mobilize more rapidly than any other army in the world." He recommended the Swiss model for England.[50]

In Switzerland herself, fortifications continued to rise. Numerous forts were built along the German border and, "for appearances' sake," two were erected on the French border. In the summer of 1939, the world had yet to witness the devastating power of a German blitzkrieg, but the Swiss were already intent on employing their resources to make any invasion exceedingly costly.[51]

On August 19, it was reported from Basel that the heightened anti-Swiss propaganda campaign and the uncommonly large German troop concentrations in southern Germany during the preceding few weeks had prompted the Swiss to further strengthen garrisons along the German and Italian frontiers. One German rumor making the rounds at the time was that homes of German citizens in Basel had been ransacked by Swiss mobs. Though patently false, this was the same type of propaganda lie that had preceded Hitler's aggression in such places as the Sudetenland. Over 20,000 motorized German troops were concentrated in the Black Forest, just north of the Swiss border, within easy striking distance of Basel.[52]

Meanwhile, Hitler was using the status of the Baltic port and "Free City" of Danzig, which was ruled locally by Nazis, as a pretext to justify an aggression against Poland.[53] In June, the Führer had approved a secret military plan to eradicate Poland's army and to occupy the country.[54] On August 23, the Nazi and Soviet governments shocked the world by announcing a non-aggression pact, signed by Foreign Ministers von Ribbentrop and Molotov. Little did the world know, until after the war, of the two parties' secret protocol for carving up Poland and eastern Europe between them.[55] Yet, by seeming to free Germany from concern with the totalitarian behemoth to its east, the pact alarmed the Swiss and made them even more determined to prepare for war.

With total war rapidly approaching after the Nazi-Soviet pact, it is instructive to compare how the small neutral countries of Europe were preparing for the coming storm. The following table includes the populations and the numbers of men under arms for selected European countries during the period 1937–39. The "peace army" includes those on active duty or on maneuvers; in some cases this service was only seasonal. The "war army," for all countries except Switzerland, was purely theoretical. It included the number of soldiers who could be mobilized given sufficient time. As events in early 1940 would demonstrate, a small country could be taken over in a few hours, before a mobilization order could even be issued. In the case of Switzerland, the figure for the "war army" was real, in that every soldier already had all equipment at home and could begin fighting at any time. In this sense, it may be said that Switzerland's "war army" was really the same size as her "peace army."

Men Under Arms, 1937–39[56]

Country	Population	"Peace Army"	"War Army"	% Pop.
Belgium	8,276,000	100,000	650,000	8
Denmark	3,764,000	4,000–10,000	150,000	4
Finland	3,762,000	30,000–100,000	300,000	8
Netherlands	8,640,000	39,000	400,000	5
Norway	2,884,000	18,000–30,000	110,000	4
Switzerland	4,183,000	25,000–36,000	400,000	10

The last column shows the percentage of the population included in the "war army." As will be seen, during the war Switzerland would mobilize as many as 850,000 soldiers and local defense troops, which would raise her proportion of men under arms from 10% to 20% of the population. The low number of men under arms in Denmark, the Netherlands and Norway corresponded with their subsequent inability to resist invasion.

Finland effectively resisted the Russians in 1939. The Finns, like the Swiss, were by reputation a nation of riflemen. But Belgium, with the same proportion of men under arms (albeit under the hypothetical "war army"), was unable to resist the Germans in 1940. In addition, Belgium (like the Netherlands) had colonies which could distract from its national defense in Europe. Switzerland, of course, had no colonies.

The above data are taken from a 1937 Austrian publication and a 1939 German publication, respectively, using the 1939 data when available. The statistics changed little if at all between those two years.

As is obvious from these sources, those planning the expansion of the Third Reich were well informed of which countries were weak militarily and which were stronger.

In the last week of August, with her citizen soldiers undergoing summer training, Switzerland had nearly 100,000 men on active service.[57] On August 25, several units of elite frontier troops were called to their posts.[58] On the 28th, the Federal Council decreed mobilization of an additional 100,000 troops.[59]

On August 29, the Federal Council proclaimed a state of active service throughout the country, automatically invoking the far-reaching provisions of the military code. Civilians who committed certain offenses were to be tried by military courts. These offenses included incitement to desertion from the army, demoralization of the army, spreading false information to countermand military orders, and violation of military secrets.[60]

On August 30, anticipating that general war was imminent, the Swiss Parliament unanimously elected Colonel Henri Guisan as commander-in-chief of the army. The appointment of this French Swiss had been agreed on since the Munich crisis of 1938. Reflecting the country's anti-militarist tradition, in peacetime the highest rank in the army was colonel, but in wartime Parliament was empowered to elect the commander-in-chief, with the rank of general. Guisan had been Commander of the III Corps and was a native of the canton of Vaud in French-speaking western Switzerland. Colonel Jakob Labhart, from a German-speaking area, was appointed Chief of the General Staff.[61]

As general, Guisan would represent the ordinary citizen-at-arms. During the course of the war, this common man and inspirational military leader would come to symbolize the Swiss spirit of resistance.[62]

At that time, the militia included all males aged 20–60 and had female volunteers for special duties. The Elite troops were aged 20–36, the Reserve were in the 36–48 age group, and the Home Guard were aged 48–60.[63] Frontier guards were put in place, explosives installed in bridges, and the air force called out—it had 150 obsolete Swiss airplanes and 50 Messerschmitt Me-109 fighters purchased from the Germans.[64] The Me-109, an aircraft similar in overall performance to the British Spitfire, was the mainstay of the Luftwaffe fighter arm. The

Germans would soon come to regret their sale of these 50 planes to the Swiss.

On August 31, together with its call for a general mobilization, the Federal Council issued a formal declaration of neutrality similar to that which it had issued at the beginning of World War I.[65] The declaration began:

> The international tension which has motivated the Swiss Confederation to take military measures obliges it to declare anew its unshakable will not to depart in any way from the principles of neutrality which have for centuries inspired its policy and to which the Swiss people are profoundly attached. . . .[66]

The National Exposition, popularly called the "Landi," was taking place at this time in Zurich. It demonstrated Swiss values, unity in diversity and readiness to meet future challenges. An area called the "Höhenweg" was an elevated path under the open sky over which, in a breathtaking display, hung 3,000 different flags representing every Swiss city, town and village. Large numbers of Swiss found reassurance and solidarity at the Exposition.[67]

An English visitor to the National Exposition heard such statements as: "There'll be no talk of a 'Munich' here" and "If anyone attacks us, we will know how to repel the invader."[68] While a year earlier an occasional voice would defend the Führer, today he symbolized evil to virtually everyone in the country. "The Third Reich, from being disliked, has come to be hated. Hitler is generally regarded as a war-obsessed politician, self-perjured and a trickster, a bully given to sudden and unprovoked attacks on his smaller neighbors."[69]

On September 1, 1939, Hitler launched World War II in Europe by invading Poland. For the first time, the world witnessed the tactics of blitzkrieg—lightning war—in which tanks would slice into and surround an enemy's front and planes would swarm behind the enemy lines as mobile artillery. The Poles fought bravely, but within a week it was clear that strategic points of their front had been irreparably broken and their major units had been outmaneuvered by German armor.

Despite the Nazi threat that had been evident for years, Poland was woefully unprepared for war. In some cases, orders to give out ammunition to riflemen or artillerymen had not been issued. In one telling incident, the commander of a unit found only enough cartridges to kill himself and his horse.[70] Much of the Polish air force was caught by surprise and destroyed on the ground by German bombers. As the Wehrmacht closed in on Warsaw, already terror-bombed by the Luftwaffe, the Polish government surrendered.[71] To preclude civilian resistance, the Nazis conducted house-to-house searches for arms.[72] Persons found in possession of firearms in defiance of the invaders were executed.[73]

On the morning the German invasion of Poland began, a telegram in Switzerland at 11:00 A.M. announced that the entire Swiss armed forces were mobilized. Recalls one soldier, "We grasped our sharpened bayonets, sharpshooting ammunition, and Totentäfeli [dog tags], and swore to sacrifice life and limb for the defense of the fatherland and its Constitution."[74]

Switzerland faced two threats against which the country would have to defend herself. The first was the fear of a German attempt to incorporate Switzerland forcibly into the Third Reich or to invade in conjunction with the Italians to divide the country among themselves. The second threat—more immediate now with the advent of general war in Europe—was that a belligerent would invade a portion of Switzerland in an attempt to reach an enemy's territory more quickly.

By September 3, when Britain and France declared war on Germany, 435,000 Swiss—out of a mere 4.2 million people—were mobilized. Most were stationed in the north in anticipation of a German-French war in which those powers would attempt to outflank each other by violating Swiss neutrality.[75] The Swiss could mobilize quickly because every man had his arms and equipment at home. By contrast, in France, aside from its standing troops, it took weeks to mobilize the reserves.[76]

Recalling Hitler's threat in *Mein Kampf* to seize new territories in the East, the *Journal de Genève* commented:

> Bound to his adventure but prisoner of his method, Chancellor Hitler must push to the brink; the plenipotentiary of

Warsaw not coming to Berlin to receive the Diktat that was put to Mister Hácha, the German troops were launched against Poland to impose the dictator's will.[77]

On September 17, the Russians moved into Poland to occupy the territory agreed upon in the Nazi-Soviet Pact.[78] The cynical secret protocol between Hitler and Stalin to divide Poland was not then known, and many Polish officers surrendered their units intact to the Soviets, thinking Stalin had moved his army forward to prevent further German aggression. Eight thousand of these Polish officers would later be found buried in mass graves in the Katyn Forest near Smolensk; thousands of others in Soviet custody were never heard from again.

The blitzkrieg which crushed Poland in just 20 days led General Guisan to intensify his planning for the expected attack against Switzerland. The Swiss now made plans in the event of "Case West," in which the French would invade en route to Germany, and for the more likely event of "Case North," in which the Germans would loop down into Switzerland under the Maginot Line.[79] On the 18th, the Federal Council authorized the army high command to reduce the age for military training from 20 to 19. The first year of military training entailed 88 days.

On September 21, General Guisan rejected a request by political leaders for partial demobilization so that soldiers could return to their farms. Concentrations of foreign troops on the border still required the army to prepare for "any eventuality."[80] At the same time, economic pressure from the warring parties began—Switzerland depended on France and Italy for foodstuffs and on Germany for fuel.[81]

That same day the normally reserved lower house of Parliament cheered Federal President Etter when he warned that Switzerland was ready to resist any invasion. Europe had recognized Swiss neutrality in the Treaty of Vienna of 1815 only "on condition we defend it ourselves." Pointing out that the army was "entirely mobilized on the first day of this war,"[82] Etter added that if "war extends to our country, it will find us ready—men, women, soldiers, civilians, old and young, all of whom swear to give their life to their country, preferring death rather than slavery."[83]

The next day, September 22, Swiss anti-aircraft batteries fired on two or more German planes flying over Schaffhausen, Switzerland's northernmost canton, and also fired at two French warplanes near Basel.[84]

As reported from Paris on September 23, the French anticipated German flanking movements over and below the Maginot Line via Belgium and Switzerland. The Swiss mountains would be difficult to pass through, but one possible route included the Basel Gap, where Germany, France and Switzerland meet. Since Napoleon's fall and the signing of the Treaty of Paris in 1815, France had honored its pledge not to build fortifications within three leagues (nine miles) of Basel. While the Maginot Line did not reach the Swiss border, the gap was protected by works set up further west, including the strongly fortified position of Belfort.[85]

Another possible invasion route was through Switzerland's Aare Valley, located east of the Jura Mountains. German military writers had frequently spoken of a blitzkrieg through the Aare Valley, beginning by crossing the Rhine over the nineteen bridges between Basel and Schaffhausen and thrusting southwest to Geneva and into France.[86]

It was reported on September 25 that a thousand veteran sharpshooters, all over 60, asked General Guisan to accept them in the army for auxiliary service. The General thankfully wired the group that they could do as they desired. Leaders of the sharpshooters' organization declared that almost all of their 3,000 members would serve if Switzerland were attacked.[87]

A large map published in the *New York Times* on October 1 illustrated possible German invasion routes through the neutral states of the Netherlands, Belgium and Switzerland. The Dutch had a unique military strategy involving the flooding of the lowlands, which would turn them into swamps, and the placement of fortifications behind the inundated areas.[88] Their plan, however, would not be executed when the Germans attacked.

The *Times* map showed invasion routes under France's Maginot Line at the Basel Gap, and another route southwest into Switzerland under the Jura and then past Geneva toward Lyons in France. While the Swiss had no Maginot Line, the country was filled with field fortifications, artillery positions, tank traps, hidden concrete-covered trenches and machine-gun nests. Bridges were mined and road obstacles were in place.[89]

As the French and Germans engaged in artillery duels on the Rhine-Moselle front, German troops massed near the Swiss frontier between Basel and Schaffhausen and also at Vorarlberg. On October 3, all Swiss army leaves were canceled and fortifications were strengthened.[90]

Operations Order No. 2, which General Guisan issued on October 4, 1939, described critical positions in the north that must be held, and then asserted that the fight would be to the death:

> At the border and between the border and army position, the border troops and advance guard persistently delay the advance of the enemy. The garrisons at the border and between the border and the works and positions making up the defensive front *continue resistance up to the last cartridge, even if they find themselves completely alone.*[91]

The order also provided that obstacles of all types and destruction of bridges would slow down the advance of the aggressor.[92]

This astonishing order—that the Swiss militiaman *must* fire every cartridge and, implicitly, fight to the death without surrender—was in sharp contrast to the policies of other European countries, which surrendered to Hitler either with a command that their troops not resist, or after a short fight.

The October 4 plan of General Guisan and General Staff Chief Labhart was to mass infantry along a line of rivers, lakes, and mountains parallel to Germany. Modern artillery was in short supply, so nineteenth-century 84mm and 120mm pieces were put in place.[93] Most importantly, the individual marksman with his rifle was the key element. There was no reserve—it would be a fight to the finish.[94]

In front of the massed riflemen was a chain of blockhouses and forts built between 1934 and 1939, with machine guns, anti-tank obstacles, minefields, and artillery. This chain ran through the Alps in the south and east, along the Rhine River and through the Jura Mountains toward Geneva. The main line of resistance, utilizing the lakes and mountains as natural barriers, would stop the German panzers.[95]

Britain and France had declared war on Germany, but, unprepared, they failed to open an aggressive front. Their window of opportunity to attack while the bulk of the Wehrmacht was occupied in Poland closed by the end of September. After the Polish capitulation the major elements of the fully mobilized German Army were quickly moved to the west. Britain at this time had only 158,000 troops in France.[96] By October 10, Hitler was pushing for an offensive against the unprepared Allies, although his cooler-headed generals advised him that, in view of the lateness of the year, it would be better to wait until spring.[97]

British military leaders told newspaper correspondents in London on October 20 that the Allies foresaw a German offensive on the Western Front supported by 1,500,000 troops. They anticipated that the Germans might attack through Belgium, the Netherlands or possibly Switzerland in order to avoid a frontal assault on the Maginot Line.[98]

American war correspondent William Shirer, then stationed in Berlin, wrote in his diary after returning from a visit to Switzerland: "The country has one tenth of its population under arms; more than any other country in the world. . . . They're ready to fight to defend their way of life." He had asked a Swiss businessman on the train "whether he wouldn't prefer peace at any price (business is ruined in a Switzerland completely surrounded by belligerents and with every able-bodied man in the army) so that he could make money again." The Swiss replied: "Not the kind of peace that Hitler offers." When the train crossed the Rhine from Switzerland into Germany, Shirer described the eerie sight: "the same unreal front. Soldiers on both sides looking but not shooting."[99]

Despite the extremely dangerous situation, the French decided that the deteriorating weather would suffice to stall the Germans, and on October 29 demobilized 100,000 men. On the same day, the Swiss increased their military preparations. The General Staff shifted troops to meet a new situation created by the concentration of German forces between Constance and Munich and around Freiburg. Agricultural leaves for Swiss peasant soldiers were canceled, and troops on leave were recalled to the Basel area. Then early snows arrived to assist the Swiss defenses. Three to four feet of snow blocked most Alpine passes, and the Jura highlands, which extended into France, became impassable.[100]

The Germans continued to mass troops along all borders with Switzerland, from the region near France all the way to the Tyrol by Italy.[101] Sixty to a hundred Wehrmacht divisions were reported to be concentrated along the Western Front. Switzerland continued to be discussed as an invasion route, but Allied observers believed that the Swiss Army could make a successful defense.[102]

At the recommendation of General Guisan, on November 10 the Federal Council called up an unannounced number of troops. Since the army's full mobilization at the beginning of the war, some units had been released and various leaves approved, always with the understanding that the troops would be recalled immediately if the army was needed at full strength. The next day, the Federal Council empowered General Guisan to call all able-bodied men whenever he decided that the defense of the nation required it. Previously, orders for full mobilization required the government's approval before they could be issued.[103]

Meanwhile, the Führer narrowly escaped an assassination attempt which might have spared the world what was to come. Georg Elser, a private citizen, placed a bomb at the Bürgerbräukeller in Munich on November 8, but Hitler finished his speech early and left before the explosion. Elser was apprehended while attempting to escape over the Swiss border.[104] The German press trumpeted that Elser's tracks led to Switzerland, alarming the Swiss of a possible retaliatory action by the Nazis. These polemics coincided with the further build-up of German troops in southern Germany and the Black Forest.[105]

"Something's in the wind," wrote William Shirer from Berlin. "Party gossip about a mass air attack on England. A drive through Holland and Belgium. Or one through Switzerland."[106]

On November 20, Hitler told his generals that they had little to fear from the United States, because it was neutral, and that "I shall attack France and England at the most favorable and earliest moment. Breach of the neutrality of Belgium and Holland is of no importance."[107]

Nor, to Hitler, was that of Switzerland. There had been repeated violations of Swiss neutrality by German aircraft and anti-aircraft fire, which had wounded Swiss border residents. German planes had even staged a "pamphlet bombing" over Switzerland, dropping propaganda leaflets. German Minister Otto Köcher apologized for these events.[108]

In November, the French High Command warned General Guisan that they anticipated a German attack proceeding through Switzerland. When the French brought up troops near Basel, Guisan feared that the French intended to invade first. He warned them that the Swiss would resist invasion by *any* party. Guisan soon learned from Swiss intelligence that Hitler had postponed the offensive.[109]

In the north, the Soviet Union attacked Finland on November 30, 1939, and Hitler officially approved of the deed, although his true feelings were doubtless more complex.[110] The Swiss were encouraged by the resistance of the Finns from the Mannerheim Line and their forests against Russian armored attacks.[111] The Finns demonstrated that a small population could, in fact, successfully resist a strong aggressor.[112] Swiss journalist August Lindt, who would later advocate radical measures for Swiss resistance, reported on the action at the Finnish front.[113] Like the Swiss, the Finns were known as a nation of riflemen and skiers.

Through the winter of 1939–40, the period known, except in Finland, as the "Phony War," Swiss defenders dug into what became known as the "Army Position." The Army Position anticipated resistance in the north from the Austrian border to an area near the Maginot Line. If defeated there, the Swiss forces would retreat south into the Alps for their last stand.[114] From the *Réduit National* (literally, the "National Redoubt") or mountain fortress, centered on the St. Gotthard massif, the Swiss could control the transportation routes across the Alps.[115]

On December 28, General Guisan ordered the formation of a new army corps to be ready before the border foothills were cleared of snow in the spring. This would be the fourth corps, and it would consist of 100,000 men under the command of Colonel Labhart. As Chief of the General Staff, Labhart had authored the reorganization, which, along with the extended eligibility for service from 48 to 60 years, had increased the size of the Swiss militia to 600,000. Virtually everyone was considered fit to serve—even the blind, who listened for planes in anti-aircraft units.[116]

As 1939 ended, *Contemporary Review* recalled Machiavelli's statement, "the Swiss are most armed and most free," along with Napoleon's dictum, "Nature destined Switzerland to become a League of States; no wise man would attempt to conquer it."[117] During that winter, many French, Britons and even Germans retained hope that Europe could still be spared a major conflagration on the level of 1914–18. To the Swiss, however, the point was moot. If the Allies and the Reich did call off their war, unallied Switzerland would remain as much threatened from the Nazi behemoth as ever.

Switzerland had the largest percentage of soldiers in the world compared to overall population—600,000 soldiers in a country of 4 million. That number would continue to grow in the years to come. Just as important, and heard everywhere inside Switzerland, was the slogan *geistige Landesverteidigung,* the concept best expressed in English as "spiritual national defense."[118] Evoking the nation's proud heritage of freedom and independence, and the utter determination of the average Swiss to defend his homeland, the term became a rallying cry for the nation as it faced the most powerful threat in its history.

Chapter 4

Spring 1940
All Fall But One

NEW YEAR'S DAY, NORMALLY A HOLIDAY OF HOPE AND CELE-
bration, was in 1940 an occasion for the people of Europe to wonder
what horrors awaited them. Nazi Germany no longer disguised its
aggressive designs in diplomatic language, historical rationales or
covert intimidation. After the invasion of Poland, questions of national supremacy were referred to the battlefield. During the winter,
German U-boats had slid out into the Atlantic to wreak their havoc in
the cold seas. The British were pouring strength into the continent to
support the defense of France. The French continued to work on their
Maginot Line, correctly assuming the enemy would not dare a frontal
assault. The German General Staff, in secret as always, laid out its specific plans for conquest. The question on the minds of the Allies at this
point was when the Nazis would strike next, and where.

In London, *The Times* quoted military analysts who predicted
that if the Germans attempted to outflank the Maginot Line through
Switzerland, their thrust would not succeed. An attack through the
former Austrian border, between Ragaz and the eastern end of Lake
Constance, would require crossing the Rhine, which was protected by
forts and pillboxes. The next logical target would be Appenzell and St.
Gallen, mountainous cantons with few roads, where small forces
might pin down a more numerous enemy. If the invaders made it to
the open regions east of Zurich, they would be confronted by Lake
Zurich and the Limmat River, the banks of which were fortified.[1]

If the Wehrmacht made it past these obstacles, it would find itself
at the Swiss Plateau, which extends 100 miles southwest to the Lake

of Geneva. Only 40 miles at its maximum width, the hilly area containing forests and rivers (the Reuss, the Aare and the Sarine) was flanked by two mountain ranges: the Alps on the south and the Jura on the north. A large army might squeeze through, but without room for maneuver and exposed along the way to Swiss troops who would fight from the Jura and the Alps as well as from the fortifications along the rivers. If the invaders reached Lake Geneva, French forces would be waiting at the fortifications on the Haute Savoie and in the Jura Mountains.[2]

Confronting the Germans would be a 600,000-man-strong Swiss Army, said The Times, "well armed and so abundantly equipped with machine guns, infantry guns and other automatic weapons that it possesses the highest relative firing power on the Continent." The French would back up the Swiss troops.[3]

By early 1940, the Swiss could mobilize 650,000 men on short notice, a number that would continue to rise in succeeding years.[4] The German General Staff estimated that it would take forty days to cross Switzerland and that "it would be necessary to oppose five Germans to one Swiss to achieve that result."[5] It was common knowledge that the Swiss would mount a stubborn defense. The Times reported: "All able-bodied men are individually trained to be defenders of their native mountains. Like the Finns, they are a nation of marksmen and of skiers."[6]

The "Winter War" in Finland demonstrated that a small, armed country could defend itself against superior numbers. The Finns learned their shooting skills from the Swiss, who now had much to learn from the Finns. In Switzerland, large numbers of women began to practice marksmanship skills.[7]

When the Military Department found it necessary to restrict the issuance of practice ammunition to 24 cartridges per civilian shooter, the Swiss Shooting Federation expressed concern. The campaigns in Poland and Finland had devoured enormous amounts of ammunition. However, as noted at that time by National Councillor Valloton in a meeting of the Swiss Parliament, the value of the Finnish Army's shooting effectiveness consisted not in mass fire but in single shots. Finnish army commander General Field Marshal von Mannerheim asserted in an interview: "Rifle shooting has played an important role in this war. Our best shooters had special tasks. Look after shooting in Switzerland!"[8] Rudolf Minger, head of the Swiss Military Department, stated:

> We learn from the fate of the Finnish, a small but heroic people. . . . A military mission should be sent to Finland. Concerning shooting in Switzerland, I can assure you we stand on the ground that individual shooting is very important. Everything is adjusted to it.[9]

"The offensive seems imminent," wrote correspondent William Shirer on March 1. "From what I saw in the Netherlands, the Dutch will be easy pickings for the Germans. Their army is miserable. Their famous defensive waterline is of doubtful worth." (Dutch military plans called for flooding areas to bog down tanks, not anticipating air attacks and paratroopers.) By contrast, Shirer continued, "Switzerland will be tougher to crack, and I doubt if the Germans will try.[10]

In deepest winter, when an invasion was unlikely, many Swiss soldiers had been released to go back to their homes and jobs. On March 4, however, Switzerland advanced a scheduled remobilization. Bavarian and Austrian formations were moving into areas opposite the Swiss frontier from the Rhine to Lake Constance.[11] Additional mobilization orders were issued as increased German troop concentrations were reported. Switzerland called up 400,000 men in response to the build-up.[12]

Meanwhile, the Swiss press expressed skepticism regarding both Anglo-French and Nazi professions of goodwill toward neutrals, although Switzerland was regarded as distinctly sympathetic to the Allies.[13] Swiss papers also continued to provide their own analyses of German public opinion.

For instance, the *Basler Nachrichten* (*Basel Evening News*) opined on February 9 that Germans blamed the Nazis for their suffering.[14] Hitler had lost popularity because he exposed Germany to armed conflict.[15] In Bavaria, the paper argued, anti-Nazi sentiment was engendered by traditional animosity toward the Prussian mentality: "All this does not imply that Germany is ready for a revolution. Civilians are disarmed, and so powerless." Some Germans thought

Germany would profit from defeat, which would destroy Nazism and Prussian militarism, while others thought victory would generate a military dictatorship and then a monarchist restoration. Germans longed for, it was asserted, the return of legality, freedom and human dignity.[16] The ongoing analysis in the uncensored Swiss press of German domestic sentiment, accurate or not, was closely followed by the Nazi leadership in Berlin, Goebbels in particular.

Propaganda Minister Goebbels demanded that the press and even the public opinion of neutrals must be truly "neutral"—in other words, never critical of National Socialism. The Nazi press asserted that Switzerland granted her citizens a license to abuse Germany. Newspapers in major German cities joined in waging the campaign of criticism against Switzerland. Elizabeth Wiskemann, in *Fortnightly* magazine, commented: "So systematic has the German press campaign been that it has appeared not altogether unlike the journalistic artillery-fire which is apt to precede a Nazi invasion."[17]

Nazi-Soviet cooperation continued during 1939–40 as Germany traded manufactured goods for foodstuffs and raw materials from Russia.[18] The Germans were also heavily dependent on the import of iron ore from Sweden. In Finland, the Soviet Union continued to take heavy losses as its attacking armies flailed helplessly in the thick northern forests, but during February they finally breached the Mannerheim Line in the south, presenting the Finns with a crisis. In one of the great ironies of the war, the Allies in response prepared an expeditionary force of British, French and Polish troops to aid Finland, a future German ally, in its war against Germany's future antagonist, the Soviet Union. The Royal Navy prepared to transport troops to Norway, from which point they would march to support the Finns. On March 6, however, Finland sued for peace with Russia and on the 12th agreed to Russia's terms, the most important of which was the handover of the Karelian isthmus north of Leningrad.[19] Against long odds, the Finns had held out heroically since November 1939.

While the Allied troops earmarked for Finland awaited new orders, Norway now became the focus of attention. The German Navy had already recommended to Hitler that he seize the Norwegian coast, if only to deny the use of its many excellent harbors to the

British, who had already violated Norway's territorial waters in search of German ships. Hitler was reluctant, but after the Allies assembled their expeditionary force and collected its naval transport, he decided there was no other choice. Aside from the advantages the Norwegian coast would offer the German Navy, a potential Allied occupation of Norway would have cut off the Reich's supply of iron. To facilitate the operation against Norway, and to strengthen Germany's strategic supply line to Sweden, the Nazis would also occupy Denmark.

At the end of March, a Swiss spy with connections to Hitler's headquarters warned Colonel Roger Masson, Swiss Intelligence Chief, that Germany would attack Denmark and Norway in April. This information was leaked to the Allied Chiefs of Staff, who discounted it.[20] Despite further warnings from dissident German diplomats and military officers, and obvious German troop movements, the governments of Denmark and Norway failed to mobilize and did nothing to prepare for invasion.[21]

On April 9, 1940, at 4:20 A.M. in Denmark and at 5:20 A.M. in Norway, German diplomats gave the ultimatum to these two countries that they agree to become German protectorates. They were told that they needed protection from impending Anglo-French occupation.[22] From Copenhagen, a German diplomat telegraphed Foreign Minister Ribbentrop at 8:34 A.M. that Denmark acceded. However, the German diplomat in Oslo reported that Norway would defend herself.

In Denmark, a flat land with no mountain sanctuaries, General and Commander-in-Chief W. W. Pryor recommended resistance. King Christian X and Premier Thorvald Stauning rejected his advice, just as a day earlier they had rejected the General's plea for mobilization. The Navy could have successfully bombarded and possibly sunk passing German ships but did nothing.[23] The King, backed by the government, then capitulated and prohibited any resistance. There was minor fighting, nevertheless. Thirteen Danes were killed.[24]

At 2:00 P.M., Wehrmacht General Kurt Himer visited the King, who declared that he and the Danish government would work to keep order and to eliminate friction between German troops and Danes. The King's only request was to keep his bodyguard. General Himer answered that "the Führer would doubtless permit him to retain them." The King was relieved, and told the General what a magnificent military operation the Germans had conducted. Denmark became a model state in the Nazis' New Order, until the tide of war changed and resistance was sparked.[25]

This could not have happened in Switzerland, which had no king and no central authority to negotiate the surrender of the army or the nation. Denmark had a very small army in 1939, numbering only 6,600 men. By 1940, the number had increased to 30,000, but that figure was still hopelessly inadequate.[26]

By contrast, in Norway the German invaders encountered heroic resistance. Coastal defense forces opened fire, sinking the ship that was transporting the would-be Nazi occupation authorities. Oslo and other major cities fell within a couple of days, but resistance continued and the government fled to the mountains in the north. Vidkun Quisling named himself head of the government, prompting rebellion within the populace.[27]

Norway had a "king," Haakon VII, but he was elected to his position by the people. Ironically, his brother was Christian X, King of Denmark, who had just surrendered to the Nazis. German Minister Curt Bräuer met with King Haakon to persuade him to surrender as his brother had done the day before. The King refused, as did the rest of the government. The British Royal Navy was already present in force off the coast and would inflict serious losses on German ships. Allied troops who had been readied earlier for intervention in Finland were disembarking at key points to assist in the Norwegian defense. The German minister was told that "resistance will continue as long as possible." The three million people of Norway were instructed by a radio broadcast from the King and political leaders to fight the invaders.[28]

They did so bravely. Unfortunately, unlike the Swiss, the Norwegians were not well armed, nor were they well trained in martial skills. It was reported on April 17 from Norway's southern front between Kongsvinger and the Swedish frontier that, "owing to a complete lack of arms, ammunition, and organization, the Norwegians have not been able to put up a serious fight."[29] Indeed, following World War I, Norway had pursued disarmament and social programs rather than defense, and was perceived as an easy prey. Though she shared Switzerland's neutrality, Norway never had the type of citizens army that the Swiss could muster.[30] In 1940, her army consisted of only 13,000 soldiers.

After they had reduced Norwegian coastal defenses, the German invaders fought their most difficult battles against the British and French contingents sent to aid in the defense of Norway. However, the Wehrmacht, reinforced with men and supplies flown in on transport aircraft, won a series of sharp clashes. As the Germans consolidated their grip on the country, the last Allied troops were evacuated from Norway in May to help stave off the even larger disaster looming in France.

While the poor training of the small Norwegian Army prevented serious resistance (the King had been evacuated to England where he maintained a government in exile), guerrilla war in the mountains waged by small groups with sharpshooting skills had an effect. Wehrmacht General Eduard Dietl conceded that the Norwegians "fought with excellence, although one clearly noticed their defective training. But the Norwegians were excellent marksmen, and that plays the key role in a war of this type!"[31] While the Norwegian resistance never became very active, later in the war enough arms to equip 35,000 men were smuggled in on British fishing boat runs.[32]

Contrasting reactions of the various neutral countries produced vastly different results. While Denmark had only 30,000 men under arms and Norway an even more meager 13,000, Switzerland could muster 650,000 militiamen within a day or two. Hundreds of thousands more Swiss had arms at home. Also, Switzerland had undertaken enormous efforts to build a network of fortifications, obstacles and mines. Denmark and Norway had done little.

Still, the Norwegian campaign caused uneasiness in Swiss military circles. The heroic fight of the Finns against the Soviet Union, which incurred losses of 200,000 killed, had created some confidence that Swiss arms could perform at least as well against a numerically superior invader. But the Germans in Norway displayed far more military skill and flexibility than had the Russians against Finland. And Germany, not Russia, was the foreign threat the Swiss would have to confront.

In Poland in 1939, as in nearly all the battles of the Great War, German military prowess had been demonstrated with massed armies and firepower. These were the tactics the Swiss anticipated, for which their trained marksmen and difficult terrain, backed by their mountain positions, would be an antidote. In Norway, however, for the first time in history, air transport had played a major role in an offensive, placing Nazi forces in key positions behind and among the defenses. Further, the Germans had enjoyed no numerical superiority in the initial stages of the campaign but nevertheless had won. Dietl's mountain troops at Narvik had numbered only 4,500 against the Allies' 25,000, until the British, French and Poles evacuated. Though uncowed, the Swiss knew that a German attack on the Swiss Alps and the Jura, employing paratroops, gliders, specially trained mountain divisions and airpower, would be formidable.

In the following months, fearing attack, Sweden allowed the Nazis to transport troops over its soil to Norway. It would later allow the transport across its neutral territory of an entire German army division, to be used in the attack on the Soviet Union.[33]

The Swiss press denounced Germany's aggression against Denmark and Norway, leading Goebbels to rant in his diary that the Swiss "are either bought or Jewish."[34] Rumors spread that Germany was preparing to attack Switzerland, the Netherlands and Belgium. The Swiss military was prepared for an attack.[35] Fifteen Wehrmacht divisions had returned to their positions just north of Switzerland's frontier, where they had been stationed before being withdrawn when Germany invaded Scandinavia.[36]

On April 18, 1940, the Federal Council and General Guisan issued joint orders for the "general mobilization of the entire army for resistance."[37] Reflecting on the lessons learned from the Polish and Norwegian experiences, they also issued, in an order signed by Federal President Pilet-Golaz and General Guisan, "directions concerning the conduct of the soldiers not under arms in event of attack."[38] Intended also as a warning to foreign countries, this remarkable document was plastered on walls all over the country. The joint order began by describing how the population would be informed of an invasion:

> With combat activity at the border or in neighboring countries, there will be ordered the "*war-mobilization in event of*

attack." The proclamation will be communicated through poster, radio, courier, town crier, storm bells, and the dropping of leaflets from airplanes.[39]

The joint order prescribed the action to take against surprise attack and fifth column subversion:

All soldiers and those with them are to attack with ruthlessness parachutists, airborne infantry and saboteurs. Where no officers and noncommissioned officers are present, each soldier acts under exertion of all powers of his own initiative.[40]

The distinctive Swiss command for the individual soldier to act on his own initiative is an ancient and deeply rooted Swiss resistance tradition which evidenced unique confidence in the ordinary man.[41] Under no condition, the order continued, would any surrender be forthcoming, and any pretense of a surrender must be ignored:

If by radio, leaflets or other media any information is transmitted doubting the will of the Federal Council or of the Army High Command to resist an attacker, this information must be regarded as lies of enemy propaganda. Our country will resist aggression with all means in its power and to the bitter end.[42]

This astonishing order was broadcast by radio and published in the international press.[43] The *New York Times* entitled its report "Swiss Alert for Invasion by Hoax," and included the subtitle "People Told to Ignore Rumors Questioning Government's Will to Resist."[44] Noting that under the order "the entire nation would be mobilized in event of an invasion," the report continued that mobilization upon the announcement of an invasion would be "instantaneous for all men with weapons in their home who are not already in service."[45]

In Switzerland, there would be no surrender. Every man had orders to fight to the death. And every man was trained with and possessed a rifle. This was the only radically democratic system of national defense in Europe. The Nazis were well aware that invasion meant fighting on every inch of ground (much of which was vertical) in every city and village, in every pasture and mountainside.

Over fifty years later, former Swiss machine-gunner Willi Gautschi remembered the order as natural and ordinary. Any officers present would take charge, but, if not, soldiers would use their own initiative. They kept 48 cartridges at home and had six more loaded in the rifle when on duty. The rifles in the home were visible and easy to operate, and Swiss women would not have hesitated to use them in event of an invasion if the man was not present. While women's auxiliaries were not armed, many women would have fought in the event of an invasion.[46]

The German minister in Bern, Otto Köcher, reported to the Foreign Ministry in Berlin that the April 18 order "for mobilization in case of a surprise attack . . . is addressed not only to the soldiers, but to the entire population." He indicated that the Swiss were "deeply shocked by Germany's military operations in Denmark and Norway," that "the Norwegian Major Quisling has become a symbol here of internal corruption and treason" and that "spies and traitors have been suspected everywhere in this country." The Swiss press, he added, was advocating replacement of the Hague Convention on land warfare with "a Swiss national statute on land warfare, which would legally oppose total war with total defense, in which the civilian population would be obliged to take part." In the citizens army, the German minister noted, junior officers had organized themselves so that if, "in an invasion, a commanding officer showed signs of giving way before overwhelming enemy forces, these officers have mutually pledged themselves to shoot such a commander on the spot."[47]

The German minister was privy to good intelligence, although much of it could be found by reading the strongest pro-defense newspapers, such as that of the quasi-official SSV shooting federation. Warning of a fifth column and quoting from the no-surrender order, the SSV envisioned a true people's war with universal participation:

> In every Swiss house is a rifle, and every village, even the small villages, has a shooting association. . . . Our marksmen know how to shoot. . . . They want to defend their homes. They have the necessary weapons, if they can get the

ammunition. Give our shooters who are in the country the opportunity to defend the nation.[48]

Fearing a paratroop attack, the SSV requested the distribution of more ammunition and the creation of local defense (*Ortswehr*) units in all communities, composed of old men, young boys and women.[49] Having learned of the Nazi tactics in Denmark and Norway, the SSV also demanded that any Nazis in the Swiss officer corps be eliminated and replaced by those with a pure Swiss spirit, and that, for total resistance, "the weapon of the civilian must also be loaded." As for traitors in the army, as was seen in Norway, "in our country, we must know where the first shots are to be fired"—that is, at any Swiss traitors.[50]

General Guisan became the symbol of the *Widerstandsgeist*, the resistance spirit.[51] He enjoyed this status because he embodied the determination to resist to the last drop of blood.

The Swiss General Staff announced on April 23 that many Swiss were receiving requests from abroad for various maps and photographs of the country. It forbade compliance and warned of whisper campaigns organized to promote Nazi propaganda, the purpose of which was to divide the Swiss people and encourage defeatism. Rumors were circulated that many Swiss army officers admired the Reich and would assist the Germans in event of an invasion; these stories were spread by Germans under the direction of the German Legation in Bern, which had a staff of over 200, and by fifth columnists.[52]

The Nazis organized a propaganda campaign attacking the Swiss as being pro-Allies and characterizing the Swiss press as a tool of the Jews. Swiss Intelligence Chief Roger Masson worried that the anti-Nazism of the Swiss press would in itself provoke a German invasion.[53] Colonel Rudolf Fueter, head of the military's press and radio section, countered that the press must defend democracy and independent thought, and that it was "the duty of our press to reject the domestic and foreign policies of the National Socialists clearly and forcefully."[54]

In anticipation of a German offensive against France through Switzerland, General Guisan entered into secret defensive plans with the French. Compromising neutrality was extremely risky, because the Nazis could use the fact as a pretext to attack. The Swiss, however, saw such planning as consistent with neutrality. In fact, Defense Minister Minger had previously encouraged Guisan to discuss mutual defense with French military leaders.[55] These prewar understandings now developed into full-scale plans in which, only if requested by the Swiss, French troops would enter Switzerland and assist in fighting the Germans.[56]

Neutrality ends when a country is attacked, but defense preparations must precede that contingency. Thus, it did not violate the common international understanding of neutrality for Switzerland to make plans for French assistance in the event of a German invasion. A similar agreement need not have been made with Germany, because no French invasion was anticipated.

In April, a Swiss military mission visited the Maginot Line and returned depressed about the lack of preparations of the French, the only major power left on the continent not allied, or otherwise cooperating, with Germany. Once the Germans attacked the French and won, the invasion of Switzerland seemed inevitable.[57]

In the stillness before the storm, a writer for the British *Fortnightly* observed the centuries-old democratic *Landsgemeinde* assemblies taking place in the Swiss countryside. She visited "the assembly of sworded freemen" in Trogen, Appenzell canton, and the citizens' meeting in Glarus canton. "All pledged themselves afresh to protect their liberty and their laws to the death," she wrote.[58] While German troops seemed poised for invasion, "it was evident that the people of Appenzell and Glarus were indulging in quiet defiance of military despotism."[59]

On May 10, 1940, the German offensive against France was launched in the north, the Germans choosing to disregard the military option of flanking the Maginot Line through Switzerland. On countless occasions, Hitler had promised to respect the rights of the neutral countries. Belgium and the Netherlands had nevertheless been warned of the coming invasion by German Major-General Hans Oster, an anti-Hitler plotter. The Belgians mobilized while the Dutch, who had not taken part in the Great War, still trusted that their neutrality would be respected.[60] On May 10, Ribbentrop in Berlin summoned diplomats of Belgium and the Netherlands and informed them that German troops would be moving in to safeguard those countries from an Anglo-French attack. He demanded a guarantee that no resistance would follow. The same message was delivered in Brussels and at The Hague.[61] At dawn that same day, attacks were launched against those countries and also against France.

Though Switzerland escaped becoming the invasion route to France, her territory nevertheless remained under threat. Before daybreak on May 10, Swiss anti-aircraft guns drove away a German bomber that had flown over Basel. A squadron of twenty Luftwaffe planes roared over that city to engage French fighters over the region of Delémont in the west as Swiss anti-aircraft guns blazed away. Twenty-seven bombs were dropped by the Luftwaffe on northern Switzerland, damaging a railway.[62]

A Swiss squadron of pursuit planes engaged the Luftwaffe, and a Swiss Me-109 from Olten shot down a German Heinkel-111 twin-engine bomber that had flown near Solothurn in the region of Brugg in northeastern Switzerland.[63] This was the first of several instances in which the Swiss used aircraft purchased from Germany to shoot down Luftwaffe planes.

A German aircraft believed to be equipped with cameras flew low over the St. Gallen region in eastern Switzerland, the location of new forts on the "Winkelried Line" (named for the hero of the medieval Battle of Sempach) and was driven off by Swiss fighter fire.[64] The Swiss already had 300,000 soldiers in the Winkelried Line facing Germany, and large forces of crack frontier troops rushed to reinforce them. A general mobilization, beginning at dawn the next day (the 11th), was ordered. The communiqué stated that the army was ready "for any eventuality . . . to face any menace from whatever side it may come."[65] It would take the Swiss only one day to mobilize and one more day to get into position.[66]

"The Swiss were calling up every available male," wrote William Shirer. "When will it be Switzerland's turn?"[67] The question became *when*, not *whether*, the Wehrmacht would attack the Alpine republic.

Before and during the Wehrmacht attack on Belgium, the Netherlands and France on May 10, deception maneuvers created the impression that German forces in the Black Forest would also execute an "Operation South" by striking into Switzerland to bypass the Maginot Line. The ploy operated like a gigantic movie set: during the day, German troops would march toward the Swiss border; at night, they would move back. The next day, the same troops would march toward Switzerland again, giving the impression, day after day, that a gigantic army was moving south. French General Maurice Gamelin thought 30 elite units would encircle his right wing, when in reality there were only 13 German units in the area, mostly reserves. Thus 19 French divisions were uselessly diverted to the south while the Germans attacked in the north.[68]

A personal account of these events was related to the author by Ernst Leisi, who had been a young rifleman in Company I, 74th Battalion, stationed with frontier troops near Lake Constance. Of the 200 men in his company, Leisi believed there was not a single man with Nazi sympathies. One day a soldier came looking pale holding a telegram. German landing craft were preparing on the other side of Lake Constance, and troops were moving toward Switzerland. Parachutists were expected. German troops would march with great noise south, and would then return north at night. This ruse lasted eight days and fooled both the French and the Swiss. The Germans were so meticulous that they would attack on the hour—or at least so the Swiss thought. According to Leisi, the Swiss troops were full of anxiety every time the hour struck.[69]

On May 13, news sources reported that the Swiss were keeping a steady armed watch against any move by the Germans, who had heavy concentrations in the southern part of the Black Forest.[70] The Swiss suspected that the German intention was to strike between Basel and Lake Constance toward the Rhône Valley of France, and that such a move might bring Italy into the war.[71] Swiss fighters patrolled the frontier skies with orders to shoot down any belligerents who ignored a first warning.[72]

By now, some 700,000 soldiers between the ages of 20 and 60—nearly 20% of the Swiss population—were mobilized. Boy scouts and aged women were posted in rear areas for support duties.[73] Hundreds of families were fleeing from Basel, which was within rifle shot of both the German Westwall and the French Maginot forts.[74]

The same day, it was reported that Mussolini was planning to invade Ticino, Switzerland's Italian-speaking canton on the southern slopes of the Alps.[75] Italian troops were massed at the border. If the assault had taken place, the Swiss planned to retire to the main Alpine passes, from where they could resist indefinitely against large forces with machine guns and mountain artillery.[76] The Swiss were concerned that in case of an Italian attack, Germany would seize the Basel area, creating a diversion at the southern end of the Maginot Line. Even while battling Belgium and Holland, the Germans had sufficient troops to thrust through Switzerland between the Jura and the Alps, all the way to Lake Geneva.[77] Assuming the Wehrmacht was able to overcome initial Swiss resistance, Germany would then occupy the passes through the Jura into France while the Italian army pursued its own objectives in the south. With Hitler being the primary threat, the argument ran, the Allies would not add to their troubles by declaring war on Italy.[78]

On May 13, the same day these reports appeared, and as German panzers and paratroopers battled in Holland, Hitler issued a secret directive that noted "the power of resistance of the Dutch Army has proven to be stronger than was anticipated." Savage bombing strikes were ordered, leading to the destruction of the center of Rotterdam with heavy civilian casualties. The city surrendered, soon to be followed by the entire Dutch Army. The Queen and the government escaped to London. On May 14, just five days after the German attack, Dutch Commander-in-Chief H.G. Winkelmann ordered the troops to surrender their arms. He signed the capitulation the next day.[79]

Also on that day, the real German plan was revealed. Despite the feints to the south, and the heavy engagements to the north, the main offensive strength of the Wehrmacht—seven panzer divisions under Guderian, Reinhardt and Rommel—had been cutting through Belgian and French frontier units in the Ardennes Forest to emerge at the Meuse River near Sedan in France. The Germans forced a crossing, and the panzers began their drive toward the English Channel. The French had no strategic reserve.[80]

With the battle for France approaching its climax, the Swiss government ordered that armed local units, composed of men not liable for military service, make themselves ready to protect rear areas in case of paratrooper assaults or German breakthroughs.[81] Wehrmacht artillery and motorized units, meanwhile, were being massed across from Schaffhausen on the Rhine and by sundown appeared ready to attack Switzerland. The Swiss Army worked feverishly on the Winkelried Line fortifications. The front page of the *New York Times* announced: "Thousands of women, boys and aged men volunteered for 'home-guard' duty and received rifles and forty cartridges each."[82] The Swiss regular army was estimated to include 600,000 men and the home guards 200,000.[83] That evening, fear of invasion swept the country. Many were leaving Zurich; even the American Consul fled Basel.[84]

With hindsight, we see that France was defeated and Britain expelled from the continent as the result of one massive operation, culminating in the panzer dash to the Channel. However, at that time it was inconceivable that the war would not involve other thrusts, fronts or flanking campaigns. The Seventh German Army was headquartered in Freiburg, just thirty miles from the Swiss border and stood in readiness.[85] German divisions were massed at the Rhine, and the attack on Switzerland was expected early on May 15.[86]

On that May 15, when the German armor went over the Meuse and routed the French at Sedan, General Guisan issued yet another remarkable command to the army. The latest war news demonstrated, he declared, that had the soldiers (he meant the French) resolved to hold fast, they could have stopped hostile advances. Instead, defections allowed the enemy to penetrate through gaps, which quickly widened. Guisan thus recalled the high duty of the individual soldier to resist at his position. The General continued:

> Everywhere, where the order is to hold, it is the duty of conscience of each fighter, even if he depends on himself alone, to fight at his assigned position. The riflemen, if overtaken or surrounded, fight in their position until no more ammunition exists. Then cold steel is next. . . . The machine-gunners, the cannoneers of heavy weapons, the artillerymen, if in the bunker or on the field, do not abandon or destroy their weapons, or allow the enemy to seize them. Then the crews fight further like riflemen. As long as a man

has another cartridge or hand weapons to use, he does not yield.[87]

Guisan's order to the army was published in the press and restored confidence to the civilian population—much of which was understandably close to panic—that Swiss resistance to German attack would be total.[88] It informed the Swiss officers and soldiers that no one was authorized to surrender. Most emphatically, it was a stern warning to the Wehrmacht that, unlike its other enemies, the Swiss would die fighting, even if only with the bayonet.

A similar order had been issued on October 4, 1939.[89] The Swiss military histories treat these orders as nothing unusual. So did Swiss soldiers who commented on the orders in interviews a half-century after the war.

Hans Senn, a lieutenant in the frontier troops who would become a lieutenant general in the postwar years, commanded a strongpoint behind the Rhine. He and his men had only rifles and machine guns but no defense against panzers. He stated that the soldiers were prepared to follow the order and sacrifice themselves. Senn commented that the individual soldier was skilled but that unit coordination was inferior—a situation which improved as the war continued.[90]

Ernst Leisi, whose unit was stationed at the border, recalls that Swiss soldiers thought they would be dead in a day or maybe a week. No one thought of retreat; even if they were surrounded, surrender was out of the question. Everyone had taken the oath at the mobilization site to sacrifice his life for the country. The no-surrender order expressed exactly what the soldiers felt.[91]

Frontier troops had so much ammunition available that they would have been killed before exhausting their cartridges and resorting to the blade. Later in the war, even after the troops in the Swiss Plateau were moved to the mountains, leaving only the border troops to face the Wehrmacht, the order remained the same: Keep fighting, no retreat, no surrender.[92]

On the same day as these events, May 15, the Swiss Army Command declared that full mobilization had been achieved in record time and that all units were in place, thereby assuring the protection of Swiss neutrality and independence. It was reported that the populace expressed disappointment about the Netherlands' surrender but retained confidence in an Allied victory.[93] An expected raid by saboteurs on General Guisan's headquarters did not materialize.[94]

The Luftwaffe continued its violations of Swiss air space, and on May 16 a German bomber near Winterthur was downed by a Swiss fighter.[95] Two German bombers found flying south of Schaffhausen were chased away by other fighters.[96]

Because of invasion threats, the League of Nations closed its Geneva offices on the evening of May 16. It planned a move to the city of Vichy, France.[97]

"I believe Hitler will bomb Geneva to destruction just out of personal hate for the League and what Geneva stands for," wrote William Shirer from Berlin that day. "Today there are reports of more German activity along the Swiss border. The Nazis may break into Switzerland any moment now." Shirer was worried about his wife Tess and their baby, who were living in Geneva, from which the women and children attached to the American consulate were departing. "The American government has advised Americans in Switzerland to leave immediately for Bordeaux, where they'll be picked up by American ships."[98]

On May 19, the Germans moved their armored cars and light tanks away from the Swiss border. This may have been a ruse to trick the French into sending their mountain forces to the battle then taking place in the north, and the withdrawal may have been only a short distance. The Swiss remained fully mobilized and continued anti–fifth column activity.[99]

By May 24, the Allied armies in France and Belgium had been cut in two. Counterattacks against the German "panzer corridor" from the south by General Charles de Gaulle had been repulsed, and Rommel had parried a larger attempt by the British from the north. The British had decided that their only hope was to evacuate their army from the continent. On May 25, King Leopold III of Belgium rejected the demands of his cabinet that he go into exile and continue the struggle as commander-in-chief. He refused, saying all was lost. On the 27th, the King sought a truce with the Germans, who replied that the Führer insisted that weapons be laid down unconditionally. Leopold accepted those terms an hour later.

Belgium, a nation of cowards –

The King's surrender allowed the Germans to pour through Belgium and deploy overwhelming strength against the French and British who were falling back to their last remaining Channel port, Dunkirk. The Allies were shocked. Winston Churchill would remark that Leopold made the decision "without prior consultation, with the least possible notice, without the advice of his ministers and upon his own personal act."[100] The King did not have the constitutional authority to surrender unilaterally, but did so anyway. The Belgian Army had fought heroically.[101] *Why did the army obey?*

Hitler was able to conquer much of Europe by bluffing the central authority of various countries into capitulation. In some cases, after a few meetings and threats, Hitler's henchmen convinced the political leaders of a nation to surrender and to direct their armed forces not to resist. In other cases, the surrender would come after a brief fight, for which the armies were unprepared. There was no need to order the people not to resist, because they were, by and large, unarmed.

By contrast, Switzerland had a weak central government; as a direct democracy, power was decentralized. The first unit of authority was the individual and the family. Then came the village or city, then the canton, and finally the Federal Parliament. Power was exercised from the bottom up, not the top down.

The creation of the *Ortswehren,* or local defense units, exemplified the Swiss policy of total resistance by the entire population. By the end of 1939, the Swiss Army command had been studying how the strength of the people could be used for the national defense. The Wehrmacht operations against Denmark and Norway in April 1940 gave the army command insights into Germany's new techniques of warfare. The command wished to avoid the potential degeneration of a "total popular resistance" into an "unorganized popular uprising." That would have given the aggressor the occasion to treat each resistance fighter as an outlaw sniper, meaning that, if captured, he would not be protected by the international rules governing warfare and could be shot on the spot.[102]

At a Swiss Army conference on April 29, Chief of the General Staff Jakob Huber expressed the need to have volunteer *Ortswehren* to reinforce the troops and to combat saboteurs and paratroopers, declaring that "only a total defense can oppose total war." General Guisan noted that the Munitions Administration had a surplus of 70,000 old rifles with ammunition that could be put at the disposal of the *Ortswehren*.[103]

1940   On May 4, the General applied to the Federal Council for immediate formal recognition of these armed reinforcements, whose tasks would be "prevention of sabotage, immediate combat against any foreign invader, maintenance of silence, and security in the community." The Federal Council gave its authorization three days later.[104] The *Ortswehren* were instituted none too soon, for the Germans launched their Western offensive on May 10, at which time the Swiss also expected to be attacked.   *D into France*

The *Ortswehren* not only filled actual military needs, but also satisfied the desire of a growing number of Swiss to make a personal contribution to the defense of the country. These local units, helping to unify the country militarily and politically, were an immediate success, and volunteers were plentiful. They consisted primarily of former soldiers no longer liable for service, the *Jungschützen* (young shooters), those who were not capable of military service but who were capable marksmen, those with emergency service duties, and others who had been exempt from the military, as well as suitable women who were in the medical service and fire brigades.[105] The recruits were so numerous that arms and equipment were insufficient.[106]

Later, the Federal Council promulgated the administrative aspects of the *Ortswehren*. As members of the army, they were sworn in and instructed in military law. Those without an old military uniform wore civilian clothing. To protect against treatment as guerrillas, those without uniforms received the Swiss armband. It was decreed that the *Ortswehr* soldiers would arm themselves either with their own rifles or carbines or, if available from army reserve stocks, the Model 1889 long rifle would be handed over.[107]

On May 28, German Minister Köcher complained to Berlin that the Swiss military was disbursing munitions and organizing local groups to wage partisan war if invaded. Guisan was again sending a strong message to the Nazis.[108] On the same day, another message was also being sent: The military penal code was amended to provide for the death penalty for betrayal of military secrets and for treason. It was applicable to soldiers and civilians alike.[109]

Eventually the *Ortswehren* came to number 200,000 and would have provided armed civilian resistance in every locality of Switzerland, no matter how remote. The historical significance of the *Ortswehren* was that they demonstrated the fundamental national attitude to resist an invasion by the Nazi dictatorship at all costs.[110]

As a neutral, Switzerland was entitled by international law to trade with any belligerent. The international treaty of October 13, 1909, had required the Swiss to allow transportation of commodities other than arms between Germany and Italy on the Simplon and St. Gotthard railroads.[111] This traffic was absolutely vital to Switzerland's economy. The Allies protested, but isolated Switzerland had no choice. However, the Swiss made clear to the Germans that any invasion would result in the demolition of the Simplon and St. Gotthard tunnels and railways. Unlike the Swedes, the Swiss disallowed the passage of German troops across their territory. Swiss customs guards and American spies effectively enforced this prohibition.[112]

On April 25, 1940, the Allies and the neutrals signed the War Trade Agreement. The Allies guaranteed the transit of Swiss imports across their territories and the seas. The Swiss agreed to limit export of certain items to Germany to agreed quantities.[113]

On May 27, trade negotiations began in Berlin. The Germans strongly protested Swiss exports of war materials to France and England, and sought the abrogation of the Swiss-Allied War Trade Agreement.[114] Germany attempted to enforce its will on June 18 by prohibiting all coal exports to Switzerland, partly in retaliation for the Swiss shooting down of Luftwaffe aircraft.[115] With their economy heavily dependent on the import of coal, now only available from Germany, the Swiss were pressured into making concessions to the Germans such as increased deliveries of arms, aluminum, and dairy products. However, they upheld their right as a neutral to export arms to the Allies and refused to abrogate the War Trade Agreement.[116] The Germans even agreed with the compensation deals under which the Swiss could import German parts, manufacture them into machine tools and other items necessary for war, and export them to the Allies.[117]

Aerial border skirmishes with the Luftwaffe continued. Some 36 German bombers penetrated Swiss air space on June 1 and were attacked over Lake Neuchâtel. Swiss Me-109s shot down two German He-111 bombers. Orders found in the downed planes read: "Caution when flying over Swiss territory!"[118] The next day, one of several He-111s coming from Geneva-Rolle was shot down by a Swiss fighter near Yverdon.[119]

By June 4, the last remnants of the British Army arrived in England after evacuation from Dunkirk. Winston Churchill made his famous speech to the House of Commons that day, in which he declared, "we shall defend our island, whatever the cost may be. We shall fight on the beaches, we shall fight on the landing grounds, we shall fight in the fields and in the streets, we shall fight in the hills; we shall never surrender."[120] Having seen almost all of continental Europe swallowed up by tyranny, the Swiss took heart from this cry of defiance. It expressed their attitude precisely.

As Churchill spoke, 29 German planes—He-111 bombers and Me-110 Destroyers—were engaging a dozen Swiss planes, mostly Me-109s, over Chaux-de-Fonds in western Switzerland. Two of the Luftwaffe planes and one Swiss plane were shot down. This time, the German aircraft had the following order: "Lure the Swiss fighters into battle and shoot down as many as possible."[121]

On June 8, it was David against Goliath again: 15 Swiss aircraft engaged 28 Luftwaffe planes, resulting in the downing of an old Swiss biplane and a Swiss Me-109 and on the German side one crash and two forced landings.[122] The Germans claimed that the Swiss had attacked first over France, but the claim was inconsistent with evidence of the location of the Luftwaffe crashes. Diplomatic notes threatened that "the German Reich reserves the right to take any measures necessary for the prevention of attacks of this nature," and warned: "In event of any repetition of such incidents, the Reich will dispense with written communications and resort to other means of safeguarding German interests."[123]

The Swiss General Staff replied on June 9 that no Swiss plane had flown over foreign territory. That same day, a Swiss observation plane was shot down ten miles inside Switzerland by six Luftwaffe fighters.

A German plane was forced down in the same vicinity. Ten miles west of Bienne, a Swiss pilot was hit by two bullets in a dogfight. Near Triengen, another German plane was forced down.[124]

On June 9, in Berlin, a memorandum by the Luftwaffe General Staff, entitled "neutrality violation in Switzerland," noted "the Führer himself has taken care of the further treatment of this issue. The Führer should be supplied directly with all material detailed from Luftwaffe General Staff concerning the dogfights with Swiss planes."[125]

In retaliation, Hermann Goering devised "Operation *Wartegau*," under which German intelligence sent terrorists to blow up aircraft and other targets. "*Wartegau*" meant a future Nazi administrative unit. On June 16, seven German and two Swiss saboteurs traveled from Berlin to blow up the Altdorf munitions plant and the Payerne and Dübendorf air bases. The plan was amateurish, and the Swiss apprehended the saboteurs with large amounts of explosives on a train. The terrorists were sentenced to life imprisonment.[126]

Meanwhile, the Germans unsuccessfully demanded the return of the Messerschmitt aircraft the Swiss had purchased before the war.[127] While the Swiss-German air war was not statistically significant in the overall Allied-Axis conflict, the Swiss victories—eleven Luftwaffe aircraft shot down to only three Swiss—inspired confidence and strengthened further the will to resist.[128]

Five Swiss were killed and fifty injured at Geneva and Renens, near the French border, from bombs accidentally dropped by the British on June 12.[129] The British apologized.[130]

The French government now fled Paris, which was occupied by the Germans on June 14. Not a shot was fired to defend the city.[131] The next day, large posters appeared all over Switzerland advising the public of what to do in the event of a parachute invasion.[132] On the 16th, Guderian's panzers circled behind the Maginot Line near the Swiss border.[133]

For some time, the Gestapo had been spying on the Swiss. Gestapo agents were ordered to gather intelligence on "everything related to the military and political war of the New Europe against the Jewish democracies and Bolshevism" and "the cooperation of the

Swiss authorities with our enemies and their intelligence services."[134] As they did for other targeted countries, the Gestapo prepared lists of Swiss citizens to be seized at the beginning of a military occupation that included politicians, journalists, Jews, army officers and any other potentially hostile persons. The individuals were divided among those who would be executed, sent to prison camps or simply kept under close surveillance.[135]

The Swiss captured one team of Nazi infiltrators, dispatched by Goering. Later in June it was found that other saboteurs had cut cables set by the Swiss to ignite mines under a bridge over the Rhine. Such activities would continue throughout the war. It was assumed that Nazi sabotage would precede a military assault. To pave the way for invasion, public buildings and newspaper offices would be torched, while bombs would explode on trains and rail stations, and in the homes of leaders. Once the fifth column prepared the way, according to Nazi theory, a blitzkrieg would finish off the Swiss.[136]

On June 17, the new French Premier, Marshal Henri Philippe Pétain, sought an armistice. Hitler replied that he would have to consult with his ally, Mussolini, who had jumped into the war after the Wehrmacht victory was all but complete.[137] In Bern that same day, German Minister Otto Köcher and Italian Minister Attilio Tamaro discussed dividing up Switzerland between their two countries.[138]

The Führer and the Duce met the next day in Munich to discuss their triumph and also the question of Switzerland. They noted that Switzerland would be totally cut off by the occupation of France and should be expected to make accommodations to the new reality in Europe.[139] There was discussion and some confusion over possible action against Switzerland.[140] Hitler desired its conquest, but Mussolini's forces had performed badly against the French, especially in the mountainous terrain adjacent to Switzerland. The time was not yet ripe for an assault, at least if the Germans expected to coordinate their attack with the Italians.[141]

For Hitler, however, the question of the conquest of Switzerland was only a matter of timing. Aside from its democratic ideology and its refusal to acknowledge the inevitable supremacy of the Reich, Switzerland irritated the Führer because of her control of the transportation routes over the Alps, allowing her to restrict Axis traffic.[142]

Beginning on the 16th, the Germans moving south in France pushed to the Swiss border. Forty-two thousand French and Polish soldiers fleeing the Germans, including the entire Polish 2nd Rifle Division, crossed into Switzerland seeking asylum.[143] They brought with them huge quantities of arms and ammunition, which they surrendered to the custody of the Swiss. It was ironic that such a large force would lay down their arms and escape to internment in a country whose soldiers were ordered never to retreat and to fight to the death with the last cartridge and the bayonet. Nevertheless, the Polish division was interned with its formations intact. An officers' school was established and the Poles continued to train in internment. If Switzerland had been invaded, the Poles would have been quickly rearmed and would have had a chance to fight the Nazis again.

On June 22, 1940, the French government capitulated, the Battle of France having lasted only six weeks.[144] The armistice was signed two days later. The final version left Switzerland with only one non-Axis border: the unoccupied area known as Vichy France. The German negotiators received a demand from the Wehrmacht High Command (OKW) just fifteen minutes too late (after the armistice was signed) that German troops occupy French territory adjacent to Switzerland in order "to lock Switzerland completely."[145] Nonetheless, the Swiss were now effectively surrounded and stood in the way of the geographical integration of the Axis powers.

The German SS intelligence service (*Sicherheitsdienst,* or SD) mocked Switzerland in its internal publication *Announcements from the Reich,* dated June 24, as a criminal "cheese state" that, because of her stand against Germany, should "vanish."[146] Three days later, the SD insisted:

> One cannot forgive this state, that it has turned into the reservoir of all restless elements, that for years to come will pose the biggest opposition against Germany. Again and again the demand is raised, "Switzerland must quickly be swallowed," "Switzerland must not be allowed to stay out of the reorganization of Europe."[147]

On June 24, the day after his triumphal march into Paris, Adolf Hitler had a celebration. Before the party began, he had been in a rage because Mussolini's inability to win on the battlefield had meant an equal inability to win in French-Italian negotiations. This obstructed Hitler's plans to surround Switzerland completely and control her external transit. A rail connection stood intact, giving the Swiss access through Vichy France. Hitler also blamed the OKW, the German military command, for this situation.[148] The Germans had been unsuccessful in a last-minute attempt, ordered by Hitler, to destroy the rail connection allowing Switzerland access to the outside world. Saboteurs would continue to try to explode rail bridges but would be unable to halt Swiss trade.[149]

Since virtually the entire Swiss population could have been expected to fight had the Wehrmacht invaded, one can easily imagine Swiss resistance as infantry units and individual sharpshooters firing at German soldiers from behind rocks in the mountains. While much resistance would have taken this form, army units were often assigned to fixed positions with orders not to retreat or surrender. Many of these fixed positions were fortified.

The principal area of Swiss mountain defenses was bounded by three immense fortified areas at key mountain passes: Sargans in the east, Gotthard in the central south, and St. Maurice in the west.[150] Instead of three single forts, each area was a series of fortifications stretching over hundreds of square kilometers, most of which were rugged and impassable mountain terrain.

The eastward stronghold of this *Réduit National* was the Sargans fortifications. Amid steep mountain rocks jutting up into the sky, the Rhine Valley opens up here at the border with Austria. The tiny principality of Liechtenstein forms part of the border. Construction of the fortifications began with the Austrian *Anschluss* in 1938 and was completed in 1943. Within the triangle made by these fortifications, all ground was within range of heavy cannon. The cannon, many disguised, peeked out of towering mountain cliffs. No matter how an invader came in, he would be greeted by heavy artillery fire aimed precisely over many kilometers.[151]

In addition to the large fortifications—which were essentially underground buildings inside mountains with scores of rooms holding hundreds of soldiers and complete with air-ventilation systems and electric generators—there were about 150 medium-sized fortifications and hundreds of small ones, all ready to spew out cannon, mortar, and machine-gun fire. Some of the Sargans fortifications are still used for military training and exercises.

This was definitely not panzer country. Tanks would have had access only through narrow valley routes, with little or no room for maneuver, and the bridges and roads were rigged with explosives. Nor were the fortifications vulnerable to Luftwaffe attacks. Positions were concealed in cliffs and protected by thick steel and several meters of concrete or rock. German espionage secured photographs and maps of some of the Sargans fortifications but were not informed about the extensive munitions reserves. Knowledge of its strength, together with ignorance of what else may have been hidden in the rocks, contributed to deterrence.

What is called the Plain of Sargans could more aptly be called the Valley of Death. German invaders attacking from Austria would have been pummeled from all sides with projectiles ranging from 7.5mm rifle cartridges to 10.5cm heavy-gun shells. The border brigades could be mobilized in a mere 6 to 10 hours and would make use of plentiful natural cover as well as bunkers and blockhouses, many disguised as cottages, from which would spew machine-gun fire.[152]

Germans coming over the hills from Lake Constance would have found themselves bogged down in a swamp, unable to move and subjected to fire from all sides. The farmland in this area had been a malaria-infested swamp in earlier times, and a system of canals and dikes had been constructed that could release water within hours to flood the entire plain. The army tried the flooding procedure as an experiment in 1940. It worked like a charm—much to the chagrin of the local farmers.

The Gotthard fortifications in central southern Switzerland are in some of the most rugged mountains of the country. The terrain features glaciers at the top, massive cliffs and rock formations, and is more vertical than horizontal. Bunkers for cannon and machine guns are still hidden today on mountainsides over the few passes where an invader could attempt to enter.

Traditionally, commerce through the Gotthard Pass was impossible except across the Devil's Bridge, near where Russian armies had defeated Napoleonic soldiers nearly two centuries earlier. Built with the help of French and German investors, the Gotthard tunnel opened rail traffic through this harsh environment in 1882. The Swiss threat to destroy the Gotthard tunnel in the event of a German invasion had to be taken very seriously in Berlin.

At the southern tip of the Gotthard, in northern Ticino, loomed Fort Airolo, its long-range guns facing in the direction of any Italian invasion. This was only the beginning of nature's vast mountain fortresses which, with the firepower of the Swiss infantry, mountain troops and artillery, would have been a death trap for any Axis invaders.

While not of the massive size as those further south, fortifications at the northern borders were extensive and sophisticated. Underground living quarters and munitions storage were built under cannon with precise, long-range firing capacity on hills or mountainsides overlooking the Rhine River. One such fortification, today operated as a private museum open to the public, is Reuenthal, near Baden in northern Switzerland. It was one of a string of fortifications along the Rhine built in September 1939 at roughly the same places where the Romans built forts for protection against barbarians some two thousand years before.[153]

Cannon in bunkers were ready to fire at crossings of the Rhine. Machine-gun positions surrounded the cannon bunkers. The purpose of the border defense was to slow down the Germans to give the main defense time to form. Despite the losses they would have inflicted had the Germans invaded, it appears likely that the Swiss defenders at these border positions would all have been killed. The soldiers assigned to the border understood their role.

In response to continued German provocations, General Guisan issued an Order of the Day to the troops on June 3 declaring that the Swiss were "an armed people willing to preserve its independence and we must and can defend ourselves." It warned the people not to be influenced by the war of nerves, apparently referring to German warnings that Swiss attacks on Nazi bombers were being investigated by the Germans to determine whether the planes were over Switzerland or France.[154] The order continued:

Nobody can conceive without horror a foreign occupation, and the Swiss can and must defend themselves. The topography of the country is a first-rate ally, and the new methods of warfare will not take the Swiss unprepared. . . . To defeatist propaganda every one should oppose the spirit which animated the mountain-folk, who in 1291, when left to themselves, placed their confidence in themselves and in God. Thus will the country be strong and the Army quite ready. One order is ample: "Hold fast!"[155]

General Guisan issued a second order on the same day expressing strong religious feelings and reminding the soldiers that "spiritual preparation" was superior to "material preparation." The General reminded the soldiers of the practice of the medieval warriors: "Our fathers knew this, and they bent the knee praying to God before every battle. If until now, nearly alone among the small countries of Europe, Switzerland has escaped the horrors of invasion, she must attribute it above all to divine protection."[156]

Chapter 5

Fall 1940

Target Switzerland

AFTER THE FALL OF FRANCE, THE GERMAN HIGH COMMAND immediately ordered preparations for an invasion to end the existence of neutral Switzerland. It had become apparent that no country in Europe could stand up to a full-blooded Wehrmacht offensive, and the time had come for the vaunted "herdsmen" to see what a blitzkrieg could do. Germany would seize the northern four-fifths of the country, and Italy would seize the area south of a line from the Lake of Geneva to the east, including the Italian-speaking canton of Ticino.[1]

Swiss intelligence obtained information that, on June 24, 1940, Hitler discussed the question of Switzerland with his principal advisers: Goering, Keitel, Ribbentrop, Hess and Goebbels. Foreign Minister Ribbentrop favored an occupation of Switzerland. General Keitel opined that the goal could be reached through preparatory measures—intimidation—"without risking the sacrifice of some hundred thousand German soldiers with it." While Swiss intelligence attempted to verify and keep abreast of the planning discussions taking place in Berlin, one fact remained clear: the Führer had his sights set on Switzerland.[2]

As the Germans celebrated the triumph over their historic antagonist, France, the guns were once again quiet; what nearly every observer and participant had expected to be a long, grueling campaign had instead concluded with an armistice after six weeks. Nevertheless, a concentration of German offensive forces began forming beyond the Swiss border between Geneva and Basel in the weeks following the

French armistice. This latest German buildup took place just as the Swiss, responding to the declared armistice and thinking the immediate crisis had passed, were demobilizing to an active troop strength of 150,000.[3]

General Walther von Brauchitsch, Commander-in-Chief of the German Army, informed his army group commanders about the intended invasion. The attack would be led by General Wilhelm Ritter von Leeb, whom Hitler would soon promote to field marshal. Von Leeb, who later commanded Army Group North in Russia, reconnoitered the terrain and gave the command for the "*Sonderaufgabe* (Special Task) Switzerland" to his Army Group C, which was allotted the 1st, 2nd, and 12th armies for the task. Various deployments proceeded near the border during the following two weeks, including the return of two mountain divisions from northern France.[4]

On June 25, the effective date of the armistice in France, Otto Wilhelm von Menges, a captain on the German General Staff, submitted a precise plan for an attack on Switzerland to the Army High Command. Proposing a surprise pincer attack by Wehrmacht troops from Germany and France and by Italian troops from the south, the idea was to fragment the Swiss Army and preclude it from being unified for further resistance in rugged mountain terrain. It would have as an objective, for political and strategic reasons, the speedy occupation of the economic resources and arms industry around Solothurn and would deny the Swiss time to destroy railroads, bridges and—especially—Alpine transit routes.[5]

The invasion plan included a detailed description of the German units and the precise points of their attack. It noted the weakness of the Swiss forces near the French border (by then there were German troops near Geneva and Lyons) and observed that reinforcing them would only weaken Swiss positions at the German border.[6]

The operation was initially created as a contingency plan that was meant to be carried out only if the armistice with France broke down. However, Swiss intelligence reported the Führer's outbursts of fury against Switzerland, which also could have led to a sudden order to attack. In either event, Menges' specific operational plan would have been executed. With the French armistice, the Führer now had sufficient forces to do so.[7]

On June 28, Leeb noted in his diary that "the 12th Army gets many mobile units and two mountain divisions. Should the total be aimed at Switzerland?" In the ensuing days, he continued to prepare for execution of his plan. At a July 11 General Staff meeting, Leeb noted that maneuvers should not be carried out under the watchful eyes of Swiss customs officials, and that the destroyed railroad bridges leading to the Swiss border had not been restored. He added in a revealing passage that these two points must be rectified "if the special task for Heeresgruppe [Army Group] C, even if at an uncertain time, is still being considered." The "special task" was, of course, the invasion of Switzerland.[8]

Always one to play off his generals against one another, Hitler ordered the creation of another plan for invasion, to be prepared by Brigadier General Bernhard von Lossberg, who served on the Wehrmacht General Staff under General Alfred Jodl from 1939 until the end of the war.[9] In a postwar book, Lossberg noted that early in the war it was recognized that passage through the Netherlands and Belgium to circle around the Maginot Line would be easier than moving through Switzerland. However, connections between the Axis countries would be better facilitated if the Swiss railroads could be made available not just for economic but also for military transport. Hitler was angry about reports of deliveries of precision engineering products from Switzerland to England. Moreover, he considered Switzerland a center of international espionage against Germany.[10]

Following Hitler's orders, Jodl assigned Lossberg the task of developing an alternate plan for an attack on Switzerland. Lossberg recognized the geographic fact that only a small part of the country was militarily accessible: the plateau between the Jura and the Alps located from Basel to Geneva. Strong resistance there was expected from 50,000 soldiers supplemented by reserve forces. Lossberg wrote: "We recognized that the mountain-habituation and the freedom-loving character of the troops would make for stubborn resistance and probably also later small wars to contend with."[11] The study was transmitted to Jodl and, probably after presentation to Hitler, stayed on Jodl's desk. The war in the East caused Swiss attack plans to be put aside for the moment.[12]

In France, repression began immediately after the armistice and German occupation. Posters appeared everywhere directing that firearms and radio transmitters be surrendered to the closest German occupation headquarters within 24 hours and also stated: "All those who would disobey this order or would commit any act of violence in the occupied lands against the German Army or against any of its troops will be condemned to death."[13]

Partisan groups would disregard these threats and take up arms against the Nazis.[14] The severity of the Nazi decree demonstrates how greatly they feared resistance by civilians.

A week before the surrender of France, German troops discovered documents abandoned by French ministers at La Charité-sur-Loire, a town west of Dijon, detailing the secret agreements between the Swiss and French for mutual assistance if the Germans attacked Switzerland, negotiated earlier by General Guisan. Because these documents could be used to challenge the "purity" of Swiss neutrality, the Germans would exploit these documents for political ends.[15] At his conference with the Italian Ambassador Dino Alfieri on July 1 in the Führer's headquarters, Hitler was outraged about the papers found at La Charité.[16] In November, German Foreign Minister Ribbentrop discussed the documents with Hitler and cited them to support the plan to liquidate Switzerland. The Swiss became aware that the plans had fallen into German hands, and General Guisan could only wonder through the rest of the war when the secret would be used as a pretext for a Wehrmacht attack.[17]

On June 25, the future looked gloomy. Not only was Western Europe overrun by Nazis but the Nazi partner in the East—the Soviet Union—had conquered Finland and occupied part of Poland. The demonstrable effect of blitzkrieg warfare was frightening and had so far swept every enemy before it. The Swiss democracy stood alone in a continent of dictatorships.

On the night of June 24–25, 1940, when the German-French armistice became effective, General Guisan met with Chief of Staff Jakob Huber and other General Staff members to plan the defense of Switzerland from the National Redoubt.[18] Guisan would write: "What mattered really was that the spiritual decision had been taken: the Chief of Staff and I had to be clear now in our own minds to what extreme degrees we must be prepared for all possible consequences of the *Réduit* policy."[19]

A *"Réduit"* in the science of fortifications means a fortress built inside another, with the goal of prolonging the defense of the main fortress and driving the aggressor out.[20] The strategy of the *Réduit* had been debated in theory since 1815. Defense at the frontier meant defense of 1,800 kilometers of border and fighting on the plateau, which the French experience against the Germans had earlier proved to be ineffective. The *Réduit* strategy, in contrast, was absolute and extreme: to concentrate the army in the most favorable defensive position, the Alps. The army would retreat to the Alps and the pre-Alps, extending east and west at the fortified zones of Sargans and Saint-Maurice, with its center the ancient fortification of St. Gotthard. Smaller forces would fight at the frontiers and in the plateau to delay the enemy's progress. The decisive battle would take place in the *Réduit*, where the army would defend to the last. This was resistance, not retreat: the *Réduit* would not be a refuge for the army, but rather its chosen place of engagement.[21]

However, the *Réduit* strategy meant abandoning, after a fight by a limited number of troops, four-fifths of the Swiss population, including women and children, most of the industry (which would be destroyed) and a large part of the national heritage—profound considerations indeed for any military planner. The strategy was based on Guisan's appreciation of the primary strategic motive of the Axis aggressors—to establish a direct territorial liaison between Germany and Italy. The *Réduit* strategy was based on the idea that the defense would be concentrated on the sector that was the principal objective of the aggressor. Using the strategy, the Swiss would destroy any hope of Axis north-south communication by controlling the St. Gotthard and Simplon passes.[22] The risk that the rest of the country would be lost would have to be taken, in view of the deterrent value of the defense plan that would deny the aggressor his most important objective.[23]

The configuration of the Alpine terrain was favorable for the execution of Guisan's plan. German blitzkriegs elsewhere in Europe had demonstrated the superiority of modern offensive weapons, especially tanks and planes. Swiss anti-tank and anti-aircraft defenses were

Swiss Defenses

△ △ △ △ Army Position
────── Réduit National

GERMANY

FRANCE

AUSTRIA

ITALY

L. Constance

Danube R.

Rhine R.

Konstanz

St. Gallen

Freiburg

Mulhouse

Belfort

Basel

Besançon

Pontarlier

St. Claude

Zurich

L. Zurich

Solothurn

BERN

Fribourg

Thun

Lausanne

Geneva

L. Geneva

Rhone R.

Chamonix

Brig

Fortress
Sargans

VADUZ

Rhine R.

L.
Lucerne

Luzern

Fortress
St. Gotthard

Fortress
St. Maurice

L. Como

L.
Maggiore

Bergamo

0 10 20 30 40
Miles

Kaumeller 1998

The "Army Position" anticipated an attack from German territory, but was no longer viable after the fall of France in 1940. The defense of the *Réduit National*, ordered by General Guisan on July 17, 1940, concentrated Swiss forces in the Alps.

insufficient, especially for defense of the plateau, so defensive terrain had to be selected which would effectively counter superior German armaments. The high mountains would make it virtually impossible for the enemy to deploy these armaments with full force.[24]

The *Réduit* strategy incorporated the previous orders that there would be no surrender. The border troops, who were supplied with ample ammunition, would resist until eliminated. The troops in the Mittelland (the Plateau) would do the same, further slowing the German advance. Finally, the troops in the *Réduit* would not only hold firm but would also conduct counterattacks in the Plateau and even the Jura. The *Réduit* was the chosen place of primary engagement and resistance, not a place of retreat.[25]

In short, as befit a small country facing far more numerous foes, Swiss strategy was one of dissuasion; total victory was not expected. Such a small nation could not win a war with Germany, but it could promise higher losses than would be worth the cost to the aggressor.[26] While the Swiss General Staff planned to wage a war in which the army, or at least the forces concentrated in the *Réduit*, would remain intact, guerrilla war would also have occurred in the Alps and the Jura. No official plans had been made for guerrilla warfare in what would be occupied territory, but it had already been discussed among young officers and even by General Guisan himself.[27]

On July 12, General Guisan wrote Minister of Defense Minger outlining the new strategy of the *Réduit National*, which would replace existing plans. In the previous phase of the war, Guisan explained, border troops had been placed in fortifications, while the main Swiss strength was in the "Army Position," stretching from Sargans in the east to Lake Zurich and the Limmat River, then along the Jura Mountains to Lake Neuchâtel, and finally to Lake Geneva. In case of aggression, prior to this point, help could have been expected from France.[28]

The fall of France and the entry of Italy into the war changed the situation. Attack could now come from any front, and there would be no assistance from any country. Further, since the signing of the French armistice, Germany and Italy had an increased interest in provoking new conflicts. The German Army in particular was at the height of its power, constantly needing new targets to showcase its strength. Democratic Switzerland already stood out in the redrawn map of Axis-controlled Europe, and both Germany and Italy coveted the transit lines across the Alps. Guisan continued:

> Switzerland cannot escape the threat of a direct German attack unless the German high command, while preparing such an attack, becomes convinced that a war against us would be long and expensive, would uselessly and dangerously create a new battleground in the heart of Europe, and thus would jeopardize the execution of its other plans. . . . If we must be dragged into the struggle, we will sell our skin as dear as possible.[29]

The new military situation made the current division of the army between the Border Position and the Army Position untenable. The value of the border troops and their fortification works remained. However, the Army Position, which had been designed to protect most of the national territory against an attack from the north, would no longer be the crucial line of defense. The risk of an attack over any border, especially using modern methods featuring armored units, required a reduction in the density of forces assigned to fixed lines. Accordingly, General Guisan decided that "the defense of the territory will be organized according to a new principle, that of staggering in depth." He instituted three main resistance echelons, including:

> —the frontier troops, which would preserve their present positions;
> —an advanced position of cover, which will use the outline of the present army position between Lake Zurich and the massif of Gempen and which will extend as a western front, bounded generally by the Bernese Jura and Neuchâtel–Morat–La Sarine until it reaches Bulle;
> —a position of the Alps, or réduit national, that will be flanked at the east, west and south by fortresses, including Sargans, St. Maurice and the Gotthard.[30]

The mission of the border troops would be to maintain their position. The troops holding the advanced position would block attacks which sought to penetrate toward the country's interior. The troops in the Alpine *Réduit* would hold their positions with the prepared stores, without retreat, for a maximum duration. Guisan also envisaged a fluid resistance:

> Between these three echelons, the intermediate defensive system will include support points of anti-tank defense, constituting redoubts or nests of resistance, kept on all fronts. Their methods of combat will be inspired by those of guerrilla warfare as well as of the most recent lessons of the war.[31]

This mobile, intermediate defense line, in the form of light detachments and territorial troops, would carry out widespread destruction of bridges, roads and factories. As an unavoidable consequence, much of the civil population could not be protected. Some Swiss could be evacuated according to local circumstances, but in no event could the entire population enter the *Réduit,* which would compromise the success of operations and expend stores.[32]

Guisan has been recently criticized for planning to "abandon" Swiss civilians to Nazi occupation. To the extent that his strategy was the inverse of the border strategies adopted by other countries under German threat, the accusation against the Swiss commander-in-chief is superficially correct. However, Guisan's strategy reflected not only the topography of Switzerland but also the reality of the Nazis' blitzkrieg warfare. The other small countries of Europe, as well as France, that massed their troops in border areas fell within a matter of days or weeks to blitzkrieg tactics. Their armies were quickly defeated and their entire populations subsequently placed under Nazi rule. By conceding that all of Switzerland's people, particularly those in the north, could not be protected against a Wehrmacht invasion, Guisan's *Réduit* strategy ensured that the Swiss Army would be able to continue the fight indefinitely. Considering Clausewitz's dictum that mere occupation of ground is useless unless the main forces of the enemy have been destroyed, occupation of Switzerland's plateau would have availed the Germans little if the Swiss Army remained intact, well supplied and capable of operations from inaccessible terrain in the Alps.

Guisan's plan presented a strategic dilemma, in turn, to the German General Staff, which, despite drawing up elaborate plans for conquest in 1940 and in future years, would never confidently advocate a commitment of German forces against the *Réduit*. Switzerland would remain the only nation among Germany's neighbors whose military preparations deterred an attempt at annexation or invasion.

The Federal Council approved Guisan's strategy, and on July 20 Operations Order No. 12 was issued to the corps commanders. Troop lines would extend from the foothills below the Alps around the fortresses of Sargans in the east to St. Maurice in the west. The southerly position would be the high Alpine border near Italy. In the center would be the St. Gotthard Pass, surrounded by valleys with some industry and tunnels filled with munitions and fuel. Only a fifth of the population lived in this area.[33]

On June 25, the same day that Guisan secretly authorized total resistance in the *Réduit*, Federal President Marcel Pilet-Golaz delivered a radio address that suggested acceptance of the new reality in Europe and advocated appeasement.[34] (One is tempted to call Pilet-Golaz the Chamberlain of Switzerland because of his ambivalence. He alternated between co-signing orders with Guisan and making accommodating remarks about the New Order.)

Defeatist in tone and in spirit, the radio speech warned the people to adapt to the new situation and urged the Swiss to rely on the leadership and authority of the Federal Council. This was a chilling recommendation for many Swiss to hear, after they had seen the leaders of nation after nation turn over their countries to the Nazis, sometimes after nothing but a closed-door meeting with Hitler. Swiss soldiers, who favored resistance to the end, questioned precisely to what Pilet-Golaz was advocating that they adapt themselves: National Socialist domination of Europe, or of Switzerland?

Pilet-Golaz' speech was inconsistent with the April 18 order—which he himself had signed—that Switzerland would never surrender and would persevere at all costs.[35] After the Pilet-Golaz statement, those who favored the absolute no-surrender policy repeatedly demanded reissuance of the order, to no avail.[36]

Even though the order was not formally reissued, it had stated that there would be no surrender no matter what the federal government said. It was not rescinded and thus remained valid until the end of the war. The Federal Council could have surrendered, yet according to the terms of the order, the army would have been obligated to disregard this and would have fought to the end.[37]

Public support for Federal President Pilet-Golaz' accommodationist tendencies was weak. A popular pun in Switzerland stated that Pilet-Golaz must go: "*den Pilet muss man go la* [short for *gehen lassen* and pronounced "Golaz"].[38] A newspaper variation went "*Dann muss der Pilet gehen.*"[39] Many regarded him with suspicion. In any event, the Swiss then and even now do not assign as much importance to the office of national chief executive as we do in the United States.

Many began to fear, however, a growing sentiment of defeatism, and rumors spread that German agents planned to prevent General Guisan from issuing the necessary orders for national defense. Instead of the great medieval victories of Morgarten, Sempach, and Morat, it was believed that the Swiss might suffer a repetition of the 1798 French invasion, during which the national polity had been weak and divided. Some began to think of a coup d'état in which young officers would seize power, install a new Federal Council, and announce a new commitment to resist. The effort was unsophisticated and undemocratic but reaffirmed the abhorrence of Nazism among the military, as well as mistrust of the federal government. Sentiment grew among the soldiers to single out any Nazi sympathizers in the army and take any accommodationist officers prisoner.[40]

Within the military, the *Offiziersbund*, or *L'Alliance des Officiers*, a secret society of officers which stood for total resistance, was formed.[41] Its members pledged not to obey any orders to surrender. As a secret society, it was considered a breach of discipline when its existence inevitably came to the notice of higher commanders. Twenty of the officer members were arrested on August 3 but were subjected to lenient discipline.

General Guisan reprimanded the officers for not having confidence in him and reassured them of the high command's commitment to total resistance. Guisan later wrote that "in the event the will of resistance would have been given up under foreign pressure, these officers, by refusing to obey, would not only have been acting completely within their rights, but they also would have followed that which is the highest duty of every soldier."[42] When it became known that the officers had been willing to compromise their military careers in support of a total-resistance policy, and that the General had reassured them of his agreement, the people responded with new confidence in the army.[43]

Another secret society, the *Aktion Nationaler Widerstand*, or *L'Action de Résistance Nationale*, was formed by junior members of the General Staff to support the policy of total resistance. Many officers and nationally prominent citizens joined and signed the promise to refuse any order by the government to surrender. If senior officers did not oppose a German invasion, junior officers would seize their commands. If surrender was ever suggested, these underground groups were pledged to engage in armed revolt.[44]

Members of the resistance groups committed themselves, in the event of Nazi occupation, to engage in partisan or guerrilla warfare, with all the risks that would have entailed. They planned active resistance to the Gestapo and all potential occupation forces.[45]

The *Aktion* movement was a lawful, albeit secret, organization of 500 members from all walks of life: the Parliament, members of all political parties, journalists, soldiers. Its members worked unstintingly to influence public opinion in favor of the policy of absolute resistance. It had meetings but no publications and was not subject to censorship. It lasted until the end of the war.[46]

Switzerland had imposed limited press censorship to protect national secrets and avoid needlessly provoking Nazi retaliation. This censorship, however, was after-the-fact, not a prior restraint, and weak. Even during the height of the war, the press could speak mostly as it wished and frequently gave great offense to the National Socialists.[47] However, not even such minimal restrictions existed regarding individual conversations.

Aktion members included Max Waibel and Captain Hans Hausamann, who operated the "Bureau Ha," a special component of Swiss intelligence. Contacts were made all over Europe, and in Switzerland the Bureau functioned to instill the spirit of resistance. Its spy network, termed the "Wiking Line" (named after a Swiss spy) reached right into Hitler's headquarters.[48]

After the French armistice, a significant portion of the Swiss forces were demobilized. However, on July 2 General Guisan issued an order which included these words: "An armistice is not peace. The war continues between Germany, Italy and Great Britain. . . . Even if we cannot win a direct victory, we will fight."[49]

At that point, the Nazis were on the verge of launching the Battle of Britain, a spectacular Luftwaffe offensive across the English Channel that would ultimately fail to pave the way for a land assault. The panzers were still idle. German troops were again concentrated at the Swiss border.[50]

On American Independence Day in 1940, William Shirer was not celebrating. In Geneva with his wife and baby, the famous correspondent confided to his diary:

> Everyone here is full of talk about the "new Europe," a theme that brings shudders to most people. The Swiss, who mobilized more men per capita than any other country in the world, are demobilizing partially. They see their situation as pretty hopeless, surrounded as they are by the victorious totalitarians, from whom henceforth they must beg facilities for bringing in their food and other supplies. None have any illusions about the kind of treatment they will get from the dictators.

The newspapers advised preparing for hardship and loss of freedom. "The Swiss do not realize what the dictators really have in store for them," wrote Shirer, adding: "And now that France has completely collapsed and the Germans and Italians surround Switzerland, a military struggle in self-defense is hopeless."[51] Demoralization had infected not only many Swiss, but also one of America's leading correspondents. But in the face of such defeatism, General Guisan developed additional plans.

To instill and reaffirm the will to resist, General Guisan decided to muster the army's key leadership—commanders, higher officers, and the Chief of the General Staff—on July 25 at the Rütli Meadow.[52] The officers rallied at and disembarked from Lucerne, all traveling on the same boat. Despite the risk of sabotage, Guisan did not want to divide them.[53]

The eastern side of Lake Lucerne is an area surrounded by steep bluffs. From a dock, a footpath proceeds up to the Rütli Meadow. According to tradition, it was here that in 1291 Switzerland was founded.

On a beautiful day, Guisan faced the senior officers of the army standing in a semicircle on the Rütli Meadow, facing the lake. Canton Uri's flag of the Battalion 87 flew above. Addressing the measures taken "for the resistance in the *réduit*," Guisan ordered "resistance to all aggression coming from the outside, and to the various internal dangers, laxity, defeatism, as well as confidence in the value of this resistance."[54] He continued:

> Here, soldiers of 1940, we will inspire ourselves with the lesson and spirit of the past to envisage resolution of the present and future of the country, to hear the mysterious call that pervades this meadow.[55]

Guisan then gave the officers an order to pass on to the troops. Noting the importance of secrecy to a disciplined army and to the national defense, Guisan stated that many questioned the reason for recent modifications in the grouping of the forces and their mobilization. Recalling that on August 29, 1939, the Federal Council had ordered the mobilization of border troops, and soon thereafter the general mobilization, he continued that the army must safeguard the country's independence. Their neighbors, he said, had "respected this independence so far, but we must see to it that it is respected to the end." He warned:

> Currently there are, beyond our borders, more troops—and excellent troops—than ever before. We can be attacked on all fronts at the same time, which was not really conceivable a few weeks ago. The army must adapt itself to this new situation and take a position that allows it to hold on to all the fronts. It will thus fulfill its invariable, historic mission.[56]

Guisan prophetically stated: "In Europe, for a long time to come, millions of men will remain under arms, and as considerable forces can attack us from one moment to the next, the army must remain ready." Complimenting the army on the value of its past efforts and disdaining doubters, he urged renewed confidence in "the effectiveness of our resistance."[57]

Guisan later reflected: "The spirits and hearts were brought closer by the magnitude of the place, the cohesion and the camaraderie of leaders in this grand assembly." That evening, each returned to his command post or his home reminded that "the task is hardly begun."[58]

Portions of the speech were broadcast on the radio and printed in newspapers.[59] New hope arose as the military directives took shape and additional fortifications were constructed. The Nazis were incensed that Guisan insinuated the Wehrmacht might attack and that he had defiantly asserted that any aggression would be stoutly resisted.[60] Any German hopes that Switzerland would surrender without a fight, or would give up after brief resistance, were shattered.[61]

On July 30, German Minister Köcher wired Berlin from Bern that a strong protest should be lodged against this "renewed incitement of Swiss public opinion against Germany and Italy." Both Axis capitals did so shortly thereafter. A few weeks later, Köcher met with Pilet-Golaz, who replied that Guisan at Rütli had not sought to "describe Germany as the possible attacker or to incite public opinion against Germany," but only intended "to exhort officers and men to the unqualified fulfillment of their duties."[62] Yet both men knew this statement bordered on the ridiculous, when the Axis powers posed the only possible threat to Switzerland.

On August 1, Swiss National Day, hundreds of fires, the historic symbol of Swiss independence, blazed from Alpine peaks as leaders expressed their determination to defend the nation.[63] General Guisan and President Pilet-Golaz pledged that the armed forces and the government would fight "to the end."[64]

At the National Day celebration at the ongoing World's Fair in New York, speakers "compared the Swiss ideals of liberty, tolerance and neutrality to those of the United States." Swiss Consul General Victor Nef noted that the Swiss had their own militia for defense, "and they always have relied exclusively on [their] own strength. These people follow the good-neighbor policy [and] exchange spiritual as well as tangible goods with their neighbors. Otherwise they would starve." New York City's Mayor LaGuardia issued the following statement to Dr. Nef:

> The determined and long-continued aloofness of Switzerland from the turmoils of Europe tells the story of the greatness of your people, towering above the jealousies and selfish greeds of nations even as your mountains tower above their neighbors. Peace and liberty, these are almost synonymous in Switzerland. It is my prayer, shared by my countrymen everywhere, that the peace and liberty which you enjoy may remain as constant and secure as your Jungfrau and your Matterhorn.[65]

Meanwhile the Führer's Luftwaffe pounded away at London. Frustrated by the efforts of the RAF, and because it had become too late in the season to launch an invasion, the Germans had resorted to wreaking havoc on the great city on the Thames. International skier Arnold Lunn, referring to "the creeping leprosy of the Nazi infection," expressed the common attitude of English and Swiss alike as follows:

> When France fell and when we watched the fires of burning dockland on the night of September 7th, 1940, and wondered whether England could continue to take it, second only to the supreme horror of Hitler's evil face gloating over conquered London from the balcony of Buckingham Palace was the possibility that the swastika might fly from the roofs of Bern.[66]

As the military situation and the location of German troops changed, so too did German plans to invade Switzerland. Hitler was constantly changing his mind. It behooved the German General Staff to continue to update attack plans against Switzerland, in case the command should come unexpectedly. A revised plan of the German Army high command, the OKH, dated August 8, conceded: "The single [Swiss] soldier is a tough fighter and a good shot." Nine German divisions and additional Italian forces would be used.[67]

Captain Menges, drafter of the June 25 plan, submitted a revised plan entitled "The German Attack Against Switzerland" to the High Command on August 12. It again proposed a simultaneous Wehrmacht attack from Germany and France along with an attack from the south by the Italians. It would be a lightning invasion from several directions with the same goals as before: fragmentation of the Swiss Army and prevention of its withdrawal into the *Réduit*; seizure of the industry and arms production around Solothurn and Zurich; and preservation of the transportation system from destruction by the Swiss.[68]

Menges described the Swiss Army—underestimating it—as having a strength of 220,000 soldiers divided into six infantry divisions, three mountain divisions, three mountain brigades, one border brigade and a border battalion. It had no tank troop, and its air force was weak. Because of internal politics and economic factors, further demobilization would continue. However, remobilization could take place quickly, and the Swiss needed only five hours to mobilize the border troops. Menges proceeded to describe Swiss defenses in great detail:

> [The Swiss have] a functionally organized and quickly mobilized armed force. The level of training will have been raised by the long time they have been mobilized. Leaders only theoretically schooled. Methodical leadership. Shortcomings in weaponry (artillery, tanks, anti-tank defenses, air force, anti-aircraft guns). The individual soldier is a tough fighter and a good sharpshooter. The mountain troops are said to be better than those of their southern neighbor. The fighting value of the western Swiss (French type) is limited, while those living south of Constance (Communists) will be bitter enemies. Final evaluation: an army suitable only for defensive purposes and completely inferior to its German counterpart.[69]

German Plan for Conquest
"von Menges"

- – – – Future German–Italian Border
- △ △ △ Swiss Frontier Brigades
- ⋀⋀⋀⋀ Swiss Main Defense Lines
- Swiss Fortified Areas
- ⊠⊠ Swiss Corps

Korsimdes 1998

The plan for a German attack from the north and west and an Italian attack from the south, submitted by Captain Otto Wilhelm von Menges of the General Staff to the German Army High Command on August 12, 1940. (Adapted from Fuhrer, "Renseignement," *Relations Internationales*, Summer 1994, No. 78, 236.)

Menges also mentioned that, in armistice commission discussions, the Germans had attempted to persuade Vichy France to change the demarcation line to allow the Germans to envelop Switzerland. Vichy refused.[70]

It was reported from Bern on September 16 that the Swiss were anxiously awaiting the results of the Vichy-Berlin negotiations. Completely surrounded by Axis powers and their conquered territories, the Swiss feared loss of trade access with the nonbelligerent world. Economic strangulation was believed to be as likely as armed invasion. Still, that same day, the Federal Council approved a referendum for an amendment to the Constitution to make premilitary training a requirement for all males over 16, setting December 1 for the public vote.[71]

For some time the Germans had been thoroughly angered by General Guisan—for his secret agreement with the French for a joint defense against a Wehrmacht invasion, for his influence in keeping troops mobilized, and for his known determination to wage total war against any German aggression. Max Waibel, head of the Swiss "N1" intelligence unit, learned that Berlin was attempting to hatch an intrigue against Guisan, whom the Germans found "unbearable," and to replace him with a commander-in-chief who was more friendly to Germany. German Minister Otto Köcher attempted to instigate a cabal in Bern against Guisan and to convince the government to demobilize the troops.[72] Not surprisingly, this unsuccessful effort coincided with the preparation of more invasion plans against Switzerland.

A series of plans codenamed "Tannenbaum" was drafted for the German General Staff. On August 26, General Franz Halder, Chief of the General Staff, ordered planning for an assault to be undertaken by Field Marshal von Leeb's Army Group C.[73] At least two plans resulted from this command.

The operations plan dated September 6 recognized that Switzerland would resist with all her might. The 12th Army under Field Marshal Wilhelm von List would spearhead the German attack, which would include winged movements centered on Bern.[74] In contrast, the plan of October 4, to be executed by von Leeb, would have used extraordinarily short deployment times but relied on 21 divisions.[75] While driving along the Swiss border from Germany to France on October 6, General Halder reflected:

The Jura frontier offers no favorable base for an attack. Switzerland rises, in successive waves of wood-covered terrain, across the axis of an attack. The crossing points on the river Doubs and the border are few; the Swiss frontier position is strong.[76]

The next day, Operation Tannenbaum was sent to the General Staff, which, after reviewing it, ordered a new study that would use only half as many German divisions.[77]

Besides all the foregoing plans, there was the "Plan Zimmerman" of October 4, prepared for the German High Command, which did not even acknowledge the existence of the plan of the same date for Army Group C. This study realistically anticipated that resistance and fighting would continue under a German occupation.[78]

General Halder, as is known by his October 17 note, continued to focus on an invasion of Switzerland. He contemplated two major operational zones using eleven divisions. First, an infantry attack would be feinted in the Jura to pin down the Swiss Army, which would then be cut off from the Alps by a new assault and smashed on the plateau. The concept was not unlike the plan that defeated France, which involved an initial assault into Belgium to flush out French and British forces, while the main thrust emerged on their rear flank from the Ardennes. According to the plan against the Swiss, army remnants in the Gotthard and other parts of the *Réduit* would initially be left alone, for they could not survive over time.[79]

However, the Swiss Army was already concentrating arms and supplies in the *Réduit*, about which General Halder stated: "The immobilization, for an indefinite time, of powerful forces without hope surrounding the central position of Switzerland, and the certainty of being deprived of a vital, favorable liaison with the Italian ally is insupportable."[80] The Chief of the German General Staff clearly preferred the benefits of limited usage to the complete cessation of transit across the Alps.

All of these invasion plans were being developed during a period of intense focus on Switzerland by Hitler and Mussolini. The two met at the Brenner Pass on October 4, and the Duce wrote the Führer on the 19th: "I am sure you will not be surprised to find Switzerland on my list of remaining English outposts on the continent. With its incomprehensible hostility, Switzerland poses itself the problem of its existence."[81]

In sum, at least five separate German attack plans were devised in 1940. Three of the plans would have been directed from the north, east and west and placed the center of gravity in the pre-Alps in order to attempt to separate the Swiss Army from the Alps and destroy it in the Plateau. The Germans knew that if the Swiss Army were in the Alps, its infantry would be extremely difficult to dislodge.[82]

The other two attack plans, "Operation Switzerland" of August 12, and the Zimmerman study of October 4, would have been launched against western Switzerland from France in the rear of the Limmat River position of the Swiss Army.[83] There were also attack plans from Italy, including the plan of General Vercellino of June 10 and others. The Duce intended to seize large parts of southern Switzerland.[84]

The German attack plans variously called for between 10 and 21 divisions, each division typically including some 12,000 to 15,000 soldiers. If 15 Italian divisions were added, that would make between 25 and 36 divisions.[85] Thus, the Axis would have found it necessary to attack Switzerland with 300,000 to 500,000 trained men—a massive force in contrast to previous German invasions of small countries.

The Wehrmacht invasion plans were drafted by at least three different groups working independently of one another and with differing hypotheses. The plans differed dramatically on the capacity of the Swiss for resistance, the size of the forces necessary for an invasion, and the foreseeable duration of the campaign. The Germans agreed, however, that the Swiss Army would put up a strong, albeit unsuccessful, resistance, expressed a marked respect for the mountains, and feared popular resistance after hostilities officially ended. On the whole, the German experts advised against an attack, knowing that a war in the mountains would be a long-term enterprise with doubtful results.[86]

On October 19 the Swiss Army announced that home defense soldiers, including men aged 42–60, were being recalled to relieve younger troops who had been on duty since the war started.[87] On October 26, the Swiss government announced the arrest of officials and employees

of the Swiss Union of Friends of Authoritative Democracy, a Nazi
group directed from Germany. Federal police simultaneously conducted raids in several cities.[88]

At the same time, Germany was tightening its economic stran-
glehold on Switzerland. The United States was still not in the war,
allowing William Shirer to continue reporting from Berlin. His wife
and baby living in Geneva, to which he commuted regularly, were subject to the same privations as the Swiss, which Shirer described:

> This winter the Germans, to show their power to discipline
> the sturdy, democratic Swiss, are refusing to send Switz-
> erland even the small amount of coal necessary for the Swiss
> people to heat their homes. The Germans are also allowing
> very little food into Switzerland, for the same shabby rea-
> son. Life in Switzerland this winter will be hard.[89]

Scarcities led to the imposition of rationing in early November.
The "cultivation battle," a plan authored by Dr. F. T. Wahlen, chief of
crop production for the Federal war bureau, was initiated to employ
every available town square, yard, soccer field and other piece of land
in food production. Virtually every family participated with great
enthusiasm and a sense of patriotism. A typical family might transform the backyard into a potato, bean or tomato field and plant herbs
in the flower beds.

In the fall, townspeople would harvest wheat and corn planted
outside town. In the evening, they would return with a pound of
ground flour which they received in return for their harvest, a wel-
come supplement to their meager rations. With these efforts land cultivation almost doubled. The cultivation battle, often waged by
women and children while the father (and for rural families, the horse
too) was away on a mobilization order, was an essential part of the
program of spiritual national defense and led to sizable crops throughout the war years.[90]

On November 9, the Italian press and radio denounced the Swiss
for allegedly allowing flights of British RAF bombers over Switzerland
on their way to Italian targets. Basel's *National Zeitung* quoted the
Italian radio: "The Swiss must not think themselves inviolable—this is

our last warning." The Swiss high command confirmed that the British had violated Swiss air space and noted that Swiss anti-aircraft guns had fired at the planes. Swiss newspapers also asked why the Swiss should be blamed for the half-hour flights over their territory if the Axis could not stop the RAF pilots in their three-hour flight over German-occupied territory.[91]

On November 15, 1940, a petition with 105 names was filed with the Federal Council advocating appeasement of Germany. By April 1941, it had 173 signatures, although it came to be known as the infamous "Petition of the Two Hundred." Its demands included abolition of a free press and revocation of criminal sentences for pro-German treason.[92] The Federal Council never responded to the petition, and its signers were subjected to criminal investigation. The petition had the opposite of its intended effect—it outraged the press and the majority of Swiss, who reacted with an increased determination to resist.[93]

The same day the petition was submitted—November 15, 1940—the fifth-column *Nationale Bewegung der Schweiz* (NBS, or National Movement of Switzerland) issued an "ultimatum" to the Federal Council and President Pilet-Golaz.[94] The NBS ultimatum was referred to the Department of Justice and Police. Police had already acted against this organization four times earlier in the year, but it kept reappearing under different names. It was believed that the group, which brought leaflets into Switzerland attacking the Federal Council and advocating the triumph of National Socialism, would be prosecuted for subversion.

On November 17, General Guisan reported that the NBS did in fact endanger the security of the state.[95] Two days later, the Federal Council dissolved the NBS. Finding that the organization was attempting to overthrow democracy, the Federal Council forbade its activities, prohibited its publications and prohibited it from reorganizing under a different name. Violators would be tried under the decree of December 5, 1938, which meant trial before military tribunals. A recent military tribunal had sentenced seven defendants to life terms at hard labor for plotting to sabotage the country's defense.[96] Switzerland's action in banning the NBS at the height of Nazi power took courage in the face of Berlin's military might.

On November 27, the Federal Council also banned the Communist Party and any branches or renamed groups as a threat to democracy. Like the Nazis, the Communists were weak and not represented in the Parliament.[97]

The German press continued to wage a propaganda campaign against Swiss neutrality and its free press. Nazi journalists denounced the reporting in the *Neue Zürcher Zeitung* of German night bombings of England while ignoring British bombing of German hospitals and civilian targets. In a headline article entitled "Switzerland in Churchill's Service," the *Frankfurter Zeitung* stated:

> Never will the German people forget the attitude of the Swiss during this war. A nation of 80,000,000, while fighting for bare existence, finds itself almost uninterruptedly attacked, insulted and slandered by the newspapers of a tiny State whose Government claims to be neutral.[98]

The *Strassburger Neueste Nachrichten* (*New Evening News*), claiming that Switzerland was once part of the Reich and was now within the "field of force" of the Third Reich, similarly stated that "Switzerland cannot prevent the penetration of the idea of the new order of Europe." European politics would no longer be dominated by the British policy of the balance of power but would be based on an "unbalance," under Axis leadership. To this new order, Swiss neutrality must bow, since Europe "is no longer interested, especially from the strategic and political viewpoint, in maintaining the isolation of certain anomalous regions."[99]

Few military analysts believe that Switzerland, outside the *Réduit*, could have held out for long against a multi-directional, combined-arms attack by Germany and Italy, no matter how bravely the Swiss fought. Occupying the country afterwards, of course, would have been a different problem for the fascists. An unidentified Swiss officer expressed the sentiment in his country as follows: "Even if Germany was irresistible, we were determined to resist. It was a character test. Are we men or dirty dogs?"

Defeat would be only a matter of months, perhaps weeks, but the Swiss believed that they could kill 200,000 Nazis before surrendering and thus contribute a noble service to the cause of all free men. And even in 1940, when it seemed as if resistance was futile and Hitler invincible, the Swiss took the long view and knew that they would not die in vain, if they preferred death to surrender. Their children and their children's children would still be proud to be Swiss, and from the seed of their pride would flower the spirit of resistance that would one day liberate enslaved Europe from the Nazi tyranny.[100]

Consistent with this theme, a publication of the SSV (Swiss Shooting Federation) ended the tension-filled year with the question, "What happens now?" The simple answer: "Learn to shoot, Swiss, learn to shoot."[101]

Chapter 6

1941
The New Order in Europe

FEDERAL COUNCILLOR ERNST WETTER, SWITZERLAND'S PRESIDENT for 1941, opened the new year with the commitment that the country's 650-year tradition of independence would survive the "dark future."[1] The new year also saw the retirement of Rudolf Minger, the tough head of the Military Department who had been responsible for ever stronger defensive measures since the Third Reich came into existence in 1933. An accomplished marksman, Minger also had promoted rifle competitions throughout the country for defense training and readiness.[2]

From 1941 until the war was nearly over, Switzerland would be encircled by the Axis powers, subjected to regular air-raid alarms, and isolated from the outside world. The country remained subject to a Nazi media barrage, which, although meant to intimidate the Swiss, only engendered a stronger spirit of resistance involving not only marksmanship but also comradeship. "These weapons and these ties will never fail," the SSV's publication insisted.[3] It was the soldier and his morale, not the blitzkrieg or the Luftwaffe, that were decisive.[4]

In February 1941, British Foreign Minister Anthony Eden sent apologies to the Swiss for bombs accidentally dropped over the Swiss border. Four civilians were killed in Basel and eleven other people in Zurich.[5] Eden wrote that the British were "anxious to maintain in all circumstances the ancient ties of friendship and goodwill" with the Swiss. He asked for the forbearance of the Swiss to the British, "fighting as they are for the traditions of freedom and resistance to tyranny, of which the Swiss Confederation has in former times been the protagonist in European history."[6]

On March 22, Federal President Wetter told his party in Bern that the government would cooperate economically with the new European order, but only on Swiss terms. "In accepting economic collaboration with the rest of Europe we would not be accepting any new ideal." New restrictions had been placed on the former policies of world trade and a liberal trade policy. "But we can make the condition that the new order be based on the principle of collaboration of free States."[7]

A group of eleven Swiss journalists touring the Reich made it clear that Switzerland was not eager to join the New Order. This led Nazi Propaganda Minister Goebbels to deliver a speech on March 25 in which he stated: "If Switzerland has decided to remain outside of our orbit under any circumstances, I cannot prevent it, but in that case Switzerland should remember that it will be excluded from all the advantages which the New Order will give to Europe." The Bern *Nation* responded: "We hope that Dr. Goebbels will keep his word. That would be the most beautiful message possible for our country, which has only one desire—to be left alone."[8]

Meanwhile, the Soviets supported and praised Hitler's conquests. The U.S.S.R. was grabbing up the parts of Eastern Europe awarded it in the Nazi-Soviet Pact and German-Soviet trade continued. Stalin, despite irritating the Germans with his avarice for territory, made every effort to solidify his relationship with Hitler.[9] During this period, Communist agitation had also heated up in Switzerland, with Moscow's agents instigating dissent and calling for the overthrow of the Swiss government.[10]

On March 26, 1941, the government in Yugoslavia entered into a pact with the Axis and was promptly deposed in a coup with popular support. The new government proclaimed unconditional neutrality.[11] The Swiss vocally supported the coup.

One Socialist newspaper urged Swiss Foreign Minister (one-time Federal President) Pilet-Golaz to "take note" of the revolt in Yugoslavia and warned against "dangerous pilgrimages," such as to Berlin. "The people and army form one indivisible thing, so that even in small countries strong diplomats are nothing," said the paper. The article quoted a warning from a Swiss folk song: "Today you proudly ride your horse; tomorrow you are shot in the chest."[12]

The elation of the Swiss people at being joined in their defiance of Nazi Germany by the Yugoslavs was unfortunately short-lived. On April 6, German, Italian and Hungarian armies invaded Yugoslavia; at the same time, Germans (from Bulgaria) and the Italians (from Albania) attacked Greece.

The Swiss press and people condemned the invasions and cheered on the beleaguered states.[13] The Yugoslavs had a million men under arms, as well as mountainous terrain that should have greatly assisted their defense. Nevertheless, their army collapsed in the face of the assault, and by the 17th, after only 11 days, the country had capitulated. The Yugoslavs had bravely, if foolishly, deployed their army to defend their entire 1,000-mile border—a tailor-made opportunity for blitzkrieg. Once the panzers cut through selected points of impact, outflanked or surrounded Yugoslav divisions panicked, thus prompting a general collapse. Elements of the Yugoslavian confederation, primarily from Slovenia and Croatia, declared for the Nazis when the attack began, further hastening the dissolution of resistance.

In the light of the Yugoslavian debacle, General Guisan's plan to fight at the border, delay in the Plateau and pre-Alps, and concentrate in the *Réduit National,* seemed more astute than ever. The cliché "he who defends everything defends nothing" was entirely applicable to defense against blitzkrieg, and though the Swiss military strategy would have "cold-bloodedly" conceded large portions of the country and large civilian population centers to Nazi domination, such pragmatism would have assisted greatly had it been applied to the Yugoslav cause.

The Wehrmacht, which lost only 151 men killed in the entire campaign against Yugoslavia, had a harder time against Greece, which was backed by three full-strength British divisions with modern equipment. Unfortunately, giving the lie to the admonition against trying to defend everything, the Greeks had cleverly arrayed their strength against anticipated points of Axis attack. But they had no defenses on their Yugoslavian border. When the panzers came streaming down on their left flank, after the sudden collapse of their neighbor, the Greek defense became unhinged. Hard fighting took place in the retreat down the Greek peninsula, including a brief stand at Thermopylae, and then the survivors of the British divisions performed another Dunkirk-like retreat, to Crete. Athens surrendered on April 27.

The evening after the Greek surrender, Athens radio called on all residents "to surrender all arms immediately and to fly the German flag wherever the Greek flag is flown."[14] In Switzerland, many citizens were despondent at what seemed to be the invincibility of the Third Reich and its allies and its growing network of conquered territory.[15]

Karl Megerle, a Nazi commentator, had warned Switzerland in the April 9 issue of Berlin's *Börsen Zeitung* "to take note of what has happened to Yugoslavia." Megerle claimed that civil unrest in Yugoslavia had "sabotaged a foreign policy of common sense." He attacked a recent article in the Swiss press which praised the honor and bravery of the Yugoslavs and warned that Switzerland might find herself in a situation similar to Yugoslavia's. Switzerland, he argued, could not be truly neutral if her press was allowed to continue to express "resentment and enmity toward Germany."[16]

The Swiss, however, remained unshaken in their desire for unconditional independence and continued to place great faith in the power of the individual citizen soldier to preserve the country's freedom. The Swiss Shooting Federation, ever on the scene, exhorted:

> The best and first guarantor of our neutrality and our independent existence is the defensive will of the people, the well-trained and armed army, and the proverbial marksmanship of the Swiss shooter. Each soldier a good marksman! Each shot a hit![17]

Heer und Haus (Armée et Foyer—"Army and Home"), an information and communications center, was initiated by the Aktion Nationaler Widerstand (the secret national resistance society) to focus the will of the people to resist and to further cement the bond between citizen and soldier.[18]

Heer und Haus entertained soldiers, but its real function was to instill the spirit of resistance into soldiers and the public alike. Conceived by intelligence operative Hans Hausamann and the journalist August Lindt, Heer und Haus was headed by Oscar Frey, a vocal spokesman in favor of resistance against Hitler's New Europe. Private lectures were not subject to censorship, and every Saturday afternoon and Sunday through the rest of the war, lectures would be held on subjects such as the military situation, the *Réduit* concept, and the will to fight. Lecturers stated explicitly that Hitler was the enemy. Persons who attended lectures spread the word. Thus, an entire communications network, free of censorship, pervaded the country.[19]

The April *National Geographic* featured a picture of a Swiss couple in their home, with the heading "Swiss 'Minutemen' Keep Their Guns at Home, Ready for Instant Action." The caption read: "Under his wife's supervision, this citizen soldier sews on a uniform button and inspects rifle, helmet, and cartridge bandoleer." "A Sword Symbolizes His Ancient Right to Vote and Bear Arms" ran the caption on another picture, with the explanation: "The custom dates back to the days when only those entitled to vote were permitted to carry arms in peacetime."[20]

This feature accurately depicted Switzerland. On May 4, 1941, the shooting association of the Canton of Fribourg admonished its members not to waste the "precious cartridges" they were allotted. For the Swiss, accurate shooting was a science. In May, the army published a manual entitled *Shooting Instructions for the Infantry* (*Schiessvorschrift für die Infanterie*) filled with mathematical formulae and scientific data for firing the rifle, carbine, light machine gun, heavy machine gun, anti-aircraft gun and anti-tank gun. Distances ranged, depending on the weapon, from 50 to 4,000 meters. One diagram demonstrated the great efficiency of single rifle shots over machine-gun fire: a 6-shot group with a spread of 30cm from the carbine versus a 250-shot group with a spread of 90cm from the machine gun, both fired in 30 seconds at 300 meters.[21]

On April 27, state-controlled Rome radio had sternly warned Switzerland that her "existence" would be jeopardized unless she observed the Axis definition of strict neutrality. "The Swiss must not forget that if they continue to eat it will be due to Italy's benevolence," said Enzio Mario Gray, a member of the Supreme Fascist Council and Mussolini's mouthpiece. He charged that "the majority of the Swiss press is paid by British Jewry and serves British interests. Locarno has become a center of espionage. Switzerland must be careful."[22]

In another account of this radio address, Gray said: "Your neutrality is not a divine privilege, and so under no circumstances can it be considered eternal." The Swiss government was responsible for the "criminal outbursts of the press" which "treat Italy's victories with extreme flippancy" while reporting British victories in detail. At carnival time, Swiss marchers insulted fascism, he said. "All this leads the Axis Powers to realize that Switzerland has no intention of accepting and subordinating itself to the New Order which is meant for the whole European Continent." His voiced boomed: "Neither Hitler nor Mussolini will allow the survival of such a dangerous nest of conspirators of the old, defeated world."[23]

The German press similarly attacked the Swiss press and people on April 30 for anti-Nazi statements and Swiss aloofness from the New Order, warning that "one day our patience will come to an end." The *Börsen Zeitung* described world-famous Swiss theologian Karl Barth as "a fanatic enemy of Germany" and said that "if such people are allowed to preach public hatred against Germany, then it is useless to argue with the Swiss press about the conception of neutrality."[24]

The Axis attack continued, as the Italian press predicted that "Switzerland's turn was coming" because her press had "played up the Italian retreat in Cyrenaica, yet scarcely mentioned the Italian troops' glorious efforts to regain lost terrain." (In early 1941, General Erwin Rommel and his Afrikakorps had arrived in North Africa and immediately reversed recent Italian defeats.) In another attack, the *Börsen Zeitung* wrote: "As the result of previous experience with other European countries, we hold the Swiss government responsible for public opinion. However, this warning does not seem to help."[25]

Yet such threats only hardened the Swiss will to resist. "The Swiss are united that in case of attack, they will fight to the last man on every line."[26]

In his "Eagle's Nest" at Berchtesgaden on May 11–12, in a meeting with Vichy Admiral Darlan, Hitler expressed his disappointment with France's collaboration and stated that Germany would obtain permanent possession of several French ports as well as of Alsace and

Lorraine. In return, France would be allowed to take Belgium's Wallonia and French Switzerland, albeit without the Reich's assistance. The Vichy Régime was hardly in a position to attack the Swiss; however, Hitler's promise demonstrates his assumption that Switzerland would soon be another territory of the Reich, to be divided as he saw fit.[27]

By May 1941, the entire Swiss field army of nine divisions—358,000 soldiers and 46,000 horses—was concentrated in the *Réduit* with provisions for both the people and the army in this region to last for five months. There was just a small number of troops left at the frontier, and only three light brigades stationed in the Plateau for purposes of demolition and the destruction of factories, tunnels and bridges.[28] A blitzkrieg would at that time have mostly hit thin air—the Germans would instead need to contemplate combat with the Swiss Army on its chosen ground, in the Alps.

The *Réduit* utilized vast, concealed underground storage facilities. The prospect of a five-month siege would have dissuaded Germany or any other invader, and in any event the Swiss could likely have conducted raids to acquire more supplies. Further, there would have been nothing worth taking. The Gotthard and Simplon railroad lines would have been destroyed. Factories would have been stripped of essential components. Losses would have been high, especially in the mountains, and the invader would not be able to count on a short campaign. In the Alps, with its narrow passages and vertical terrain, the defending infantry could resist both panzers and the Luftwaffe. The mountains were pocked with heavy fortifications and camouflaged positions.[29]

As Swiss defense tactics became more refined, so did German offensive tactics. On May 20, the Germans practiced a new form of offense, albeit one they had demonstrated on a smaller scale before, in Norway and the Netherlands: they launched an airborne invasion of the island of Crete. Over 600 German transports and gliders skimmed across the Mediterranean to deliver 7,000 parachutists and mountain troops, against a British Empire garrison of 40,000 men. The carnage on the drop zones was horrendous; many paratroopers of the first wave were killed by ground fire before they even came to earth. But by the end of the week 22,000 Germans had landed while some 600 bombers and fighters of the Luftwaffe supported the assault and attempted to keep the Royal Navy at bay. By June 1, in a familiar story, 18,000 British troops were evacuated, this time to Egypt. The Third Reich had won again.

The news of Crete, history's first conquest by airborne invasion, resonated in Switzerland, as did the seeming German willingness to pay any price in blood, against whatever odds, in pursuit of a quick victory. In fact, Hitler had been repulsed by the steep price his paratroopers had paid for Crete and resolved not to attempt an airborne invasion again. But the Führer's attitude was unknown to the Swiss, who more than ever wondered what the Nazis had in store with their combined arms that could force a decision in the Alps.

That month's issue of London's *Contemporary Review* noted that Switzerland had maintained her liberty, despite being surrounded by the most powerful enemies of freedom in European history. After the shocking defeats of 1940, the Swiss recommitted themselves to resist and steadily improved their defenses.[30] The article went on to surmise, "little use the Nazi army could make of holding Zurich and the lower hills of the Jura, while a few divisions of Swiss snipers could hold the peaks of the Alps for an almost indefinite period."[31]

Despite flattering comments in the British press, however, the Swiss had yet to witness a successful land operation performed by the British Army against the Germans. In mid-1941, of course, the United States was still neutral, largely unarmed and remote. With the exception of Franco's Spain and Salazar's Portugal, the entire continent, except for democratic Switzerland, was an Axis domain. Who knew if the "Thousand Year Reich" was indeed an irrevocable fact? Even if the Nazis were reluctant to attempt a direct conquest, how soon would it be before Switzerland would be economically strangled or starved?

On June 22, 1941, the Germans launched the greatest offensive in history, against the Soviet Union. The Führer's former friend Stalin, Hitler's accomplice in the Nazi-Soviet non-aggression pact, now had his turn to see blitzkrieg at first hand. This was a lucky break for the Swiss. Nazi plans to invade Switzerland had been drafted around the same time as plans to attack Russia were being developed. An Italian plan during this period would also have unleashed three armies with 15 divisions on Switzerland. Had Hitler not launched his legions at Russia, Switzerland would surely have been the continued obsession of the German General Staff. Instead, "Operation Barbarossa" meant a delay in the assault on Switzerland.[32]

While most Swiss had no sympathy for Soviet totalitarianism, the Aktion Nationaler Widerstand, Switzerland's total-resistance purists, cheered the Russian resistance and thanked God that Hitler had decided to divert his forces elsewhere in Europe.[33]

Nevertheless, despite Germany's attack on the Soviet Union, planning continued for an assault on Switzerland. In July, Colonel Adolf Heusinger presented to the Chief of the German Army Operations Department an invasion plan named "Operation Wartegau" (not to be confused with 1940's sabotage plan of the same name). The plan included not only paratrooper, panzer and Luftwaffe attacks, but also the transportation of forces on hydroplanes which would land on lakes in Switzerland. Informed by good intelligence, General Guisan would plan for just such an attack in the coming months.[34]

This plan was not consummated, but Hitler did not lose sight of his ambition to destroy the Swiss nation. No one, including Western military observers, expected the Soviet Union to withstand the German onslaught, and a Wehrmacht victory would free up troops for an attack on Switzerland. During 1941, Swiss traitors continued to be trained by the Waffen SS and other Nazi groups in sabotage and espionage for the purpose of carrying out Nazi activities against their homeland.[35]

However, the Führer believed that the Swiss would not be fit citizens of the Reich. Reflecting on the need to colonize his conquests with racially pure peoples, Hitler insisted: "we must attract the Norwegians, the Swedes, the Danes and the Dutch into our Eastern territories. They'll become members of the German Reich. Our duty is methodically to pursue a racial policy." The Germans created a new Waffen SS division, "Viking," composed of Scandinavian volunteers and also recruited young men from the Low Countries. Despite the reputation of the Swiss, earned over hundreds of years, as the best infantry and the most intrepid fighters in Europe, however, the Führer was never able to attract more than a handful of Swiss to his endeavors. Himmler's SS eventually created independent units of various European nationalities from French to Latvian (and also a formation of East Indians), but it was never able to recruit enough Swiss to form a self-standing unit. Regarding the "inferior" people to Germany's immediate south, Hitler griped: "As for the Swiss, we can use them, at the best, as hotel-keepers."[36]

At the June 2 conference between Hitler and Mussolini on the Brenner, the two dictators took turns expressing their hatred for the Swiss. Hitler went first:

> The Führer characterized Switzerland as the most despicable and wretched people and national entity. The Swiss were the mortal enemies of the new Germany. . . . They frankly opposed the Reich, hoping that by parting from the common destiny of the German people, they would be better off. . . . Their attitude is determined as it were through the hate of renegades.[37]

Elsewhere in this harangue, Hitler made an obscure reference apparently expressing resentment against the Swiss for their victory against the Germans in the Swabian War of 1499. He saw Switzerland as the historic enemy of the First as well as the Third Reich.

Mussolini agreed, complaining that the Swiss opposed the Axis nations without regard to language group and sounded out Hitler on dates for an invasion:

> On a question of the Duce, what was in store in the future for Switzerland, which is but an anachronism anyway, the German Foreign Minister [Ribbentrop] replied, smiling, that the Duce must talk about it with the Führer. The Duce observed that only the French Swiss in Switzerland stood by France, while the Italian Swiss stood against Italy and the German Swiss against Germany. On the Jewish Question, the Führer said that after the war all Jews would have to get out of Europe completely.[38]

Thus Hitler managed to link his hatred for both the Swiss and the Jews in the same diatribe. He called for the killing of Swiss until they submitted and the eradication of all Jews, whether or not they submitted.

The Führer held Switzerland in particular contempt because of her policy in favor of peace. On August 20, 1941, he stated: "If one wants to wish the German people something good, it would be to have a war every fifteen to twenty years. An army whose only goal is to secure peace, one is led to observe, becomes playing at soldier—one only needs to look at Sweden or Switzerland—or it is in danger in the sense of a revolutionary setting."[39]

In September 1941 Heinrich Himmler communicated with his lieutenant Gottlob Berger regarding who might be named Reichsstatthalter (governor) in a conquered Switzerland. Himmler's papers include a document entitled "Reichsführer SS, SS Hauptamt, Aktion S[chweiz]," which was a detailed plan for a Nazi takeover in Switzerland.[40] It is unclear whether Himmler actually chose a Reichsstatthalter for Switzerland.

Nazi aversion to the Swiss stemmed in part from the Swiss tolerance for different languages, cultures, religions and ethnic groups. *Contemporary Jewish Record*, a publication of the American Jewish Committee (AJC), commented that in 1941 Switzerland's 18,000 Jews "have preserved their socio-religious existence, and have still become completely absorbed within the Swiss body-politic. This is the cardinal reason for the fact that there is no anti-Jewish movement in Switzerland worthy of such designation." Germany tried to finance Nazism in Switzerland, but "when the source of these incomes dries up, Nazi activities and the spread of anti-Semitic poison cease at once." Almost all anti-Semitism in Switzerland stemmed from German citizens living there, and the authorities vigorously suppressed Nazi activities.[41]

The umbrella for Jewish groups in Switzerland was the Swiss Union of Jewish Communities (Schweizerischer Israelitischer Gemeindebund). The AJC publication also stated: "Having found no difficulty in synthesizing their lives as Swiss citizens and as Jews, being left in peace at least for the time being, Swiss Jewry is consolidating its cultural and socio-religious activities with a remarkable degree of success."[42]

An article in the American magazine *Commonweal* commented that Switzerland was the most international country of Europe while at the same time, with her system of local autonomy, the most decentralized. Since the Middle Ages, "the Swiss were a sort of European militia, and their country was recognized as free because it was an 'Imperial Domain,' not a feudal state like the others." The Swiss still represented the same ideals:

> Switzerland, at present encircled by the Axis powers, is a living refutation, a concrete and indisputable denial, of the totalitarian ideal. The Swiss have never asked for any other "living space" than liberty. By its very existence Switzerland proves that several races can live together in harmony, and on a footing of scrupulous equality; that it is possible to unite, in a freedom of diversity, various languages, various modes of life, and that this union is far more truly human than the enforced unity of the dictatorships. By its very existence it refutes the racial and nationalistic theories.[43]

On August 11, Federal Councillor Karl Kobelt, head of the Federal Military Department, defined Switzerland's double task in the midst of the European war as that of safeguarding her national defense and her food supply. To survive, commercial treaties with other nations had to be undertaken. At the same time, it was necessary to keep spending the three and a half million francs per day to keep mobilized for defense.[44]

Before France fell, Swiss arms exports were almost equally divided among the warring camps; the defeat of France cut Switzerland off from Allied markets. In 1939, 42 of 64 million francs' worth of arms exports went to France and Great Britain. In 1940 the official figures were, in millions of Swiss francs: France 26, Great Britain 21, Germany 33, and Italy 34; in 1941, Germany 122, Italy 61, and the Allied countries 0.[45] These official figures, though, obscure the major (and often surreptitious) Swiss exports of defense items to the Allies, which would continue for the entire war, as was acknowledged in secret British documents in 1943. Not surprisingly, despite Swiss trade with the Axis, Admiral William D. Leahy, the American Ambassador to Vichy France, found the Swiss in August 1941 to be "in complete sympathy with the cause of the democracies."[46]

Wolf, M. "What People Are Saying," in *Nineteenth Century*, 126 (Sept. 1939).

PERIODICALS

(Specific articles from the following sources are cited in the Chapter Notes.)

Allgemeine Schweizerische Militärzeitung
Boston Gazette
Congressional Record
Der Angriff
Journal de Genève
Neue Volkszeitung
Neue Zürcher Zeitung
New York Times
Reichsgesetzblatt
Schweizerische Schützenzeitung
The Times (London)

Under the Hague Conventions governing war between nations, the commercial enterprises of a neutral may engage in free trade, including trade in arms, with belligerents. A neutral state may not supply one warring party with arms, but a private firm may.[47] Hague Conventions 5 and 13 of 1907 concerned the rights and duties of neutrals in war, including the right of all belligerents to equal treatment.[48] During the war, Switzerland strictly followed international law and prohibited state-owned firms from selling weapons to belligerents. Private commercial transactions, including those in arms, took place and were consistent with international law.

As a small, landlocked nation surrounded by the Third Reich and its allies, the Swiss, from necessity, traded with the only market available to them—the Axis. More puzzling was the ongoing trade between the Third Reich and the neutral United States. A document written by Major Charles A. Burrows of Military Intelligence addressed to the American War Department on July 15, 1941, stated:

> A report has been received from Cleveland, Ohio . . . to the effect that the Standard Oil Company of New Jersey now ships under Panamanian registry, transporting oil (fuel) from Aruba, Dutch West Indies, to Teneriffe, Canary Islands, and is apparently diverting about 20% of this fuel oil to the present German government.[49]

The September 1941 issue of *Fortune* magazine noted that the Swiss were denounced at least twice a week at the Wilhelmstrasse press conferences in Berlin. This was because the Swiss, who were "outspoken democrats and antifascists," had "the only oasis of democracy, free speech, and civilized living in all Europe today." Surrounded by the Axis, landlocked Switzerland was "a continental island blockaded by the British and counterblockaded by the Germans, *yet dependent on foreign trade to live.*" Of its four language groups, "the German-speaking, German-descended *Volksdeutsche* are readiest to fight if Hitler should try to violate their democratic soil." Yet "nations other than Switzerland, Sweden for example, have taken their place in the Nazi New Order without visible resistance. But the Swiss have shown that they will never peaceably submit to *Gleichschaltung.*"[50]

Economic strangulation, *Fortune* continued, forced the Swiss to trade with the Axis. "For to fight Germany they must meantime live and work and produce—and because of their economic isolation they can do so only on German sufferance. The ironic result is that by arming themselves, they are forced to arm Germany as well."[51]

Before the war, Swiss trade with England accounted for 17% of total foreign trade, but this was now almost totally blocked. Switzerland had imported foodstuffs, tobacco, rubber goods, and machinery from the United States, but England, fearing that the goods might find their way to the Nazis, had in the previous April stopped issuing permits for U.S.-Swiss trade in bulk foods and many materials.[52] With Switzerland's markets now severely restricted, *Fortune* described the situation:

> The Axis sets its own prices, and the Swiss say that their profits have been cut to the bone. But nothing can be done. The factories must go on producing if Switzerland is to implement its own defenses. They must produce at full blast or there will be unemployment—and unemployed men are open targets for Nazi propaganda. The factories can run at all only because Germany sells, or permits others to sell, coal, iron, copper, and other necessary raw materials, and the supplies come through only because Germany receives war materials in return.[53]

In a telling incident showing the attitude of the average Swiss, the authors of the *Fortune* article had recently returned from Germany via Switzerland, and observed the following rather humorous phenomenon seen at movie houses that showed both American and German newsreels:

> The Nazi reels move with a peculiar jerkiness, a result of the removal of all "*heiling*" for the Swiss market. The Germans are still puzzled, but they found that Swiss audiences laughed uproariously at every sight of a grim-faced German shooting up his hand like a railroad signal and grunting "*Heil, Hitler!*" One theatre had to stop the film to restore

calm after a scene in which Hitler himself had said *"Heil, Hitler!"*[54]

As the brutal nature of German occupation of foreign territories unfolded during 1941, it became clear how the Nazis might have responded to a nation of armed citizens, of which Switzerland was the best—indeed, the only—example. The Germans took the sternest measures against the few citizens who possessed arms in the occupied countries. At year's end, the Nazis decreed:

> The death penalty or, in less serious cases, imprisonment shall be imposed on any Pole or Jew . . . if he is in unlawful possession of firearms . . . or if he has credible information that a Pole or a Jew is in unlawful possession of such objects, and fails to notify the authorities forthwith.[55]

This decree was related in part to the activities of the Einsatzgruppen, Nazi killing squads that exterminated Jews and others in the East. A half-million Soviet Jews were murdered in the second half of 1941. In Riga, Latvia, a mere 23 men killed 10,600 people. As Raul Hilberg observed in his 1985 book: "The killers were well armed. . . . The victims were unarmed."[56] The Einsatzgruppen killed two million people between fall 1939 and summer 1942.[57]

Six Einsatzgruppen of a few hundred members each, and divided into Einsatzkommandos, operated in Poland and Russia. Their tasks included arrest of the politically unreliable, confiscation of weapons, and extermination.[58] The Einsatzgruppen reports to superiors in Berlin during 1941–42 are enlightening. Interspersed with report after report of thousands executed were accounts of snipers. For instance, Einsatzgruppe C reported in September 1941 that, besides liquidating Jews and Communists, its operations included, "above all, the fight against all partisan activities, beginning with the well-organized bands and the individual snipers down to the systematic rumor mongers."[59]

Typical executions were that of one woman "for being found without a Jewish badge and for refusing to move into the ghetto" and of another "for sniping." Persons found in possession of firearms were shot on the spot. Reports of sniping and partisan activity increased over time.[60]

Even under the most repressive conditions, a small proportion of the citizens who had arms gave the Nazis great anguish. The Nazis did not overlook the "sniping" to be expected should an incursion into Switzerland be ventured. If they needed a reminder, they could read about it in the Swiss Shooting Federation's newspaper: "Swiss weapons are part of the Swiss mentality. . . . The government has the confidence to give the people weapons and even ammunition to save us from any surprise."[61] Swiss Jews received arms just like all other citizens.

It was reported from Bern on December 2 that Germany was expected to demand that the Swiss expel all British nationals. Britain's offensive in Libya and the resistance of the Russians were believed to have delayed the Nazis' "Swiss revisionist plan" to integrate Switzerland into the New Order. The Swiss were prepared to resist any new push to become part of an economically and politically related Nazi bloc.[62]

Switzerland's role as a neutral in World War II concerned not merely military defense and trade policy but also, continuing an age-old tradition, diplomacy. The United States remained neutral until forced into the war by the Japanese attack on Pearl Harbor on December 7, 1941. Three days later, it was announced that Switzerland would likely represent the interests of the United States in Japan. Her first duty would be to arrange the exchange of officials and nationals of each country.[63]

On the 11th, the German and Italian ambassadors notified the American government that their countries had entered into a state of war with the United States. The Germans appointed the Swiss to represent their interests in the United States, beginning with the exchange of nationals.[64] Six days later, the State Department announced that Switzerland would in turn represent American interests in all belligerent countries and all occupied countries. While the Swiss would represent the Americans in Japan, Japan selected Spain to represent her in the United States.[65]

By the following month, Switzerland was representing the interests of twenty belligerents, a function that included the exchange of wounded prisoners.[66] In Germany, the Swiss represented the interests of the United States, Britain, Canada, Australia and New Zealand, among others.[67]

Throughout the war, Hitler continued to exhibit both hatred and fear of things Swiss. One incident from 1941 illustrates the point. In June, Hitler personally forbade Schiller's play *Wilhelm Tell* from being performed in Germany or read in the schools. Tell was a freedom fighter, and his killing of a tyrant reminded Hitler of the 1938 attempt of the Swiss citizen Maurice Bavaud to kill him. Bavaud, though he had not succeeded, resembled a modern Tell.[68] Schiller's play, however, could still be performed at theatres in Switzerland, the only free German-speaking theatres left in Europe.

The Isolation of Switzerland

Großdeutschland – Greater Germany

Occupied/controlled by Germany or German allies

Occupied/controlled by the Allies

Neutral nations or territories

Karminder 1998

Chapter 7

1942
"Oasis of Democracy"

AS 1942 UNFOLDED AND AN ALLIED VICTORY SEEMED REMOTE, the battle for hearts and minds was at a critical stage. On January 5, the Swiss arrested an artillery soldier and his co-conspirators whom German intelligence had paid to steal certain Swiss weapons and munitions and to make maps of Swiss Army positions. By a judgment on October 9, he became the first Swiss soldier sentenced to death for treason.[1]

The Führer's intent to impose Nazi rule on Switzerland at some future date was evident again during a discussion on his policy toward Jews on January 27. A week after the notorious Wannsee Conference, where the plan to annihilate the Jewish people was settled, Hitler insisted: "The Jew must get out of Europe! . . . Out of Switzerland and out of Sweden, they must be driven out."[2]

Nazi spies and propagandists were busy, but the Swiss were equally vigilant, as a sampling of reports for the first quarter of 1942 reveals. Two workers at the Altdorf Munitions Works were convicted of communicating fortification plans to a foreign power.[3] Six Nazi agents were sentenced to prison for revealing military secrets.[4] In Lucerne, Swiss police arrested nineteen National Socialists, followers of Swiss Nazi propagandist Franz Burri, for distribution of prohibited propaganda.[5] Burri had already fled from Swiss authorities and was in exile in Vienna. In Zurich, two were sentenced to prison for violation of military secrets and eleven were jailed for organizing unlawful propaganda.[6]

The two founders of the Swiss National Socialist movement, which had been dissolved in 1940, were convicted by a Zurich court in absentia of threatening national security and were sentenced to prison.[7] Several men were convicted of revealing military secrets to a foreign state and stealing ammunition and weapons parts from the military, some receiving life sentences.[8]

Also in January, General Guisan took steps to make official the collaboration between the security service and the public communications section known as Heer und Haus (Army and Home). That organization was invited to "commence the struggle against all extremist propaganda for the purpose of instruction and dissuasive activities."[9] This meant that nothing was barred by the censor for fear of Nazi retaliation—lecturers could explicitly discuss the advantages of Swiss democracy over National Socialism, and of shooting as many Wehrmacht invaders as possible.

In the January 9th issue of *Reich* magazine, Nazi Propaganda Minister Goebbels attacked "the remaining so-called neutrals in the European hegemony" and charged that "Switzerland and Sweden are lacking in the most elementary appreciation of the security of their nations and their future existence." Goebbels insisted:

If these neutrals are not prepared to fight with us for the German victory, they should at least pray God for that victory. But they have not even enough sense for that. . . . Their political tendencies incline them toward bolshevism.[10]

As Goebbels wrote those words, for the first time in the war he might have been growing nervous. German Army Group Center, surprised by both the Russian weather and Soviet reserves, was just barely staving off a huge counteroffensive outside Moscow. Still, in the preceding months the Nazis had surrounded Leningrad, occupied the Baltic states, and taken Kiev and most of Ukraine.

The January 25th *New York Times Magazine* included an article on Switzerland entitled "Oasis of Democracy" which argued that while the Swiss took every measure to guarantee peace, they never followed an appeasement strategy. "Dependent though they are upon

The historic Rütli Meadow on July 25, 1940, just after the fall of France.
On the very spot where the "Companions of the Oath" had formed the Swiss
Confederation in 1291, General Henri Guisan summoned his highest officers
to stand before him and receive his orders: Switzerland would never surrender!

1

"If my first arrow had my dear child struck, The second arrow I had aimed at you, And this, I swear, would not have missed its mark. "—William Tell to the tyrant Gessler (Schiller, 1804). From a painting by Ludwig Vogel.

1315: The Battle of Morgarten, where 1,400 Swiss peasants defeated 20,000 Habsburg knights and infantry. Pummeled with huge stones and driven into the lake, 2,000 Austrians were killed to only 12 Swiss. The painting is by Ferdinand Wagner.

Henri Guisan, Switzerland's wartime leader, has been compared to Winston Churchill for the inspiration he gave his people during times of crisis.

August 30, 1939: At the Federal Parliament in Bern, General Guisan is made commander-in-chief of the Swiss Army. With Guisan are, from left to right, Federal Councilors Marcel Pilet-Golaz, Philipp Etter and Rudolf Minger.

General Guisan reviews a unit of troops. Swiss soldiers traditionally keep their arms and equipment at home, allowing for rapid mobilizations.

The Ortswehren *(Local Guards), consisting of older men from the shooting associations, as well as teenaged marksmen, carried the old Model 1889 rifle. Armbands identified them as members of the Swiss military.*

German troops enter a Belgian town in May 1940. Belgium, the Netherlands and France would fall and the British would evacuate the continent after a campaign that lasted only six weeks.

June 18,1940: Hitler and Mussolini in Munich, where they discussed plans to attack and carve up Switzerland.

Nazi Propaganda Minister Joseph Goebbels fumed about the Swiss press throughout the war. In May 1942 he called Switzerland "this stinking little state."

The German attacking force under the 1940 von Menges plan would have been Army Group C commanded by General Wilhelm Ritter von Leeb.

Allan W. Dulles arrived in Bern in November 1942 to establish the Office of Strategic Services (OSS), the American intelligence network. Switzerland was an ideal location to spy on the Axis, encourage French and Italian partisans and communicate with Germany's underground.

The Swiss
applied a fluid
defense between
the border and the
the Alps. Each
mobile 11-man
squad was
equipped with a
light machine gun
(right), a subma-
chine gun and nine
K31 carbines.
The main strength
of the Swiss Army,
however, awaited a
German attack in
fortified Alpine
positions (below).

Although Switzerland has been called a country where marksmanship is the "national sport," the Swiss Army also trained in other martial skills.

When the men were under mobilization orders, the rural women, helped only by the children, were left with all of the farm work.

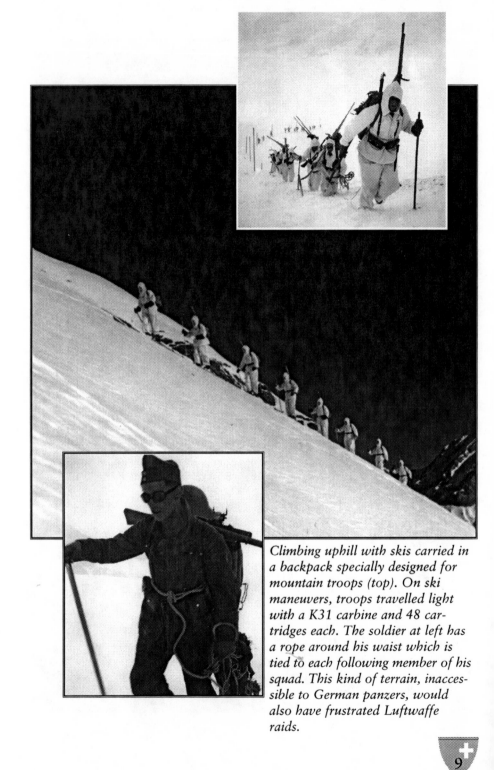

Climbing uphill with skis carried in a backpack specially designed for mountain troops (top). On ski maneuvers, troops travelled light with a K31 carbine and 48 cartridges each. The soldier at left has a rope around his waist which is tied to each following member of his squad. This kind of terrain, inaccessible to German panzers, would also have frustrated Luftwaffe raids.

9

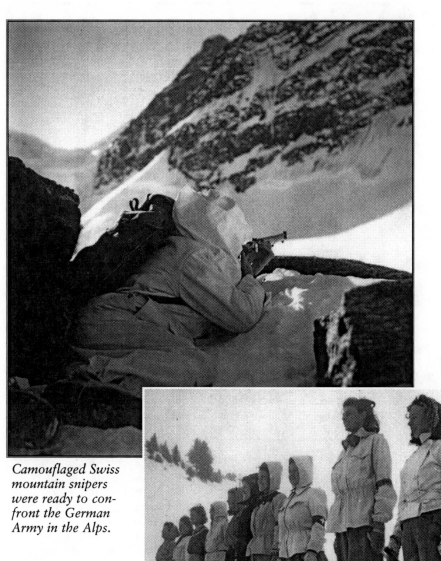

Camouflaged Swiss mountain snipers were ready to confront the German Army in the Alps.

Women in the auxiliary forces, identified by the armband with the Swiss flag—white cross on red background (not to be confused with the Red Cross emblem of a red cross on a white background).

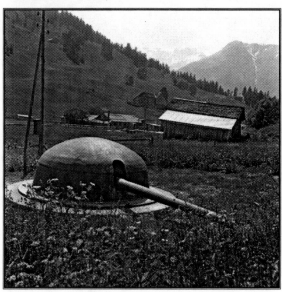

A 75mm mountain cannon (above) and a 105mm turret cannon (left). Such artillery was typically placed at high positions overlooking valleys through which an invader would have to pass.

This Swiss-made 20mm anti-aircraft gun fired 250 rounds per minute with a range of 4,500 meters.

Swiss Messerschmitt fighters originally purchased from Germany. In 1940, Swiss pilots shot down 11 Luftwaffe planes and lost only 3 of their own.

The Luftschutz (air raid defense), which included many female members, detected and plotted the paths of intruding bombers and fighters.

Scrambling into the cockpit during an air raid alarm (below). The plane appears to be armed with a Model 1925 light machine gun.

The woman standing points to the Gotthard fortification on the map at a military communications office.

The tragic bombing of Schaffhausen on April 1, 1944 by thirty American Liberators, whose pilots thought they were over Germany, killed scores of Swiss. The Swiss forgave the attack and provided a safe haven for 1,700 downed American pilots.

A Swiss infantry combat unit. The Swiss feared, and stayed in readiness for, a German attack from the beginning of the war in 1939 until the end in 1945.

The Swiss hosted over 100,000 interned soldiers during the war, 65 percent of whom were Allied. French Colonial troops pictured above found refuge in Switzerland after the fall of France.

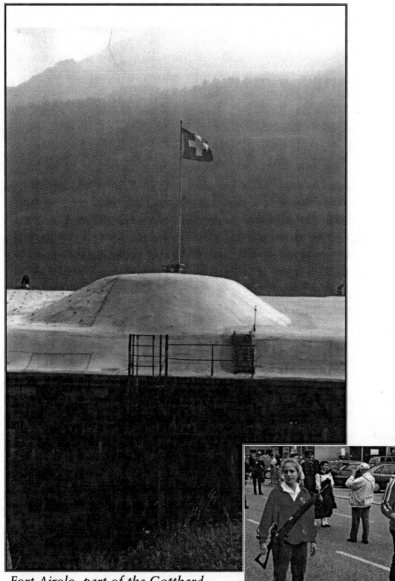

Fort Airolo, part of the Gotthard fortification located in northern Ticino, pointed its long-range guns in the direction of a probable Italian invasion. The flag flies peacefully today.

July 16, 1995: A young woman with a Sturmgewehr 90, the current service rifle, and a young man with a Sturmgewehr 57, a now obsolete military rifle, march in a parade in Thun celebrating the Federal Shooting Festival.

their Axis neighbors for everything, the Swiss, democrats and independents to the core, have never acquiesced in Germany's 'New Order'."[11]

Nevertheless, Switzerland was feeling the effects of the war. There was only enough coal to heat one room per house, the article noted. Most commodities were rationed, and there were three meatless days a week. Both private and public grounds, including soccer fields and, in at least one case, the front lawn of a library, were given over to growing potatoes. The Swiss survived only through foreign trade, and all exports required a German permit. Yet their trade with Germany paradoxically allowed them to defend themselves from Germany. Indeed, "by manufacturing arms for Germany they have been able to make arms for themselves."[12] In any event, Swiss manufactures accounted for only a miniscule part of German weapons acquisitions. For the entire war period, Swiss arms deliveries to Germany accounted for 0.6% of Germany's total armaments.

Despite protests from the Reich, Switzerland refused to recognize Axis conquests and allowed the occupied countries to maintain their embassies in Bern. This policy corresponded to the British policy of permitting similar embassies, as well as entire governments-in-exile, to operate in London. The Swiss were ready for an invasion, according to the *Times*: "Their citizen army is tiny by comparison with the millions mustered by its neighbors, but its equipment is excellent and it is highly trained."[13]

While far too few partisans in the occupied East had guns, the small number who did continued to wreak havoc. Propaganda Minister Goebbels made the following diary entry on March 16, 1942:

> The activity of partisans has increased noticeably during recent weeks. They are conducting a well-organized guerrilla war. It is very difficult to get at them because they are using such terrorist methods in the areas occupied by us that the population is afraid of collaborating with us loyally any longer. The spearheads of this whole partisan activity are the political commissars and especially the Jews.[14]

Jews with rifles waging guerrilla warfare were obviously hampering the activities of the Nazis. Similarly, the Swiss Shooting Federation believed that despite the role of the panzers and heavy weapons on European battlefields, the rifle-carrying infantryman remained invaluable: "The calm individual single shot is still the most important thing. . . . A little war behind enemy lines is being fought with well-aimed, single shots by infantrymen. Our purpose is confirmed: we must make every effort to heighten the training of marksmen." Swiss marksmen thus promised the same treatment to Wehrmacht invaders as was meted out by the Russian partisans.[15]

German military training as of 1942, and probably long before, emphasized marksmanship skills at 100 meters.[16] The Swiss population at large, whether of military age or not, regularly participated in rifle competitions at 300 meters, although military training entailed distances of anywhere from 50 to 600 meters. Although the Germans were formidable foes on the battlefields of other European countries, none of these countries had a reputation for good marksmanship.

In a March 16 speech, Military Department chief Karl Kobelt stated that "Switzerland does not want peace at any price and never at the price of her honor."[17] Addressing marksmen in eastern Switzerland, Kobelt referred to the founding of the country six-and-a-half centuries earlier:

> It was the supreme goal, the fight for freedom, that gave the small mountain people the strength to win. . . . If we lose our freedom, it will have to be won again, because the Swiss can only live in freedom.[18]

A report in Fribourg Canton typifies the Swiss preparations for a war of all the people against an invader:

> On April 11, the chief of the I Division spoke at Fribourg on the role of the noncommissioned officers and the shooters in the event of rapid mobilization and under enemy fire, wherein orders perhaps will be lacking or not delivered to them. This raises the value and importance of shooting as applied to the specific terrain that the troops of our canton will have to defend.[19]

As explained in the *Training Manual for the Infantry 1942* (*Ausbildungsvorschrift der Infanterie 1942*), the Swiss infantry combat unit consisted, at full strength, of a squad leader and ten soldiers. The unit was armed with a light machine gun, a submachine gun, and nine carbines, one of which featured a telescopic sight. Two soldiers carried equipment for the launching of anti-tank shells and two anti-tank weapons. The unit might also have had hand grenades and, in exceptional cases, land mines.[20]

The light machine gun was the primary weapon for the firefight. It could be shot at 600 meters and, in favorable conditions, at 800 meters with success. The submachine gun was not only the automatic weapon for use under the arm at the shortest distances, but also offered good hit probabilities at targets up to 200 meters. Normally the shooter fired in quick single shots or bursts at short distances.

The telescopic-sight carbine belonged in the hands of a superior marksman. This rifle could be used at distances over 500 meters when sufficient time existed for carefully aimed shots or when ammunition was low. The regular carbines could be used out to distances of 600 meters, if the targets were at all recognizable.[21]

The unit was well supplied with ammunition. Excluding the two anti-tank weapons supplied with five rounds each, the squad of eleven soldiers could shoot around 1,800 bullets at the enemy before drawing new supplies from their parent unit or arms caches.

Given the natural cover in the Alps and the Jura, the countless hills, crevices, and bodies of water at the border and in the Plateau, these combat units would have been deadly against any German invasion. Roughly half a million soldiers would have been divided into units of just eleven. One can imagine the damage a seemingly infinite number of swarms of these units could have inflicted on the Wehrmacht.

Yet for the time being, the war between Germany and Switzerland continued to be waged with words instead of bullets. Nazi Propaganda Minister Goebbels complained in his diary on May 7 that the Swiss had recalled their representative to a film organization. "This stinking little state [*dieser kleine Dreckstaat*] is trying to provoke the International Motion Picture Association." He insisted that the association impose a general boycott on the Swiss.[22]

The press, especially in Switzerland's German-speaking areas, strongly opposed National Socialism and criticized any concessions the government made to the Reich. Berlin's *Vlkischer Beobachter* attacked Switzerland as "the reservation park of democracies," peopled by "*Berg-Semiten*," mountain Jews. A popular Nazi song went:

> Switzerland is a porcupine,
> We will take her as dessert;
> Then we'll go to the wide world
> And get us Roosevelt.[23]

The Swiss joked that only the Nazis would eat porcupine.

The Nazi assault on the Swiss press continued. In mid-October, Dr. Paul Schmidt, Press Chief of the German Foreign Office, charged that the Swiss press had a "negative attitude" toward the New Order. As Swiss reporters listened, he continued: "There will be no place for such editors in the new Europe. We will make short shrift of them. Perhaps they will find their future home in the steppes of Asia, or maybe it would be best simply to send them off into the Great Beyond."[24]

From Switzerland, the *Neue Berner Zeitung* shot back: "The National Socialist conception of a new European order is absolutely incompatible with the freedom of Europe's states and peoples." Under a headline "*Wir machen nicht mit!*" (loosely, "We won't play ball"), Zurich's *Volksrecht* also responded: "The prospect of death can scare no one who must imagine what the 'New Europe' of tomorrow will be like, from the way it looks today."[25] The Federal Council protested Schmidt's death threats through the Swiss minister in Berlin.[26]

Dr. Schmidt was at it again on November 21, blaming the Swiss for allowing British bombers to fly over their territory en route to targets in northern Italy. Schmidt claimed that Switzerland, which "flatters itself on being a democratic country and flaunts particular sympathies for Britain," tolerated the flights, which resulted in the deaths of women and children.[27]

On June 15, 1942, it was reported that the Swiss were preparing for full mobilization. Domestic trouble in the Reich was anticipated; Italian soldiers had not been paid and were clamoring for food, and traffic on the "underground railroad" by which refugees and deserters from the German military forces escaped into Switzerland had greatly increased. Interned German soldiers confirmed that an "escape organization" existed in the German Army, just as one existed for civilians. Two German airmen from the faraway Russian front deserted into Switzerland.[28]

On July 5, Hitler attacked the Swiss press for glowing reports about Soviet military power, deploring that "not only in England and America, but also in Stockholm and in Swiss cities the population believes in Jewish claptrap." The Führer fumed that Jews must have special influence in Switzerland because her people cared only about matters such as milk-interests, grain prices and clocks. In addition to all the other characteristics of the Swiss that Hitler disliked, he hated them because of their free market capitalism, which he associated with Judaism.[29]

The Swiss National Day celebration on August 1 was marred by air-raid sirens and a blackout. General Guisan's order of the day stated: "Soldier of Switzerland of 1942! To remain master of your own destiny, sole master after God, hold to the watchword I gave you at the beginning of the year: Stand firm and faithful."[30] Three days later, on August 4, the Federal Council decreed that military tribunals rather than civil courts would try all persons, including civilians, accused of crimes against state security.[31]

In August, the British staged a large amphibious raid against the French port of Dieppe. Using a Canadian division, Churchill had intended to demonstrate that Nazi-held Europe was vulnerable to surprise attacks made possible by the strength and mobility of the Royal Navy. The Canadians, however, were met by a wall of fire from German tanks and guns. Most of the invaders were killed or captured before the remnants were rescued in a hasty evacuation. It would be almost two years before the Allies would attempt another invasion of northern Europe.

On August 26, Hitler, in one of his harangues to his military advisers, stated bluntly: "A state like Switzerland, which is nothing but a pimple on the face of Europe, cannot be allowed to continue." Hitler denounced the Swiss as a racial miscarriage, "a misbegotten branch of our *Volk*."[32]

For all his threats and the numerous General Staff operational plans to attack Switzerland, Hitler hesitated to commit the Wehrmacht to combat on Swiss ground. Nazi military intelligence was well aware of the military prowess of this "pimple." It prepared a Little Swiss Information Manual (*Kleines Orientierungsheft Schweiz*), issued September 1, 1942, to acquaint German soldiers with Swiss defenses. The manual stated:

> The Swiss militia system enables a complete use of all those fit for military service with relatively low expense. It invariably results that the warrior spirit arises in the Swiss people and allows the installation in the small country of a very strong and expedient organization, resulting in the quick readiness of the army for war.[33]

The Swiss soldier, the manual continued, is characterized by love of home, toughness and tenacity. His shooting performance is good. He dedicates himself to the great care of arms, equipment, uniforms, horses and pack animals. "Particularly the German Swiss and the Alpine soldier would be good fighters."[34]

After Hitler launched World War II in 1939 by invading Poland, the Swiss decreed that foreigners in their country must have a visa.[35] Early in the war, French civilians and Belgian and Dutch soldiers found refuge in Switzerland. Many left again through Vichy France. Once the Axis occupied Vichy France and thus completely surrounded the Swiss in November 1942, however, there was no longer any escape route, and the Swiss government, fearing food shortages, became reluctant to accept new refugees. It was known that other countries such as the United States would not accept refugees. In the first half of 1942, the United States granted only 30 visas.[36]

Meanwhile, Switzerland continued to play her traditional humanitarian role. The International Committee of the Red Cross in Geneva handled millions of letters to and from prisoners and provided assistance to wounded soldiers.[37] It resisted Axis pressure to extradite political refugees and, while an "independent" Vichy France existed, Swiss officials helped endangered persons to escape from it and through it.

In August, the Swiss border was briefly closed to Jewish refugees. Heinrich Rothmund, police chief of the federal Ministry of Justice and Police, commanded his men to prevent persons from entering Switzerland, especially over the French border. This drastic policy change led to such a public outcry, however, that within days border guards were ordered to accept Jews under sixteen, families, and the elderly.[38] Once again, the Swiss people had protested successfully against policies established by government bureaucrats. Edgar Bonjour, the preeminent scholar on Swiss neutrality, notes:

> Left to themselves, the Swiss people would have swept away all frontier barriers and taken in all the thousands who were striving to save their lives, if nothing else, from fury at their persecutors. But the government was soon warning the people of the dangers of the "overcrowded boat," and stressing the inexorable limits set to the granting of asylum.[39]

Wartime immigration policy was debated in the National Council, the lower house of Parliament, on September 22. The government's anti-immigration policy was attacked. A government spokesman warned that fifth columnists could infiltrate the country if the borders were opened. However, he acknowledged that numerous refugees were being granted asylum.[40]

Swiss citizens resorted to ingenious methods to assist refugees. A Swiss doctor bandaged a Jewish woman as a ruse and, crying emergency, took her right past the guards on both sides of the German border. She then stayed in a Swiss home which took in several other Jewish refugees until she could make her way to the United States.[41]

During this period, the average number of refugees fleeing into Switzerland was 175 per night, for a total of more than 14,000 by October 3, 1942. The mostly destitute refugees, in particular those seeking to escape slave labor, came from the north and from Vichy France in the southwest. Soon the previously lax border control was tightened and a Commissioner for Refugees was appointed.[42]

For purposes of comparison, it is instructive to examine American refugee policy during this period. In July 1940, the U.S. State Department directed its consuls not to issue visitors' or transit visas unless the person had an exit permit from his home country. An

American edict of June 1941 made it all but impossible for refugees with relatives in the Reich to come to the United States. At that time the Vichy government unsuccessfully sought the resettlement of thousands of French Jews in the United States. The State Department did not recognize Jews, as such, to be political refugees. It was later decided that *children* from Vichy could enter, but between March 1941 and August 1942 only 309 refugee children were admitted into the United States. Of the 460,000 visas available for admission to the United States between 1938 and 1942, only 228,964 were issued.[43]

On November 8, 1942, the Allies invaded North Africa, prompting the Nazi occupation of Vichy France so that the Germans could guard the Mediterranean coast. Premier Pétain objected, but offered no resistance.[44] The noose thus tightened around Switzerland.[45] The Nazi takeover of Vichy France included an incident that illustrated what it meant for Switzerland to be a protecting power for the interests of belligerents. A Wehrmacht soldier with a submachine gun took over the United States Embassy in Vichy just before the arrival of the Swiss representative, Minister Walter Stucki. Stucki burst into the embassy brandishing his only weapon—a Swiss Army knife—with which he managed to drive the soldier from the building.[46]

The Nazis seemed to be postponing an invasion of Switzerland until they could defeat the major powers. Germany could, of course, also invade when the Gotthard and Simplon tunnels were no longer of military value. Meantime, the Germans kept Swiss industry supplied with coal.

The Allies restricted imports from Switzerland and threatened to blacklist Swiss firms.[47] The Swiss spent most of the year negotiating with the Allies over trade terms. Without coal from Germany, Swiss industry would collapse, and an unemployed work force would be a seedbed for National Socialist agitation. To get coal, Switzerland had to export products to Germany. Yet this Swiss-German trade also allowed Switzerland to manufacture goods for the Allies. The Swiss obtained transit permits from Berlin and Rome allowing shipment of goods to the Allies, who in turn would ship raw materials to the Swiss. The Allies and the Axis were both concerned, of course, that their raw materials not be used to manufacture goods for their enemies.

Controls could not be strictly implemented, however, and in fact the Allies and the Axis, both of which needed Swiss products, had to approve trade agreements allowing Swiss trade with their enemies.

The chief American negotiator, Winfield Riefler, promoted trade with the Swiss for the purpose of employing the Swiss work force to produce for the Allies and of strengthening the Swiss military. He argued against some of his British colleagues that refusing to trade with Switzerland because the Swiss traded with Germany would only force the Swiss to trade more with Germany. At the end of 1942, it was agreed that, in the first four months of 1943, Switzerland would export goods valued at two and a half million Swiss francs to the United States and Britian. In return, the British and Americans would supply specified raw materials for the exclusive use of the Swiss Army. This trade allowed the Swiss to *decrease* shipments to Germany.[48]

Now that the United States had been forced into the war by the Japanese attack on Pearl Harbor, some Americans suddenly took a dim view of neutrality on the part of other countries.[49] Yet despite Germany's influence over Swiss imports and exports, American public opinion still recognized, as *Newsweek* reported, that "Nazism never was able to take deep root among the freedom-loving mountaineers."[50]

The burgeoning American war effort now required Swiss goods more than ever before. Machine tools, ball bearings, and especially jewel bearings (almost all made in Switzerland by watchmakers) were much-needed imports. This trade reflected the real feelings of most Swiss. In a telling example, while the Germans would not allow the Swiss to export chronographs, which the Allies used for air bombings, the Swiss smuggled them out disguised as ordinary watches. Diamond dies were also surreptitiously exported to Britain. Swiss customs agents were in collusion with the manufacturers.[51] U.S. Assistant Secretary of State Dean Acheson noted that the delivery of industrial diamonds to Allied countries "required more than cooperation by the Swiss, often complicity in illegality or indifference to it."[52]

In response to the new dangers posed by the sudden Nazi occupation of Vichy France, in November 1942 General Guisan and the Federal Council issued "Orders to the Population in Case of War," which was a revised version of the no-surrender order of April 18, 1940. It began with the usual admonition:

1. Switzerland will defend itself in an attack with all its powers *to the end.*

2. Any news that doubts the will to resist of the Federal Council or the Army leadership, or that portrays it as broken, are inventions of enemy propaganda and *false.*[53]

Just as when originally issued, this order was remarkable. It asserted that there would be no surrender—ever—and that any statement or broadcast of surrender by the government or the military must be considered false. It made surrender impossible. It reaffirmed to the populace the high duty to resist to the death and sent a message to the Nazis that any invasion would be very costly in blood.

The order further instructed that any men who were capable of fighting but not enlisted, and who wished to volunteer to defend the country, should report immediately to the *Ortswehren*, the local defense organizations created in 1940. Persons who were not members of an officially recognized armed force were told not to participate in armed hostilities. These directives were intended to make sure that every armed man or boy would have the Swiss armband and thereby be entitled to treatment, if captured, as a prisoner of war and not be shot on the spot. However, the order continued: "Everyone will otherwise support the actions of our troops *with all his power.*"[54]

Allen Dulles became the last American to enter Switzerland legally before the Nazi occupation of Vichy France. Although he was officially attached to the American legation, Dulles described his real tasks as an assignment to "gather information about the Nazi and Fascist enemy and quietly to render such support and encouragement as I could to the resistance forces working against the Nazis and Fascists in the areas adjacent to Switzerland."[55]

Dulles established the Office of Strategic Services (OSS) in Bern. As the only neutral nation bordering Germany and Italy, Switzerland was the perfect location for his spy mission—the American window on the Reich. Numerous refugees had found asylum there in the six prewar years of the Reich, and some continued to make the perilous border crossing. According to Dulles, certain German officials and citizens who traveled to Switzerland on business were also willing to give information about conditions in Germany.[56]

One of Dulles' first tasks was to gather intelligence about underground anti-Nazi movements in Germany. Besides refugee labor and church leaders, Dulles soon came into contact with Hans Bernd Gisevius, a Gestapo official who would later conspire with Wehrmacht officers in an attempt to assassinate Hitler. Assigned to the German Consulate General in Zurich, Gisevius was actually sent to Switzerland by the conspirators to make contact with the Allies. As Dulles wrote, such men "felt that a victory of Nazism and the extinction of liberty in Europe, and possibly in the world, was a far greater disaster than the defeat of Germany." They wanted to hasten that defeat before Germany was totally destroyed.[57] Bern became a center not only for anti-Hitler plots but also for smuggling currency to assist Jewish refugees.[58]

Aid and encouragement to resistance movements in France and northern Italy were also primary objectives of the OSS. The American legation helped the French *maquis* (resistance fighters) in the mountains south of Lake Geneva communicate with arms suppliers. Sam Woods, American Consul General in Zurich, assisted interned U.S. soldiers and airmen in escaping from Switzerland through Axis lines.[59]

The Nazis suspected Swiss intelligence of passing Axis secrets to the Allies. They rightly saw General Guisan as their enemy and an Allied sympathizer, although Guisan scrupulously honored his duties as military chief of a neutral country.[60]

With the Vichy French state, Switzerland's last corridor to the outside world, under Gestapo jurisdiction, many Swiss feared that the Führer would complete the process of controlling the entire continent and invade. *Time* magazine commented:

> Less doggedly independent lands would have toppled long ago, but Switzerland's reaction to the new situation was to answer the obvious question before it was asked. Said the democratic *Volksrecht*: "It is of the greatest importance that we leave no doubt in anybody's mind that not even the most hopeless situation will make us capitulate voluntarily, and before we can be commanded we have got to be beaten."[61]

Without saying which was the first, *Time* commented: "Man for man, Switzerland probably has the second best army in Europe today."

In late November, seven Swiss soldiers were sentenced to death for treason. Infantryman Ernst Leisi watched one evening as a platoon of 20 soldiers marched by. They carried carbines, but no packs or helmets. He thought that they must be going to a shooting match. Not so. These were members of the same platoon as artilleryman Ernst Schrämli. They were acting as a firing squad, and they would execute their former comrade a few minutes later. Schrämli was convicted of passing military secrets to the Germans concerning a new type of armor-piercing ammunition. The Parliament upheld his death sentence, although a few leftists voted for life imprisonment.[62]

During the war, thirty-three death sentences for treason or espionage would be pronounced by the Swiss. Seventeen Swiss would finally be executed for treason. Once the appeal was denied, the traitor would be shot immediately by a firing squad composed of his own army unit. A total of 245 Swiss, 109 Germans and 33 others would be convicted of treasonous offenses. These measures helped deliver the message to Berlin that any attempts to coerce Switzerland into the New Order would be met with strenuous resistance.[63]

Despite repeated press barrages, as the year ended the Nazis were more pessimistic than ever about winning over public opinion in Europe's remaining neutral nations. On December 15, Goebbels wrote in his diary: "Sentiment has turned very much against us in Sweden and in Switzerland. . . . My articles in the *Reich* are for the present about the only source of information on which the elements friendly to Germany in the neutral countries can depend for their moral uplift."[64]

By contrast, there was growing optimism elsewhere. On Christmas Eve, international skier Arnold Lunn mused about the preceding years in Switzerland and England: "There were months when we faced the peril of losing something even more precious than the mountains, our island fortress, and with that fortress the last hope of enslaved Europe." Still, Lunn retained "unquestioning faith in final victory."[65]

During the year the bread ration in Switzerland had averaged only 225 grams a day—less than the ration in Germany, Sweden, and occupied France and Denmark. While their standard of living continued to deteriorate throughout the war, the Swiss stubbornly maintained their spirit and the military capacity to resist any invasion.

Chapter 8

1943
"A Pistol at Their Heads"

"SWITZERLAND, AXIS CAPTIVE"? DESPITE SWISS RESISTANCE WHICH had thus far deterred an invasion of their country, such was the portait offered by writer Charles Lanius in the *Saturday Evening Post* in January 1943. He began with a dramatic, if inaccurate, statement: "I've just escaped from a Nazi-occupied country. The name of that country is Switzerland." Switzerland's four million people were surrounded by 125 million hostile neighbors. "The Swiss are a people living with a pistol at their heads." According to Lanius, German Minister Hans Sigismund von Bibra really ran Switzerland.[1] The theme of the article was the domination of the Swiss economy by Germany. Lanius conceded that the majority of the Swiss hoped for an Allied victory.[2]

Outraged by Lanius' article, Walter Lippmann published a reply in the *New York Herald Tribune* which could be considered the most significant statement in American journalism on Switzerland's role in the war. A founder of *The New Republic*, Lippmann had influenced Woodrow Wilson's concept of the League of Nations and would later win two Pulitzer prizes for journalism. Lippmann began by suggesting that Lanius "certainly did not mean to do an injustice to a nation which is of such moral importance to America and to all the United Nations," yet "unintentionally he has wronged the Swiss and hurt our own cause."[3] Lippmann wrote:

What was not so obvious to Mr. Lanius, though it should have been, is that the Swiss nation which is entirely sur-

rounded by the Axis armies, beyond reach of any help from
the democracies, that Switzerland which cannot live without trading with the surrounding Axis countries, still is an
independent democracy. The "engulfing sea of 125,000,000
hostile neighbors" has not yet engulfed the Swiss.

That is the remarkable thing about Switzerland. The
real news is not that her factories make munitions for
Germany but that the Swiss have an army which stands
guard against invasion, that their frontiers are defended,
that their free institutions continue to exist and that there
has been no Swiss Quisling, and no Swiss Laval. The Swiss
remained true to themselves even in the darkest days of
1940 and 1941, when it seemed that nothing but the valor
of the British and the blind faith of free men elsewhere
stood between Hitler and the creation of a totalitarian new
order in Europe. Surely, if ever the honor of a people was
put to the test, the honor of the Swiss was tested and proved
then and there. How easy it would have been then for them
to say that they must hasten to join the new order, and lick
the boots of the conqueror of Europe. Their devotion to
freedom must be strong and deep. For no ordinary worldly
material calculation can account for the behavior of the
Swiss.[4]

The behavior of the Swiss was of critical importance, Lippmann
continued, because the majority were, "by Hitler's standards, members of the German race," who lived on Germany's border and within its economic jurisdiction. He concluded:

Yet they have demonstrated that the traditions of freedom
can be stronger than the ties of race and of language and
economic interest. Could there be a more poignant, a more
dramatic, a more conclusive answer to the moral foundations of Nazism than that which Switzerland has given?[5]

In Switzerland the *Journal de Genève*, commenting on these articles, compared the persistence of the Swiss to endure in the present

war, which the Americans praised, to "the spirit of the American pioneers."[6]

The Nazis themselves certainly did not consider Switzerland to be, as Lanius put it, "Nazi-occupied." Two days after his article was published, the Swiss Federal Council ordered the seizure and forbade the sale of the latest edition of the German publication *Meyers Konversations Lexikon,* Volume 9, for "insulting language towards this country." The book presented "appreciations of Switzerland today" in these words, according to the *New York Times:*

> A country that, like London and Paris, is no longer anything but a dumping place for doubtful individuals who abuse their liberty. . . . It is peopled by a medley of criminals, particularly Jews.
>
> The Switzerland of today is a backward State detached from the German Empire. But even today the greater part of its inhabitants belong to the 'German body' [*Deutscher Volkskörper*].[7]

"Switzerland stands today an island in a Nazi ocean," a *Times* editorial commented. While forced by economic necessity to produce for the Nazi war machine, "spiritually they refuse to be conquered." The *Times* continued:

> Perhaps the Swiss didn't mind being called "a medley of criminals, particularly Jews." To be called a criminal by a Nazi is to receive a high compliment. To be called a Jew by a Nazi is to be classed with those who have suffered martyrdom for freedom's sake.[8]

Even with Nazi bombers minutes away, the Swiss had suppressed Nazi organizations in their country. Their pastors denounced anti-Semitism. While the Swiss protested Allied flights over their territory, they would shoot down Nazi planes. "Hitler may yet, in some last despairing thrust, occupy their country. He won't conquer it."[9]

The Swiss were able to continue shipping highly strategic products to the Allies throughout the war, either with German approval or by smuggling. Of the strategic war materials, the most important items were jewel bearings, used in the flight instruments of bombers. In March, American Minister Leland Harrison urged that Swiss requests for military supplies be favorably considered. Secretary of State Cordell Hull told the Joint Chiefs of Staff regarding the shipment of supplies to Switzerland: "It is in our vital interests that the Swiss Army be maintained at the highest possible standard of military preparedness and efficiency. While supply routes to Switzerland are still open, advantage should be taken to bring the Swiss Army up to the level essential for the defense of Switzerland, regardless of any present or pending agreement of a compensatory nature." The State Department understood that the Swiss Army needed to remain strong to resist German demands to send troops through Switzerland or otherwise violate her neutrality.[10]

On January 6, 1943, General Guisan sent a confidential report to the federal cabinet on the increased danger of a future "Fortress Europe," in which the Nazis would attempt to seize the passes and tunnels of the Alps along with its defensive positions. An invader would try to seize these key points in a surprise attack, before the Swiss had time to destroy them.[11]

The American military attaché in Bern prepared an intelligence message dated January 29 that the German General Staff was "studying [a] new plan [for the] invasion of Switzerland" and that, on an Allied invasion of Italy, "Germany could not have large parts of a mountainous frontier held by a nation which was," in the words of this American officer, "only [an] advance guard of [the] Allies." The German plan was a "surprise air invasion before the Swiss could concentrate in their National Redoubt," in which "parachute and air landings troops neutralize troop concentrations" and "motorized and mechanized ground invading forces" make an assault across the borders. The Germans had prepared a scale map of the *Réduit*, a copy of which was obtained by Allied intelligence.[12]

By February 2, the last German holdouts in Stalingrad had laid down their arms. An entire army of a quarter-million men had been wiped off the map. Thus released from the siege, half-a-million Soviets were added to the westward offensive that threatened to destroy the entire German Army Group South. During the days of heady German expansion, the Swiss had been in the Nazis' sights; now Switzerland's neighbor had become a wounded animal that might do anything to survive. If the Germans continued to fall back from Russia pursued by the Red Army, all of central Europe could become a desperate battleground.

In February and March, 1943, OSS operative Allen Dulles met secretly with two German spies, one of whom worked under General Walter Schellenberg, the chief of SS foreign intelligence. The content of the meeting is unknown, but it took place at the time when Wehrmacht generals were plotting assassination attempts against Hitler.[13]

On March 3, General Guisan had a secret meeting with Schellenberg, whose organization conducted espionage against Switzerland and areas nearby. The Swiss had all bases covered. As Allen Dulles noted, he (Dulles) had lines of communication open with Swiss intelligence officer Max Waibel, while Colonel Roger Masson of the Swiss General Staff had contact with Schellenberg, head of Himmler's intelligence service.[14] Masson set up Schellenberg's meeting with Guisan.[15]

Schellenberg's motive for meeting with the General was apparently to size up the Swiss leader for purposes of planning future operations to incorporate the Swiss Alps into Germany's defenses.[16] Guisan explained his own purpose as follows: "I did not want to neglect any occasion to confirm in our northern neighbor's mind the sentiment, which was evidently not strong at all, that our army would fulfill its mission under all circumstances and would fight against anybody attacking our neutrality."[17]

Meeting at the Bären Inn in the town of Biglen in northern Switzerland, Guisan told Schellenberg in no uncertain terms that Switzerland would resist any invader and that a Nazi assault would result in instant destruction of the Alpine railroads.[18]

In early 1943, Italian planners continued to discuss an invasion of Switzerland.[19] Hitler retained similar designs, partly because of his concern about an Allied invasion of Italy. On March 14, the Führer warned his commanders that "the loss of Tunisia will also mean the loss of Italy." Plans for "Case Switzerland" were therefore revived in the event that a collapse in Italy allowed the Allies to reach the Alps.

Schellenberg reminded the commanders that Switzerland would succumb, if at all, only through conquest.[20]

In Munich on March 20, 1943, General Eduard Dietl, who had commanded mountain troops in the invasion of Norway, and more recently on the Murmansk front in alliance with the Finns, prepared a "Switzerland command" that would use air transport and parachute forces.[21] The day before, Swiss intelligence, with its "Wiking Line" source in the German high command, reported to Bern that the Germans were planning an invasion. It was believed that German mountain troops were concentrating in Bavaria. This episode became known as the *März-Alarm* (March Alarm).[22]

The German General Staff had, indeed, been discussing a strategic retreat from Russia into "Fortress Europe"—of which Switzerland could be made a pillar. The SS had orders to prepare such a plan and wished to incorporate the Swiss Alpine positions. Fortunately for the Swiss, Hitler decided against a strategic retreat in the East at this time because of recent German success there.[23] German Field Marshal Erich von Manstein had halted the huge Soviet offensive in the southern sector, rolled it back, and on March 12 the Germans had retaken the Soviet Union's fourth-largest city, Kharkov.

According to one account, a week later it was learned that the warning resulting in the *März-Alarm* may have been planted by the Germans to encourage the Swiss to keep their troops mobilized in order to deter an Allied invasion through Switzerland. The rumor may also have been started as leverage for the benefit of German trade negotiators then engaged in talks with the Swiss, who had recently reduced credit and exports to Germany.[24]

According to another account, when "Wiking" warned Swiss intelligence of "Case Switzerland," Swiss Colonel Masson naïvely asked Schellenberg if it was true. This tipped the latter off to the fact that a leak existed in Hitler's headquarters. Since any element of surprise was lost for a German attack, which the Swiss were now preparing to defend against, Schellenberg later told Masson that he had persuaded the German command against launching an invasion.[25]

OSS operative Allen Dulles was aware that the Nazis made plans to invade Switzerland in 1943 during the last stages of the battle for North Africa. Dulles later reflected:

At the peak of its mobilization Switzerland had 850,000 men under arms or standing in reserve, a fifth of the total population. . . . That Switzerland did not have to fight was thanks to its will to resist and its large investment of men and equipment in its own defense. The cost to Germany of an invasion of Switzerland would certainly have been very high.

During his tenure as the chief American agent in Switzerland, Dulles made clear to the Swiss that "the stronger they were in their preparations against a German attack, the better we liked it."[26]

As the German position in North Africa neared liquidation by the Allies, and Russia hung in the balance, increased talk of a "Fortress Europe" led Guisan to believe that a very real danger of invasion loomed. Himmler and his colleagues began to contemplate a last stand that could join the Swiss *Réduit* with the Black Forest, the Arlberg and the Bavarian Alps, the Brenner Pass and the Dolomites. A coup against the Swiss, whose troops were outnumbered six to one, would prolong the war.[27]

Perhaps in reaction to this tension, the SSV shooting federation encouraged heightened vigilance. To the Swiss, freedom was the "highest good on earth," but only power and force could secure it.[28] The SSV printed a message from Federal Councillor Karl Kobelt, head of the Military Department, encouraging every person to join an official defense organization. Kobelt stated:

Every Swiss who is able to fight and shoot can participate in the fight for our country. But in order not to be regarded as *Heckenschuetze* [outlaw sniper], he must join an official military organization, the military service, *Ortswehr* [local defense], or *Luftschutz* [anti-aircraft defense] and be subject to their rules. . . . The civil population not organized in battle corps . . . must stay out of active armed participation in battle.[29]

Switzerland was thus relying on the Land War Law of the Hague Convention, which protected a member of a military organization, if captured, from being shot on the spot as an unofficial partisan. Had an invasion actually occurred, it is unclear whether the Germans would have respected this rule; they seemed to have done so more in their Western than their Eastern campaigns. It seems unlikely that Swiss who were not members of an official organization would have foregone resistance activities for that reason. Then again, virtually every Swiss capable of bearing arms was already a member of an officially recognized organization. This raised the question, which the German foreign minister mentioned in 1940, of whether almost the entire population of a country must be recognized under international law as being in a military force.[30] In the event of capture, would armed civilians with military armbands be treated as prisoners of war or would they be shot?

Many German military professionals, excluding the SS, recognized the principles of international law. However, the German Army had traditionally abhorred partisan or guerrilla warfare, so it was important that Swiss fighters be recognizable as national soldiers rather than irregulars in any combat with the Wehrmacht. There were no guarantees. The Führer himself had never been greatly impressed with any laws of warfare or nations.

In a May 8 diary entry, Nazi Propaganda Minister Goebbels described Hitler's address to the conference of the Reichsleiters and Gauleiters, the Nazi Party sub-leaders. "The Führer deduced that all the rubbish of small nations [*Kleinstaaten-Geruempel*] still existing in Europe must be liquidated as fast as possible."[31] Hitler defended Charlemagne, even though he was branded the "Butcher of the Saxons," and asked:

> Who will guarantee to the Führer that at some later time he
> will not be attacked as the "Butcher of the Swiss"? Austria,
> after all, also had to be forced into the Reich. We can be
> happy that it happened in such a peaceful and enthusiastic
> manner; but if [Austrian Chancellor] Schuschnigg had
> offered resistance, it would have been necessary, of course,
> to overcome this resistance by force.[32]

Hitler had not yet ventured to become the butcher of the Swiss, in part because the Swiss had the arms and capacity to kill an unacceptably large number of invaders. Indeed, in this period the Swiss Military Department reissued the famous order requiring a fight to the end and prohibiting surrender. On May 24, General Guisan recalled the directions "concerning the conduct of the soldiers not under arms in event of attack" that had been issued on April 18, 1940, and that since then had been printed in the soldiers' Service Books. The General now directed that the particular portions of the order be adapted to reflect the replacement of certain guarding tasks of the soldiers by Auxiliary Patrol Companies, *Ortswehren*, air raid defense organizations and factory guards.[33] The general provisions of the remarkable no-surrender order remained the same.

On May 31, General Guisan addressed the meeting of the Swiss Society of Noncommissioned Officers in the town of Arbon. Warning that the war would be fought ever closer to the Swiss borders, he noted that preparations for combat must be adjusted accordingly. The strategy must "offer to inflict heavy losses on the potential enemy." Promising that "the first to penetrate into our country will be our enemy," Guisan stated that "the people and the army are united more than ever. There are no French, Italian or German Swiss; there is only an indivisible Switzerland."[34]

As has been shown, a crucial part of the Swiss strategy was widespread armed resistance on the part of individuals or small units. Elsewhere in Europe, populations had little means with which to fight back against German forces, even after the murderous policies of the occupying power had become clear. The heroic Warsaw ghetto uprising demonstrated that a small population with arms in its hands could effectively resist the Nazis. The second Warsaw *aktsia*, meaning the violent roundup and deportation of Jews to death camps, which began in early 1943, sparked resistance. Simha Rotem, a member of the Jewish Fighting Organization (Zydowska Organizacja Bojowa, or ZOB), described the situation:

> I and my comrades in the ZOB were determined to fight, but we had almost no weapons, except for a few scattered pistols. . . . In other places, where there were weapons, there was shooting, which amazed the Germans. A few of them

were killed and their weapons were taken as loot, which apparently was decisive in the struggle. Three days later, the *aktsia* ceased. The sudden change in their plans resulted from our unforeseen resistance.[35]

ZOB members obtained more pistols and some grenades by the time of the April 19 *aktsia*. Rotem recalled that, despite the Germans' heavy arms, after an SS unit was ambushed:

> I saw and I didn't believe: German soldiers screaming in panicky flight, leaving their wounded behind. . . . We weren't marksmen but we did hit some. The Germans took off. But they came back later, fearful, their fingers on their triggers. They didn't walk, they ran next to the walls.[36]

Dozens of Germans were killed, but partisan losses were few. In the first three days not a single Jew was taken out of the buildings. Finally, the Germans resorted to artillery and aerial bombings to reduce the ghetto to rubble. On the tenth day, the ghetto was burned down. Many fighters escaped through sewers and into the forests. There they continued the struggle in cooperation with non-Jewish partisans.[37]

The great Warsaw ghetto uprising of Passover 1943 is described by the U.S. Holocaust Memorial Museum in Washington, D.C. in the following succinct manner:

> More than 2,000 heavily armed German soldiers and police were backed by tanks and artillery. The 700 to 750 ghetto fighters had a few dozen pistols and hand grenades. Yet in three days of street battles, the Germans were unable to defeat the Jewish combatants.[38]

During the fighting, 24-year-old Mordecai Anieleicz wrote to his liaison with the Polish underground: "Jewish self-defense in the Warsaw ghetto has become a fact. Jewish armed resistance and revenge have become a reality."[39] Ironically, this was confirmed in Joseph Goebbels' May 1 diary entry about the occupied areas:

The only noteworthy item is the exceedingly serious fights in Warsaw between the police and even a part of our Wehrmacht on the one hand and the rebellious Jews on the other. The Jews have actually succeeded in making a defensive position of the Ghetto. Heavy engagements are being fought there. . . . It shows what is to be expected of the Jews when they are in possession of arms.[40]

The uprising was defeated but it demonstrated the viability of armed resistance. As *Notre Voix* (*Our Voice*), a French Jewish partisan paper, stated:

The Warsaw Jews have given to their brothers, and to the whole world, an admirable example of courage. . . . Let us arm ourselves; let us form defense groups to fight back all attempts at arrest and deportation; let us strengthen the Resistance organization. . . . Let us attack the enemy wherever he may be.[41]

In retrospect it is tragic that the means, both physical and spiritual, forcibly to resist Nazism had not been engendered years before among the groups and nationalities conquered by Hitler. However, before the war and even during the years of German conquests, 1939–41, few people had fully recognized the magnitude of the horrors to come. (The infamous Wannsee Conference took place in January 1942.) Whole countries were surrendered by their leaders to the Führer without a fight, and this attitude of defeatism infected individuals, groups and nations. By 1943, universal resistance, of the kind that Switzerland planned in her own defense, was no longer possible in Europe at large, even though increasing numbers of partisans were fighting back with whatever weapons were at hand. In picking up arms to resist the Nazis, the heroes of the Warsaw ghetto were acting with the same philosophy that had inspired and would save the Swiss.

Polish Jews who fought back from the forests—their equivalent to the Alps in terms of defensive terrain—also illustrated how anti-Nazi defenders with only a few firearms could successfully combat the Wehrmacht. In 1942, resistance leader Harold Werner met about 40

Jews waiting to go to the ghetto, and recruited 15 of them to hide in the forest. They had not a single gun and were even attacked by wild boars and wolves. Eventually they purchased sawed-off shotguns and other firearms from local villagers.[42]

The Jews entered into alliances with Russian partisans. Werner stated that the "Russians had weapons, and the Germans knew that they were armed. The Germans were more cautious in attacking when they knew there would be resistance." The Jews' first attack "was a tremendous uplift to our morale to be able to hit back at the Germans. It was also important to us to show the villagers that Jews, once armed, would strike back."[43]

The group tried to persuade Jews at the Adampol slave labor camp to join them in the forest, but the inmates feared the Germans would kill them. The partisans explained that the Germans had superior forces, "but our bullets were just as deadly as theirs, and they were just as afraid of us as we were of them. I explained that the woods were our protection, and that it was easy to disappear into them. . . . I showed them my gun and said: 'Only this will save us.' "[44]

An armed partisan who escaped from the Warsaw ghetto uprising joined the group. "It made us feel fortunate to be in the woods, free and armed with weapons with which to defend ourselves." In a typical ambush, the partisans killed 20 Germans and lost only one of their own.[45]

By the summer of 1943, the group numbered three hundred fighters, both men and women, all armed. Many of the arms were World War I leftovers. In one incident, the Germans ambushed the forest hideout. Some forty boys and elderly men with rifles held the enemy at bay. The armed Jews effected the escape of many and held off the Germans, although most of the defenders were ultimately killed. In other fights, the Jews and other partisans prevailed over the Germans.[46]

As a non-belligerent, Switzerland had a prominent humanitarian role to play in the war. That role was featured in the May 1 *Saturday Evening Post*, which began, "Other people make wars and the Swiss pick up the pieces." The Swiss had shipped food and medical supplies into desperate areas like Greece and Yugoslavia, brought in French,

Belgian and Dutch children for rehabilitation, and had sent nurses and doctors to dangerous war zones. The International Committee of the Red Cross in Geneva maintained records on 1,600,000 war prisoners and sent out countless letters each day. The Swiss safeguarded the rights of both Allied and Axis war prisoners, thereby earning the trust of both sides.[47] The Swiss themselves bore three-fourths of the costs of their humanitarian efforts, mostly from voluntary contributions. As an example, 10,000 children brought in for rehabilitation stayed in private homes.[48]

As a neutral, Switzerland also served as an important financial center to which funds for the resistance in occupied Europe could be transferred. The American Joint Distribution Committee funneled money for the Jewish Resistance in France through the *Vaad Hatzalah* (Palestine Rescue Funds) in Istanbul, from which funds were transferred to Switzerland.[49]

Marc Jarblum, a founder of the French Jewish Resistance, escaped from the Gestapo over the Swiss border in April 1943. From Geneva, he informed the world of the needs of the French Resistance, both Jewish and non-Jewish. Saly Mayer, the Joint Distribution Committee head in Switzerland, transferred funds to Jarblum, who distributed them to the Jewish Army, the Communists, and other resistance groups.[50]

The Intergovernmental Committee on Refugees was reorganized in April 1943 at the Bermuda Conference to consider the refugee problem. Nothing was solved because none of the countries, including the United States, was prepared to absorb the refugees. In proportion to her population, tiny Switzerland gave asylum to more refugees than any other country.[51]

Switzerland pleaded with the United States to allow an increase in Swiss foreign trade so that the beleaguered nation could afford to admit more refugees. The U.S. Department of State promised to give sympathetic consideration to the request, acknowledging:

> The United States Government is aware of and appreciates greatly the generous reception which the Swiss Government has extended to the large numbers of refugees who have made their way to Swiss territory.[52]

French Jewish resister Anny Latour wrote that, despite Swiss border guards preventing entry to many adult Jews, "On the brighter side, however, there was an attempt made to rescue the children—they were not sent back, but arms were outstretched to them, and many were thus saved from slaughter." Rescuers would slip past German soldiers and Vichy police, snip the barbed wire, and send the children running through the opening. "Once on Swiss soil, they were safe—Switzerland, sanctuary for Jewish children."[53]

Smuggled children needed both a false and a real identification, the latter to present to Swiss authorities and to the Relief Organization for Children in Geneva, which would care for them. Swiss border guards sometimes also permitted adults with small children to cross the border.[54]

Georges Loinger smuggled some 600 children into Switzerland. He would take children to a soccer field fifty meters from the border. Some would play while others sneaked across the border. When the Gestapo became suspicious, Loinger managed, just a hundred meters from a German patrol, to throw his wife and two children over the barbed wire. Swiss soldiers helped them escape. Loinger continued his rescue work until the Liberation.[55]

The Swiss Army's Adjutant General issued an official pamphlet entitled *Die Judenfrage* (*The Jewish Question*) on May 25. It noted that extremist, nationalist movements had persecuted Jews from the Middle Ages to the present. After an analysis of the historical role of Jews in Switzerland and present demographics, the article stated:

Article 4 of the Federal Constitution states that every Swiss is equal before the law. Democracy is based on the principle of tolerance, tolerance of different views, but also—and to be sure, nowhere like in Switzerland—vis-à-vis different races, different languages and different religions. Mass, race, and class hatred [*Massen-, rassen-, und Klassenhass*] are fundamentally undemocratic principles.[56]

Allowing a political doctrine based on racial hatred to be espoused in Switzerland meant letting in an irreconcilable ideology. "Anti-Semitism is simply intolerance," the Swiss Army publication asserted. "It is therefore undemocratic and tears at the roots of our democratic way of thinking." The *Judenfrage* pamphlet concluded: "Anti-Semitism is an invasion of foreign propaganda."[57]

On July 7, the Federal Council banned two additional National Socialist parties: Rassemblement Fédéral and National Gemeindschaft Schaffhausen. Two members of these groups had previously been executed by military order for giving military information to a foreign power. The decree of dissolution applied to any organization that would replace these groups.

The *New York Times* noted that the government adhered to neutrality, but the people were overwhelmingly anti-Axis. "Switzerland, acting strictly within her rights as a neutral, sells Germany goods that Germany needs." However, "the Swiss are just the people, if pushed a mite too far, who would prefer to starve or die fighting rather than give in. Because they are that kind of people they may not have to prove it in action."[58]

In May the Allies sought assurances from the Swiss regarding Axis use of the Gotthard railroad. At the Gotthard Convention of 1909, the Swiss had guaranteed that use of the railroad would not be interrupted.[59] On June 29, the Federal Council stated to the U.S. Department of State that it adhered to the declaration of neutrality and would never allow foreign troops or military stores to pass through the country. The Council asserted: "As for the transit through Switzerland, the Swiss government is resolved to observe conscientiously the rules of the Law of Nations, as well as International Conventions and to take care that [the transit] is handled in conformity with Switzerland's policy of neutrality."[60]

These assertions would soon be put to the test. On July 9 a mammoth Anglo-American invasion force landed in Sicily. The Italian Army made only a half-hearted defense, and it soon became clear that the Germans alone could not hold the island. Italy would soon become a theater of war. On July 25, Hitler received the news that Mussolini had been deposed. He immediately dispatched eight divisions from Army Group B under Rommel's command to northern Italy to secure the Alpine passes. This would ensure the supply pipeline to the Wehrmacht forces already in Italy and those still fighting in Sicily.[61]

Once again, the Nazis threatened to pass through Switzerland, this time to keep Italy in the Axis—a threat that would worry the Swiss profoundly in the months to come. If the Germans had carried out this plan, the Swiss made it clear that they would defend their borders, then fight from the *Réduit*, where resistance would continue indefinitely. The tunnels would be destroyed and with them rail linkage with Italy, thus defeating the military purpose of any invasion. The Germans were again deterred.[62]

In the Soviet Union, the Germans had made one last attempt to deal a crippling blow to the Red Army, at Kursk, resulting in history's greatest tank battle. On July 15, after ten days of heavy casualties, the attack was called off, and the Soviets immediately launched a series of counteroffensives. Even as the panzers gave ground, key units were pulled from the front and transferred to Italy. The Germans would never regain the strategic initiative in the East. Although the Swiss cheered any Wehrmacht defeat, the spectre of the main Nazi armies falling back on central Europe for defense implied a new and dangerous development.

With its "unlimited will for independence," Switzerland would have been a rebellious province had she been in the New Order, and in any event was "an enemy to the Reich" and was in "solidarity with the suppressed nations," in the words of the Swiss Shooting Federation (SSV).[63] These published comments no doubt confirmed to the Gestapo that the names of the SSV leadership must be on the list of persons to execute when the invasion came.

The Allies completed their liberation of Sicily on August 17, although the German defenders had effected an evacuation to the mainland with most of their equipment during the preceding week. Mussolini's fall intensified bombings of Italian ports, including Genoa, from which the Swiss had shipped goods for the American market. *Business Week* reported that "Swiss trade may now be reaching the end of the line."[64]

The British Eighth Army landed on the boot of southern Italy on September 3. Five days later the American Fifth landed farther up the coast, at Salerno, south of Naples. That same day the secret armistice between the Allies and Italy was announced. The security of northern Italy now became critical for Germany, and its factories ran overtime to turn out munitions for the Wehrmacht.[65] Shortly after the capitulation, almost 4,000 Italian civilians and thousands of escaped Allied prisoners of war entered Switzerland.[66]

After the Allied invasion of Italy, the Germans concluded that a decisive battle would eventually take place for "Fortress Europe," in which Switzerland might be forced to play a role.[67] The Germans continued to debate their Italian strategy. Field Marshal Rommel advocated falling back to defend the Alpine mountain passes in the north—a strategy that would have put Switzerland near the front line. Field Marshal Albert Kesselring, however, convinced Hitler that the Allies could be held off during the coming winter in the mountainous terrain south of Rome.

On September 13, the SS accomplished the daring rescue of Mussolini, who was being held captive and waiting to be turned over to the Allies. The Führer set up a new fascist government in northern Italy under the Duce.[68] Since Italy's surrender could have sent German or Italian troops rushing into Swiss territory, on September 15 partial remobilization was ordered in Switzerland. The Swiss anticipated that the Wehrmacht might launch a surprise attack to seize the key positions protecting the passages to the center of the Alps in an attempt to keep transit lines open.[69]

A broadcast to America from the Swiss Schwarzenburg station on September 16 asserted:

> Now that Italy has capitulated and the northern Italian territories have been occupied by German troops, the Swiss situation has become very difficult. She is now dealing not with just one coalition, but with just one country. The customs officers of that one country control all possible openings with the outside world. Switzerland must, therefore, now suffer from the effects of the counter-blockade and stop all economic exchange with America. It is not yet possible to measure fully all the consequences of this new situation. In any case, just one word describes it: "Encirclement."[70]

On September 17, officials in Bern denied a rumor that the Swiss government had received an ultimatum demanding transit privileges for German troops through Switzerland. Messages communicated by means of diplomatic circles in Stockholm contained information that, after setbacks to the Allies at Salerno, the Germans had demanded passage for the Wehrmacht. It was believed that the Swiss refused, but that the Germans would not take no for an answer. Even if the Swiss blew up the St. Gotthard and Simplon tunnels, the German high command was said to have planned to use the roads across these passes, built by Napoleon, which could carry artillery. The routes through Austria and France by which reinforcements could be sent were considered vulnerable to Allied air attack. While German control over northern Italy isolated Switzerland more than ever before, in the face of this imminent danger the Swiss mobilization demonstrated the nation's resolve to maintain neutrality and prevent any passage by belligerents through her territory.[71]

Now that the war was at their doorstep, the Swiss were never more determined.[72] Heretofore, Hitler believed Guisan's warnings that Switzerland would be defended at all costs, allowing her to avoid the fate of the other neutrals. But Switzerland was now even more of a prize than in 1939–40, for she separated the Reich from its own forces in Italy.[73] Switzerland was a natural path for both reinforcements and retreat.

On September 26, Federal Councillor Karl Kobelt, chief of the Department of Defense, told a gathering of women in St. Gallen:

> There can never be and must never be any doubt but that we will categorically reject any demand for passage through Switzerland by troops of a foreign country. Should an attempt be made to force such a passage, we will resist with arms.[74]

The Swiss predicament was treated with understanding in the September issue of the *Yale Review*, which contended that "Swiss political sympathies . . . are reflected by the relative accuracy of her anti-aircraft batteries. Only two British planes have been shot down, but some fifteen German planes have been brought down by their fire."[75]

While forced to conform to numerous German economic demands, Switzerland's independence was protected by her ability to destroy her mountain tunnels and by her democratic army, which could hold out for a very long time:

> Stores of ammunition have been hidden in rocks and crevices, during the past four years, large enough to enable the Swiss to carry on a savage guerrilla warfare. . . . Swiss artillery is embedded in crevices at an altitude of 10,000 feet, where it is inaccessible to tanks and unassailable from the air.

The author of the article noted that if a poll were taken "to determine whether the Swiss people want a victory of the Anglo-Americans or of the Germans, 95 percent would be in favor of the United States and Great Britain."[76]

Due to the change in Switzerland's position after the German occupation of northern Italy, trade by the Swiss again became a vital question for the Allies. In a secret memorandum dated November 29, entitled "Trade with Switzerland," representatives of the British Chiefs of Staff pointed out to their American counterparts:

> 1. The British Chiefs of Staff attach considerable importance to the military advantages they now derive from Swiss neutrality and are anxious that our policy towards Switzerland should aim at ensuring that these advantages are neither discontinued nor curtailed.
>
> 2. These advantages include the following:
>
> a. Switzerland is an important source of intelligence.
>
> b. Switzerland is the protecting power for prisoners of war. In addition to their official duties as protecting power the Swiss render many valuable services to our prisoners, e.g., the distribution of parcels to prison camps and assistance to escaped and escaping prisoners.
>
> c. Certain valuable materials of importance to the war effort find their way to us from Switzerland with the connivance of the authorities. These materials include special R.A.F. plotting equipment, jewels for instruments, machine

tools, stop-watches and theodolites to the value of some £300,000 per year.

    3. The British Chiefs of Staff accordingly hope that the U.S. Chiefs of Staff will support the proposals which have been made by the British Government for the dispatch of certain supplies for the Swiss Army."[77]

Tough negotiations over trade issues persisted throughout the year. Winfield Riefler, America's chief negotiator, warned the Department of State about blacklisting: "When we threaten to list such firms, therefore, we simply force them to choose between Axis orders which they have the ability to fill and overseas orders, the continuation of which are uncertain because of Germany's counter-blockade."[78]

In the trade agreement of December 19, 1943, the Swiss met most Allied demands.[79] Swiss exports to Germany, particularly arms and machine parts, were sharply curtailed. The Allies restored the quotas for food, but could not guarantee the supply of scarce items needed for survival. Thus, as a result, trade with Germany was decreased without equivalent increases in Allied trade.[80]

As late as 1943, the Waffen SS had not abandoned its earlier plans for an attack. The circles around Himmler hoped for an opportunity to retaliate against Switzerland for her anti–National Socialist stance. Preparations for an invasion plan were assigned to SS General Hermann Böhme, who became chief of the Austrian military intelligence service after the *Anschluss*. Böhme, who was knowledgeable about Switzerland as a result of his intelligence work, drafted his plan, entitled "Thoughts Concerning the Defense Situation of Switzerland in Event of a German Armed Intervention," in late 1943.[81] It is a highly important document, demonstrating how high-ranking Nazis regarded Switzerland during the war. In brief, they were both impressed with her capacity for resistance and angered at her refusal to be drawn into the New Order and particularly at her support for the Allies.

Böhme analyzed the changing military situation since 1938 and how it had affected the Swiss. Germany's 1940 victory in France had

had profound effects on Switzerland. Deeply impressed by the great efficiency of the German Army, the Swiss Army leadership tried to adapt its forces to new military realities. Switzerland had two difficulties: first, she had to impress Germany with the speed of her military adaptability, and second, she had to obtain German approval to import the material required for her armament. Böhme described the Swiss rejection of the New Order:

> Although expectations would have been that the new military-political situation in Europe would also lead to a total alteration of Swiss politics in all areas, reports only showed too clearly, however, that internal politics degenerated into a peculiar defensive posture. The visible consequence is the *Réduit*: fight, instead of putting itself entirely into the concerns of the new Europe.[82]

As a result of her rejection of the "New Europe," Böhme noted, Switzerland failed to join the crusade against the Soviet Union. No significant number of Swiss volunteers joined. Yet Switzerland should have known that the realities of political power in 1941 made survival "dependent in first instance on the will of the German Reich." The Reich's late 1942 seizure of Vichy France demonstrated again that Switzerland was surrounded on all sides by territory under German control. Yet the Swiss continued their efforts to decrease dependence on German influence. Their food supply in particular was rearranged, as much as possible, to rely on domestic production.[83]

One could not expect, Böhme continued, a reversal of the Swiss mood after 1942 brought the Allied invasion of North Africa and the German setbacks in the East. Yet the Swiss resistance to Germany's potential power remained baffling, as the following demonstrated:

> 1. The defense against Allied flights over Swiss territory is insufficient in view of the existing possibilities.
> 2. A bulk of news reporting in broadcasting and the press is anti-German. Germany has no good press in Switzerland.
> 3. The granting of asylum to so-called refugees and the

presence of large numbers of Allied intelligence services greatly damage German-Swiss relationships.

4. By its numerous interconnections of Swiss capital with foreign countries, Switzerland is organized in the interests of the Allied forces more and more. A German victory in Europe would have disastrous consequences for that Swiss capital.

5. Members of German-friendly army circles, who always give an assurance of strict neutrality, fall cold.[84]

Anticipating that the Allies might include Switzerland within their strategic plans, Böhme asked: "How can Switzerland be conquered quickly by military force under the present realities?" He proceeded to consider in detail the strength of Swiss national defense, recognizing that the Swiss Army had a great tradition which utilized the power of the people. While there were 470,000 soldiers to contend with in 1939, there would be 550,000 by the end of 1943. He calculated four corps with 10 to 12 divisions, including light brigades, mountain brigades and border troops. The troops were geared toward infantry. Domestic industry supplied the army with good quantities of firearms, machine guns to 34mm, cannon to 120mm, ammunition and motor vehicles. The air force had only 250 planes and no bombers. Fortifications both in the interior and at the borders had greatly increased.[85]

Swiss weaknesses, on the other hand, included the inexperience of the army in combat, insufficient tanks and air power, and the nearness of industry to combat zones. Yet the value of the Swiss Army should not be underrated. Böhme wrote:

> The *fighting spirit* of Swiss soldiers is very high, and we will have to equate it approximately to that of the Finns. A people that produces good gymnasts also produces good soldiers. The unconditional patriotism of the Swiss is beyond doubt. Despite the militia system, the shooting instruction is better than, for example, in the former Austrian Federal Army with 18 months term of service.[86]

General Böhme obviously had a high regard for the resistance spirit of Switzerland.[87] In stressing that losses would be heavy because the Swiss were first-class shots, Böhme's impressions reflected exactly what Swiss defensive strategy aimed to make known to potential enemies.[88]

Since 1939, Böhme continued, numerous Swiss units of all weapons types had the opportunity to become proficient. While the Swiss lacked combat experience, they would be fighting in familiar terrain. If Switzerland could survive the critical first weeks, numerous combat-experienced troops would be available.[89]

Swiss armament was insufficient in many ways, he observed, but the high command effectively promoted up-to-date training and arming, and, just as the Germans, the Swiss would improvise in making the best possible use of arms. Strong border fortifications which had been built since 1938 were an obstacle and would make up for other deficiencies. Thorough destruction near the border would create serious barriers. The *Réduit* would provide a strong defense and guarantee reserves.[90]

The goal of an attack, Böhme was certain, must be to take complete possession of an intact Switzerland. An armed intervention was not profitable unless Swiss industry was captured undamaged, electric power and railways were intact and there was a population willing and able to work. The reprovisioning of Germany being a high priority, it would not be advisable to undertake a military operation that would transform Switzerland into a desert.[91]

The German planner anticipated that it would take a large number of Axis forces to overcome the resistance of the Swiss troops defending the steep Alpine *Réduit*.[92] Even after the conquest of the Swiss, Böhme acknowledged, permanent German security forces would be required to guarantee the pacification of the country.[93]

Böhme detailed two operations to be executed independently of each other. Operation I would have the main focus of attack in the north with occupation of the Mittelland, swift occupation of the Swiss airfields, and capture of the mass of the Swiss Army. Operation II would penetrate the *Réduit* with paratroopers, mountain troops, and ground forces. It would be incumbent that, in the first 72 hours, the

German Plan for Conquest
"Böhme"

SS General Hermann Böhme's attack plan against Switzerland completed in December 1943 after the Germans had occupied northern Italy. Recommended for execution in August 1944, the Allied invasion of Normandy in June rendered the plan moot. (Adapted from Kurz, *Die Schweiz in der Planung*, 51.)

paratroopers cut off the Plateau from the *Réduit*. The Luftwaffe would fend off any possible Allied bomber attacks.[94]

The actual operations and places of attack proposed by Böhme were highly detailed. He recommended a surprise attack from all sides with fifteen divisions. Casualties were expected to be twenty percent. The attack would be conducted in the summer of 1944, preferably in August.[95]

The Allied invasion of Normandy in June 1944, two months before the recommended time of Böhme's plan of operations, would render the plan inoperable.[96] But that was in the unforeseeable future. For now, General Guisan's Christmas message to the soldiers at St. Gotthard included the watchwords: "Double our vigilance, hold the rifle tightly in our hand!"[97]

Chapter 9

1944

War at the Border

THE NEW YEAR OPENED WITH A DRAMATIC CONFIRMATION OF
the continuing Nazi threat. A Luftwaffe twin-engine plane flying over
the Bernese Jura Mountains responded with gunfire to Swiss orders to
land. In the dogfight that followed, Swiss fighters shot it down.[1]

War Department Minister Karl Kobelt, in a speech at Winterthur
on January 24, expressed confidence that Switzerland could protect
her independence because of

> an extraordinarily high number of small strongpoints,
> countless mined objectives, and sufficient quantities of
> arms, ammunition and war materials, including food, all
> stored at scientifically chosen central points, to enable us
> not only to bring the battle to the enemy if we are attacked
> but also to live, fight and hold in the interior of Fortress
> Switzerland. We are on guard and are ready for anything.[2]

The same day, the government announced that "in view of the present
necessities, a large part of the 19-year-old class will receive military
instruction immediately."[3]

At the beginning of 1944, there were 16,000 German nationals
in Switzerland. Desperate for manpower, Berlin called almost all able-
bodied citizens home from various countries for war conscription that
year. It is noteworthy that the Germans allowed some 12,600 to
remain in Switzerland, the fifth column card that they believed might
need to be played.[4]

Swiss trade with the belligerents continued during 1944. Both the Allies and the Axis needed Swiss products and had an interest in allowing Switzerland access to raw materials. Both sides had servicemen interned in Switzerland and thus had greater incentive to preserve Swiss neutrality.[5]

On March 29, OSS operative Allen Dulles prepared a report on a conference he had had with General Guisan, who wanted to know whether France would be invaded soon. "He fears the threat to Switzerland present in the fact that the Nazis may wish to use Swiss railroads to transport Nazi forces into safety in the event of a retreat of the Germans from the south."[6]

The Germans occupied Hungary on March 30 in response to an advance by the Red Army on the Carpathians and because they suspected a movement in the Hungarian government to hand the country over to the Soviets. To the Swiss, this proved once again that Hitler could suddenly launch the Wehrmacht into Switzerland any time it suited him or whenever he felt German strategic interests would be served.[7]

The April 1944 issue of *American Mercury* included an intriguing article entitled "If Switzerland Is Invaded." As his attack on the Soviet Union demonstrated, the Führer could do unexpected things. But if Switzerland managed to stay out of the war, said the magazine, it was only because of her ingenious military preparations.[8]

If Switzerland were to be attacked, demolition would begin in seconds. "Terrific explosions [would] rend the air all along the Swiss frontiers, as if hundreds of avalanches were thundering down the mountain slopes of the land." All bridges over the Rhine would collapse, and mines would await invaders who tried to cross by rafts or amphibious tanks. The Simplon and the St. Gotthard tunnels would be immediately destroyed. Roads, railways, bridges, power stations and air fields would be blown up. Camouflaged tank traps and electric barbed-wire fences would stop many panzers and infantry.[9] Just as they had done at the Battle of Morgarten in 1315, when they launched boulders down the mountain sides to crush the Austrian invaders, the Swiss could use modern technology to cause landslides and avalanches that no infantry and armored divisions could survive.

Both World War I and Hitler's blitzkrieg tactics demonstrated to the Swiss General Staff the need for lightning mobilization. As soon as the order was broadcast, every soldier not already on duty would grab his rifle and report to a nearby post. *American Mercury* continued:

> It is the pride of the country that every citizen is allowed to keep his army rifle and ammunition in his house. So orderly and ethically advanced is the population of this model country that there is rarely a case where this officially sanctioned and encouraged custom leads to violence.[10]

American B-17 Flying Fortresses and B-24 Liberators conducted major raids over southern Germany on March 18, destroying a factory that produced the Messerschmitt 109 fighter. Prompting an air-raid alarm, sixteen of the bombers flew into Swiss air space. Most had been damaged in the raids and crash-landed, their crews parachuting to safety and then being interned. Swiss pursuit planes brought down one bomber which appeared to be fleeing.[11]

Fifty Swiss were reported killed and over 150 seriously wounded on April 1 when thirty American Liberator bombers dropped explosive and phosphorus incendiary bombs on the Swiss city of Schaffhausen, which lies north of the Rhine. Six factories were destroyed and the busy marketplace was hit. The American target was apparently Singen, a German town and rail junction eleven miles away. No Swiss fighters pursued the American bombers. Astonishingly, while grieving for their dead, the people of Schaffhausen reportedly expressed no hard feelings toward the United States for what they truly believed to be a tragic mistake.[12]

Leland Harrison, American Minister to Switzerland, expressed his deepest regrets for the accidental bombing. A mass funeral was planned. American fliers, when told of their mistake, were exceedingly distressed, remembering that Switzerland provided a safe haven for American airmen interned there. "There are a lot of our airmen alive today because they were able to come down there instead of in enemy territory," said Lt. Howard McCormick of Michigan.[13] Speaking of conditions in Switzerland for interned American airmen, Lt. Robert A. Long of New Jersey said, "The Swiss people were good to us."

Insisting that measures be taken to prevent a repetition of the disaster, the *New York Times* commented:

> The tragic error through which the peaceful and friendly Swiss town of Schaffhausen was laid waste by American Liberators shows that our precision bombing is not always as precise as we have assumed. . . . The reaction of the Swiss themselves is characteristic. Only an admirably self-disciplined people could grieve without anger over so unnecessary a calamity.[14]

Secretary of State Cordell Hull and Secretary of War Henry Stimson offered their apologies and promised that steps would be taken to prevent a recurrence, even as bodies continued to be found in the smoldering rubble.[15]

American Minister Harrison called on former President, now Foreign Minister, Pilet-Golaz on April 4 in Bern to communicate the American apology and to assure the Swiss that the tragedy would not be repeated. The meeting was interrupted by another air raid alert, however, as U.S. bombers once again strayed over the border. While official American explanations blamed the April 1 mistake on bad weather, the Swiss press noted that the sky over Schaffhausen had been clear, with excellent visibility, and nearby Lake Constance and the Rhine falls were definitive landmarks.[16] The final report of the official investigation cited malfunctioning of the navigational equipment of the leading plane and high winds. Directives were revised to prohibit bombing targets in Germany that were not positively identified if within 50 miles of the Swiss border.[17]

On April 13, thirteen American bombers flew over Switzerland after attacks on southern Germany. Twelve of the planes obeyed instructions issued by the formations of Swiss fighters intercepting them and landed safely. The thirteenth plane was shot down by the fighters in the canton of Schwyz, in central Switzerland, after it refused to obey Swiss instructions. Its crew members parachuted out.[18]

That day, Swiss radio announced more details of the accidental Schaffhausen bombing. A total of 331 incendiary and explosive bombs had been dropped. The number reported dead was revised downward to 39, although several of the wounded were near death, and others were invalids. Some 438 Swiss citizens lost their homes.[19]

In an article published in American and Swiss newspapers, Walter Lippmann called upon President Roosevelt to take the occasion of the Schaffhausen tragedy to reexamine and liberalize America's economic policies toward Switzerland, arguing that Switzerland was a neutral, not a German satellite. By maintaining their democratic freedoms while surrounded by fascism in the darkest days of the war, the Swiss "contributed to humanity." Americans, Lippmann concluded, should appreciate the positive role played by Switzerland, which in the future would have a role to play in the recovery of Europe.[20]

On June 4, the American Army entered Rome. Two days later the greatest invasion fleet the world had ever seen landed at Normandy in France. After years of battling the German Army in the Mediterranean theater, the strongest Allied army yet had attacked in northern Europe, breaching Hitler's "Atlantic Wall." The next day, General Guisan requested the Swiss cabinet's authorization for a mobilization of troops based on continued reports of hostile intentions on the part of the Nazis. Public opinion welcomed the Allied landing, and the mobilization was favorably received.[21] Military leaders had long expressed concern that Switzerland would face increased danger as the borders of the Reich constricted—a fear confirmed by Wehrmacht disengagement actions in Italy.[22]

On June 10, as Swiss soldiers mobilized, a battalion of the 2nd SS Panzer Division claimed to have discovered explosives in the village of Oradour-sur-Glane, near Limoges, France. The Germans rounded up and executed 642 people, almost the entire population.[23] The Nazis were as unpredictable and ruthless as ever.

General Guisan warned Swiss soldiers on June 15 that the threats to Switzerland "might be progressively discernible or could appear quite suddenly," thus requiring new forces to be called up. Guisan's order of the day stated:

> The risk to which this country is exposed does not of a necessity—as many pretended to believe—spring from the threat from this or that group of belligerents. Neither does

it apply to this or that frontier, or always present itself in this or that concrete form.

It can come quite slowly and progressively increase, or it can break out with startling suddenness. It can even take on a form you have never imagined, but one which it is the duty of your leader who is entrusted with defense to reflect upon and measure in all its consequences.

To parry this danger, determination, courage, the best troops, armaments and fortifications alone will never suffice, unless we are ready in time. It is far better, therefore, that we are ready too soon than too late. It is far better to watch all outposts, even those deemed unimportant, than to find that we have neglected a single one.[24]

The Nazis were still capable of dangerous surprises. As General Guisan spoke, the first of the German "Vengeance" rockets—the Vergeltungswaffe 1—exploded over London. In rocket technology, Nazi scientists had leapfrogged their Allied counterparts. The big question then being asked by a select few in the United States and Britain was: how close were the Nazis to developing an atomic bomb?[25]

"As the war in Europe reaches its climax the position of Switzerland becomes more precarious," said Werner Richter in the July 1944 issue of Foreign Affairs. Unlike Nazi-encircled Switzerland, all of the other neutrals—Spain, Portugal, Ireland, Turkey and Sweden—had a seacoast and thus the capacity for contact with the Allies. If the Wehrmacht was expelled from the Po Valley or from eastern or southern France, however, it might attempt to overrun and then to resist from Switzerland. Further, the Reich's plans for its final stand on the "inner line" could entail seizure of Swiss railways connecting France with Austria and Germany with Italy.[26] Allied tactics of blanketing German forces with massive firepower, especially from artillery and bombers, would have grave implications for Swiss cities and civilians if the Nazis fought from Swiss territory.

Richter noted that the Swiss were determined to prevent any such invasion. The Swiss militia was equivalent to a superior standing army and, until the Allied invasion of Italy, was the only armed force in continental Europe not subject to Hitler's orders.[27]

German imperialists historically stigmatized the Swiss as rebels, Richter continued. Until the seventeenth century, the word "Swiss" in Germany was equivalent to the French radical term "Jacobin." The centralization of the German state under Bismarck and Wilhelm II coincided with the alienation of the Swiss. Essentially, it was the Austrian-born Führer, Hitler, who had renewed the old Habsburg claim to Switzerland. The Swiss, Hitler believed, remained traitors against their "German blood"; Nazi school maps depicted Switzerland in the "Grossdeutsches Reich." But the contrast between Germany and Switzerland had grown dramatically in the previous eighty years:

> While the Reich became more and more the incarnation of imperialism, centralism, deification of the state and nega- tion of the individual, Switzerland grew more and more firmly attached to the principles of her origin—democracy, federalism and individual freedom.[28]

Economically, according to Richter, Switzerland was in fact pay- ing tribute to Germany. Had Switzerland not traded with Germany, "she would soon have been forced by starvation into capitulation and would have become one more on the list of occupied countries, while her factories went ahead full blast under Nazi management."

The most critical internal problem was the food supply. Rations of essential foods were still far below those in the United States. Yet the Swiss resisted Nazi attempts to use commercial negotiations to extort political concessions, such as demobilization of troops. That did not prevent, of course, harangues from German loudspeakers telling Swiss frontier troops that they would be massacred within hours.[29]

By 1944, Richter wrote, Switzerland was a refuge for over 60,000 men and women who had fled from the New Order. More than 100 million francs of federal funds had been expended on help- ing refugees. The Swiss government, moreover, took measures to pro- tect the rights of Jews with interests or presence in Switzerland:

> When a German decree maintained that the property of German Jews in Switzerland was forfeited to the Reich, the Court of Appeals in Zurich—only a few minutes' flight

from German bombing bases—condemned this law and declared it to "constitute an intolerable violation of our native sense of justice." And when the Gestapo seized a Jewish refugee on Swiss territory at Basel as a spy, the Swiss Government protested and stubbornly maintained its protest, regardless of risks, until the captive was returned.[30]

Allied intelligence derived substantial benefits from operations conceived in neutral Switzerland. From his arrival in Bern until midsummer 1944, OSS operative Allen Dulles had devoted considerable effort to supporting the French Resistance. *Maquis* fighters and couriers slipped into Switzerland, where the OSS would give them funds, plan parachute drops of arms, and coordinate resistance activities with the Allied forces which had swept into France. Dulles noted that "the groups we had worked with in the Haute-Savoie region adjoining Switzerland had been instrumental in clearing the way for the American thrust northward after the landings on the coast of southern France in July of 1944." In addition, Italian partisan leaders would slip over the border into Ticino, the Italian-speaking Swiss canton, and arrange with the OSS for air drops of supplies to their mountain bases.[31]

The German underground also plotted Hitler's death from Switzerland, where Dulles served as the intermediary between the conspirators and the Allies.[32] On July 20, Colonel Claus von Stauffenberg planted a bomb at Hitler's headquarters, the "Wolf's Lair," and flew back to Berlin to stage a coup against the Nazi regime. Hitler survived the blast, however, and the discovered plotters were executed in a barbaric manner. Thousands more would be rounded up and killed. Dr. Hans Gisevius, a longtime leader of the German Resistance, escaped to Zurich with the help of OSS-forged papers.[33] Tragically, the failure of the "Officers' Plot" left Hitler with a more committed, hard-core military cadre than before. Anyone within the professional ranks of the Wehrmacht suspected of being insufficiently instilled with the Nazi cause was purged. Field Marshals Erwin Rommel and Gunther von Kluge committed suicide. Hitler now had an officer corps too intimidated to object to even his wildest and most destructive whims.

The untested but highly regarded Swiss capacity for a universal partisan war could be contrasted with the pitiful condition of the partisans in occupied Europe, who were hardly armed at all. The Allies would therefore parachute into Europe one million Liberator pistols—a cheap single-shot, smooth-bore pistol that was useless for anything except shooting a Nazi in the head at point-blank range in order to steal his arms. The partisan was lucky if the Liberator did not blow up in his own hand.[34]

The Swiss were feeling the effects of desperate Luftwaffe attacks near the frontier with France. The Swiss village of Morgins, a mile from the French border, was bombed and machine-gunned by the Luftwaffe on August 6, as the Germans were conducting an operation against the *maquis* in the French department of Haute-Savoie, where they inflicted severe damage. The population of the French village of Novel escaped injury by being evacuated into Switzerland. Luftwaffe planes also flew over the Valais in western Switzerland.[35]

On August 15, just as the German front in Normandy was cracking, the Allies landed another army on the French Mediterranean coast. Like the Normandy invasion, the Allied strike into southern France increased the danger of a desperate Wehrmacht incursion into Switzerland.[36]

In southern Germany, special forces under SS Colonel Otto Skorzeny plotted to send frogmen to blow up bridges and power plants along the Rhine. They also conspired to assassinate Free French General de Lattre de Tassigny, but the Swiss military warned the Allies in time.[37]

An American intelligence report dated August 19 noted the formation of two groups: the National Sozialistische Schweizer Bund in Vienna and the Bund der Schweizer in Gross-Deutschland in Stuttgart. These groups consisted of Swiss trained by the Nazis for the purpose of occupying and transforming Switzerland into a National Socialist state.[38]

As the battlefront neared the border, and in view of the fluid situation, the Swiss Federal Council ordered additional security measures and called up more troops on August 25.[39] That same day, American armies reached the Swiss border near Geneva. For the first time since 1940, the Axis no longer completely encircled Switzerland.

As Allen Dulles wrote: "Until American troops broke through to the frontier near Geneva in August 1944, Switzerland was an island of democracy in a sea of Nazi and Fascist despotism. Radio communication was our only link with the outside world."[40] The Swiss regarded the combat in the Lyons region as dangerous for them, which explained their additional military measures.[41]

Because they had entered as refugees, over 9,000 Allied troops who had escaped from Italian and French prison camps into Switzerland were allowed to depart and join the American units at the Swiss border, according to the terms of The Hague Convention. Airmen who had bailed out or were forced down over Switzerland while on combat missions, however, remained for the time being as internees.[42]

With the Germans falling back toward the Belfort Gap near the Swiss border, on September 5 the Federal Council ordered increased mobilization of first-line frontier troops "in preparation for all eventualities." The Germans were driven out of two of their last three strongholds in the Jura Department before the Belfort Gap, when Besançon and Pontarlier fell. The remaining German stronghold, Baume-les-Dames, midway between Besançon and Montbéliard, was surrounded. German deserters flowed into the Porrentruy pocket of Switzerland and were interned.[43]

As the Allies approached the Swiss border, the sounds of artillery fire were easily heard in Switzerland. Remobilized militiamen were taken from the *Réduit* and were positioned, without explanation, in the Plateau. To inform the soldiers of the nature of the current peril, artillery corporal August Lindt drafted a report dated September 9 entitled "Information on the Situation," which was then distributed through liaison officers to the Swiss military. Lindt gave lectures for the Heer und Haus (Army and Home) communications center and would become an ambassador after the war.

Those who thought the end of the war was imminent, the Lindt report began, must consider the still relatively high state of morale of the German troops. The Wehrmacht remained a force to be reckoned with. "It would be at the very least imprudent to conclude," Lindt wrote, "that the German army can collapse in a few weeks. The war is not finished."[44]

While the Allies had broken through the encirclement of Switzerland, transportation had not reopened to improve the economic situation. The window needed strengthening, as the subsequent German reconquest of Briançon demonstrated. The zone occupied by the Allies was very narrow.[45]

Between June 1940 and June 1944, the reasons for Swiss mobilizations and specific troop movements were cloaked in secrecy. But the present partial mobilization could be readily understood by the soldier: the sounds of combat could be heard in Switzerland, and the war was at the western border.[46]

Gigantic pincers were trying to envelop the German armies, continued Lindt: one from Marseille, the other from Normandy. Both Allied and German military operations included numerous freestanding actions. The danger of Allied or German invasion was clear: "To complete an encirclement, the commander of an armored column could decide that he would reach his objective more quickly by crossing a part of Swiss territory. On the other hand, a German detachment may be very well tempted to escape encirclement, extinction, or capture by entering our borders." Either side could conduct lightning raids into Switzerland for resupply. Lindt's report added:

> To face all these possibilities, which are not in a faraway future but can become reality from one day to the next, we must solidly protect our borders. . . . In these times, neutrality as such does not count. Armed neutrality alone counts.[47]

The Lindt report specified the threats to Swiss security in the European theater. In Burgundy, the Allies were closing in on the Germans, who might try to escape destruction by entering Swiss soil. In the region of Belfort, the part of German General Blaskowitz's army that was not annihilated in the Rhône Valley was reforming and trying to break out through a narrow passage. These troops could also overflow into Switzerland. Swiss bridges on the Rhine were also tempting to both the Germans and the Allies. "It is our duty," Lindt emphasized, "to avoid at all costs the use of Swiss territory by one or the other for its operations."[48]

In a reversal of the 1940 scenario, the Allies might intrude into Switzerland to avoid German fortified lines. The Germans might try to prevent this by a quick invasion of Switzerland. Switzerland's best hope remained that "the belligerents would be dissuaded by our will to defend our neutrality."[49]

The Lindt report illustrates the view of the most defense-minded, anti-Nazi elements of the Swiss leadership of the peril the country faced in the fall of 1944. Lindt thereafter prepared a weekly report of similar nature, hundreds of which were produced and sent to army commanders.

Once transportation with France was reopened, approximately 4,000 French children arrived in Switzerland in one week alone. Caught in the war zone, they had become destitute after retreating Germans had swept through their towns and villages.[50]

In August, the Swiss government eased immigration restrictions to let in up to 14,000 additional Hungarian Jews. This action was the result of the protests of numerous social-welfare groups, Christian churches, newspapers and political leaders who opposed the government's restrictive policies and advocated opening the borders to all fleeing Jews. Placing the Swiss record in perspective, David S. Wyman, who wrote a study of United States policies that prohibited Jewish immigration, noted:

> In relation to its size Switzerland was unquestionably more generous in taking in refugees than any other country except Palestine. At the end of 1944, some 27,000 Jewish refugees were safe in Switzerland—so were approximately 20,000 non-Jewish refugees and about 40,000 interned military personnel. . . . The country's borders were wide open to all who were in danger because of their political beliefs, to escaped prisoners of war, and to military deserters. Usually, the following categories of Jews were also allowed to enter: young children (and their parents if accompanying them), pregnant women, the sick, the aged, and close relatives of Swiss citizens.[51]

Although Switzerland maintained her centuries-old tradition as a refuge for dissidents and took pity on children and the weak, the authorities would not allow the free immigration of able-bodied adults without children who belonged to ethnic groups, including Jews and gypsies, that were being subjected to extermination. Many Swiss citizens opposed or protested this policy, which was based on the traditional view that the nation-state has an obligation to protect only her own citizens and others lawfully within her territory. From a humanitarian perspective, the governments of all the democracies, including Switzerland and even the United States, had deplorable policies regarding Jewish and other refugees during World War II.

The Swiss have not been faulted regarding their internment of Allied troops, who were thereby protected from Axis prison camps. British Foreign Secretary Anthony Eden cautioned U.S. Ambassador John Winant on August 21 against pressuring the Swiss to stop all exports to Germany and to prohibit all German transit traffic. Eden stated:

> We attach very high importance to avoiding forcing the Swiss to take action which would result in a rupture of Swiss diplomatic relations with Germany. This would necessarily mean that Switzerland would cease to act as protecting power at a moment when this may be more necessary than ever before. After the recent murder of our airmen in Germany we are genuinely alarmed at the possibility that the last moment before total defeat the Gestapo might run amok and commit wholesale murder of British and American prisoners of war. Obviously this is more likely to happen if the restraining influence of the protective power is removed.[52]

Actually, in August Switzerland had already placed a ceiling on exports to Germany. The Swiss response to American demands made clear that Allied progress would enable Switzerland to decrease trade with Germany even more:

The war as it nears the Alps changes aspects of the transit problem and has a bearing on its solution. . . . Traffic in both directions has in general decreased and not increased since spring. In the spirit of true neutrality which guides them, they will see to it that it follows the trend circumstances demand.[53]

As of October 1, 1944, the Federal Council prohibited the export of arms, aircraft parts, ball bearings, fuses, radio and telegraph apparatus, and other military supplies to any belligerent—the first total prohibition on war exports enacted by a neutral. The Simplon route through the Alps was closed to transit traffic by the end of the month.[54] Despite these concessions, in early November the Allies ordered a halt to all Swiss rail and truck traffic into France. Switzerland remained almost completely isolated.[55]

The Swiss also clarified to the Allies that Nazi leaders and Gestapo members would not be granted asylum in Switzerland. The Federal Council declared in November that, while Switzerland retained her sovereign power to grant asylum to worthy persons, "asylum could not be granted either to persons who have displayed an unfriendly attitude toward Switzerland or who have committed acts contrary to the laws of war or whose past gives evidence of conceptions incompatible with fundamental traditions of law and humanity."[56]

Emphasizing August Lindt's earlier warning that no one should consider the Wehrmacht defeated, on September 17 British Field Marshal Montgomery launched a massive air and land assault to flank the German Westwall in the north. German divisions that had been considered decimated at Normandy showed surprising new strength, and the British 1st Airborne Division was nearly annihilated near Arnhem.

From September through December, the French and Germans fought one of the last great battles of the war between the Vosges Mountains and Switzerland, whose borders extended perilously near the combat zone. General Guisan wrote: "In case we were attacked, even if it was only in this small projection of our territory, we had the duty to return fire immediately and very effectively. Our parry at this very place was of symbolic value, with considerable effect on our external and internal situation."[57] As this statement makes clear, the Swiss would have defended themselves against any aggressor, whether Axis or Allied, though any conflict with the Allies would have grieved them.

A Swiss division guarded the narrow strip near the combat zone. On November 16, the French attacked the Germans between Belfort and Swiss soil. In two days, the French liberated Delle, close to the Swiss village of Boncourt, as combat continued all along the Swiss border in the Montbéliard region. The Allies advanced 18 miles along the Swiss border in three days. Some 200 German soldiers were disarmed and interned by Swiss soldiers. On the 19th, the Americans entered the fray. The Germans retreated eastward, although shelling continued at the border. The border battle lasted until Christmas.[58]

On November 8, German V-2 rockets rained on London and Antwerp. The Führer had a seemingly unlimited capacity to keep striking back with ever more sinister weapons.

At Yalta on October 13, Stalin had proposed an invasion of Switzerland, supposedly as a strategy to circumvent Germany's Westwall, but the Allies refused. Winston Churchill called the plan both illegal and militarily senseless.[59] Churchill wrote to Foreign Secretary Anthony Eden on December 3:

> I put this down for the record. Of all the neutrals Switzerland has the greatest right to distinction. She has been the sole international force linking the hideously sundered nations and ourselves. What does it matter whether she has been able to give us the commercial advantages we desire or has given too many to the Germans, to keep herself alive?[60]

In an instruction to Eden on the same date, Churchill expressed astonishment at Stalin's "savageness" against Switzerland, adding: "He called them 'swine,' and he does not use that sort of language without meaning it. I am sure we ought to stand by Switzerland."[61] Stalin had always hated the Swiss for their capitalism and democracy.

Gestapo chief Heinrich Müller, who after the war became a paid informant for American intelligence, recalled that "the Swiss did not want any country to invade their territory and would have fought to the death to prevent it." The Swiss feared that the Allies would cross into Switzerland to flank the German lines in the west, and, as noted, Stalin advocated just that. Müller commented:

> If the West had invaded Swiss territory, the Germans might well have had to fight these people [the Allies] on Swiss land and the result would have been catastrophic, I'm sure, and I pointed this out in the right circles, that the Americans and British would bomb all the Swiss cities flat in a few days and shoot the refugees on the roads. After all, the Swiss knew what happened in Dresden and had no illusions.[62]

The cities of Dresden and Hamburg were subjected to massive Allied fire-bomb attacks that resulted in tens of thousands of civilian deaths. Cities in France, Italy and the Low Countries had also been targeted by Allied bombers if they became part of German defense lines. In any event, Müller was certain that the Swiss "would have fought to the death against you, us or the Soviets. They would have lost but it wasn't worth it. At least not as far as we were concerned."[63]

Debate continued in 1944 within the Nazi hierarchy about whether to invade Switzerland. In 1943 SS General Walter Schellenberg had secretly met with General Guisan, who convinced Schellenberg that the Swiss would resist to the end. (Allen Dulles' agents had also met with the SS general to discuss anti-Hitler matters and peace prospects.) In his self-serving memoirs, Schellenberg wrote:

> While Hitler's fortunes declined rapidly, I had to make frequent and desperate use of my position with Himmler to insure that at least Swiss neutrality was respected, and I honestly feel that it is largely due to my influence with and through Himmler, which I was never tired of exerting to the utmost, that a "preventive" occupation of Switzerland did not take place.[64]

Schellenberg claimed that his activities almost brought his doom at the hands of Müller's Gestapo, especially after it intercepted a radio message about negotiations with Allied representatives in Switzerland.

In an attempt to prevent the invasion, Schellenberg also contacted former Federal President Musy, who, he recalled, "had one aim— the saving of as many as possible of the hundreds of thousands of concentration camp inmates."[65] Secret meetings between Musy and Himmler then took place at the end of 1944 and again on January 12, 1945. Himmler agreed to a mass evacuation of concentration camp inmates in exchange for tractors, cars, medicines and other scarce items. Musy offered foreign currency, to be credited to the International Committee of the Red Cross. Himmler did not understand, according to Schellenberg, "that the freeing of thousands of Jews was important from the point of view of Germany's foreign policy; he seemed only to be concerned with the effect such an action would have on the Party clique and on Hitler." Schellenberg could tell that Himmler wanted to clear himself from his past activities against Jews. It was suggested that the United States should recognize Switzerland as a place of transit for Jews who would eventually emigrate to America. Musy agreed to confer with certain Jewish organizations in Switzerland.[66] Himmler reluctantly authorized Schellenberg to coordinate the release of a number of prominent Jews and French. Fighting Gestapo reluctance, Schellenberg arranged for the emigration of some prisoners.[67]

Saly Mayer, a prominent Swiss Jewish leader, negotiated with the SS in an attempt to rescue Jews. Between August 1944 and April 1945, he periodically met with SS Colonel Kurt Becher in St. Margrethen, Switzerland, to discuss "the price of abandoning the gassing." Becher said he had Himmler's permission to bargain for the exchange of Jewish lives for matériel and money. While the Allies were not about to provide either, Mayer dragged out the negotiations to buy time until an Allied victory and succeeded in getting numerous Jews released and brought to Switzerland.[68]

As they advanced, the Allies were more able and willing to reopen the world market to the Swiss, who were by then increasingly able to function without imports from Germany. In addition, coal shipments from Germany to Italy over Swiss rails were curtailed, and numerous other concessions were made to the Allies. On the day the agreement was signed, the Allies declared: "The Allied Governments fully understand Switzerland's unique position as a neutral, a position which they have always respected."[69]

In mid-December, the U.S. State Department's Western European experts issued a paper on current policy toward Switzerland. It stated squarely: "For political reasons and for reasons arising out of the benefits to us of Switzerland's neutral position and her future potential usefulness in the economy of Europe, it was inadvisable to place too great a pressure upon the Swiss Government at this time in order to attain pure economic warfare objectives." Agreeing with the August statement by British Foreign Secretary Eden, the American paper explained that Swiss neutrality was recognized by the major powers and was important to the Allied cause:

> As a result of this neutrality Switzerland performs certain indispensable services for all the belligerents and claims in return the right to trade with such of them as will help maintain its essential economy and internal stability. As far as the United States is concerned, Switzerland serves as the protecting power for our general interest and in particular for our prisoners of war in Germany and Japan. It is the agreed policy of the British and U.S. Governments to avoid forcing Switzerland to a break with Germany. Such a break would make it impossible for the Swiss to continue to represent British and U.S. interests in Germany and might likewise affect their position in so far as Japan is concerned. It is essential as the situation in Germany becomes more and more disturbed that we endeavor to obtain their greatest degree of protection, not only for U.S. general interests but especially in regard to matters relating to prisoners of war. But it should be remembered that the effectiveness of Switzerland's protection can be much altered by a severe deterioration of its relations with Germany short of complete rupture.[70]

The State Department report also recognized Switzerland's services in assisting refugees:

> Related to but not directly connected with the protection of U.S. interests by Switzerland are her humanitarian efforts, undertaken at the request of the U.S. Government, on behalf of the Jews in Central Europe. At our request, she has recently agreed to admit some 15,000 additional Hungarian Jews in spite of the increased strain on her general food problem.[71]

Although the Allies' high hopes of summer that the war would be over by Christmas were not fulfilled, the Allied high command nevertheless believed that Germany's collapse was imminent. France had been retaken in the west, and in the east the Soviet army had advanced into Hungary and Poland. The vise was closing, and the Reich's losses in resources and manpower surely had crippled Hitler's ability to stave off an inevitable Allied victory. On December 16, however, two German armies, comprising 300,000 men and thousands of armored vehicles, burst from the Ardennes in a surprise counteroffensive. They broke the American front and SS panzer spearheads advanced on the Meuse. Two weeks later, a Luftwaffe armada of 700 planes hit Allied airfields in Belgium and France. The Allies restructured their front, Montgomery from the north and Patton from the south rushing forces to seal the breakthrough. This Battle of the Bulge continued through January.

The new exhibition of German strength demonstrated the continued threat to the Swiss, for the German divisions launched in the Ardennes would have been sufficient, too, to invade Switzerland. The war was by no means over, and only after his death could the Führer's capabilities and limitations be accurately evaluated.[72]

As the war wore on, Swiss engineers developed improved designs for the submachine gun, the anti-tank rifle, the tank grenade launcher, the rocket tube, the flamethrower, mines, hand grenades and explosive devices. The air defense was equipped with light and heavy anti-aircraft guns. The artillery was reorganized and partially motorized. By the end of the war, anti-aircraft guns and artillery together included 5,126 guns of different calibers: 1,317 field cannons and howitzers, 696 fortress guns, 166 mountain guns and 2,947 anti-aircraft guns.[73]

While the Swiss militiamen had not actually participated in war, explained Hans Senn, who would later become a Chief of the General Staff, "the soldiers received tough physical training and were accustomed to deprivations. They mastered their arms in sharpshooting and under combat conditions."[74]

Switzerland had produced 240 million rounds of infantry ammunition in 1941, 120 million in 1942 and 60 million in 1943. Chief of the General Staff Jakob Huber explained that there was so much stored ammunition in the *Réduit* by 1944 that "if one assumes only one hit in 1,000 rounds—less would be a disgrace for the Swiss shooting people (*Schützenvolk der Schweizer*)—we could kill one million enemies with rifles and light and heavy machine guns."[75] Swiss sharpshooting skills would have been far more efficient, as the Wehrmacht well knew.

Chapter 10

1945

The Liberation of Europe

AS ONE SWISS RIFLEMAN REMINISCED YEARS LATER, SWISS
soldiers had little time to think during the entire period of the war. The
young soldier was mostly concerned with making sure his rifle was
clean. Most men and women put in double time in their jobs, and the
load kept them from thinking about what would happen next. They
had only a third of the ration of the average American G.I.; bread
could not be eaten until it was two days old, because some government official thought stale bread was more filling. Despite privations,
the Swiss did not despair but retained a strong national spirit. Hitler
was seen as an unpredictable madman, and the Swiss people feared a
German invasion until the very end of the war.[1]

As the Allied forces tightened their grip on the Nazi empire, the
question of Swiss economic relations with Germany once again came
to the fore. American Secretary of State Edward Stettinius announced
on January 3 that Swiss-American economic relations would be over-
hauled. According to one report, the Allies sought a prohibition on all
Swiss exports to Germany. The Swiss were still selling Germany a
reduced quantity of machine tools, precision instruments, and other
non-war items. They allowed the transit of coal to northern Italy but
barred the movement of all goods from Italy. During this period, it
should be noted, Germany was also still trading with Sweden.[2]

The Swiss interpreted Secretary Stettinius' announcement as an
attempt to force their country to become a weapon against Germany.
The socialist Bern *Tagwacht* (*Daily Watch*) newspaper asserted that
American pressure was part of a plan that started with the Soviet

Union's refusal to open diplomatic relations with Switzerland. The *Neue Zürcher Zeitung* noted:

> The American demands, as announced, suggest a reckless disregard for the naked material existence of a nation of 4,000,000 people that for the past five years has been defending its independence and neutrality with a firm hand and even in the most critical hours today is housing and feeding more than 100,000 refugees.[3]

The press emphasized the fact that the United States had not offered to replace essential German coal with Allied deliveries.[4]

President Roosevelt dispatched his special assistant Lauchlin Currie to Switzerland to negotiate economic matters. The Americans recognized that Switzerland had a commercial treaty with Germany and appreciated Swiss diplomatic services representing the United States to that country.[5] In fact, Secretary Stettinius' remark about the "overhaul" of American-Swiss economic relations was misunderstood; the Department of State clearly recognized the advantages of Swiss neutrality to the Allied cause.[6]

To counter press reports critical of Switzerland, the Department issued a declaration to the United Press affirming that friendly relations would be maintained between Switzerland and the United States. It noted that Switzerland had to maintain diplomatic relations with the belligerents in order to serve as protecting power for the United States, and that Switzerland's democratic system, as well as her traditional friendship with America, continued to be appreciated.[7]

Why the sudden objections to Swiss trade? According to *Newsweek*, reports critical of Swiss trade with Germany "came from certain government quarters whose objective is to align United States policy with that of the Soviet Union." The accusations did not represent the policy of the State Department, however, and when Secretary Stettinius asserted that the U.S.-Swiss economic relationship was under discussion, his aim in fact was to strengthen ties. An American military mission in Bern was at that time negotiating the purchase of watches and precision instruments for use by U.S. troops in France. While these purchases would deprive the Germans of such goods and compensate the Swiss for German trade losses, they were not contingent on Switzerland's severance of economic ties with Germany.[8] Furthermore, Switzerland could not protect American interests in Germany, including looking after war prisoners and arranging exchange of the wounded, if she compromised her neutrality.[9]

The Department of State, recognizing the benefits of Swiss neutrality, favored a balanced approach. The Treasury Department and other agencies narrowly concerned only with issues such as trade with Germany and German assets, instigated various measures against the Swiss toward the end of the war and even after cessation of hostilities.[10]

The French exile newspaper *Pour la Victoire (For Victory)* deplored the attacks on Switzerland, which had been, since 1940, "an oasis in the fascist desert." In the "moral confusion" engendered by six years of war, the Anglo-American press was "launching poison arrows against the only democratic country to hold its own in the face of the passions of its neighbors."[11]

Allied-Swiss trade talks, which began on February 12, culminated in agreement on all issues on March 9. The agreement included Swiss trade with belligerents, carriage of goods by rail, export of electricity (which would assist French reconstruction), prevention of the concealment by defeated belligerents of looted property, and the supply of food and raw materials to Switzerland. The report concluded that "the Allied delegates were able to see for themselves how deeply rooted democracy is in the minds of the Swiss." Under the agreement, trade with Germany was reduced to negligible proportions, and Germany was denied transportation facilities to and from northern Italy.[12]

The Swiss also revoked their bank privacy law for deposits by Nazi officials, froze German assets, and prohibited exchange of German gold for Swiss francs. American negotiator Currie remarked: "This really ends the last hope of the Nazis for establishing themselves through the safe haven of property held abroad."[13]

The greatest aerial assaults on rail systems in history took place against Germany on February 22. American planes attacking southern Germany just north of the Swiss frontier, between Basel and Stein-am-

Rhein, also accidentally dropped bombs on five Swiss villages and towns, killing 16 persons. The bombs hit minutes before American economic delegation head Lauchlin Currie arrived in Schaffhausen to lay wreaths on the graves of the victims of the earlier disaster. The State Department expressed shock and distress at the latest bombing accident.[14] The same day, hundreds of American airmen were released from internment in Switzerland and returned to the ranks in Britain.

Hitler continued to launch surprise offensives. On February 17, the Sixth SS Panzer Army, which had been transshipped from the Ardennes, attacked with 600 tanks against the Soviets around Lake Balaton in Hungary.

In Switzerland, again, on March 4, 6 were killed and 50 injured in Basel and Zurich when American Flying Fortresses and Liberators dropped explosives and incendiaries and machine-gunned cars on freight-yard sidings. Numerous houses burned or were blasted. Swiss radio called the bombings precision work and not an "accidental release of bombs by a crashing plane."[15]

Lt. General Carl A. Spaatz of the U.S. Army Air Force spent 24 hours in Bern to meet with General Guisan and the Swiss high command concerning the prevention of further Allied bombardments, a problem he called "even more urgent than his conduct of Allied aerial operations over the Western Front." Swiss Councillor Karl Kobelt of the Military Department expressed the "grave revulsion of feeling" by the public of the bombings of Zurich and Basel, which were easily identifiable from the air.[16] Four more Swiss were killed and extensive damage done on March 11, when a single plane bombed Basel and six planes bombed Zurich.[17]

Also in March, the Swiss investigated subversives responsible for a pamphlet which falsely claimed that it was being distributed in the name of Swiss officers, non-commissioned officers and soldiers. The pamphlet accused the Federal Council of considering Allied demands that Switzerland enter the war on their side, allow free transit of Allied armies through Switzerland to attack Germany from the south, and the use of Swiss airfields for Allied attacks on Germany. This propaganda piece came in response to the Swiss government's blunt refusal of a German request for 200 "asylum safe-conducts pending transfer to Argentina" for prominent Nazis.[18]

The Swiss refusal coincided with an immediate increase in border patrols to prevent political undesirables from entering the country. Recalling Germany's surprise attacks on neutrals, as well as considering the Nazis' increasingly desperate position, the Swiss were not taking any chances.[19]

Indeed, the Nazis could still be expected to take the most inhumane and unexpected measures. In late March, after partisans wounded an SS-Obergruppenführer who headed the Gestapo in the Netherlands, German police executed 400 Dutchmen.[20] Nazi V-1 and V-2 rockets continued to rain on London, Antwerp and other cities until March 27. Thousands of the rockets remained in the Wehrmacht inventory and could easily have been launched against Switzerland.

A quarter-of-a-million German civilians and foreign worker refugees, the *New York Times* reported on April 18, were headed for Switzerland's borders. In response, the Federal Council ordered the recall of army formations to watch for "undesirable individuals." Strong measures were being prepared to keep out war criminals such as Gestapo and Elite Guard (SS) men.[21]

On the 20th, thousands of refugees fleeing the Reich in search of asylum in Switzerland reached the border at Lake Constance. Some French, Polish and Russian workers were allowed into the country. Panic spread on the German side as the French First Army made its way toward the Swiss frontier, where it was expected to cut off the Reich's province of Baden, from which six divisions of Wehrmacht, Volkssturm and SS forces were attempting to escape. Small arms and light artillery combat could be heard just across the border.[22] In the coming days, thousands of foreign workers continued to stream into Switzerland and were cared for by the International Committee of the Red Cross. No Germans were allowed in. The French advance into Baden accelerated the flow.[23]

By April 22, the French had reached the Swiss border at Schaffhausen, cutting off Baden from the Reich 120 kilometers to the north. The Germans prepared an all-out defense of the "Baden Redoubt." Explosions rocked Basel the next day as the Wehrmacht blew up rail facilities in southern Germany. German deserters seeking to enter Switzerland were treated curtly, since it could not be determined whether they were war criminals. Refugees being admitted were examined for contagious diseases, and several cases of smallpox were discovered. The increasing dangers and the massing of SS troops in Austria's Vorarlberg caused the Swiss to close their eastern frontier.[24]

The Allies also continued to advance against the Germans in northern Italy in early 1945. The Swiss received intelligence from partisans, who crossed into the Swiss canton of Ticino where they received material support, that the Germans might retreat with a scorched earth policy. The Swiss feared that Germany's best combat force, the same Army Group C that had figured prominently in earlier Nazi invasion plans, now led by Field Marshal Kesselring, might finally bring the war into Switzerland in an effort to reach the suspected Nazi mountain redoubt in the Alps of Austria and Bavaria.[25]

By March 11, General Eisenhower had also received reports that Hitler would command a last stand in the "National Redoubt" in the Alps. General Omar Bradley wrote that "this legend of the Redoubt was too ominous a threat to ignore and in consequence it shaped our tactical thinking during the closing weeks of the war."[26] Allen Dulles noted that German forces on the Italian front were considered to be as intransigent as those in Berlin. As the Wehrmacht desperately attempted to hold on to the Apennines, German troops in Italy were expected to play a decisive role in a last stand of the Nazis in an Alpine redoubt.[27]

Just as the Allies feared the Nazi war machine to the end, it is hardly surprising that the Swiss feared a possible Nazi attack until the final days of the war. When Hitler saw the inevitability of defeat, he ordered that Europe be destroyed—not only Italy and France, but Germany itself. Known to be moody and impulsive, he could have easily given the order to attack Switzerland.[28] The Red Army was advancing in Austria, and Germany's strategic options were narrowing. German armies retreating from northern Italy would have been the troops best placed, and with the most incentive, to attempt a breakthrough of the Swiss border.

To prevent further catastrophes, Swiss intelligence, acting in a private capacity, began to mediate a possible surrender of the German force in northern Italy. Acting on his own and not as the representative of neutral Switzerland, Major Max Waibel, head of the "N1" intelligence bureau in Lucerne, contacted Allen Dulles in Bern.[29] Dulles credited Waibel with playing a major role in orchestrating the early surrender of the German troops in Italy, which was a great relief to Allied war planners:

> As we later proceeded to develop our secret and precarious relations with the German generals early in 1945, we would have been thwarted at every step if we had not had the help of Waibel in facilitating contacts and communications and in arranging the delicate frontier crossings which had to be carried out under conditions of complete secrecy. In all his actions Waibel was serving the interests of peace.[30]

On March 3, emissaries met in Lugano to discuss the unconditional surrender of the Germans. On March 8, SS General Karl Wolff met Allen Dulles in Zurich and agreed to recommend surrender to Field Marshal Kesselring.[31] To show good faith, Wolff promised to discontinue warfare against Italian partisans, to release to Switzerland hundreds of Jews from Bolzano and to guarantee the safety of hundreds of American and British prisoners.[32]

On March 15–19, American and British representatives together with Major Waibel met SS General Wolff at Ascona, on Lake Maggiore in Switzerland, and agreed that the surrender would take place on March 21 at Caserta, headquarters of the Allied high commander for Italy, British Field Marshal Sir Harold Alexander. The Soviets, who had not known about the negotiations, were invited to attend.[33]

Stalin, convinced that the Western Allies were negotiating behind his back, suspected betrayal. Ever since the German attack on the Soviet Union, he had feared the West would make a separate peace. Stalin's pressure on the Allies killed the possibility of a March surrender. In April, the Germans were again ready to surrender. After exchanges between Stalin and Roosevelt, however, on April 21 Dulles was again ordered to inform the Swiss to cease negotiating the surrender of German Army Group C in Italy. Thus, because of Soviet pressure on the White House, surrender was delayed once more, and the war continued.[34]

Dulles confided to Waibel that Stalin sought to delay the German surrender in Italy in order to give the Communists more time to organize and seize political power in eastern Europe. The Soviets were also worried that a quick German surrender would allow the Western Allies to occupy Trieste, key to the Adriatic. If the Germans delayed a surrender, however, and continued fighting in the area west of Venice, in the shadow of the Alps, then Soviet or Yugoslav Communists could seize Trieste first. Stalin had encouraged Marshal Tito to move quickly across northern Italy all the way to the French border, where the Yugoslavs could link up with French Communist partisans. The result would be a Soviet-controlled belt in western and southern Europe. The spilling of the blood of his American and British allies occasioned by a delay in the German surrender hardly mattered to the Soviet dictator when such objectives were at stake.[35] Given Stalin's historic perfidy, such as his previous pact with Hitler and Soviet territorial ambitions, such motives would have been entirely in character.

General Wolff called a meeting of German commanders, who decided that Army Group C should consider itself free to surrender. However, Gauleiter Hofer, who commanded the Tyrolean mountains, suggested an armed retreat into Switzerland and a surrender to the Swiss. Wolff replied that the southern Swiss defenses would repel such a move.[36]

Thus, a Wehrmacht retreat to Germany through Switzerland, or even surrender there (which meant internment and not prison), was impossible.[37] Though Switzerland was not a belligerent on the Allied side, her strong defenses nevertheless assisted the Allies in blocking a Wehrmacht retreat. In contrast, had the Nazis been able to occupy the Swiss *Réduit* and make it a part of a German National Redoubt, the war might have lasted longer.

On April 23, General Wolff appeared at the Swiss border and requested a meeting with Major Waibel, who may have obtained General Guisan's confidential approval to continue assisting surrender negotiations. Allen Dulles obtained permission to attend the negotiations, which took place in Lucerne. Field Marshal Alexander instructed that they fly to Naples. On April 29, two envoys from German Army Group C, whose forces were estimated at between 600,000 and one million men, signed surrender documents in Caserta, near Naples. This was the best remaining German combat force and the first to surrender unconditionally.[38]

There was a last-minute hitch. The surrender papers were signed and in the hands of the two German envoys, but the documents needed to be delivered to German headquarters in Bolzano, in northern Italy, to be verified by the high command there. The envoys flew back to Switzerland with Waibel with the intent to drive through Austria and from there to Bolzano. Reaching Allen Dulles' home at 23 Herrengasse in Bern at midnight, they found themselves at the Austrian border the next morning, but Swiss border guards would not allow them to pass. Dulles called on Walter Stucki, acting Swiss Foreign Affairs Minister, early on the morning of April 30, explaining to him that

> two German envoys with the signed surrender of the German armies in North Italy were waiting at the Swiss frontier. If they passed quickly and safely to the German headquarters in Italy, the war in North Italy would be over—without further destruction and bloodshed. Guerrilla warfare in the mountains surrounding Switzerland would be avoided.[39]

Stucki understood that the emergency precluded formal consultations and dispatched orders to let the German envoys pass. Once over the border into Austria, the envoys eluded the Gestapo—which wanted to arrest them—and reached Bolzano with the surrender documents that night. At last Army Group C would be authorized to lay down its arms when the armistice took place on May 2.

According to Waibel's account—credited as accurate by former American Ambassador Hugh Wilson—the delays in negotiating the surrender caused by Stalin's pressure on Roosevelt cost Allied lives. Waibel wrote:

> For over two months we tried to work out as quickly as possible a cease fire. On March 7, weeks before the end of

the war, our goal seemed reached. In April it was possible to end the war five to seven days earlier had not the Combined Chiefs of Staff in Washington, on April 21, given orders to break off negotiations a day before the Germans came in to surrender. On April 23, when the authorities from the German Army arrived in Switzerland, the Allies were still south of the Po. Much blood and destruction could have been saved if the Allied attack across the Po had not been carried out.[40]

In any event, the surrender, assisted by private Swiss citizens, avoided a bloodbath in northern Italy and encouraged the capitulation of the remaining forces. This helped prevent what SS General Wolff himself called the "madness" of a last-ditch German Alpine Redoubt stand. It protected Switzerland from the German armed horde and hastened the end of the war, saving thousands of lives of Allied soldiers and Italian civilians alike.[41]

Adolf Hitler commited suicide in his Berlin bunker on April 30. Benito Mussolini had been captured by Italian partisans and killed on April 28. In early May, the French occupied the Vorarlberg in western Austria, and the threat of war for Switzerland finally ceased. The Reich unconditionally surrendered on May 8, and the war officially ended at midnight.[42]

On the date of surrender, the Swiss Federal Council announced that it no longer recognized the Third Reich as the government of Germany and Swiss authorities proceeded to expel all foreigners considered inimical to the national interest. The Swiss had fought Nazi subversion ever since Hitler came to power, and the closing of the Reich Embassy made it possible to suppress completely the espionage it generated. Immediate action was taken to expel Nazis and Fascists. Anyone who had been a member of a foreign organization known for violence, such as the Gestapo, and anyone who would continue to promote National Socialism by unlawful methods was to be expelled, as would persons likely to engage in sabotage or assassination. The U.S. State Department, in a report entitled *Swiss Policies on Purge of Axis Supporters*, clearly recognized Swiss efforts to rid their country of Nazi sympathizers.[43]

Though the direct military threat to Switzerland had ended, as in the rest of Europe the economic and social effects of the war were far from over. In May 1945 there were 115,000 people in refugee centers in Switzerland, and thousands of others elsewhere. During the entire war, 400,000 refugees and emigrants came to the country, and one billion Swiss francs were spent on related assistance.[44] The *Atlantic Monthly* commented:

> To these, as to the refugee problems, the country has steadily responded with generous gifts and help of all sorts, including the providing of temporary shelter during the war for 35,000 Jews. (If we had made a comparable effort, we should have taken in 1,225,000, since our population is 35 times that of Switzerland; actually, we did not take as many as Switzerland.)[45]

Refugees included interned soldiers, sick and wounded, escaped prisoners of war, civilians who escaped either from concentration camps or had fear of being imprisoned, and the frontier fugitives at the end of the war. Throughout the war, the number continued to increase despite repatriation measures.[46] Between August 13, 1943 and April 20, 1945, 166 American planes landed or crashed in Switzerland. Allied planes sometimes flew to Switzerland as a place of refuge after being damaged in battle or because of spent fuel or mechanical failure. By contrast, Axis planes that landed there did so because they were shot down or made navigational mistakes.[47] Some 1,700 American airmen would be safely interned in Switzerland during the war.[48]

As a protecting power between nations which had severed diplomatic relations, Switzerland interned civilians and wounded prisoners of war, and facilitated POW exchanges between the Allies and the Axis. Many thousands of prisoner exchanges took place without the public being aware of them.[49]

The following table sets forth the national origins and numbers of foreign soldiers interned in Switzerland from June 20, 1940 through December 31, 1945, as reported by the Commission for Interned and Hospitalized Military Persons.[50]

Country of Origin	Soldiers
France	32,621
Italy	29,213
Poland	14,972
Russia	8,415
Germany & Austria	7,532
Britain	5,139
Yugoslavia	2,921
United States	1,742
Greece	846
Belgium	783
Czechoslovakia	516
Finland	105
Diverse	81

By interning these soldiers Switzerland fulfilled her obligations as a neutral under international law, but more importantly, demonstrated singular humanitarian concern as the numbers were great in proportion to the Swiss population. Fully 68,141, or 65 percent, of the internees were Allied soldiers, most of whom had been interned since 1940. Most of the Axis internees were Italians, not Germans, and they were interned relatively late in the war. (By being interned, many of these Italians escaped having to fight for the Germans.) Large numbers of Allied soldiers would have lost their lives had they been kept in Nazi prisoner-of-war camps.

Headquartered in Geneva, the International Committee of the Red Cross (ICRC) is a voluntary association of citizens recognized by governments for its humanitarian work in war zones around the world. When the war began, the Central Agency for Prisoners of War was established pursuant to the Geneva Convention Relating to the Treatment of Prisoners of War. Beginning with 50 volunteers in September 1939, by the end of the war the ICRC employed over 2,500 workers in Switzerland.[51]

The ICRC kept lists of all prisoners of war and transmitted messages between prisoners and their families. Millions of communications involving both civilians and prisoners were generated during the war. Besides locating missing persons, ICRC personnel visited prisoner camps, sent relief packages to military and civilian prisoners, provided information about violations of the Geneva Conventions, supplied medicine and protected captured partisans. Except for the Soviet Union, all warring nations relied on the ICRC,[52] which assisted or registered 477,000 Americans, most of them POWs and a few civilian internees, during the war. A total of 10 million Allied prisoners and civilian internees were assisted overall by this uniquely Swiss organization.[53]

The ICRC also succeeded in convincing the Germans to recognize Free French partisans as legitimate armed forces, thereby preventing some massacres. As rumors of the Holocaust spread, the ICRC sought access to concentration camps to seek freedom for children and the aged and to provide relief. After a period of refusal, in 1942 the ICRC gained permission to provide food parcels to the Theresienstadt concentration camp, which imprisoned 40,000 Jews, and to other camps. However, the Allies prohibited the use of food imported into Switzerland for these prisoners. It took two years of work before the ICRC could overcome Allied objections. Not until 1944 was permission granted for such provisions.[54] By the end of the war, ICRC delegations had conducted 2,200 visits to prison camps. Delegates helped arrange the surrender of German concentration camps to the Allies and prevented last-minute executions.[55]

Swiss diplomats, particularly Carl Lutz and delegates of the ICRC in Budapest, were able to save thousands of Jewish lives in late 1944 and early 1945 by extending Swiss diplomatic protection.[56] A total of 1,355 inmates, mainly Hungarian Jews, of the Bergen-Belsen concentration camp arrived in Switzerland in December 1944. As their destination was Palestine, the U.S. Department of State argued to the British in January 1945: "This is an excellent opportunity to demonstrate to the Swiss our good faith in promising to find temporary havens for all refugee Jews arriving in Switzerland from Hungary."[57]

Acting Secretary of State Joseph C. Grew cabled Bern that the United States "would deeply appreciate continued Swiss cooperation in this humanitarian endeavor by admitting all such refugees who may be able to reach Switzerland, without regard to numbers." However, for months the Allies had refused to permit the Swiss to use French roads and railways to import some 300,000 tons of foodstuffs warehoused in a Spanish port.[58]

The U.S. War Refugee Board asked the ICRC to "distribute food, medicine and clothing to concentration camp inmates in enemy controlled areas and to remove them, if possible, to safety in Switzerland without unnecessary delay."[59]

According to SS General Walter Schellenberg, in mid-January Himmler promised former Swiss President Jean-Marie Musy to release 1,200 Jews to Switzerland every two weeks. The program began in February. However, through a decoded message, Hitler discovered the agreement, and ordered that any German who helped a Jew or a British or American prisoner escape would be executed immediately. Schellenberg persuaded the chief of the Prisoner of War Administration not to pass on Hitler's order. He further arranged to countermand the order to evacuate concentration camp inmates liable to be liberated by the Allies, and arranged for meetings with Dr. Carl Burckhardt, the ICRC president.[60]

The end of the Pacific war also involved Switzerland. On July 22, 1945, after three-and-a-half years of war with the Western powers, Japan finally agreed to comply with international law permitting neutral observers to visit prisoner-of-war camps. As reported by the *New York Times*, the Swiss had recently agreed to represent Japan in the United States (replacing Spain) only on condition that Japan allow Swiss observers to visit all camps where Americans were held.[61] After the atomic bombs fell on Hiroshima and Nagasaki, Japan capitulated on August 14. The Swiss transmitted Japan's surrender offer to the United States and handled the subsequent dispatches between those powers.[62]

Between 1939 and 1945, Switzerland spent 4 billion Swiss francs for arms and another 4 billion to maintain the army, for a total of 8 billion francs or, at today's rate, 80 billion francs.[63] In 1940, defense expenditures were fully 12 percent of the entire Swiss national income as Switzerland concentrated her efforts on fortifications and the *Réduit National*; in 1945, the figure remained high at 7 percent.[64] The monetary costs of defense and preparedness, together with the personal efforts related to the mobilizations, required great sacrifices on the part of Swiss citizenry during the war. When the average Swiss man was at his military post along with the farm's pack animals, his wife and children had to do all of the grueling farm work alone. Urban workers likewise lost wages.

The National Defense Commission concluded at the end of the war that the SSV shooting federation would continue to promote rifle skills for the entire nation in the interest of national defense.[65] The armed citizen had played a deterrent role against invasion and would remain the cornerstone of Switzerland's democratic army.

The army demobilized in July 1945, and active service officially ended on August 20. In Bern, Guisan spoke of future defense as the nation celebrated.[66]

While the Allies had accepted Swiss neutrality through most of the war because it suited their interests, some became critical of Switzerland toward the end of the war and afterward. At the Swiss National Day on August 1, 1945, Foreign Minister Max Petitpierre responded to this criticism:

> Those who reproach us today for our neutrality forget that this country, even when in mortal danger and practically alone as the representative of democratic ideals in the sub-jugated continent of Europe, resisted all pressure from the outside (Axis) and maintained that independence of which she is justly proud today.[67]

Petitpierre asked rhetorically: "As a belligerent state, invaded as the other countries of the continent, would we have been more useful than by remaining neutral?"[68]

On October 4, 1945, Federal Councillor Karl Kobelt gave an account of the Swiss perception of Nazi Germany's wartime threat and revealed some wartime secrets to the Swiss public. Kobelt noted that Swiss intelligence "stretched right into the *Führer's* headquarters" and kept the Military Department informed of Wehrmacht plans. The danger of invasion was greatest after the fall of France, after the Italian surrender, and as the war approached its end. The German General Headquarters also planned an invasion in March 1943, when 30 German divisions were massed on the Swiss frontier, but it was canceled at the last moment, according to Kobelt.[69]

Beginning almost immediately after Hitler's rise to power, Switzerland expended large sums of money and human effort to arm herself and to have the capacity to resist a Nazi invasion. Most other European nations failed to make these expenditures or efforts and would become prey to Nazi military invasion and, afterward, economic exploitation and worse.

European nations that failed to resist or that were quickly defeated and occupied contributed to the Nazi war effort, albeit involuntarily—clearly far more than any neutral country that traded with Germany. The Nazis plundered every country they occupied. Production of goods, crops, slave labor—all was free. The Nazis extracted immense resources from the occupied countries: France, Belgium, the Netherlands, Austria, Denmark, Italy, Yugoslavia, Hungary, Czechoslovakia, Greece, Poland, the Baltic states, Ukraine, large portions of Russia and the Caucasus, Norway, Bulgaria and parts of North Africa.

Switzerland is now being criticized for not joining the war on the side of the Allies and for trading with Germany. Yet this relationship of trading partners required Germany to pay for what it purchased, instead of getting valuable resources at little or no cost. By sustaining her economy through trade, Switzerland maintained the strength to resist a Nazi takeover. Had Switzerland declared war on Germany, she would have been overrun from the borders to the Plateau, and the Swiss Jews and the Jewish refugees in Switzerland, as well as resisters in general, would have been exterminated. Nazi control of the Alpine transit routes, as well as the superb defensive terrain of the Swiss Alps, would also have greatly damaged the Allied cause.

As the war neared, Switzerland at first embargoed all arms exports, but lifted the embargo in April 1939 at the insistence of the Allies. The Swiss munitions industry then exported sizable amounts of matériel to France and Great Britain and virtually none to Germany, until the surrender of France in June 1940. The Swiss did supply some armaments to Germany after the fall of France, but for the duration of the war Swiss arms deliveries amounted to less than one percent of Germany's total armaments. Albert Speer, the Reich Minister of Armaments and Munitions, does not even mention Switzerland in his lengthy memoirs, although he wrote extensively on how Germany harnessed industry in France and other occupied countries to serve the Reich's war needs.[70]

Speer also wrote of the importance of Germany's trade for raw materials with other neutrals. In December 1943, Speer informed Hitler that, should supplies of chromium from Turkey be cut off, the manufacture of tanks, planes and U-boats would become impossible and that the war would end about ten months after the loss of the Balkans.[71] His prediction came true. Iron ore from Sweden was just as important to Speer's efforts, and keeping open Germany's supply route from Sweden was an important factor in Hitler's decision to invade and occupy Norway and Denmark.

In every country they occupied, the Nazis seized the gold in the national bank. They also imposed occupation costs on these countries, which by the end of the war amounted to a cumulative total of 60 billion marks ($15 billion). France paid over half. Banks were also forced to grant "credits" to the Nazis. The total occupation costs and credits extracted from all occupied countries totaled 104 billion marks ($26 billion). This does not include the value of crops, raw materials and products which were taken. From France alone, those amounted to about 185 billion francs.[72] The Nazis stole no manufactured or agricultural products from the Swiss. Nor did the Swiss pay occupation costs.

At the end of September 1944, Germany held 7.5 million foreign slave laborers from occupied nations who were simply kidnapped and railroaded there. There were also two million prisoners of war, half a million of whom worked in munitions plants.[73] Switzerland supplied no slave labor force to the Third Reich.

The Nazi arms industry could not have functioned without this human war booty. Even the subjects of the Final Solution were fodder for the Nazi war machine. Emmanuel Ringelblum of the Warsaw ghetto, writing in 1942, described the plight of Jews in Eastern Europe:

> Only those Jews have a right to live who work to supply the German Army. . . . Never in history has there been a national tragedy of these dimensions. A people that hates the Germans with every fiber of its being can purchase its life only at the price of helping its foe to victory—the very

victory that means the complete annihilation of Jewry from
the face of Europe, if not of the whole world.[74]

Many of these workers were literally worked to death or died
from starvation. It bears repeating that Switzerland was almost the
only country in the whole of continental Europe where such horrors
did not occur.

The collective determination to resist, at any cost, at the national, group and individual levels throughout Europe might have stopped
Adolf Hitler far earlier. There should have been more and earlier resistance, including armed resistance, by states and peoples alike. More
than most European countries, the Swiss prepared themselves for such
resistance. Spiritually, they made the commitment to expend the
national resources to make their military preparedness credible.

General Henri Guisan symbolized the spirit of the Swiss citizen—the
citizen who was a trained marksman since youth and who gained confidence from the announcement that surrender was never an option.
The genius of Guisan was that he masterminded a strategy that was
entirely within Swiss historical traditions. Throughout the war, the
Führer had simply not been willing to pay the bloody price that the
Swiss would have extracted. Both when Germany was at the peak of
its power and later, when it sought to create a "Fortress Europe," the
Nazis declined to launch the Wehrmacht against Switzerland. Guisan,
the Swiss riflemen and their mountains, alone out of all Europe,
deterred Hitler from swallowing them up.

A half-century later, the place of General Guisan in history is
indisputably positive. He will be remembered forever as the leading
figure of Switzerland who led the nation honorably through its
darkest hour by fostering the will to resist.[75] While military leaders are
usually remembered for their combat activities, Guisan will be remembered as the general who stood up to Hitler and made him blink—
saving the country from devastation.

Chapter 11

ARMED NEUTRALITY TO
THE 21ST CENTURY

IT WAS ONLY A MATTER OF TIME BEFORE WORLD WAR WOULD
be replaced by the Cold War, and an economically and militarily
strong Switzerland continued to be vitally important to Europe. In a
1950 policy statement, the U.S. State Department praised the Swiss
contribution to the reconstruction of Europe and confirmed American
endorsement of Swiss armed neutrality:

> The Swiss Confederation is an important factor in Euro-
> pean economic recovery and a positive force in the maint-
> enance of free democratic institutions in Europe. While
> traditional neutrality precludes their political or military
> alignment with the West, the Swiss can nevertheless be
> relied upon to defend their territory resolutely against any
> aggressor.[1]

The Swiss emerged from World War II convinced of the value of
their militia system. A decade after the end of the war, now retired
General Henri Guisan praised the virtues of military rifle shooting as
the national sport: "It is not for nothing that in every Swiss house is a
firearm with its ammunition, always ready to defend our freedom and
independence." In no other country was "keeping a weapon by everyone the symbol of free men." The present generation was obliged,
Guisan continued, to impart shooting skills to their youth.[2]

Total Resistance (Der Totale Widerstand) by Swiss Major H. von
Dach, written in 1958 with the Nazi experience still fresh in mind,

expressed the Swiss philosophy: "We believe it is better to resist until the last. We believe that every Swiss woman or man must resist."[3] Civilian resisters would have no shortage of arms, because practically every Swiss family had either a Model 1911 rifle or K31 carbine, not to mention the arms held by hunters and marksmen.[4]

Most of von Dach's work concerned how to organize and wage guerrilla warfare and conduct underground operations. He admonishes that the arms found in every household "must be cleverly concealed as their illegal possession may mean a death sentence." The enemy will set a deadline for surrender of arms, will assure those who comply that they will not be punished, and will initially adhere to this policy, to create trust. The sense of security will be false:

> Should you be so trusting and turn over your weapons, you will be put on a "black list" in spite of everything. The enemy will always need hostages or forced laborers later on (read: "work slaves") and will gladly make use of the "black lists." You see once again that you cannot escape his net and had better die fighting.[5]

In such a struggle, the imperative for the Swiss must be: "Death rather than slavery!"[6] Some Swiss authorities looked askance at von Dach's thesis because it did not consider international law, under which partisans not in an official force are not protected if they become prisoners of war and can be executed.

However, this was the philosophy successfully applied by the Swiss in the war to dissuade a Nazi attack. It must be surmised that many Swiss civilians, men and women, would have resisted a Soviet invasion in the Cold War era, just as they would have resisted a Nazi invasion a decade before, by waging partisan warfare. The official *Soldier's Book* (*Soldatenbuch*) of the postwar period equated the citizen and the soldier and instructed on how to wage total war.[7]

After the Soviet Union swallowed up one Eastern European country after another—some of them not very far away—Swiss defense policy was directed toward protection from Soviet aggression. The air force, tanks, and artillery were modernized. The growing nuclear threat led to increasing civil defense measures, including massive construction of fallout shelters. Civilian defense was professionally organized and taught to the population at large.[8]

The threat was real. As Czechoslovak General Jan Sejna would later disclose, in the 1970s the Warsaw Pact planned, in the event of a European war, to make strategic air landings in Switzerland and to capture all vital centers within three days.[9]

To this day, the Swiss Constitution provides that every Swiss male is subject to military service and is to be issued arms which he may retain. "In this, Switzerland is unique in the world, exhibiting a remarkable degree of trust in her citizens, whose right to bear arms is considered as natural as the right to vote, and as such showing that Swiss direct democracy, armed and based on the idea of a social contract between rulers and ruled, is real."[10]

In the late 1950s, the Model 1931 bolt-action carbine was declared obsolete and the Model 1957 Sturmgewehr (Stgw 57 assault rifle) began to be issued to the citizen soldiers. Using a 24-round magazine, the Stgw 57 is selective fire, meaning that it shoots in semiautomatic (one shot per trigger pull) or full automatic (continuous fire as long as the trigger is held back), at the option of the user.[11]

Following the adoption of a new service rifle, the roughly 200,000 Stgw 57 rifles remaining at arsenals, pursuant to the 1997 Federal firearms regulation (the first ever passed by the Swiss Parliament), are being rendered exclusively semiautomatic and are being sold to Swiss citizens, male and female, at the bargain price of about 60 Swiss francs each.

The current service rifle is the Model 1990 Sturmgewehr (Stgw 90 assault rifle). This handy selective-fire rifle, which also features a three-shot burst, holds twenty 5.6mm cartridges (which are interchangeable with 5.56mm NATO cartridges), has a folding stock, a bipod, high-tech plastic, and precision diopter sights.[12]

The K31 carbine and the models Stgw 57 and 90 rifles are the three rifles typically used in 300-meter rifle competitions that are held every weekend all over Switzerland except in winter. These rifles are commonly seen being carried by ordinary citizens on trams and buses or on the shoulders of pedestrians and bicyclists en route to and from shooting ranges. Swiss shooting traditions also live on in the annual

Feldschiessen, shooting festivals held everywhere in the country on the same weekend each year, except in Geneva, which holds its festival a few weeks later. There are also countless cantonal and local matches, in which women have been participating in increasing numbers. Historical shoots are held to commemorate the great events of the Swiss past—the Rütli, Morgarten, and St. Jakob an der Birs shoots are only a few.[13]

The Federal shooting festival (Schützenfest) is conducted over a three-week period once every five years. Last held in Thun in 1995, it attracted 72,000 competitors, over one percent of Swiss citizenry, making it by far the largest rifle match in the world.[14] By comparison, the 1995 National Matches at Camp Perry, Ohio, America's "World Series" of the shooting sports, in which both civilians and military personnel participated, had only 4,000 competitors. Had the same percentage of the population participated as in the Swiss matches, 2,500,000 Americans would have shot at Camp Perry.

As has been the tradition since medieval times, the young are instructed in the use of weapons. One of the highlights of the year in Zurich is the Knabenschiessen. The city closes down for the afternoon as boys and girls compete with the Stgw 90 rifle. In 1997, the shooting queen and king, aged 15 and 17, respectively, won out over some 4,000 other teenagers and were crowned in the traditional festive ceremony.[15]

Swiss male citizens, with few exceptions, serve in the army and keep their arms at home, even after retirement. Major bus stops display not only the bus schedule but also a large poster with the training schedule of every unit of the Swiss Army for the year. Uniformed soldiers carrying their assault rifles are regularly seen at train stations and in other public places. Today, climbers in the Swiss Alps may witness army helicopters darting among the peaks on maneuvers. A close look at a rocky mountainside might also reveal a hidden bunker with a cannon.

Despite the prevalence of arms in the population, Switzerland is an exceptionally peaceable and safe society—not in any sense militaristic. Her tradition of defense preparedness and a citizenry trained in martial skills is allied to her tradition of nonaggression and neutrality. Virtually the only European country able to stay out of

European wars since the fall of Napoleon, Switzerland renounced all imperialist ambitions as long ago as the Battle of Marignano in 1515. Evidence of World War II defenses abound. Concrete tank obstructions litter the cow pastures along the Rhine. Bunkers for heavy machine guns dot farms and hillsides. Almost all bridges still have cavities to hold explosives; the major ones are still wired. Fortifications consisting of scores of rooms carved inside mountains are still maintained, either as museums or for current training and defense.

Today, Switzerland's citizens army is equipped with state-of-the-art weapons that include a wide array of advanced-design machine guns, mortars, rocket launchers, anti-tank guns, Stinger missiles, tanks, artillery, helicopters and anti-aircraft guns. Jet fighters include the Mirage, the Tiger II and, most recently, the American-built F/A-18 Hornet.[16]

Switzerland has banned, however, the use of antipersonnel land mines. The Federal Law on War Matériel prohibits the use, production, or possession of these weapons.[17]

The robust Swiss democracy provides for citizen initiatives at the Federal level to be voted on by the populace. In 1989, the year the Berlin Wall fell, 64.4 percent of the voters rejected an initiative to abolish the army outright. Majorities in all cantons other than the Jura and Geneva voted no. The supporters of this initiative then adopted a piecemeal strategy, but the voters again, in 1993, rejected initiatives to preclude purchase of the F/A-18 fighter jet from the United States and to deny funds for the building of a military training facility. More recently, attempts have been made to bring initiatives to cut military expenditures by one-half and to prohibit exportation of armaments.[18]

The portion of the Swiss political spectrum consisting of pacifists has thus gone full circle. After campaigning against the army in the 1920s and early 1930s, the pacifists, who were mostly socialists, finally entered into a coalition with the other political parties to strengthen defense against the threat of the Third Reich. This alliance created the will and ability of the entire populace to resist Nazism and Fascism to the end. The Socialist Party had resolved in 1942 that "the Swiss should never disarm, even in peacetime."[19] Opponents of the 1989 initiative to abolish the army thus contended that the lessons of World

War II were being completely disregarded. Once again, it was argued, pacifists were willing to believe in the inherent goodness of surrounding governments and to assume that Switzerland needed no defense.[20]

A current Swiss armed forces publication, *The Army of a Small, Neutral Nation: Switzerland*, explains the militia system of national defense, with the purpose of convincing foreigners that any aggression would be extremely costly and not worthwhile to the aggressor.

The militia army is also a force for social cohesion in the nation. Active units consist of 20- to 30-year-olds, although soldiers to age 50, and officers to age 55, can be called. "The acceptance of a superior, especially an officer, by his men," says the publication, "is less a problem than might be expected in an egalitarian society where one is accustomed to making his own political decisions, right down to the last detail." This democratic militia takes advantage of the experience and skills of its members in their civilian capacities, resulting in appropriate assignments to specific weapons or services. Bank presidents and farmers serve together, and this provides important unifying experience in the society at large. For total mobilization, the Swiss Army can rely on over 600,000 soldiers, including a number of specialized women volunteers.[21]

Based on its Constitution and international law, Swiss defense incorporates permanent neutrality and the pledge never to start a war: "The nation's goal is peace in freedom." The repulsion of armed aggression against Swiss territory is the imperative. "Should the army suffer reverses, it is to continue resistance in the form of guerrilla warfare. The aim of such action is to 'make it impossible for the aggressor to control the occupied area and to prepare that area for liberation.'"[22]

The policy of dissuasion which kept the Nazis out of the country in World War II continues today:

> The army clearly contributes to the avoidance of war by demonstrating its ability and readiness to fulfill the tasks expected of it under the conditions just described, by convincing foreign observers that the Swiss army is capable of maintaining long-term resistance and inflicting heavy losses on an aggressor, by minimizing a potential aggressor's

chances of success in view of the will of the Swiss people to resist and the material means of resistance available to their army.[23]

The Swiss armed forces today are organized according to the concept of "Army 95," named after its reorganization program, which became effective in 1995. As formulated in the Federal Council's report leading to the adoption of this program, Swiss security goals include: peace in freedom and independence; maintenance of freedom of action; protection of the population; defense of the national territory; and contribution to international stability, mainly in Europe.[24]

According to former Chief of Staff of the Swiss Armed Forces Hans Senn, the "Army 95" plan will reduce the army from 800,000 to 400,000 by the year 2005, by reducing the age of active service. The plan, however, retains the important principle that every male will continue to serve, and the maintenance requirements of technologically complex weaponry will increase the small number of full-time professionals.[25]

The lessons of World War II remain relevant today. As Dr. Senn states, timely preparation and the will to defend are decisive. Why did Switzerland have the means and will to resist and others did not? She was not a kingdom; she had her traditions of democracy, a citizens army and independence.

As a youngster in 1933, Dr. Senn recalls that the Swiss were already anti-Nazi. That year, he was engaging in military exercises with his fellow cadets in the canton of Aargau. A Berlin newspaper published a picture of the youngsters with the caption: "The Swiss make propaganda of their defense capability." That "propaganda" would inspire the nation to keep the Nazis out, and it has kept out most intruders since 1291.

In a 1997 interview, Lt. General Arthur Liener, Chief of Staff, explained the character of the Swiss armed forces. The Swiss system is unlike any military force in the world. Nor does it bear any resemblance to the American National Guard. Composed primarily of civilians, its members are professional in that their military duties often reflect their jobs in civilian life. Military duty is not mere training for some other occupation.[26]

"There are 400,000 small arsenals in Switzerland," stated Liener. "Personal arms and ammunition are kept in the home of every militiaman." The ammunition consists of 50 rounds of 5.6mm cartridges for the Stgw 90 assault rifle, sealed in what looks like a thin coffee can. Given that 400,000 militiamen possess their own small arsenal at home, the entire army can be mobilized in 24 hours, and much of it can be mobilized in as little as 4 hours. All matériel is dedicated to a fixed unit. This is unlike all other military forces in the world; Germany, for instance, has an armed force of 330,000 but matériel for 650,000. (By comparison, the U.S. Army numbers 480,000 active-duty soldiers. While this does not include other branches of service, the Army is by far the largest.)

Unlike World War II strategy, mobility rather than fixed position is emphasized. Military forces can reach anywhere in Switzerland within two hours. The new fleet of F/A-18 fighter jets purchased from the United States is the backbone of the air defense.

Why does Switzerland need a military force, in view of the peace that currently prevails in Europe? Who are Switzerland's potential enemies? These are questions asked today by Swiss youth for whom World War II is a distant memory. Liener replied that Switzerland, as a neutral, belongs to no traditional alliances. The armed forces must be able to defend the country against *any* aggression. As long as other countries have armed forces and the potential for aggression, Switzerland must be able to defend herself. For evidence of turmoil not too far away, one need only look at the Balkans or the former Soviet Union.

Liener was being diplomatic when he failed to mention the historic enemy to the north. Although a peaceful neighbor now, Germany's sheer size and might, particularly since the reunification of the country, raises questions that go to the heart of Swiss defense preparedness. How can a small nation like Switzerland permanently maintain her independence in the shadow of such a powerful neighbor? For much of its history, Germany has not shared Switzerland's democratic tradition, and its overwhelming economic power is potentially threatening.

Soviet Russia was a bitter enemy of Switzerland during much of this century. The end of the Soviet empire, which held Swiss democracy and capitalism in contempt, does not, however, mean that Switzerland will not be threatened from the east in the future.

Consistent with her policy of neutrality, Switzerland is not a member of NATO, which is now expanding into Eastern Europe. Referenda voted on by the people have also mandated that the country remain outside the European Union and the United Nations, although this could change in the future. Switzerland's lack of membership in the UN has not prevented her from participating in initiatives against chemical warfare or providing medical assistance in war-torn areas. Switzerland also contributes sizable sums to various UN humanitarian organizations. Membership in NATO would allow the armed forces to participate more fully in joint training exercises, but the historic commitment to strict neutrality has prevented this. Still, the Swiss military has played certain roles outside the country in cooperation with NATO, including the Partnership for Peace program, and has participated in certain United Nations activities. Whether the Swiss armed forces should join other countries in armed intervention in countries torn by civil war, such as the former Yugoslavia, continues to be debated.

The deeper political question is whether Switzerland should continue to maintain her traditional neutrality in the absence of an immediate threat. Some in Switzerland endorse membership in NATO while others call for the abolition of the Swiss Army because there is no further need for it. Yet neglect of defense in times of apparent calm is an act of naïveté in view of the volatile nature of people and governments. The threat that Switzerland parried in the 1940s—because of its will to prepare for the worst—arose in a blink of the eye in the context of history. The question of membership in a binding military alliance is, ultimately, a question of sovereignty. Switzerland's robust independence has worn well—for Switzerland, for Europe and for much of the world. It should not be too readily compromised.

Epilogue

IF THE EXAMPLE OF SWISS RESISTANCE IN WORLD WAR II PROVES anything, it proves that federalism, with its concomitant idea of limited government, and democracy, with its distrust of rule by the few, go hand in hand. During the years 1938–41 country after country was served up to Hitler, as if heads on a platter, after a political elite decided, either following brief resistance or no resistance at all, to surrender. The radically democratic Swiss, by contrast, retained their tradition of the armed citizen and refused to recognize a Führer, whether their own or someone else's. Instead, they prepared, beginning at the level of the individual citizen, to resist with arms to the end.

Although Germany originally consisted of a collection of states, after 1933, as noted by William Shirer, Hitler "abolished the separate powers of the historic states and made them subject to the central authority of the Reich, which was in his hands." Reichsminister Frick explained: "The state governments from now on are merely administrative bodies of the Reich."[1]

The benefits of direct democracy are clear. At the cantonal level, the ability of citizens to vote on the laws that affect them means that the people are sovereign. At the federal level, the initiative and the referendum offer the people the ability to govern themselves.

Again, federalism and direct democracy go hand in hand. True democracy means power from the bottom up rather than from the top down. In Switzerland, the individual and the family influence local affairs at the community and cantonal levels. The cantons govern according to the will of their citizens. The federal government is simply the unified cantons. In this system of federalism, the U.S. Constitution parallels that of Switzerland in that limited sovereignty is delegated to the federal government, but residual sovereignty is retained by the states or the people.

To defend her independence and unique system of government, Switzerland continues to maintain a citizens army, which by its very nature could never be used to institute tyranny or to wage imperialist wars against her neighbors. Though not militarist, this militia was strong enough to successfully deter aggression in World War II, while the standing armies of almost every other European army either collapsed or were ordered not to fight by fainthearted ruling elites.

In the United States, the original federal and state militias were abandoned. Although the armed populace was considered the militia, it was supposed to be "well regulated" and trained under federal and state law. The maverick private groups in the United States today calling themselves "militias" are not what the Framers had in mind when they affirmed the concept of a unified citizenry in arms. Switzerland's citizens army is equivalent neither to America's National Guard, the membership of which is restricted, nor, of course, to the so-called "militia" movements.

The institution of neutrality means, in theory, that one fewer country is available to initiate, or to participate in, a potential war. Historically, wars are started by rulers, who order commoners who have nothing against each other to kill or be killed. Swiss armed neutrality has been dictated by necessity but has also been a benefit to the world in that it enabled Switzerland to work in humanitarian causes and provided a site where conflicts could be resolved among belligerents in a climate of security.

World War II was the supreme test of these fundamental principles. The Swiss capacity for universal armed resistance by the entire population and spiritual resolve to resist to the death were major factors in deterring Adolf Hitler's anticipated attack. This proved the success, not the failure, of Switzerland's institutions of federalism, the citizens army and limited government.

For over two centuries, the United States and Switzerland have been recognized as "Sister Republics" because of their common ideals. Americans admire the little man standing up to the big bully. And

Americans of the war generation were well aware of the story of how the Swiss stood up to Hitler. They read the newspapers and saw the maps of Nazi Europe as it expanded from 1938 onward, always making democratic Switzerland seem ever smaller in the sea of Nazi tyranny. The fiftieth anniversary of the end of World War II captured great public interest, but the Swiss story has not heretofore been widely shared with the postwar generation. Many Americans seem to be only vaguely aware of Switzerland's reputation as a democratic nation of riflemen who offered armed deterrence to the prospect of an *Anschluss* by the Führer.

Influenced by English writers, America's Founding Fathers, who made the Revolution and then adopted the Federal Constitution and Bill of Rights in the late eighteenth century, were inspired by the Swiss example. The Founders depicted Switzerland as a democracy standing alone in a continent of tyrannical monarchies.

The American republic was founded on the principles of federalism, democracy and neutrality, which were strongly influenced by the Swiss model. Switzerland's policy of armed neutrality in World War II, which stemmed from these ideals, was morally sound because it did not constitute moral neutrality. The Swiss well understood what a Nazi victory would have meant for all of Europe and publicly opposed Nazism despite the threat of invasion. The ideals of human rights and the sanctity of individual life remained the motivating ideals of Switzerland throughout the war, even as they were abolished elsewhere in Europe wherever the Third Reich and the Soviet system advanced.

Switzerland has entered her eighth century as Europe's only direct democracy. Since 1291, this country has preserved her independence by mobilizing her entire population of armed men to resist any and all foreign aggressors. In recent centuries, with the exception of the Napoleonic incursion, Europe's tyrannies have been deterred from attempting to invade Swiss soil.

From the late eighteenth through the early twentieth centuries, Americans have studied the Swiss militia as the model of a democratic fighting force. The Swiss model required every man to serve in the militia and to keep a rifle at home. When World War II came, Switzerland was the only country in Europe whose entire populace had the capacity to wage a partisan armed struggle against an invader. Over three-fourths of a million soldiers, out of a population of just over four million, were mobilized, and boys and old men were armed in local defense organizations. Women, too, would have fought in the event of a Nazi aggression, just as they did when Napoleon invaded.

Switzerland's institutions played a key role in her being the only country on continental Europe to be surrounded but never conquered by the Nazis. The Nazis despised Switzerland because of her democratic traditions. Propaganda Minister Goebbels called Switzerland "this stinking little state," while Hitler implored that "all the rubbish of small nations still existing in Europe must be liquidated."

Had the Germans attacked, the Swiss were instructed to disregard any alleged "official" surrender as enemy propaganda and, if necessary, to fight individually. A nation of sharpshooters was prepared to snipe at German soldiers at long range from every mountainside.

Switzerland had few heavy arms, although any Nazi panzers that made it past mined roadways would have found the mountains impassable. During the war, Swiss fighter planes shot down 11 Luftwaffe aircraft over border skies.

The Warsaw Ghetto uprising exemplified what a small number of oppressed people could do by obtaining even a few arms. Jewish resistance fighters drove the Nazis from the Ghetto and inspired the free world with their heroism. While the revolt was crushed, its participants killed many Nazis. Similarly, Switzerland, with the highest percentage of trained citizen soldiers in the world, posed an obstacle that was unacceptably costly to the Nazis.

The Swiss strategy of defense from their *Réduit National* was simple: An opposition to the death by select troops at the border would be followed by a relentless war conducted from the Alps—the place the Swiss chose to engage the invader. The vast majority of Swiss strongly opposed Nazi ideology. There was no Holocaust on Swiss soil.

As so often in the history of World War II, the final verdict belongs to Winston Churchill: "Of all the neutrals Switzerland has the greatest right to distinction. . . . She has been a democratic State, standing for freedom in self-defense among her mountains, and in thought, in spite of race, largely on our side."

For centuries, Switzerland has symbolized the ideals of individual rights, direct democracy, federalism and armed strength for defense, never for aggression. She has been neutral in military conflicts, but was never morally neutral; her people have always sided with freedom. Swiss traditions were put to the supreme test during World War II and were vindicated.

Chapter Notes

PREFACE

[1] William L. Shirer, *Berlin Diary* (New York: Alfred A. Knopf, 1941), 114.
[2] Ibid. at 137.

PROLOGUE

[1] *Rapport du Général Guisan à l'Assemblée Fédérale sur le Service Actif, 1939–45* (Bern, 1946), 203.
[2] Julius Caesar, *De bello Gallico,* I. 1–29.
[3] John J. Zubly, *The Law of Liberty: A Sermon on American Affairs* (Philadelphia, 1775), 35.
[4] Ibid. at 35–36. Spellings are as in the original.
[5] Ibid. at 36-37.
[6] John Adams, *A Defence of the Constitutions of Government of the United States of America* (London 1787), I, 47–48.
[7] Ibid. at 32.
[8] Zubly, *The Law of Liberty,* 38; John McCormack, *One Million Mercenaries: Swiss Soldiers in the Armies of the World* (London: Leo Cooper, 1993), 7. See Oberst M. Feldman and Hauptmann H.G. Wirz eds., *Schweizer Kriegsgeschichte* (Bern: Oberkriegskommissariat, 1915–1935), I, Heft 1, 74–78.
[9] McCormack, *One Million Mercenaries,* 8. See Feldman & Wirz eds., *Schweizer Kriegsgeschichte,* I, Heft 2, 15.
[10] Zubly, *The Law of Liberty,* 38.
[11] Ibid. See Feldman & Wirz, *Schweizer Kreigsgeschichte,* I, Heft 2, 26–32;

McCormack, *One Million Mercenaries*, 9.

[12] Adams, *A Defence of the Constitutions*, I, 28–30. The above uses the original spellings. See Feldman & Wirz, *Schweizer Kriegsgeschichte*, I, Heft 2, 33–37.

[13] McCormack, *One Million Mercenaries*, 27–29; Feldman & Wirz, *Schweizer Kriegsgeschichte*, I, Heft 2, 154–62.

[14] McCormack, *One Million Mercenaries*, 29–32; Feldman & Wirz, *Schweizer Kriegsgeschichte*, I, Heft 2, 162–95.

[15] Feldman & Wirz, *Schweizer Kriegsgeschichte*, I, Heft 2, 203–76; James Murray Luck, *A History of Switzerland* (Palo Alto, CA: Society for Promotion of Science & Scholarship, 1985), 107–08; McCormack, *One Million Mercenaries*, 33–34.

[16] Niccolò Machiavelli, *The Discourses*, L. Walker, trans. (New York: Penguin, 1970), 332. See Feldman & Wirz eds., *Schweizer Kriegsgeschichte*, I, Heft 2, 354–71.

[17] Niccolò Machiavelli, *The Prince*, trans. L. Ricci (New York: New American Library of World Literature, 1952), 73.

[18] Machiavelli, *The Discourses*, 308, 321, 309–310.

[19] Machiavelli, *The Art of War*, E. Farneworth transl. (Indianapolis: Bobbs-Merrill, 1965), 46–47.

[20] F. Freymond, "Neutrality and Security Policy as Components of the Swiss Model," in Marko Milivojević and Pierre Maurer, eds., *Swiss Neutrality and Security* (New York: St. Martin's Press, 1990), 180; James Bryce, *The Holy Roman Empire* (London: MacMillan, 1889), 308.

[21] McCormack, *One Million Mercenaries*, 173.

[22] *Boston Gazette*, April 1, 1771, 3.

[23] Charles S. Hyneman & Donald S. Lutz, *American Political Writings During the Founding Era* (Indianapolis: Liberty Press, 1983), I, 238.

[24] James H. Hutson, *The Sister Republics: Switzerland and the United States from 1776 to the Present* (Washington, DC: Library of Congress, 1991), 9. See "The Sister Republics," *Rapport Annuel 1992* (Bern: Bibliothèque Nationale Suisse, 1993), 41–57.

[25] Adams, *A Defence of the Constitutions*, 38–39.

[26] Robert A. Rutland, ed., *The Papers of George Mason* (University of North Carolina Press, 1970), III, 896–97.

[27] *Documentary History of the Ratification of the Constitution* (Madison: State Historical Society of Wisconsin, 1981–93), IX, 966.

[28] Ibid. at 1040–41.

[29] See Stephen P. Halbrook, *That Every Man Be Armed: The Evolution of a Constitutional Right* (Oakland, CA: The Independent Institute, 1994).

[30] Jürg Stüssi-Lauterburg, *Föderalismus und Freiheit* (Brugg: Effingerhof,

1994), 19.

[31] Luck, *A History of Switzerland*, 282–85.

[32] *Chronik der Schweiz* (Zürich: Chronik-Verlag, 1987), 315.

[33] Interview with Jürg Stüssi-Lauterburg, Sept. 1996.

[34] Feldman & Wirz eds., *Schweizer Kriegsgeschichte* (Bern 1923), III, Heft 8, 8–31; Luck, *A History of Switzerland*, 305–06.

[35] McCormack, *One Million Mercenaries*, 163; Luck, *A History of Switzerland*, 308; *Chronik der Schweiz*, 319; Feldman & Wirz eds., *Schweizer Kriegsgeschichte* (Bern 1923), III, Heft 8, 31–38

[36] Luck, *History of Switzerland*, 310–11.

[37] Ibid. at 318–29.

[38] Jürg Stüssi-Lauterburg, "A History of Change," *Army 1995: The Past and Future of the Swiss Army* (Genève: Intermedia Com, 1997), 61.

[39] *Commentaires de Napoléon Premier* (Paris: Imprimerie Impérile, 1867), III, 464–65, quoted in Stüssi-Lauterburg, "A History of Change," *Army 1995*, 65.

[40] Hans Rudolf Kurz, *Histoire de l'Armée suisse* (Lausanne: Editions 24 Heures, 1985), 13, 18–19.

[41] Robert C. Brooks, *Civic Training in Switzerland: A Study of Democratic Life* (Chicago: University of Chicago Press, 1930), 365.

[42] Ibid.; Feldman & Wiwrz, *Schweizer Kriegsgeschichte*, IV, Heft 11, 36, 43, 57.

[43] Joachim Remak, *A Very Civil War: The Swiss Sonderbund War of 1847* (Boulder, CO: Westview Press, 1993), 157.

[44] Kurz, *Histoire de l'Armée suisse*, 24–26; John Hitz, *The Military System of the Republic of Switzerland* (Washington, DC: Franck Taylor, 1864), 11; Luck, *History of Switzerland*, 390–93.

[45] Stüssi-Lauterburg, "A History of Change," *Army 1995: The Past and Future of the Swiss Army*, 70.

[46] Christian Reinhart, Kurt Sallaz, & Michael am Rhyn, *Die Repetiergewehre der Schweiz: Die Systeme Vetterli und Schmidt-Rubin* (Dietikon-Zürich: Stocker-Schmid, 1991), 11–12; Edward C. Ezell, *Small Arms of the World* (Harrisburg, Pa.: Stackpole, 1983), 676; Schweizerischer Schützenverein, *Hand- und Faustfeuerwaffen: Schweizerische Ordonnanz 1817 bis 1975* (Frauenfeld: Huber, 1971), 67–69.

[47] Reinhart, Sallaz, & am Rhyn, *Die Repetiergewehre der Schweiz*, 110; Feldman & Wirz eds., *Schweizer Kriegsgeschichte*, IV, Heft 12, 127.

[48] Stüssi-Lauterburg, "A History of Change," *Army 1995*, 69.

[49] Luck, *History of Switzerland*, 406.

[50] Kurz, *Histoire de l'Armée suisse*, 36–37; Stüssi-Lauterburg, "A History of Change," *Army 1995*, 69; Feldman & Wirz, *Schweizer Kriegsgeschichte* IV,

Heft 12, 117; Christopher Hughes, *The Federal Constitution of Switzerland* (Oxford: Clarendon Press, 1954), 17.

[51] Remak, *A Very Civil War*, 175.

[52] Stüssi-Lauterburg, "A History of Change," *Army 1995*, 73.

[53] Richard Munday, *Most Armed and Most Free?* (Brightlingsea, Essex: Piedmont Publishing, 1996), 16.

[54] George W. Wingate, *Why School Boys Should Be Taught to Shoot?* (Boston: Sub-Target Gun Co., 1907), 6–7.

[55] Reinhart, Sallaz, & am Rhyn, *Die Repetiergewehre der Schweiz*, 154–59, 203, 164.

[56] *The Officers Training Corps: The Australian System of National Defense, The Swiss System of National Defense*, Senate Document No. 796, 63rd Cong., 3rd Sess. 1915, 123.

[57] Kurz, *Histoire de l'Armée suisse*, 60; Georg Thürer, *Free and Swiss* (London: Oswald Wolff, 1970), 143.

[58] Luck, *History of Switzerland*, 793–94.

[59] Kurz, *Histoire de l'Armée Suisse*, 60.

[60] Edgar Bonjour, *Swiss Neutrality: Its History and Meaning* (London: Allen & Unwin Ltd, 1952), 108.

[61] Kurz, *Histoire de l'Armée Suisse*, 70–71.

[62] Bonjour, *Swiss Neutrality*, 103, 106.

[63] Kurz, *Histoire de l'Armée Suisse*, 64.

[64] *The Military Law and Efficient Citizen Army of the Swiss*, Senate Document No. 360, 64th Cong., 1st Sess. (1916), 77.

[65] Ibid. at 78.

[66] Julian Grande, *A Citizens' Army: The Swiss System* (London: Chatto & Windus, 1916), 9.

CHAPTER 1

[1] William L. Shirer, *The Rise and Fall of the Third Reich* (New York: Simon & Shuster, 1990), 190–91.

[2] Ibid. at 184–86, 191–92.

[3] Ibid. at 194.

[4] Ibid. at 199–200.

[5] Ibid. at 203.

[6] *Journal de Genève*, Mar. 20, 1933, 6, and Mar. 26, 1933, 12.

[7] Ewald Banse, *Germany Prepares for War: A Nazi Theory of "National Defense"* (New York: Harcourt, Brace and Company, 1934), iii.

[8] Ibid. at iii–iv.

[9] Ibid. at 310.

[10] Ibid. at 311.

[11] Ibid. at 312–13.

[12] Ibid. at 313–14.

[13] Ibid. at 314.

[14] Ibid.

[15] Ibid. at 314–15.

[16] Ibid. at 315.

[17] *New York Times*, May 13, 1933, 7; *The Times* (London), May 13, 1933, 11g.

[18] Jürg Stüssi-Lauterburg, "Die Entstehung der Direktion der Militärverwaltung," *Entstehung und Wirken der Direktion der Militärverwaltung (MDV)*, ed. Jürg Stüssi-Lauterburg (Brugg, Schweiz: Verlag Effingerhof, 1989), 39.

[19] Lieut.-colonel Marietti, *Mon Fusil: Manuel du Fantassin* (Berne: Hallwag, 1933), 3.

[20] Ibid. at 22.

[21] Ibid. at 23.

[22] Ibid. at 24.

[23] Ibid. at 28.

[24] Ibid. at 30.

[25] *Schweizerische Schützenzeitung*, Aug. 24, 1933, 34:306.

[26] *Schiessprogramm für die Schulen und Kurse der Infanterie* (Eidg. Militärdepartement genehmigt am 7. April 1932).

[27] Hugh R. Wilson, *Switzerland: Neutrality as a Foreign Policy* (Philadelphia: Dorrance, 1974), 6.

[28] *New York Times*, Aug. 10, 1933, 11.

[29] *New York Times*, Aug. 29, 1933, 1.

[30] Ibid.

[31] G.E.W. Johnson, "Switzerland is Next," *The North American Review*, vol. 237, 523 (June 1934).

[32] "Un plan d'invasion de la Suisse?" *Journal de Genève*, Sept. 27, 1933, 1.

[33] *North American Review*, vol. 237, 529 (June 1934).

[34] *Journal de Genève*, Sept. 27, 1933, 1.

[35] Ibid.

[36] Ibid.

[37] Ibid. at 2.

[38] Ibid.

[39] Ibid.

[40] Hans Rudolf Fuhrer, "'Augur': Angriffspläne gegen die Schweiz schon 1933," *Schweizerzeit*, May 16, 1997.

[41] Jürg Fink, *Die Schweiz aus der Sicht des Dritten Reiches, 1933–1945*

(Zürich: Schulthess Polygraphischer Verlag, 1985), 51.

[42] *North American Review*, vol. 237, 523 (June 1934).

[43] Interview with Hans Senn, Sept. 17, 1997.

[44] Interview with Hans Rudolf Fuhrer, Sept. 17, 1997.

[45] *North American Review*, vol. 237, 529 (June 1934). *New York Times*, Oct. 12, 1933, 1, stated the appropriation to be 20,000,000 Swiss francs ($5,940,000).

[46] Kurz, *Histoire de l'Armée Suisse*, 75.

[47] *North American Review*, vol. 237, 529 (June 1934).

[48] *The Times* (London), Oct. 19, 1933, 12c.

[49] Ibid.

[50] *North American Review*, vol. 237, 529 (June 1934).

[51] Jules Sauerwein, "Main Entrances Blocked, Side Doors Worry France," *New York Times*, Dec. 10, 1933, Section IV, 1.

[52] Ibid.

[53] Ibid. at Section IV, 2.

[54] Ibid.

[55] *New York Times*, Dec. 15, 1933, 15.

[56] Ibid.

[57] Adolf Hitler, *Mein Kampf* (München: N.S.D.A.P., 1934), 1.

[58] Ibid.

[59] *North American Review*, vol. 237, 521, 526 (June 1934).

[60] Ibid. at 521.

[61] Ibid. at 522.

[62] Ibid.

[63] Ibid.

[64] Ibid. at 523.

[65] Ibid.

[66] Ibid.

[67] Ibid. at 524.

[68] Ibid.

[69] Ibid. at 525.

[70] Ibid. at 526.

[71] Ibid.

[72] Urs Schwarz, *The Eye of the Hurricane: Switzerland in World War II* (Boulder, CO: Westview Press, 1980), 4.

[73] Ibid. at 5.

[74] Shirer, *The Rise and Fall of the Third Reich*, 279–80.

[75] *New York Times*, Nov. 18, 1934, Section VII, 6.

[76] *New York Times*, July 28, 1934, 2.

[77] *Tir Fédéral, Fribourg 1934, Journal de Fête*, 101, 17, quoted in Munday,

Most Armed and Most Free?, 22. See *Schweizerische Schützenzeitung*, 1934, 32:280–81.

[78] *New York Times*, July 28, 1934, 2.

[79] *New York Times*, Nov. 18, 1934, Section VII, 6.

[80] Jacob B. Glenn, "The Jews in Switzerland," *Contemporary Jewish Record* (New York: American Jewish Committee, 1941), IV, 286.

[81] *New York Times*, Nov. 18, 1934, Section VII, 6.

[82] Ibid.

[83] Ibid.

[84] *New York Times*, February 25, 1935, 6.

[85] *Schweizerische Schützenzeitung*, 1935, 7:40.

[86] Th. Jenny, *Unsere heutigen Militärausgaben im Lichte der schweizerischen Volkswirtschaft*, 118. The figure for Belgium has been recalculated to correct the conversion rate of Belgium francs to Swiss francs.

[87] Shirer, *The Rise and Fall of the Third Reich*, 284–86.

[88] *New York Times*, April 5, 1935, 2.

[89] Ibid.

[90] *New York Times*, May 20, 1935, 9.

[91] *New York Times*, May 26, 1935, 19.

[92] *New York Times*, June 3, 1935, 1.

[93] *New York Times*, June 2, 1935, 24.

[94] *New York Times*, June 9, 1935, Section IV, 8.

[95] Hansjörg Siegenthaler & Heiner Ritzmann, *Historische Statistik der Schweiz* (Zurich 1996), 1045.

[96] Jon Kimche, *Spying for Peace: General Guisan and Swiss Neutrality* (London: Weidenfeld & Nicolson, 1961), 156.

[97] Hervé de Weck and Pierre Maurer, "Swiss National Defence Policy Revisited," *Swiss Neutrality and Security: Armed Forces, National Defence and Foreign Policy*, ed. Milivojević and Maurer, 66.

[98] *New York Times*, Feb. 5, 1936, 1.

[99] *New York Times*, Feb. 6, 1936, 1.

[100] Ibid. at 1, 14.

[101] *New York Times*, Feb. 7, 1936, 13.

[102] *New York Times*, Feb. 19, 1936, 13.

[103] Ibid.

[104] Ibid. See also "Swiss-German Crisis Intensified," *The Literary Digest*, 121 (February 29, 1936), 13.

[105] Schwarz, *The Eye of the Hurricane*, 8.

[106] *New York Times*, Oct. 7, 1936, 20.

[107] Shirer, *The Rise and Fall of the Third Reich*, 291.

[108] *New York Times*, Mar. 28, 1936, 8.

[109] *Schweizerische Schützenzeitung*, 1936, 17:123–33.

[110] *New York Times*, July 10, 1936, 17.

[111] Ibid.

[112] Ibid.

[113] Kimche, *Spying for Peace*, 156.

[114] *New York Times*, Sept. 21, 1935, 8.

[115] Ibid.

[116] "Swiss Doors: European War-Scare Leads 'Isle of Peace' to Fortify Its Frontiers," *The Literary Digest*, 123 (Jan. 23, 1937), 13.

[117] Ibid., quoting Gordon Reud, *Military and Naval Digest*.

[118] *New York Times*, Mar. 18, 1937, 9.

[119] *New York Times*, Mar. 22, 1937, 1, and Apr. 2, 1937, 8.

[120] Lothrop Stoddard, "Europe's Balance of Neutrals," *Christian Science Monitor*, Apr. 14, 1937, 3, 12.

[121] *New York Times*, Apr. 29, 1937, 7.

[122] *New York Times*, June 14, 1932, at 14.

[123] "Three Minor Characters," *Living Age*, 352 (Aug. 1937), 503.

[124] Reinhart, et al., *Die Repetiergewehre der Schweiz*, 171–79, 205; Law, *Karabiner 98k*, 1934–1945.

[125] Philipp Etter, *Geistige Landesverteidigung* (Schweiz. Studentenverein, 1937).

[126] Ibid. at 5.

[127] Ibid. at 14.

[128] Oskar Felix Fritschi, *Geistige Landesverteidigung während des Zweiten Weltkrieges* (Fabag + Druckerei Winterthur AG, 1971), 39; interview with Dr. Fritschi, Sept. 22, 1997.

CHAPTER 2

[1] Shirer, *The Rise and Fall of the Third Reich*, 296.

[2] Ibid. at 325–28.

[3] Ibid. at 337.

[4] Ibid. at 338.

[5] Ibid. at 341.

[6] Ibid. at 342.

[7] Ibid. at 347.

[8] Anton Gill, *An Honourable Defeat: A History of German Resistance to Hitler, 1933–1945* (New York: Henry Holt, 1994), 74.

[9] *New York Times*, Mar. 13, 1938, 36.

[10] Shirer, *The Rise and Fall of the Third Reich*, 347.

[11] R.A. Friedman, "Switzerland Fights Against a New 'Anschluss,'" *Contemporary Review*, 154 (Sept. 1938) 312.

[12] Ibid.

[13] Ibid. at 312–13.

[14] Ibid. at 313; "Switzerland," *Time*, July 4, 1938, 17.

[15] Bonjour, *Swiss Neutrality*, 134.

[16] *New York Times*, Mar. 16, 1938, 5.

[17] Joseph Conrad Fehr, "Fascism in Switzerland," *The Commonweal*, 27 (Jan. 28, 1938), 370.

[18] Ibid.

[19] J.B. Rusch, "Swiss Forebodings," *Living Age*, 354 (May 1938) 202. (Translated from the *National-Zeitung*, Basel Liberal German-Language Daily.)

[20] Schwarz, *The Eye of the Hurricane*, 112–13.

[21] William E. Rappard, "Switzerland in a Changing Europe," *Foreign Affairs*, July 1938, XVI, 679, 687-88.

[22] Ibid. at 688.

[23] Hans Senn, *Erhaltung und Verstärkung der Verteidigungsbereitschaft zwischen den beiden Weltkriegen* (Basel: Helbing & Lichtenhahn, 1991), 292 (map).

[24] Freymond, "Neutrality and Security Policy as Components of the Swiss Model," *Swiss Neutrality and Security: Armed Forces, National Defence and Foreign Policy*, ed. Milivojević and Maurer, 184.

[25] Antoine Fleury, "Switzerland and the Organisation of Europe: An Historical Perspective," *Swiss Neutrality and Security: Armed Forces, National Defence and Foreign Policy*, ed. Milivojević and Maurer, 103, citing *Feuille fédérale suisse*, 1938, Vol. 1, pp. 845–55.

[26] C. L. Sulzberger, "National Defense Speeded By Swiss," *New York Times*, July 24, 1938, 16.

[27] Ibid.

[28] Kurz, *Histoire de l'Armée Suisse*, 83–84.

[29] T.R. Ybarra, "Switzerland Rallies Again for Freedom," *New York Times*, Aug. 14, 1938, 8.

[30] Ibid.

[31] *New York Times*, Aug. 25, 1938, 3.

[32] *Contemporary Review*, 154 (Sept. 1938) 312, 318.

[33] Willi Gautschi, *General Henri Guisan: Die schweizerische Armeeführung im Zweiten Weltkrieg* (Zürich: Neue Zürcher Zeitung, 1989), 58; Tom Bower, *Nazi Gold* (New York: HarperCollins, 1997), 263.

[34] Shirer, *The Rise and Fall of the Third Reich*, 359.

[35] Ibid. at 383.

[36] Ibid. at 386.

[37] Ibid. at 390–91.

[38] Ibid. at 400.

[39] Heinz K. Meier, *Friendship Under Stress: U.S. - Swiss Relations 1900-1950*, (Bern: Lang Druck., 1970), 254.

[40] Ibid. at 254; *New York Times*, September 30, 1938, 6.

[41] Shirer, *The Rise and Fall of the Third Reich*, 420–22.

[42] Ibid. at 423.

[43] Ibid. at 424.

[44] Ibid. at 426.

[45] *New York Times*, Oct. 1, 1938, 2.

[46] Shirer, *The Rise and Fall of the Third Reich*, 428.

[47] William B. Chamberlain, "Nazi Shadow Over Switzerland," *Christian Century*, Mar. 22, 1939, L, 378.

[48] *New York Times*, Nov. 6, 1938, 2.

[49] *New York Times*, Nov. 11, 1938, 4.

[50] *Chicago Daily Tribune*, Nov. 12, 1938, 5f.

[51] Jacob B. Glenn, "The Jews in Switzerland," *Contemporary Jewish Record* (New York: American Jewish Committee, 1941), IV, 286.

[52] *New York Times*, Nov. 9, 1938, 24.

[53] *Neue Zürcher Zeitung*, Nov. 8, 1938, 2.

[54] *Der Angriff*, Nov. 9, 1938, 14.

[55] *Reichsgesetzblatt* 1938, I, 265, §15.

[56] *Der Angriff*, Nov. 10, 1938, 7; *Neue Zürcher Zeitung*, Nov. 11, 1938, 2.

[57] *New York Times*, Nov. 11, 1938, 1.

[58] Ibid.

[59] Ibid. at 4.

[60] *Neue Zürcher Zeitung*, Nov. 10, 1938, 2.

[61] *Reichsgesetzblatt* 1938, I, 1571. Printed in *Berliner Börsen Zeitung*, November 12, 1938, 12.

[62] Glenn, "The Jews in Switzerland," *Contemporary Jewish Record*, IV, 286.

[63] *New York Times*, Dec. 3, 1938, 8.

[64] Ibid.

[65] Ibid.

[66] Receuil Officiel, LIV, 880 (1938), in U.S. Dept. of State, *Swiss Policies on Purge of Axis Supporters* 7 (Washington, DC, 12945). See *The Times* (London), Dec. 12, 1938, at 13e.

[67] *Christian Century*, Mar. 22, 1939, L, 378.

[68] Ibid.

[69] *New York Times*, Jan. 1, 1939, 16.

[70] Kurz, *Histoire de l'Armée Suisse*, 82.

[71] *New York Times*, Dec. 28, 1938, 6.

[72] Gill, *An Honourable Defeat: A History of German Resistance to Hitler, 1933–1945*, 149. See Klaus Urner, *Der Schweizer Hitler- Attentäter* (Frauenfeld: Huber, 1980).

[73] Hans Kohn, *Nationalism and Liberty: The Swiss Example* (London: Unwin Brothers Limited, 1956), 128, quoting *Neue Zürcher Zeitung*, Dec. 12, 1938.

[74] Ibid. at 129.

[75] Ibid.

[76] Interview with Oskar Felix Fritschi, Sept. 22, 1997.

[77] Henri Guisan, *Notre Peuple et son Armée* (Zürich: Ed. polyg., 1939); General Henri Guisan, *Unser Volk und seine Armee* (Zürich, 1940).

[78] Interview with Dr. Willi Gautschi, Sept. 24, 1997. See Gautschi, *General Henri Guisan: Die schweizerische Armeeführung im Zweiten Weltkrieg*.

[79] Guisan, *Notre Peuple et son Armée*, 8.

[80] Ibid. at 8–9.

[81] Ibid. at 9.

[82] Ibid.

[83] Ibid. at 10.

[84] Ibid. at 11.

[85] Ibid. at 10–11.

[86] Ibid.

[87] Ibid. at 15.

[88] Ibid.

[89] Ibid. at 16.

[90] Ibid. at 22.

[91] Ibid.

[92] Ibid. at 23–24.

[93] Ibid. at 25.

[94] Ibid. at 26.

[95] Ibid. at 27.

[96] Ibid. at 30.

[97] Ibid. at 31.

[98] Ibid. at 31–32.

[99] Ibid. at 32.

[100] Ibid.

[101] Ibid. at 33.

[102] Ibid.

[103] Ibid. at 34.

[104] Ibid. at 37.

[105] Ibid. at 38.

[106] Ibid.

CHAPTER 3

[1] *The Times* (London), Jan. 23, 1939, 12b.
[2] *New York Times*, Jan. 31, 1939, at 5:2.
[3] Kurz, *Histoire de l'Armée Suisse*, 92.
[4] *Schweizerische Schützenzeitung*, Feb. 1939, 8:55.
[5] Shirer, *The Rise and Fall of the Third Reich*, 440.
[6] Ibid. at 445–46.
[7] Ibid. at 447–48.
[8] Ibid. at 441–42.
[9] Ibid. at 450.
[10] *The Times* (London), Mar. 16, 1939, 16b.
[11] Interview with Milan Kubele, Uherský Brod, Czech Republic, Mar. 16, 1994.
[12] Ibid.
[13] *The Times* (London), Mar. 16, 1939, at 15c; *Journal de Genève*, Mar. 16, 1939, 1.
[14] Edgar Bonjour, *Geschichte der Schweizerischen Neutralität* (Basel 1967), III, 320–21. See *New York Times*, Mar. 18, 1939, 1.
[15] *New York Times*, Mar. 19, 1939, 36.
[16] *New York Times*, Mar. 21, 1938, 8.
[17] Ibid.
[18] R. de Craon-Poussy, "Switzerland is Ready," The *Commonweal*, 30 (July 7, 1939), 273.
[19] *New York Times*, Mar. 24, 1939, 3.
[20] *New York Times*, Mar. 26, 1939, 33.
[21] *New York Times*, Mar. 27, 1939, 5.
[22] Ibid.
[23] *The Times* (London), Mar. 27, 1939, 11a.
[24] Schwarz, *The Eye of the Hurricane*, 69.
[25] Ibid. at 67.
[26] Gerhard L. Weinberg, *A World At Arms* (Cambridge University Press, 1994), 26.
[27] Quoted in Wilhelm Viola, "The Position of Switzerland," *Contemporary Review*, vol. 156, 695–96 (1939).
[28] Ibid. at 696.
[29] Adolf Keller, "Switzerland Will Fight," *Christian Century*, May 24, 1939, LVI, 679.
[30] *The Times* (London), Apr. 5, 1939, at 16a.
[31] *The Times* (London), May 9, 1939, at 21c.
[32] Charles F. Phillips & J.V. Garland, *The American Neutrality Problem* (New

York: H.W. Wilson Co., 1939), 74, 283, quoting Testimony of Dr. John B. Moore, U.S. Senate Foreign Relations Committee Hearings on *S*. 3474, 74th Cong., 2nd Sess. (Jan. 10–Feb. 5, 1936).

[33] Meier, *Friendship Under Stress: U.S.-Swiss Relations 1900–1950*, 260.

[34] Ibid. at 261.

[35] Ibid. at 263.

[36] Phillips & Garland, *The American Neutrality Problem*, 304.

[37] Griffin Barry, "Swiss Democracy Goes into Action," *Travel*, 73 (June 1939) 26.

[38] Ibid. at 27–28.

[39] Ibid. at 28.

[40] Ibid. at 41.

[41] *Schweizerische Schützenzeitung*, June 22, 1939, 25:1.

[42] Ibid. at 25:226.

[43] Munday, *Most Armed and Most Free?*, 23.

[44] Ferdinand Hediger, "The Fabulous Martini," *Gun Digest 1996* (Northbrook, IL: DBI Books, 1995), 182, 193.

[45] Ibid.

[46] Kimche, *Spying for Peace: General Guisan and Swiss Neutrality*, 157.

[47] Henry L. Feingold, *The Politics of Rescue* (New York: Waldon Press, 1970), 66.

[48] *New York Times*, Aug. 2, 1939, 14.

[49] Ibid.

[50] *The Times* (London), Aug. 4, 1939, at 13d.

[51] Donovan Richardson, "The Neutrals' Fight for Peace," *Christian Science Monitor*, Aug. 12, 1939, 1.

[52] *New York Times*, Aug. 20, 1939, 5.

[53] Shirer, *The Rise and Fall of the Third Reich*, 456.

[54] Ibid. at 496.

[55] Ibid. at 541.

[56] Hugo Schäfer, *Die Wehrmächte aller Staaten 1937* (Vienna, 1937); Kurt Passow, *Taschenbuch der Heere, Ausgabe 1939* (Munich: J.F. Lehmanns, 1939). Where available, 1939 figures are used.

[57] *New York Times*, Aug. 25, 1939, 3.

[58] *New York Times*, Aug. 26, 1939, 2.

[59] *New York Times*, Aug. 29, 1939, 3.

[60] Receuil Officiel, LV, 760 (1939), invoking Receuil Officiel, XLIII, 375 (1927). U.S. Dept. of State, *Swiss Policies on Purge of Axis Supporters* 7–8 (Washington, DC, 1945).

[61] *The Times* (London), Aug. 31, 1939, 7b.

[62] Kimche, *Spying for Peace: General Guisan and Swiss Neutrality*, 8–9.

[63] Ibid. at 6.

[64] Schwarz, *The Eye of the Hurricane*, 3.

[65] Luck, *A History of Switzerland*, 803.

[66] Bonjour, *Geschichte der Schweizerischen Neutralität*, IV, 23.

[67] Fritschi, *Geistige Landesverteidigung während des Zweiten Weltkrieges*, 44–45; letter from George Gyssler, Nov. 26, 1997.

[68] M. Wolf, "What People are Saying," *Nineteenth Century*, 126 (Sept. 1939), 370, 371.

[69] Ibid. at 374.

[70] Interview with Robert Dowlut, son of Cannoneer Dyonizy Dowlut, Nov. 21, 1997.

[71] Shirer, *The Rise and Fall of the Third Reich*, 626.

[72] Simha Rotem (Kazik), *Memoirs of a Warsaw Ghetto Fighter and the Past Within Me* (New Haven: Yale University Press, 1994), 10.

[73] *New York Times*, Nov. 4, 1939, 5.

[74] Ernst Leisi, *Freispruch für die Schweiz* (Frauenfeld: Huber Verlag, 1997), 63–64.

[75] Schwarz, *The Eye of the Hurricane*, 3.

[76] Interview with Hans Senn, Sept. 19, 1997.

[77] *Journal de Genève*, Sept. 4, 1939, 1.

[78] Shirer, *The Rise and Fall of the Third Reich*, 628.

[79] Kimche, *Spying for Peace: General Guisan and Swiss Neutrality*, 12.

[80] *New York Times*, Sept. 22, 1939, 7.

[81] *New York Times*, Sept. 19, 1939, 15.

[82] *New York Times*, Sept. 22, 1939, 7.

[83] Ibid.

[84] *New York Times*, Sept. 23, 1939, 3.

[85] *New York Times*, Sept. 24, 1939, Section IV, 5.

[86] Ibid.

[87] *New York Times*, Sept. 26, 1939, 16.

[88] *New York Times*, Oct. 1, 1939, Section IV, 5.

[89] Ibid.

[90] *New York Times*, Oct. 4, 1939, 2.

[91] Operationsbefehl Nr. 2, A.H.Q., Oct. 4, 1939, in *Tagesbefehle des Generals, 1939–1945* (Bern: Eidg. Militärbibliothek, n.d.) (emphasis added).

[92] See Gautschi, *General Henri Guisan*, 90.

[93] Schwarz, *The Eye of the Hurricane*, 9.

[94] Ibid. at 10.

[95] Ibid.

[96] Shirer, *The Rise and Fall of the Third Reich*, 634.

[97] Ibid. at 644.

[98] *New York Times*, Oct. 21, 1939, 1.
[99] Shirer, *Berlin Diary*, 114.
[100] *New York Times*, Oct. 30, 1939, 4.
[101] *New York Times*, Nov. 5, 1939, 4.
[102] *New York Times*, Nov. 7, 1939, 20.
[103] *New York Times*, Nov. 12, 1939, 41.
[104] Gill, *An Honourable Defeat: A History of German Resistance to Hitler, 1933–1945*, 129–30.
[105] Hans Rudolf Kurz, *Die Schweiz in der Planung der kriegführenden Mächte während des zweiten Weltkrieges* (Biel: SUOV, 1957), 10.
[106] Shirer, *Berlin Diary*, 118.
[107] Shirer, *The Rise and Fall of the Third Reich*, 658.
[108] *New York Times*, Nov. 21, 1939, 3.
[109] Kimche, *Spying for Peace*, 24–25.
[110] Shirer, *The Rise and Fall of the Third Reich*, 665.
[111] Schwarz, *The Eye of the Hurricane*, 11.
[112] Kurz, *Histoire de l'Armée Suisse*, 107.
[113] August Lindt, *Le temps du hérisson. Souvenirs, 1939–1945* (Genève: Editions Zoè, 1995), 21–32. This work was published in German as *Die Schweiz das Stachelschwein.*
[114] Ibid. at 47.
[115] Ibid. at 48.
[116] *New York Times*, Dec. 29, 1939, 6.
[117] Wilhelm Viola, "The Position of Switzerland," *Contemporary Review*, vol. 156, 695 (1939).
[118] Ibid. at 696.

CHAPTER 4

[1] *The Times* (London), Jan. 3, 1940, 5a.
[2] Ibid.
[3] Ibid.
[4] *The Times* (London), Jan. 8, 1940, 5f.
[5] Ibid.
[6] *The Times* (London), Jan. 9, 1940, 9c.
[7] *Schweizerische Schützenzeitung*, Jan. 25, 1940, 4:21–22.
[8] *Schweizerische Schützenzeitung*, Feb. 1940, 9:54.
[9] Ibid.
[10] Shirer, *Berlin Diary*, 137.
[11] *New York Times*, Mar. 5, 1940, 3.

[12] *New York Times,* Mar. 6, 1940, 13.

[13] *New York Times,* Feb. 2, 1940, 3.

[14] *The Times* (London), Feb. 10, 1940, 5e.

[15] Ibid.

[16] Ibid.

[17] Elizabeth Wiskemann, "The Swiss Confederation and the War," *Fortnightly,* 153 (April 1940) 383, 387–88.

[18] Shirer, *The Rise and Fall of the Third Reich,* 666–67.

[19] Ibid. at 683.

[20] Kimche, *Spying for Peace: General Guisan and Swiss Neutrality,* 28.

[21] Shirer, *The Rise and Fall of the Third Reich,* 694–95.

[22] Ibid. at 697.

[23] Ibid. at 698.

[24] Ibid. at 699.

[25] Ibid. at 700.

[26] Wilson, *Switzerland: Neutrality as a Foreign Policy,* 67; Carlos Caballero Jurado, *Resistance Warfare 1940–45,* (London: Osprey, 1985), 12.

[27] Shirer, *The Rise and Fall of the Third Reich,* 701–04.

[28] Ibid. at 705–06.

[29] *The Times* (London), Apr. 18, 1940, 5c.

[30] Wilson, *Switzerland: Neutrality as a Foreign Policy,* 67.

[31] *Schweizerische Schützenzeitung,* 1941, 32:223.

[32] Jurado, *Resistance Warfare 1940–45,* 8–10.

[33] Shirer, *The Rise and Fall of the Third Reich,* 711.

[34] Urner, *"Die Schweiz muss noch geschluckt werden!"* 28.

[35] *New York Times,* Apr. 13, 1940, 5.

[36] *New York Times,* Apr. 17, 1940, 5.

[37] Bonjour, *Geschichte der Schweizerischen Neutralität,* VII, 35–36.

[38] *Militär-Amtsblatt* (Eidgenössiches Militärdepartement 1940), 82–83.

[39] Ibid.

[40] Ibid.

[41] Bonjour, *Geschichte der Schweizerischen Neutralität,* IV, 70. See Gautschi, *General Henri Guisan,* 180.

[42] *Militär-Amtsblatt* (Eidgenössiches Militärdepartement 1940), 82–83.

[43] *The Times* (London), Apr. 19, 1940, at 5c.

[44] *New York Times,* Apr. 19, 1940, at 3.

[45] Ibid.

[46] Interview with Willi Gautschi, Sept. 24, 1997.

[47] Kimche, *Spying for Peace,* 30–31; Fritschi, *Geistige Landesverteidigung während des Zweiten Weltkrieges,* 186–87.

[48] *Schweizerische Schützenzeitung,* 1940, 20:142.

[49] See *Schweizerische Schützenzeitung*, Apr. 1940, 17:119.

[50] Ibid. at 18:128.

[51] Fritschi, *Geistige Landesverteidigung während des Zweiten Weltkrieges*, 188.

[52] *The Times* (London), Apr. 24, 1940, 5b.

[53] Jon Kimche, *Spying for Peace*, 34.

[54] Ibid. at 32–33.

[55] Schwarz, *Eye of the Hurricane*, 15–17.

[56] Ibid. at 18–20.

[57] Ibid. at 21–22.

[58] Elizabeth Wiskemann, "The Sword of Freedom," *Fortnightly*, 156 (August 1941) 129.

[59] Ibid. at 130.

[60] Gill, *An Honourable Defeat: A History of German Resistance to Hitler, 1933–1945*, 134–38.

[61] Shirer, *The Rise and Fall of the Third Reich*, 713–14.

[62] *New York Times*, May 11, 1940, 7.

[63] Leisi, *Freispruch für die Schweiz*, 51; *New York Times*, May 12, 1940, 40.

[64] *New York Times*, May 14, 1940, 2.

[65] *New York Times*, May 11, 1940, 7.

[66] Interview with Hans Senn, Sept. 19, 1997.

[67] Shirer, *Berlin Diary*, 155.

[68] Kurz, *Histoire de l'Armée Suisse*, 111.

[69] Interview with Ernst Leisi, Sept. 22, 1997.

[70] *The Times* (London), May 13, 1940, 5g.

[71] *New York Times*, May 14, 1940, 2.

[72] Ibid.

[73] Ibid.; Kurz, *Histoire de l'Armée Suisse*, 110.

[74] Ibid.

[75] Augur, "Switzerland Held Objective of Italy," *New York Times*, May 14, 1940, 9.

[76] Ibid.

[77] Ibid.

[78] Ibid.

[79] Shirer, *The Rise and Fall of the Third Reich*, 721–23.

[80] Ibid. at 726.

[81] *The Times* (London), May 14, 1940, 5g.

[82] *New York Times*, May 16, 1940, 1.

[83] Ibid. at 5.

[84] *The Times* (London), May 15, 1940, 6b.

[85] Kimche, *Spying for Peace*, 36.

86 Schwarz, *Eye of the Hurricane*, 26.
87 Gautschi, *General Henri Guisan*, 183.
88 Ibid. at 189; see *Rapport du Général Guisan*, 195–96.
89 Ibid. at 90.
90 Interview with Hans Senn, Sept. 17, 1997.
91 Interview with Ernst Leisi, Sept. 22, 1997.
92 Interview with Robert Vögeli, Sept. 20, 1997.
93 *The Times* (London), May 16, 1940, 5d.
94 Kimche, *Spying for Peace*, 36.
95 Ibid.
96 *New York Times*, May 17, 1940, 1.
97 Ibid.
98 Shirer, *Berlin Diary*, 156.
99 *New York Times*, May 20, 1490, 6.
100 Shirer, *The Rise and Fall of the Third Reich*, 729.
101 Ibid. at 730.
102 Kurz, "Vor vierzig Jahren: Aufstellung der Ortswehren," *Der Fourier*, June 1980, 211.
103 Ibid.; Gautschi, *General Henri Guisan*, 182.
104 Gautschi, *General Henri Guisan*, 182.
105 *Der Fourier*, June 1980, 211–12.
106 Ibid.
107 Ibid. at 212.
108 Kimche, *Spying for Peace*, 40.
109 Receuil Officiel, LVI, 556 (1940), in U.S. Dept. of State, *Swiss Policies on Purge of Axis Supporters* 7–8 (Washington, DC, 1945) 8. See also *The Times* (London), May 29, 1940, 5f.
110 Hans Rudolf Kurz, "Vor vierzig Jahren: Aufstellung der Ortswehren," *Der Fourier*, June 1980, 214.
111 Bonjour, *Geschichte der Schweizerischen Neutralität*, VI, 271.
112 Schwarz, *Eye of the Hurricane*, 64–65.
113 Ibid. at 89.
114 Ibid. at 84.
115 Ibid., citing Bonjour, *Geschichte der Schweizerischen Neutralität*, VI, 211.
116 Ibid.
117 Ibid. at 86.
118 Leisi, *Freispruch für die Schweiz*, 51.
119 Ibid.; see also *The Times* (London), June 3, 1940, 5d.
120 Shirer, *The Rise and Fall of the Third Reich*, 738.
121 Leisi, *Freispruch für die Schweiz*, 52.
122 Ibid. at 52.

[123] Ibid. at 52–53.

[124] *The Times* (London), June 10, 1940, 5d.

[125] Klaus Urner, *"Die Schweiz muss noch geschluckt werden!"* Hitlers *Aktionspläne gegen die Schweiz* (Zürich: Neue Zürcher Zeitung, 1990), 137.

[126] Kurz, *Histoire de l'Armée Suisse*, 114; Leisi, *Freispruch für die Schweiz*, 53.

[127] Leisi, *Freispruch für die Schweiz*, 53.

[128] Ibid. at 54.

[129] *The Times* (London), June 13, 1940, 5f, and June 14, 1940, 5b.

[130] *The Times* (London), June 29, 1940, 5d.

[131] Shirer, *The Rise and Fall of the Third Reich*, 745–46.

[132] *New York Times*, June 16, 1940, 25.

[133] Schwarz, *Eye of the Hurricane*, 27.

[134] Jakob Huber, *Bericht des Chefs des Generalstabs an den Oberbefehlshaber der Armee über den Aktivdienst 1939–1945* (Bern 1946), 482.

[135] Schwarz, *Eye of the Hurricane*, 114.

[136] Huber, *Bericht des Chefs des Generalstabs*, 493–94; Schwarz, *The Eye of the Hurricane*, 114–16.

[137] Shirer, *The Rise and Fall of the Third Reich*, 745–46.

[138] Urner, *"Die Schweiz muss noch geschluckt werden!"* 39.

[139] Fink, *Die Schweiz aus der Sicht des Dritten Reiches, 1933–1945*, 28. See Urner, *"Die Schweiz muss noch geschluckt werden!"* 144–45.

[140] Urner, *"Die Schweiz muss noch geschluckt werden!"* 39–41.

[141] Ibid. at 45–47.

[142] Ibid. at 29–30.

[143] Hans Rudolf Kurz, *Die Schweiz in der Planung der kriegführenden Mächte während des zweiten Weltkrieges* (Biel: SUOV, 1957), 13–14.

[144] Shirer, *The Rise and Fall of the Third Reich*, 745–46.

[145] Urner, *"Die Schweiz muss noch geschluckt werden!"* 45. For the positions of the German, Italian, and French armies, see Hans Senn, *Anfänge einer Dissuasionsstrategie während des Zweiten Weltkrieges* (Basel: Helbing & Lichtenhahn, 1995), 514.

[146] Urner, *"Die Schweiz muss noch geschluckt werden!"* 27.

[147] Ibid.

[148] Ibid. at 56–58.

[149] Ibid. at 59–61.

[150] See Hans Senn, "Entre-deux-guerres et Seconde Guerre Mondiale," *Forts et Fortifications en Suisse* (Lausanne: Payot, 1992), 155–95.

[151] Information on Sargans was provided in a guided tour by Adj. Uof Malnati and Major i Gst Peter C. Stocker, Sept. 18, 1997. See *Die Festung Sargans im Wandel der Zeit* (Mels: Sarganserländer Druck, 1994).

[152] Information on the defenses at the Plain of Sargans was provided in a guided tour by Oberstlt. i Gst D. Lätsch on Sept. 18, 1997.

[153] Robert Vögeli et al., *Festungsmuseum Reuenthal* (Reuenthal, 1989).

[154] *New York Times*, June 7, 1940, 8.

[155] *The Times* (London), June 7, 1940, 5e. The complete text is in *Tagesbefehle des Generals, 1939–1945* (Bern: Eidg. Militärbibliothek, n.d.).

[156] *Rapport du Général Guisan*, 198.

CHAPTER 5

[1] Weinberg, *A World At Arms: A Global History of World War II*, 173–74.

[2] Urner, *"Die Schweiz muss noch geschluckt werden!"* 62–63.

[3] Ibid. at 64–65.

[4] Ibid. at 66–69.

[5] Ibid. at 52–55, 151.

[6] Ibid. at 151–52.

[7] Ibid. at 55.

[8] Ibid. at 70–71.

[9] Ibid. at 72.

[10] Bernhard von Loßberg, *Im Wehrmachtführungsstab. Bericht eines Generalstabsoffiziers* (Hamburg: H.H. Nölke, 1949), quoted in Ernst Uhlmann, "Angriffspläne gegen die Schweiz," *Allgemeine Schweizerische Militärzeitung* (Dec. 1949), LX, 841, 842.

[11] Ibid. at 842–43.

[12] Ibid. at 843.

[13] *Ordonnance concernant la détention d'armes et de radio-émetteurs dans les territoires occupés.* A photograph of an original of this poster was taken by the author at the Partisan exhibition at the Museum of the Hotel National des Invalides, Paris, on August 22, 1994. See *New York Times*, July 1, 1940, 3.

[14] Anny Latour, *The Jewish Resistance in France (1940–1944)*, (New York: Holocaust Library, 1970), 24.

[15] Kurz, *Histoire de l'Armée Suisse*, 103.

[16] Jürg Fink, *Die Schweiz aus der Sicht des Dritten Reiches, 1933–1945* (Zürich: Schulthess Polygraphischer Verlag, 1985), 28.

[17] Schwarz, *Eye of the Hurricane*, 22–23.

[18] Ibid. at 48.

[19] Kimche, *Spying for Peace*, 43–44.

[20] Bonjour, *Swiss Neutrality*, 122.

[21] Kurz, *Histoire de l'Armée Suisse*, 119–20.

[22] Ibid. at 122.

23 Ibid. at 124.

24 Ibid. at 125.

25 Interview with Willi Gautschi, Sept. 24, 1997. See Gautschi, *General Henri Guisan*, 294–328.

26 Hans Senn, *Anfänge einer Dissuasionsstrategie während des Zweiten Weltkrieges* (Basel: Helbing & Lichtenhahn, 1995).

27 Interview with Hans Senn, Sept. 17, 1997.

28 *Rapport du Général Guisan a l'Assemblée Fédérale sur le Service Actif, 1939–1945* (Bern 1946), 36.

29 Ibid. at 37.

30 Ibid. at 38.

31 Ibid. at 39.

32 Ibid.

33 Gautschi, *General Henri Guisan*, 317; Schwarz, *Eye of the Hurricane*, 49.

34 Schwarz, *Eye of the Hurricane*, 38–40.

35 Lindt, *Le temps du hérisson*, 40–41.

36 Interview with August Lindt, Sept. 23, 1997.

37 Interview with Willi Gautschi, Sept. 24, 1997.

38 Interview with George Gyssler, a schoolboy at the time, June 6, 1997.

39 August Lindt, *Die Schweiz das Stachelschwein* (Bern: Zytglogge, 1992), 69.

40 Lindt, *Le temps du hérisson*, 42; interview with August Lindt, Sept. 23, 1997. Lindt, a corporal in heavy artillery, was a member of the Offiziersbund and Aktion Nationaler Widerstand.

41 Lindt, *Le temps du hérisson*, 45–49.

42 *Rapport du Général Guisan*, 208.

43 Lindt, *Le temps du hérisson*, 50–52.

44 Ibid. at 54–59; Kurz, *Histoire de l'Armée Suisse*, 117; Allen Dulles, *The Secret Surrender* (London: Harper & Row, 1966), 26; Kimche, *Spying for Peace*, 46–48.

45 Lindt, *Le temps du hérisson*, 64–65.

46 Interview with August Lindt, Sept. 23, 1997.

47 Interview with Oskar Felix Fritschi, Sept. 22, 1997.

48 Kimche, *Spying for Peace*, 83–84, 87–88.

49 Armeebefehl, A.H.Q., 2 Juli 1940.

50 Urner, *"Die Schweiz muss noch geschluckt werden!"* 159.

51 Shirer, *Berlin Diary*, 195.

52 See Gautschi, *General Henri Guisan*, 267–93.

53 *Rapport du Général Guisan*, 202.

54 Ibid. at 203.

55 Ibid.

56 Ibid. at 203–04.

[57] Ibid.

[58] Ibid.

[59] Schwarz, *Eye of the Hurricane*, 54, citing *Neue Zürcher Zeitung*, July 29, 1940.

[60] Ibid. at 54.

[61] Marko Milivojević, "The Swiss Armed Forces," *Swiss Neutrality and Security*, ed. Milivojević and Maurer, 15–16.

[62] Kimche, *Spying for Peace*, 56.

[63] *New York Times*, Aug. 2, 1940, 7.

[64] Ibid.

[65] Robert S. Bird, "Swiss Celebrate Freedom at Fair," *New York Times*, Aug. 2, 1940, 13.

[66] Arnold Lunn, *Mountain Jubilee* (London: Eyre & Spottiswoode, 1943), vi.

[67] Hans Rudolf Kurz, *Operationsplanung Schweiz* (Thun: Ott Verlag, 1972), 39–40.

[68] Urner, *"Die Schweiz muss noch geschluckt werden!"* 161.

[69] Ibid. at 161–62, 163–64.

[70] Ibid. at 171–72.

[71] *New York Times*, Sept. 17, 1940, 4.

[72] Gautschi, *General Henri Guisan*, 372–74.

[73] Kurz, *Die Schweiz in der Planung der kriegführenden Mächte während des zweiten Weltkrieges*, 32-33.

[74] Kurz, *Operationsplanung Schweiz*, 46-50.

[75] Urner, *"Die Schweiz muss noch geschluckt werden!"* 83; Kurz, *Operationsplanung Schweiz*, 50–55.

[76] Kurz, *Die Schweiz in der Planung*, 39.

[77] Ibid. at 28, 40.

[78] Senn, *Anfänge einer Dissuasionsstrategie während des Zweiten Weltkrieges*, 251–53.

[79] Kurz, *Die Schweiz in der Planung der kriegführenden Mächte während des zweiten Weltkrieges*, 38; Urner, *"Die Schweiz muss noch geschluckt werden!"* 83.

[80] Kurz, *Histoire de l'Armée Suisse*, 123.

[81] Alberto Rovighi, *Un Secolo di Relazioni Militari Tra Italia e Svizzera 1861–1961* (Roma 1987), 560.

[82] Interview with Hans Senn, Sept. 17, 1997.

[83] Senn, *Anfänge einer Dissuasionsstrategie während des Zweiten Weltkrieges*, 516, 520.

[84] Ibid. at 521–22; Georges-André Chevallaz, *Les Plans Italiens Face à la Suisse en 1938–1943* (Morges: Pully, 1988).

[85] Senn, *Anfänge einer Dissuasionsstrategie während des Zweiten Welt-*

krieges, 255; interview with Hans Senn, Sept. 17, 1997.

[86] Kurz, *Histoire de l'Armée suisse*, 126–28.

[87] *New York Times*, Oct. 20, 1940, 32.

[88] *New York Times*, Oct. 26, 1940, 3.

[89] Shirer, Berlin Diary, 230.

[90] Fritschi, *Geistige Landesverteidigung während des Zweiten Weltkrieges*, 126–29; letter from George Gyssler, Nov. 26, 1997.

[91] *New York Times*, Nov. 10, 1940, 48.

[92] Lindt, *Le temps du hérisson*, 77–79; Schwarz, *Eye of the Hurricane*, 44.

[93] Ibid. at 84–85; Schwarz, *Eye of the Hurricane*, 44–45.

[94] Schwarz, *Eye of the Hurricane*, 8.

[95] Bonjour, *Geschichte der Schweizerischen Neutralität* (1976), IV, 393.

[96] *New York Times*, Nov. 20, 1940, 3.

[97] *New York Times*, Nov. 28, 1940, 4.

[98] *The Times* (London), Dec. 10, 1940, 5f.

[99] Ibid.

[100] Lunn, *Mountain Jubilee*, 277.

[101] *Schweizerische Schützenzeitung*, Dec. 1940, 51:350.

CHAPTER 6

[1] *New York Times*, Jan. 2, 1941, 4.

[2] *Schweizerische Schützenzeitung*, Jan. 9, 1941, 2:1.

[3] *Schweizerische Schützenzeitung*, Jan. 1941, 3:15.

[4] Ibid., Mar. 1941, 11:69.

[5] *New York Times*, Feb. 19, 1941, 10.

[6] Bonjour, *Geschichte der der Schweizerischen Neutralität* (1970), V, 122.

[7] *New York Times*, Mar. 24, 1941, 2.

[8] Bonjour, *Geschichte der Schweizerischen Neutralität*, V, 250–51; *Living Age*, Aug. 1941, 525, 526.

[9] Shirer, *The Rise and Fall of the Third Reich*, 793, 839–41.

[10] *New York Times*, Mar. 23, 1941, Section IV, 5:7.

[11] Lindt, *Le temps du hérisson*, 88.

[12] *New York Times*, Mar. 31, 1941, 4.

[13] "The New Lebensraum," *Neue Volkszeitung*, in *The Living Age*, 525, 526 (Aug. 1941).

[14] *New York Times*, April 29, 1941, 2.

[15] Lindt, *Le temps du hérisson*, 89.

[16] *New York Times*, Apr. 9, 1941, 3.

[17] *Schweizerische Schützenzeitung*, April 1941, 17:110.

[18] Lindt, *Le temps du hérisson*, 90.

[19] Interview with August Lindt, Sept. 23, 1997. See Philipp Wanner, *Oberst Oscar Frey und der Schweizerische Widerstandswille* (Münsingen: Tages–Nachrichten, 1974), 157–60.

[20] "Swiss Cherish Their Ancient Liberties," *National Geographic*, 79 (Apr. 1941) 481, 495.

[21] Schweizerische Armee, *Schiessvorschrift für die Infanterie* (Bern 1941), 24.

[22] *New York Times*, Apr. 28, 1941, 3. The radio address was published in the *Gazzetta del Popolo* (Turin), Apr. 29, 1941. *New York Times*, Apr. 30, 1941, 2.

[23] "The New Lebensraum," *Neue Volkszeitung*, in *Living Age*, Aug. 1941, 525, 526–27.

[24] Ibid.

[25] *New York Times*, May 4, 1941, Section IV, 4.

[26] *Living Age*, Aug. 1941, 525, 527.

[27] Wilson, *Switzerland: Neutrality as a Foreign Policy*, 55–56.

[28] Senn, *Anfänge einer Dissuasionsstrategie während des Zweiten Weltkrieges*, 338.

[29] Interview with Hans Senn, Sept. 17, 1997.

[30] W.W. Schütz, "The Independence of Switzerland," *Contemporary Review*, 159 (June 1941), 658, 660.

[31] Ibid. at 660–61.

[32] Gerhard L. Weinberg, *Germany, Hitler, and World War II* (Cambridge University Press, 1995), 161.

[33] Interview with August Lindt, Sept. 23, 1997.

[34] Senn, *Anfänge einer Dissuasionsstrategie während des Zweiten Weltkrieges*, 376–77.

[35] *Neue Zürcher Zeitung*, July 13, 1945; U.S. Dept. of State, *Swiss Policies on Purge of Axis Supporters* 11 (Washington, DC, 1945).

[36] *Hitler's Secret Conversations, 1941–1944*, intro. by H.R. Trevor-Roper (New York: Signet, 1976), 53.

[37] Andreas Hillgruber, *Staatsmänner und Diplomaten bei Hitler* (München: DTV, 1969), 275–76.

[38] Ibid.

[39] Fink, *Die Schweiz aus der Sicht des Dritten Reiches, 1933–1945*, 25.

[40] Norman Rich, *Hitler's War Aims: The Establishment of the New Order*, (London: André Deutsch Limited, 1974), 402, citing Berger to Himmler, September 8, 1941, T175/123/2648463 [U.S. National Archives]; Swiss government report of December 28, 1945, on antidemocratic activities, 1939–45, NG [Nuremberg trial document] 4137.

[41] Jacob B. Glenn, "The Jews in Switzerland," *Contemporary Jewish Record*

(New York: American Jewish Committee, 1941), IV, 283, 286–87.

[42] Ibid. at 285, 287.

[43] Denis de Rougemont and Charlotte Muret, "What Switzerland Teaches," 34 *Commonweal* (1941), 511–12.

[44] *New York Times*, Aug. 11, 1941, 4.

[45] Meier, *Friendship Under Stress*, 273–74.

[46] Ibid. at 310.

[47] Jürg Martin Gabriel, "Switzerland and Economic Sanctions: The Dilemma of a Neutral," *Swiss Neutrality and Security*, ed. Milivojević and Maurer, 235.

[48] Schwarz, *Eye of the Hurricane*, 83.

[49] Charles Higham, *Trading with the Enemy: The Nazi-American Money Plot, 1933–49* (New York: Delacorte Press, 1983), 242.

[50] "Switzerland Sits Tight," *Fortune*, 24 (Sept. 1941), 74.

[51] Ibid.

[52] Ibid.

[53] Ibid. at 75.

[54] Ibid. at 112.

[55] *Reichsgesetzblatt*, I, 759 (Dec. 4, 1941).

[56] Raul Hilberg, *The Destruction of the European Jews* (New York: Homes and Meir, 1985), 341, 318, 297.

[57] Gill, *An Honourable Defeat: A History of German Resistance to Hitler, 1933–1945*, 140.

[58] Yitzhak Arad *et al.* eds., *The Einsatzgruppen Reports* (New York: Holocaust Library, 1989), ii.

[59] Ibid. at 117, 128.

[60] Ibid. at 233, 306, 257–58, 352–53, 368.

[61] *Schweizerische Schützenzeitung*, Dec. 1941, 51:361.

[62] *New York Times*, Dec. 3, 1941, 9.

[63] *New York Times*, Dec. 11, 1941, 13.

[64] *New York Times*, Dec. 12, 1941, 3.

[65] *New York Times*, Dec. 18, 1941, 7.

[66] *New York Times*, Jan. 23, 1942, 4.

[67] *New York Times*, Jan. 31, 1942, 7.

[68] Fink, *Die Schweiz aus der Sicht des Dritten Reiches, 1933–45*, 22–23.

CHAPTER 7

[1] Schwarz, *The Eye of the Hurricane*, 117.

[2] Fink, *Die Schweiz aus der Sicht des Dritten Reiches, 1933–45*, 25.

[3] *New York Times*, Feb. 4, 1942, 4.

[4] *New York Times*, Feb. 22, 1942, 6.

[5] *New York Times*, Mar. 17, 1942, 9; Rings, *Schweiz im Krieg*, 297–301.

[6] *New York Times*, Mar. 29, 1942, 4.

[7] *New York Times*, April 30, 1942, 6.

[8] *New York Times*, May 3, 1942, 32.

[9] Lindt, *Le temps du hérisson*, 106.

[10] *New York Times*, Jan. 11, 1942, 24.

[11] Percival B. Knauth, "Oasis of Democracy," *New York Times*, Jan. 25, 1942, Section VII, 8.

[12] Ibid.

[13] Ibid. at 28.

[14] *The Goebbels Diaries: 1942–1943*, ed. Louis P. Lochner, (Garden City, NY: Doubleday & Co., 1948), 126.

[15] *Schweizerische Schützenzeitung*, Feb. 1942, 7:41.

[16] *Schweizerische Schützenzeitung*, 1942, 14:98

[17] *New York Times*, Mar. 17, 1942, 9.

[18] *Schweizerische Schützenzeitung*, 1942, 33:250.

[19] Société cantonale des Tireurs fribourgeois, *Rapport de Gestion du Comité Cantonal Pour L'Exercice 1942* (Fribourg: Hodel, 1943), 6–7.

[20] Schweizerische Armee, *Ausbildungsvorschrift der Infanterie 1942* (Eidg. Militärdepartement 1948), 9.

[21] Ibid. at 10.

[22] *The Goebbels Diaries: 1942–1943*, 208.

[23] Anita Daniel, "The Miracle of Switzerland," *American Mercury*, 54 (May 1942) 554–55. (In German: *Die Schweiz, die ist ein Stachelschwein, / Die nehmen wir zum Dessert ein. / Dann geh'n wir in die weite Welt / Und holen uns den Roosevelt.*)

[24] "Europe: 'Wir Machen Nicht Mit,'" *Time*, 40 (Nov. 2, 1942) 38.

[25] Ibid.; see *Journal de Gevève*, Oct. 16, 1942, 8.

[26] *New York Times*, Oct. 24, 1942, 6.

[27] *New York Times*, Nov. 23, 1942, 5.

[28] *New York Times*, June 16, 1942, 6.

[29] Fink, *Die Schweiz aus der Sicht des Dritten Reiches, 1933–1945*, 23.

[30] *New York Times*, Aug. 2, 1942, 11.

[31] *New York Times*, Aug. 5, 1942, 7.

[32] Rich, *Hitler's War Aims*, 401–02.

[33] Hans Rudolf Fuhrer, *Spionage gegen die Schweiz* (Frauenfeld: Huber, 1982), 98.

[34] Ibid.

[35] Schwarz, *Eye of the Hurricane*, 123.

[36] Ibid. at 124.

[37] Daniel, "The Miracle of Switzerland," *American Mercury*, 54 (May 1942),

557.

[38] Adam LeBor, *Hitler's Secret Bankers* (Secaucus, NJ: Birch Lane Press, 1997), xvi–xvii, 147; Schwarz, *Eye of the Hurricane*, 125.

[39] Bonjour, *Swiss Neutrality*, 128.

[40] Ibid. at 125, citing *Neue Zürcher Zeitung*, Sept. 22, 1942.

[41] Interview with Ernst Leisi, Sept. 22, 1997. The Leisi family was the family identified above that rescued Jews.

[42] "Swiss Haven," *Newsweek*, Oct. 26, 1942, 54.

[43] Feingold, *The Politics of Rescue*, 142, 131, 154, 178.

[44] Shirer, *The Rise and Fall of the Third Reich*, 924.

[45] Kurz, *Histoire de l'Armée Suisse*, 132.

[46] Interview with Paul R. Jolles, Sept. 22, 1997. See Jolles, "A Battle for Neutrality," *Newsweek*, Sept. 1, 1997, 4.

[47] Weinberg, *A World at Arms*, 397.

[48] Meier, *Friendship Under Stress*, 281–86.

[49] Ibid. at 285–86.

[50] "Isolated Swiss," *Newsweek*, Nov. 23, 1942, 45.

[51] Schwarz, *Eye of the Hurricane*, 91–92.

[52] Dean Acheson, *Present at the Creation* (London: Hamish Hamilton, 1969), 50.

[53] Walter Schaufelberger, *Armee Abschaffen?* (Frauenfeld: Huber, 1988), 39.

[54] Ibid.

[55] Allen Dulles, *The Secret Surrender* (London: Harper & Row, 1966), 12.

[56] Allen W. Dulles, *Germany's Underground* (New York: MacMillan, 1947), 125.

[57] Ibid. at 126, 129.

[58] Gill, *An Honourable Defeat*, 179–80; Shirer, *The Rise and Fall of the Third Reich*, 1018, 1024.

[59] Schwarz, *Eye of the Hurricane*, 103.

[60] Ibid. at 108.

[61] "Switzerland: Alone, Little & Tough," *Time*, Dec. 7, 1942, 40.

[62] Leisi, *Freispruch für die Schweiz*, 122–23.

[63] Bonjour, *Geschichte der Schweizerischen Neutralität*, IV, 472; Huber, *Bericht des Chefs des Generalstabs*, 501–13.

[64] *The Goebbels Diaries: 1942–1943*, 244.

[65] Lunn, *Mountain Jubilee*, vii.

CHAPTER 8

[1] Charles Lanius, "Switzerland, Axis Captive," *Saturday Evening Post*, 215 (Jan. 23, 1943) 24.

[2] Ibid. at 57.

[3] Walter Lippmann, "The Faithful Witness," *New York Herald Tribune*, Jan. 26, 1943, 21.

[4] Ibid.

[5] Ibid.

[6] *Journal de Genève*, Mar. 14, 1943, 1.

[7] *New York Times*, Jan. 27, 1943, 13. The above may have been part of the series by the Institute for the History of New Germany, which published Christopher Steding's *The Reich and the Disease of European Culture*, a 7000-page work which proved that Switzerland and other small states had no right to exist. See Werner Richter, "The War Pattern of Swiss Life," *Foreign Affairs*, July 1944, XXII, 643, 646.

[8] *New York Times*, Jan. 28, 1943, 18.

[9] Ibid.

[10] Meier, *Friendship Under Stress*, 294–95.

[11] Kimche, *Spying for Peace*, 104.

[12] Pierre-Th. Braunschweig, *Geheimer Draht Nach Berlin* (Neue Zürcher Zeitung, 1989), 269.

[13] Kimche, *Spying for Peace*, 106–08.

[14] Dulles, *The Secret Surrender*, 27.

[15] See Pierre-Th. Braunschweig, *Geheimer Draht nach Berlin*, 231–58.

[16] Kimche, *Spying for Peace*, 99–100.

[17] *Rapport du Général Guisan a L'assemblée Fédérale sur le Service Actif, 1939–1945* (Bern 1946), 50.

[18] Schwarz, *The Eye of the Hurricane*, 112. See Lindt, *Le temps du hérisson*, 128.

[19] Chevallaz, *Les Plans Italiens Face à la Suisse en 1938–1943*, 18.

[20] Kimche, *Spying for Peace*, 100–01.

[21] Ernst Uhlmann, "Angriffspläne gegen die Schweiz," *Allgemeine Schweizerische Militärzeitung* (Dec. 1949), LX, 841.

[22] Pierre-Th. Braunschweig, *Geheimer Draht Nach Berlin*, 259–94.

[23] See Senn, *Anfänge einer Dissuasionsstrategie während des Zweiten Weltkrieges*, 356–75.

[24] Schwarz, *Eye of the Hurricane*, 61–62.

[25] Kimche, *Spying for Peace*, 101–02; Lindt, *Le temps du hérisson*, 128–30.

[26] Dulles, *The Secret Surrender*, 25, 27.

[27] Kimche, *Spying for Peace*, 103, 120–21.

[28] *Schweizerische Schützenzeitung*, 1943, 18:122.

[29] *Schweizerische Schützenzeitung*, 1943, 19:127–28.

[30] Kimche, *Spying for Peace*, 30–31.

[31] Ibid. at 357.

[32] *The Goebbels Diaries: 1942–1943*, 355, 357, 358.

[33] Weisungen für die Kriegsmobilmachung bei Ueberfall, Militärdepartement, May 24, 1943.

[34] *Journal de Genève*, May 24, 1943, 2.

[35] Rotem (Kazik), *Memoirs of a Warsaw Ghetto Fighter and the Past Within Me*, 118–19.

[36] Ibid. at 25, 32–34.

[37] Ibid. at 38–39, 62, 76.

[38] United States Holocaust Memorial Museum, Washington, DC, exhibit on display on April 21, 1997.

[39] Ibid.

[40] *The Goebbels Diaries: 1942–1943*, 350–51.

[41] Latour, *The Jewish Resistance in France (1940–1944)*, 177.

[42] Harold Werner, *Fighting Back: A Memoir of Jewish Resistance in World War II* (New York: Columbia University Press, 1992), 8, 76–79, 92, 97.

[43] Ibid. at 104–05, 110.

[44] Ibid. at 139.

[45] Ibid. at 146–47.

[46] Ibid. at 155, 184–85, 190.

[47] Marquis W. Childs, "No Peace For The Swiss," *The Saturday Evening Post*, 215 (May 1, 1943) 14, 15.

[48] Ibid. at 52.

[49] Latour, *The Jewish Resistance in France (1940–1944)*, 127.

[50] Ibid. at 127–28.

[51] Meier, *Friendship Under Stress*, 299.

[52] Ibid. at 301.

[53] Latour, *The Jewish Resistance in France (1940–1944)*, 154.

[54] Ibid. at 154, 156.

[55] Ibid. at 157–58.

[56] Generaladjutantur, Sektion Heer und Haus, Die Judenfrage, Wehrbrief Nr. 26 (25 May 1943), 1, 4.

[57] Ibid.

[58] *New York Times*, July 8, 1943, 5. See August Lindt, *Le temps du hérisson*, 133–34.

[59] Meier, *Friendship Under Stress*, 326.

[60] Ibid. at 326.

[61] Shirer, *The Rise and Fall of the Third Reich*, 999.

[62] Wilson, *Switzerland: Neutrality as a Foreign Policy*, 51.

[63] *Schweizerische Schützenzeitung*, 1943, 32:225.

[64] "Goods Still Move," *Business Week*, Aug. 14, 1943, 49–50.

[65] Shirer, *The Rise and Fall of the Third Reich*, 1001–02.

⁶⁶ Schwarz, *Eye of the Hurricane*, 125–26.

⁶⁷ Kurz, *Histoire de l'Armée Suisse*, 132.

⁶⁸ Shirer, *The Rise and Fall of the Third Reich*, 1003–04.

⁶⁹ Kurz, *Histoire de l'Armée Suisse*, 133.

⁷⁰ *The Times* (London), Sept. 27, 1943, 3c.

⁷¹ *New York Times*, Sept. 18, 1943, 3.

⁷² *New York Times*, Sept. 26, 1943, Section IV 4:7.

⁷³ Milivojević, "The Swiss Armed Forces," in *Swiss Neutrality and Security*, ed. Milivojević and Maurer, 16.

⁷⁴ *New York Times*, Sept. 27, 1943, 6.

⁷⁵ Malcolm Moos, "Swiss Neutrality," *Yale Review*, 33 (Sept. 1943) 121, 123.

⁷⁶ Max Mandellaub, "The Swiss Barometer," *The Nation*, Nov. 13, 1943, 555.

⁷⁷ Memorandum by the Representatives of the British Chiefs of Staff, "Combined Chiefs of Staff Trade With Switzerland," C.C.S. 388/1 (Washington, DC), November 29, 1943.

⁷⁸ Meier, *Friendship Under Stress*, 287.

⁷⁹ Weinberg, *A World at Arms: A Global History of World War II*, 398.

⁸⁰ Meier, *Friendship Under Stress*, 290–91.

⁸¹ Ernst Uhlmann, "Angriffspläne gegen die Schweiz," *Allgemeine Schweizerische Militärzeitung* (Dec. 1949), LX, 843–44.

⁸² Ibid. at 844–45.

⁸³ Ibid. at 845–46.

⁸⁴ Ibid. at 846.

⁸⁵ Ibid. at 848.

⁸⁶ Ibid. at 849.

⁸⁷ Bonjour, *Geschichte der Schweizerischen Neutralität, Band V: 1939–1945*, 136–37.

⁸⁸ Hervé de Weck and Pierre Maurer, "Swiss National Defence Policy Revisited," *Swiss Neutrality and Security*, ed. Milivojević and Maurer, 79.

⁸⁹ *Allgemeine Schweizerische Militärzeitung* (Dec. 1949), LX, 849.

⁹⁰ Ibid. at 849–50.

⁹¹ Ibid. at 850–51.

⁹² Ibid. at 851.

⁹³ Ibid. at 859.

⁹⁴ Ibid. at 851–52.

⁹⁵ Ibid. at 858.

⁹⁶ Senn, *Anfänge einer Dissuasionsstrategie während des Zweiten Weltkrieges*, 379.

⁹⁷ *Schweizerische Schützenzeitung*, Dec. 1943, 52:359.

CHAPTER 9

[1] *New York Times*, Jan. 3, 1944, 8.

[2] *New York Times*, Jan. 25, 1944, 11.

[3] Ibid.

[4] Huber, Bericht des Chefs des Generalstabs, 649.

[5] "Business at War," *Fortune*, 29 (Feb. 1944) 46.

[6] Pierre-Th. Braunschweig, *Geheimer Draht Nach Berlin* (Neue Zürcher Zeitung, 1989), 249.

[7] Hans Senn, *Anfänge einer Dissuasionsstrategie während des Zweiten Weltkrieges* (Basel: Helbing & Lichtenhahn, 1995), 423.

[8] Edward J. Byng, "If Switzerland Is Invaded," *American Mercury*, 58 (April 1944) 488.

[9] Ibid.

[10] Ibid. at 489–90.

[11] *New York Times*, Mar. 19, 1944, 17.

[12] *New York Times*, Apr. 2, 1944, 1; see *Journal de Genève*, Apr. 3, 1944, 2–3, 10.

[13] *New York Times*, Apr. 3, 1944, 2.

[14] *New York Times*, Apr. 3, 1944, 20.

[15] *New York Times*, Apr. 4, 1944, 4.

[16] *New York Times*, Apr. 5, 1944, 10.

[17] Meier, *Friendship Under Stress*, 313–14.

[18] *New York Times*, Apr. 14, 1944, 1, 3.

[19] Ibid. For a definitive study, see James H. Hutson, "Bombing the Sister Republic," *Swiss-American Historical Society Review*, Feb. 1995, XXXI, 3.

[20] *Journal de Genève*, Apr. 5, 1944, 2.

[21] Kimche, *Spying for Peace*, 123; Lindt, *Le temps du hérisson*, 150.

[22] *New York Times*, June 11, 1944, 40.

[23] Shirer, *The Rise and Fall of the Third Reich*, 993.

[24] *New York Times*, June 17, 1944, 5. The full text is *Tagesbefehl*, A.H.Q., June 15, 1944, in *Tagesbefehle des Generals, 1939–1945* (Bern: Eidg. Militärbibliothek, n.d.)

[25] Lindt, *Le temps du hérisson*, 151.

[26] Werner Richter, "The War Pattern of Swiss Life," *Foreign Affairs*, July 1944, XX, 643.

[27] Ibid.

[28] Ibid. at 644.

[29] Ibid. at 645–46, 648.

[30] Ibid. at 647–48.

[31] Dulles, *The Secret Surrender*, 20.

[32] Dulles, *Germany's Underground*, 134–41.

[33] Ibid. at 134–41, 229–53.

[34] See Ralph Hagan, *The Liberator Pistol* (El Dorado Hills, CA: Target Sales, 1997).

[35] *New York Times*, Aug. 7, 1944, 4.

[36] Kurz, *Histoire de l'Armée Suisse*, 135.

[37] Schwarz, *The Eye of the Hurricane*, 115.

[38] U.S. Dept. of State, *Swiss Policies on Purge of Axis Supporters* (Washington, DC, 1945), 11–12.

[39] *New York Times*, Aug. 26, 1944, 3.

[40] Dulles, *Germany's Underground*, 125.

[41] *The Times* (London), Aug. 31, 1944, 3d.

[42] Ibid.; *New York Times*, Aug. 27, 1944, 21.

[43] *New York Times*, Sept. 6, 1944, 7.

[44] Lindt, *Le temps du hérisson*, 159.

[45] Ibid. at 159–60.

[46] Ibid. at 160.

[47] Ibid. at 160–61.

[48] Ibid. at 161–62.

[49] Ibid. at 162.

[50] *The Times* (London), Oct. 3, 1944, 3c.

[51] David S. Wyman, *The Abandonment of the Jews: America and the Holocaust, 1941–1945* (New York: Pantheon Books, 1984), 233–34.

[52] Stuart E. Eizenstat and William Z. Slany, *U.S. and Allied Efforts to Recover and Restore Gold and Other Assets Stolen or Hidden by Germany during World War II* (Washington, DC: U.S. Department of State, 1997), 26.

[53] Ibid.

[54] Acheson, *Present at the Creation*, 58–59; Meier, *Friendship Under Stress*, 329; *New York Times*, Sept. 30, 1944, 5.

[55] Meier, *Friendship Under Stress*, 329–30.

[56] Ibid. at 336–37.

[57] *Rapport du Général Guisan*, 65.

[58] Schwarz, *Eye of the Hurricane*, 151–52; *The Times* (London), Nov. 20, 1944, 4c.

[59] Wilson, *Switzerland: Neutrality as a Foreign Policy*, 56.

[60] Winston S. Churchill, *The Second World War* (London: Cassel, 1954), VI, 616.

[61] Ibid.

[62] Gregory Douglas, *Gestapo Chief: The 1948 Interrogation of Heinrich Müller* (San Jose: R. James Bender, 1995), 227.

[63] Ibid.

[64] Walter Schellenberg, *Hitler's Secret Service* (New York: Pyramid Books, 1977), 369.

[65] Ibid.

[66] Ibid. at 370.

[67] Ibid.

[68] Feingold, *The Politics of Rescue*, 276–79.

[69] Bonjour, *Geschichte der Schweizerischen Neutralität*, VI, 383.

[70] Eizenstat and Slany, *U.S. and Allied Efforts*, 28–29.

[71] Ibid. at 29.

[72] Lindt, *Le temps du hérisson*, 165.

[73] Gautschi, *General Henri Guisan*, 629.

[74] Ibid. at 630.

[75] Ibid. at 629–30.

CHAPTER 10

[1] Interview with Ernst Leisi, Sept. 22, 1997.

[2] *New York Times*, Jan. 5, 1945, 8.

[3] Ibid.

[4] Meier, *Friendship Under Stress*, 331, citing *Neue Zürcher Zeitung*, Jan. 4, 1945.

[5] *New York Times*, Jan. 26, 1945, 8.

[6] Meier, *Friendship Under Stress*, 333.

[7] *Journal de Genève*, Jan. 9, 1945, 2.

[8] "The Swiss War," *Newsweek*, Jan. 15, 1945, 56.

[9] Ibid.

[10] Meier, *Friendship Under Stress*, 316, 319.

[11] *Journal de Genève*, Jan. 17, 1945, 8.

[12] *The Times* (London), Mar. 9, 1945, 3d; Ibid., Mar. 10, 1945, 5b.

[13] "No Haven," *Time*, Apr. 2, 1945, 23.

[14] *New York Times*, Feb. 23, 1945, 2; Ibid., Feb. 25, 1945, 11. See *Journal de Genève*, Feb. 23, 1945, 2.

[15] *New York Times*, Mar. 5, 1945, 4. See *Journal de Genève*, Mar. 5, 1945, 8.

[16] *New York Times*, Mar. 9, 1945.

[17] *New York Times*, Mar. 12, 1945, 6.

[18] *New York Times*, Mar. 26, 1945, 8. See *Tagesbefehl*, 2.4.45, in *Tagesbefehle des Generals, 1939–1945* (Bern: Eidg. Militärbibliothek, n.d.).

[19] Ibid.

[20] *The Times* (London), Mar. 28, 1945, 3c.

[21] *New York Times*, Apr. 19, 1945, 3.

[22] *New York Times*, Apr. 21, 1945, 3.

[23] *New York Times*, Apr. 22, 1945, 4; Ibid., Apr. 23, 1945, 7.

[24] *New York Times*, Apr. 23, 1945, 7; *The Times* (London), Apr. 24, 1945, 3e.

[25] Schwarz, *Eye of the Hurricane*, 141.

[26] Shirer, *The Rise and Fall of the Third Reich*, 1006.

[27] Dulles, *The Secret Surrender*, 43.

[28] Interview with August Lindt, Sept. 23, 1997.

[29] Schwarz, *Eye of the Hurricane*, 143–44. See Wilson, *Switzerland: Neutrality as a Foreign Policy*, 29–37.

[30] Dulles, *The Secret Surrender*, 27.

[31] Schwarz, *Eye of the Hurricane*, 143–44.

[32] Dulles, *The Secret Surrender*, 99.

[33] Ibid. at 145.

[34] Schwarz, Eye of the Hurricane, 146–47; Wilson, *Switzerland: Neutrality as a Foreign Policy*, 35.

[35] Kimche, *Spying for Peace*, 148; Dulles, *The Secret Surrender*, 146–47.

[36] Ibid. at 144.

[37] Ibid. at 150.

[38] Schwarz, *The Eye of the Hurricane*, 147. On whether General Guisan or the Swiss government knew of the negotiations, see Dulles, *The Secret Surrender*, 100–01.

[39] Dulles, *The Secret Surrender*, 214–15.

[40] Wilson, *Switzerland: Neutrality as a Foreign Policy*, 33, quoting H.R. Kurz, ed., *Die Schweiz im Zweiten Weltkrieg* (Thun: Ott, 1959), 126.

[41] Dulles, *The Secret Surrender*, 119–20; Kimche, *Spying for Peace*, 151–52.

[42] Schwarz, *Eye of the Hurricane*, 153. See *Tagesbefehl*, May 8, 1945, in *Tagesbefehle des Generals, 1939–1945* (Bern: Eidg. Militärbibliothek, n.d.).

[43] U.S. State Department, *Swiss Policies on Purge of Axis Supporters* (Washington, DC, Dec. 31, 1945), 20–31.

[44] Bonjour, *Swiss Neutrality*, 127.

[45] Carl J. Friedrich, "As Switzerland Sees It," *Atlantic Monthly*, 178 (Dec. 1946) 108, 109.

[46] *The Times* (London), Aug. 27, 1945, 5f.

[47] Hans-Heiri Stapfer & Gino Künzle, *Escape to Neutrality* (Carrollton, Tex.: Squadron/Signal Publications, 1992), 3, 77.

[48] Faith Whittlesey, "Switzerland on Trial," *The Ambassadors Review*, (Spring 1997) 53.

[49] Schwarz, *The Eye of the Hurricane*, 133–34.

[50] *Schlussbericht des Eidg. Kommissariates für Internierung und Hospital-*

isierung über die Internierung fremder Militärpersonen von 1940–45.

[51] Schwarz, *Eye of the Hurricane*, 129.

[52] Ibid. at 130–31.

[53] Letter from Pierre Pont, Head of Delegation, ICRC, Washington, DC, Sept. 9, 1997.

[54] Schwarz, *The Eye of the Hurricane*, 137–38.

[55] Ibid. at 134–38.

[56] Theo Tschuy, *Carl Lutz und die Juden von Budapest* (Neue Zürcher Zeitung 1995).

[57] Meier, *Friendship Under Stress*, 302.

[58] Ibid. at 303.

[59] Ibid. at 303–04, 309.

[60] Schellenberg, *Hitler's Secret Service*, 371–74. See LeBor, *Hitler's Secret Bankers*, 199.

[61] *New York Times*, July 23, 1945, 1.

[62] Schwarz, *Eye of the Hurricane*, 134; Kurz, *Histoire de l'Armée Suisse*, 142.

[63] Hans Senn, *Anfänge einer Dissuasionsstrategie während des Zweiten Weltkrieges* (Basel: Helbing & Lichtenhahn, 1995), 440–41.

[64] Charbonney, *Considérations sur les répercussions économiques de la défense Nationale* (Lausanne 1968), Appendix 5.

[65] *Schweizerische Schützenzeitung*, 1945, 44:329.

[66] *Tages–Befehl für den 20. August 1945*, in *Tagesbefehle des Generals, 1939–1945* (Bern: Eidg. Militärbibliothek, n.d.).

[67] *New York Times*, Aug. 2, 1945, 5.

[68] Jean-Jacques de Dardel, "New Challenges Facing Swiss Foreign Policy," *Swiss Neutrality and Security*, ed. Milivojević and Maurer, 127 n. 7.

[69] *The Times* (London), Oct. 6, 1945, 3d.

[70] E.g., Albert Speer, *Inside the Third Reich* (New York: Macmillan, 1970), 369–72.

[71] Ibid. at 378, 467.

[72] Shirer, *The Rise and Fall of the Third Reich*, 943.

[73] Ibid. at 946–47.

[74] Jacob Sloan, ed., *Notes from the Warsaw Ghetto: The Journal of Emmanuel Ringelblum* (New York: Schocken, 1958), 263.

[75] Interview with Willy Gautschi, Sept. 24, 1997.

CHAPTER 11

[1] Eizenstat and Slany, *U.S. and Allied Efforts*, 113.

[2] Robert Frick ed., *Das Schiesswesen in der Schweiz* (Zürich: Gottfried

Schmid, 1955), I, 1.

[3] Statement of Central Committee of Swiss Noncommissioned Officers Association, in Major H. von Dach, *Total Resistance*, trans. Hans Lienhard (Boulder, Colo.: Paladin Press, 1965), iii. See Major H. von Dach, *Der Totale Widerstand* (Biel: SUOV, 2nd ed., 1958).

[4] Ibid. at 14.

[5] Ibid. at 104, 155, 169–70.

[6] Ibid. at 173.

[7] *Soldatenbuch* (Eidg. Militärdepartement, 1959).

[8] See Albert Bachmann & Georges Grosjean, *Zivilverteidigung* (Aarau: Miles, 1969).

[9] Stüssi-Lauterburg, "A History of Change," *Army 1995*, 79.

[10] Marko Milivojević, "The Swiss Armed Forces," *Swiss Neutrality and Security*, 39, 43.

[11] See *Das Sturmgewehr 57 und die Gewehrgranaten 58* (Schweizerische Armee, 1984); *Jane's Infantry Weapons* (Surrey, UK: Jane's Information Group, 1990), 198–200.

[12] Josepf Inauen, *Schweizer Armee 97* (Frauenfeld: Huber, 1996), 112.

[13] See Halbrook, "Switzerland's Feldschiessen," *Gun Digest* 20–26 (1996/ 50th Annual Edition); Halbrook, "Swiss Schützenfest," *American Rifleman*, 46–47, 74–75 (May 1993); Robert Frick ed., *Das Schiesswesen in der Schweiz* (Zürich: Gottfried Schmid, 1955), II, 120.

[14] Halbrook, "The World's Largest Rifle Shooting Match: Switzerland 1995," *The 1996 Precision Shooting Annual* (Manchester, CT: Precision Shooting, Inc., 1996), 91, 107.

[15] *Neue Zürcher Zeitung*, Sept. 15, 1997, 35. See Robert Frick ed., *Das Schiesswesen in der Schweiz* (Zürich: Gottfried Schmid, 1955), II, 114.

[16] Inauen, *Schweizer Armee 97*, 114–62.

[17] Jörg Köhler, "Switzerland as Champion for the Abolishment of Anti-Personnel Mines," *Swiss Peace Keeper*, Sept. 3, 1997, 8.

[18] Patrick Cudré-Mauroux, "From Yesterday to Tomorrow," *Army 1995*, 100–03; Roman Brodmann, *Schweiz ohne Waffen* (Bern: Zytglogge, 1989); Andreas Gross ed., *6. Juni 1993: Kompromiss auch bei der Armee?* (Zürich: Realotopia, 1993).

[19] Alfred Hostettler, *"Ein vom Bund aufgezwungener 'Sport'"*: *Arbeiterschiesswesen in der Schweiz* (Historisches Institut der Universität Bern, 1990), 69.

[20] See Walter Schaufelberger ed., *Armee Abschaffen?*

[21] *The Army of a Small, Neutral Nation: Switzerland* (Berne: Department of Defense, n.d.).

[22] Ibid. at 9.

[23] Ibid. at 10.
[24] *Swiss Security Policy in Times of Change: Report 90 of the Federal Council to the Federal Assembly* (1990), 29.
[25] Interview with Hans Senn, Sept. 19, 1997.
[26] Interview with Arthur Liener, Sept. 17, 1997.

EPILOGUE

[1] Shirer, *The Rise and Fall of the Third Reich*, 199–200.

Bibliography

BOOKS

Acheson, Dean. *Present at the Creation*. London: Hamish Hamilton, 1969.

Adams, John. *A Defence of the Constitutions of Government of the United States of America*. London, 1787.

Adolf Hitler: Monologe im Führerhauptquartier, 1941–1944, ed. Werner Jochmann. Hamburg: Albrecht Knaus, 1980.

Allen, William Sheridan. *The Nazi Seizure of Power: The Experience of a Single German Town 1922–1945*. New York: Franklin Watts, 1984.

Arad, Yitzhak, et al. eds. *The Einsatzgruppen Reports*. New York: Holocaust Library, 1989.

Army 1995: The Past and Future of the Swiss Army. Geneva: Intermedia Com, 1997.

The Army of a Small, Neutral Nation: Switzerland. Bern: Department of Defense, n.d.

Bachmann, Albert and Grosjean, Georges. *Zivilverteidigung*. Aarau: Miles, 1969.

Banse, Ewald. *Germany Prepares for War: A Nazi Theory of "National Defense."* New York: Harcourt, Brace and Company, 1934.

Bindschedler, Rudolf L., et al. *Schwedische und Schweizerische Neutralität im Zweiten Weltkrieg*. Basel: Helbing & Lichtenhahn Verlag, 1985.

Bodin, Jean. *The Six Books of a Commonweale*, trans. R. Knolles. London: G. Bishop, 1606.

Bonjour, E., H.S. Offler and G.R. Potter. *A Short History of Switzerland*. Oxford: Clarendon Press, 1952.

Bonjour, Edgar. *Swiss Neutrality: Its History and Meaning*. London: George Allen & Unwin Ltd, 1952.

Bonjour, Edgar. *Geschichte der Schweizerischen Neutralität.* Basel: Helbing & Lichtenhahn, 1967̶7̶6.

Bourgeois, Daniel. *Le Troisième Reich et la Suisse 1933–1941.* Neuchâel: Éitions de la Baconniè̶e, 1974.

Bower, Tom. *Nazi Gold: The Full Story of the Fifty-Year Swiss-Nazi Conspiracy to Steal Billions from Europe's Jews and Holocaust Survivors.* New York: HarperCollins, 1997.

Braunschweig, Pierre-Th. *Geheimer Draht Nach Berlin.* Zurich: Verlag Neue Zürcher Zeitung, 1989.

Brodmann, Roman. *Schweiz ohne Waffen.* Bern: Zytglogge, 1989.

Brooks, Robert C. *Government and Politics of Switzerland.* Yonkers-on-Hudson, NY: World Book Co., 1927.

Brooks, Robert C. *Civic Training in Switzerland: A Study of Democratic Life.* Chicago: University of Chicago Press, 1930.

Brooks, Thomas R. *The War North of Rome: June 1944–May 1945.* New York: Sarpedon, 1996.

Bryce, James. *The Holy Roman Empire.* London: MacMillan, 1889.

Cattani, Alfred, ed. *Shadows of World War II.* Neue Zürcher Zeitung, March 1997.

Charbonney, Marc. *Considérations sur les répercussions économiques de la défense Nationale.* Lausanne 1968.

Chevallaz, Georges-André. *Les Plans Italiens Face à la Suisse en 1938–1943.* Morges, Switz.: Pully, 1988.

Collomb, Jean-Daniel. *Les Remparts.* Genève: Editions Slatkine, 1989.

Commentaires de Napoléon Premier. Paris: Imprimerie Impériale, 1867.

Chronik der Schweiz. Zurich: Chronik-Verlag, 1987.

Churchill, Winston S. *The Second World War.* London: Cassel, 1954.

Dach, Major H. von. *Total Resistance.* Boulder, CO: Paladin Press, 1965.

Dessemontet, F., and T. Ansay. *Introduction to Swiss Law.* The Hague: Kluwer Law Int'l., 1995.

Documentary History of the First Federal Congress. Baltimore: The Johns Hopkins University Press, 198695.

Documentary History of the Ratification of the Constitution. Madison: State Historical Society of Wisconsin, 198193.

Douglas, Gregory. *Gestapo Chief: The 1948 Interrogation of Heinrich Müller.* San Jose, CA: R. James Bender, 1995.

Dulles, Allen W. *Germany's Underground.* New York: MacMillan, 1947.

Dulles, Allen W. *The Secret Surrender.* London: Harper & Row, 1966.

Durrer, Marco. *Die Schweizerisch-Amerikanischen Finanzbeziehungen im Zweiten Weltkrieg.* Bern: Paul Haupt, 1984.

Eizenstat, Stuart E., and William Z. Slany. *U.S. and Allied Efforts to Recover and Restore Gold and Other Assets Stolen or Hidden by Germany during World War II.* Washington, DC: U.S. Department of State, 1997.

Elliot, Jonathan. *Debates on the Adoption of the Federal Constitution.* Philadelphia: J.B. Lippincott, 1845.

Etter, Philipp. *Geistige Landesverteidigung.* Schweiz. Studentenverein, 1937.

Ezell, Edward C. *Small Arms of the World.* Harrisburg, PA: Stackpole, 1983.

Faesch, Captain Remy. *The Swiss Army System.* New York: G.E. Stechert, 1916.

Feingold, Henry L. *The Politics of Rescue.* New York: Waldon Press, 1970.

Feldman, Oberst M., and Hauptmann H.G. Wirz, eds. *Schweizer Kriegsgeschichte.* Bern: Oberkriegskommissariat, 1915–1935, 4 vols.

Die Festung Sargans im Wandel der Zeit. Mels, Switz.: Sarganserländer Druck, 1994.

Fink, Jürg. *Die Schweiz aus der Sicht des Dritten Reiches, 1933–1945.* Zurich: Schulthess Polygraphischer Verlag, 1985.

Fletcher, Andrew. *Political Works.* Glasgow: Robert Urie, 1749.

Frick, Robert, ed. *Das Schiesswesen in der Schweiz.* Zurich: Gottfried Schmid, 1955.

Fritschi, Oskar Felix. *Geistige Landesverteidigung während des Zweiten Weltkrieges.* Fabag + Druckerei Winterthur AG, 1971.

Fuhrer, Hans Rudolf. *Spionage gegen die Schweiz.* Frauenfeld: Huber, 1982.

Gabriel, Jürg Martin. *The American Conception of Neutrality After 1941.* London: MacMillan, 1988.

Gasser, Christian. *Der Gotthard-Bund.* Bern: Paul Haupt, 1984.

Gautschi, Willi. *General Henri Guisan: Die schweizerische Armeeführung im Zweiten Weltkrieg.* Zürich: Neue Zürcher Zeitung, 1989.

General Guisan 1874–1960. Zürich: Fretz und Wasmuth Verlag, 1960.

Gill, Anton. *An Honourable Defeat: A History of German Resistance to Hitler, 1933–1945.* New York: Henry Holt, 1994.

The Goebbels Diaries, ed. Louis P. Lochner. Garden City, NY: Doubleday & Company, 1948.

Grande, Julian. *A Citizens' Army: The Swiss System.* London: Chatto & Windus, 1916.

Gross, Andreas ed., *6. Juni 1993: Kompromiss auch bei der Armee?* Zürich: Realotopia, 1993.

Guisan, Henri. *Notre Peuple et son Armée.* Zürich: Ed. Polyg., 1939.

Guisan, Henri. *Unser Volk und seine Armee.* Zürich, 1940.

Guisan, Henri. *Bericht an die Bundesversammlung über den Aktivdienst 1939–1945.* Bern, 1946.

Gurtner, Othmar. *Schweizer Schützenbuch.* Zürich: Verkehrsverlag, 1943.

Haas, Gaston. *"Wenn man gewusst hätte, was sich drüben im Reich abspielte . . ."* *1941–1943 Was man in der Schweiz von der Judenvernichtung wusste.* Basel: Helbing & Lichtenhahn, 1994.

Hagan, Ralph. *The Liberator Pistol.* El Dorado Hills, CA: Target Sales, 1997.

Halbrook, Stephen P., *That Every Man Be Armed: The Evolution of a Constitutional Right.* Oakland, CA: The Independent Institute, 1994.

Heer, Gottlieb H. & Gessler E. A. *Armee und Volk.* Zürich: Verkehrsverlag, 1946.

Herren, A.H.L. *Der Deutsche Bund in seinen Verhältnissen zu dem europäischen Staatensystem.* Göttingen, 1816.

Hertzberg, Arthur. *Shalom Amerika! Die Geschichte der Juden in der Neuen Welt.* Munich, 1996.

Higham, Charles. *Trading with the Enemy: The Nazi–American Money Plot, 1933–1949.* New York: Delacorte Press, 1983.

Hilberg, Raul. *The Destruction of the European Jews.* New York: Homes and Meir, 1985.

Hillgruber, Andreas. *Staatsmänner und Diplomaten bei Hitler.* Munich: DTV, 1969.

Hitler, Adolf. *Mein Kampf.* Munich: N.S.D.U.P., 1934.

Hitler's Secret Conversations, 1941–1944, intro. by H.R. Trevor-Roper. New York: Signet, 1976.

Hitz, John. *The Military System of the Republic of Switzerland.* Washington, DC: Franck Taylor, 1864.

Hostettler, Alfred. *"Ein vom Bund aufgezwungener 'Sport'":* *Arbeiterschiesswesen in der Schweiz.* Historisches Institut der Universität Bern, 1990.

Howell, Captain Willey. *The Swiss Army.* Ft. Leavenworth: Army Service Schools, 1916.

Huber, Jakob. *Bericht des Chefs des Generalstabs an den Oberbefehlshaber der Armee über den Aktivdienst 1939–1945.* Bern, 1946.

Hughes, Christopher. *The Federal Constitution of Switzerland.* Oxford: Clarendon Press, 1954.

Hutson, James H. *The Sister Republics: Switzerland and the United States from 1776 to the Present.* Washington, DC: Library of Congress, 1991.

Hyneman, Charles S., and Donald S. Lutz. *American Political Writings During the Founding Era, 1760–1805*. Indianapolis: Liberty Press, 1983.

Inauen, Josepf. *Schweizer Armee 97*. Frauenfeld: Huber, 1996.

Jane's Infantry Weapons. Surrey, UK: Jane's Information Group, 1990.

Jenny, Th., *Unsere heutigen Militärausgaben im Lichte der schweizerischen Volkswirtschaft*. Zürich und Leipzig, 1938.

Jochmann, Werner, ed. *Adolf Hitler: Monologe im Führerhauptquartier, 1941–1944*. Hamburg: Albrecht Knaus, 1980.

Jones, Michael A. *Swiss Bank Accounts*. New York: McGraw-Hill, 1990.

Jurado, Carlos Caballero. *Resistance Warfare 1940–45*. London: Osprey, 1985.

Keegan, John. *The Second World War*. New York: Henry Holt, 1987.

Kimche, Jon. *Spying for Peace: General Guisan and Swiss Neutrality*. London: Weidenfeld & Nicolson, 1961.

Kobelt, Karl, et al. *Die Schweiz in Waffen: Ein Erinnerungsbuch über den Aktivdienst 1939/45 für Volk und Armee*. Zürich: Vaterländischer Verlag A.G. Murten, 1945.

Kohn, Hans. *Nationalism and Liberty: The Swiss Example*. London: Unwin Brothers Limited, 1956.

Kreis, Georg. *Auf den Spuren von "La Charité."* Basel: Helbring & Lichtenhahn Verlag, 1976.

Kuenzli, Frederick A. *Right and Duty or Citizen and Soldier*. New York: National Defense Institute, 1916.

Kurz, Hans Rudolf. *Die Schweiz in der Planung der kriegführenden Mächte während des Zweiten Weltkrieges*. Biel, Switz.: SUOV, 1957.

Kurz, Hans Rudolf. *Die Schweiz im Zweiten Weltkrieg*. Thun, Switz.: Ott Verlag, 1959.

Kurz, Hans Rudolf. *Operationsplanung Schweiz*. Thun, Switz.: Ott Verlag, 1972.

Kurz, Hans-Rudolf. *General Guisan und der Zweite Weltkrieg 1939–1945*. Lausanne: Editions Marguerat, 1974.

Kurz, Hans Rudolf. *Histoire de l'Armée Suisse*. Lausanne: Editions 24 Heures, 1985.

Large, David Clay, ed. *Contending with Hitler: Varieties of German Resistance in the Third Reich*. Washington DC: Cambridge University Press, 1991.

Lasserre, André. *La Suisse Des Années Sombres*. Lausanne: Editions Payot, 1989.

Latour, Anny. *The Jewish Resistance in France 1940–1944*. New York:

Holocaust Library, 1970.

Law, Richard D. *Karabiner 98k, 1934–1945*. Dietikon-Zürich: Stocker-Schmid, 1995.

LeBor, Adam. *Hitler's Secret Bankers: The Myth of Swiss Neutrality During the Holocaust*. Secaucus, NJ: Birch Lane Press, 1997.

Leisi, Ernst. *Freispruch für die Schweiz*. Frauenfeld: Huber Verlag, 1997.

Lemkin, Raphael. *Axis Rule in Occupied Europe: Laws of Occupation, Analysis of Government, Proposals for Redress*. Washington, DC: Carnegie Endowment for International Peace, 1944.

Lindt, August. *Die Schweiz das Stachelschwein*. Bern: Zytglogge, 1992.

Lindt, August. *Le Temps du Hérisson: Souvenirs, 1939–1945*. Geneva: Editions Zoè 1995.

Lossberg, Bernhard von. *Im Wehrmachtführungsstab. Bericht eines Generalstabsoffiziers*. Hamburg: H.H. Nölke, 1949.

Luck, James Murray. *A History of Switzerland: The First 100,000 Years— Before the Beginnings to the Days of the Present*. Palo Alto, CA: Sposs Inc., 1985.

Lunn, Arnold. *Mountain Jubilee*. London: Eyre & Spottiswoode, 1943.

Machiavelli, Niccolò *The Prince*. New York: New American Library of World Literature, 1952.

Machiavelli, Niccolò *The Art of War*. Indianapolis: Bobbs-Merrill, 1965.

Machiavelli, Niccolò *The Discourses*. L. Walker, trans. New York: Penguin, 1970.

Marietti, Lt.-Colonel. *Mon Fusil: Manuel du Fantassin*. Bern: Hallwag, 1933.

Martin, Colonel John A. *A Plan for Establishing and Disciplining a National Militia in Great Britain, Ireland, and in All the British Dominions of America*. London, 1745.

Masanti, Remo. *Die Gefahrvolle Zeit im Sommer/Herbst 1940*. Eidgenössische Technische Hochschule, 1988.

McCormack, John. *One Million Mercenaries: Swiss Soldiers in the Armies of the World*. London: Leo Cooper, 1993.

McPhee, John. *La Place de la Concorde Suisse*. New York: Noonday Press, 1983.

Meier, Heinz K. *Friendship Under Stress: U.S.–Swiss Relations 1900–1950*. Bern: Lang Druck., 1970.

Meyer, Alice. *Anpassung oder Widerstand*. Frauenfeld: Verlag Huber, 1965.

Militär-Amtsblatt. Eidgenössiches Militärdepartement, 1940.

The Military Law and Efficient Citizen Army of the Swiss. Senate Document No. 360, 64th Cong., 1st Sess. 1916.

Milivojevic, Marko, and Pierre Maurer, eds. *Swiss Neutrality and Security: Armed Forces, National Defence and Foreign Policy.* New York: St. Martin's Press, 1990.

Munday, Richard. *Most Armed and Most Free?* Brightlingsea, UK: Piedmont Publishing, 1996.

Neutrale Kleinstaaten im Zweiten Weltkrieg. Münsingen: Buchverlag Tages-Nachrichten, 1973.

Oechsli, Wilhelm. *Quellenbuch zur Schweizergeschichte.* Zürich: Schulthess, 1901.

The Officers Training Corps of Great Britain, The Australian System of National Defense, The Swiss System of National Defense. Senate Document No. 796, 63rd Cong., 3rd Sess. 1915.

Oman, C.W.C. *The Art of War in the Middle Ages.* Oxford and London, 1885; rev. ed. New York: Cornell University Press, 1953.

Passow, Kurt. *Taschenbuch der Heere, Ausgabe 1939.* Munich: J.F. Lehmanns, 1939.

Persico, Joseph E. *Piercing the Reich.* New York: Barnes & Noble, 1979.

Phillips, Charles F., and J.V. Garland. *The American Neutrality Problem.* New York: H.W. Wilson Co., 1939.

Die Pistolen: Technisches Reglement Nr. T4d. Schweizerische Armee 1949.

Rappard, William E. *Collective Security in Swiss Experience, 1291–1948.* London: Allen & Unwin, 1948.

Rapport du Général Guisan à l'Assemblée Fédérale sur le Service Actif, 1939– 1945. Bern, 1946.

Reinhart, Christian. *Pistolen und Revolver der Schweiz.* Dietikon-Zürich: Stocker-Schmid, 1988.

Reinhart, Christian, Kurt Sallaz, and Michael am Rhyn. *Die Repetiergewehre der Schweiz: Die Systeme Vetterli und Schmidt-Rubin.* Dietikon-Zürich: Stocker-Schmid, 1991.

Remak, Joachim. *A Very Civil War: The Swiss Sonderbund War of 1847.* Boulder, CO: Westview Press, 1993.

Rich, Norman. *Hitler's War Aims: The Establishment of the New Order.* London: André Deutsch Limited, 1974.

Riedmatten, Chantal de. *Général Henri Guisan: Autorité et Démocratie.* Fribourg: Institut d'Histoire Moderne et Contemporaine, 1983.

Rings, Werner. *Schweiz im Krieg, 1933–1945.* Zürich: Ex Libris, 1974.

Roberts, Adam. *Nations in Arms.* New York: St. Martin's Press, 1986.

Roesch, Werner. *Bedrohte Schweiz.* Frauenfeld: Huber, 1986.

Rotem (Kazik), Simha. *Memoirs of a Warsaw Ghetto Fighter and the Past Within Me.* New Haven: Yale University Press, 1994.

Rovighi, Alberto. *Un Secolo di Relazioni Militari tra Italia e Svizzera 1861–1961.* Rome, 1987.

Rutland, Robert A. ed. *The Papers of George Mason.* University of North Carolina Press, 1970.

Sandoz, Ellis, ed. *Political Sermons of the American Founding Era.* Indianapolis: Liberty Press, 1990.

Santschi, Catherine. *Schweizer Nationalfeste im Spiegel der Geschichte.* Zürich: Schweizerische Gemeinnützige, 1991.

Schaer, Alfred. *Kaiser Wilhelm II. in der Schweiz.* Zürich: Orell Füssli, 1912.

Schäfer, Hugo. *Die Wehrmächte aller Staaten 1937.* Vienna 1937.

Schaufelberger, Walter, ed. *Armee Abschaffen?* Frauenfeld, Switz.: Verlag Huber, 1988.

Schellenberg, Walter. *Hitler's Secret Service,* trans. Louis Hagen. New York: Pyramid Books, 1977.

Schiessprogramm für die Schulen und Kurse der Infanterie. Eidg. Militärdepartement genehmigt am 7. April 1932.

Schlie, Ulrich. *Kein Friede Mit Deutschland.* München: Langen Müller, 1994.

Schwarz, Urs. *The Eye of the Hurricane: Switzerland in World War Two.* Boulder, CO: Westview Press, 1980.

Die Schweiz in Waffen: Ein Erinnerungsbuch über den Aktivdienst 1939/45 für Vok und Armee. Zürich: Vaterländischer Verlag A.G. Murten, 1945.

Die Schweiz und der Zweite Weltkrieg. Winterthur: Herausgeber, 1990.

Schweizerische Armee. *Schiessvorschrift für die Infanterie.* Bern, 1941.

Schweizerische Armee. *Ausbildungsvorschrift der Infanterie 1942.* Eidg. Militärdepartement, 1948.

Schweizerischer Schützenverein. *Hand- und Faustfeuerwaffen: Schweizerische Ordonnanz 1817 bis 1975.* Frauenfeld, Switz.: Huber, 1971.

Senn, Hans. *Erhaltung und Verstärkung der Verteidigungsbereitschaft zwischen den beiden Weltkriegen.* Basel: Helbing & Lichtenhahn, 1991.

Senn, Hans. *Anfänge einer Dissuasionsstrategie während des Zweiten Weltkrieges.* Basel: Helbing & Lichtenhahn, 1995.

Shirer, William L. *The Rise and Fall of the Third Reich.* New York: Simon & Shuster, 1990.

Shirer, William L. *Berlin Diary: The Journal of a Foreign Correspondent, 1934–41.* New York: Knopf, 1941.

Siegenthaler, Hansjög, and Heiner Ritzmann. *Historische Statistik der Schweiz.* Zürich, 1996.

Siegfried, André. *Switzerland: A Democratic Way of Life.* London: Lowe & Brydone, 1953.

Simkin, Jay, Aaron Zelman, Alan Rice. *Lethal Laws.* Milwaukee: Jews for the Preservation of Firearms Ownership, Inc., 1994.

Sloan, Jacob, ed. *Notes from the Warsaw Ghetto: The Journal of Emmanuel Ringelblum.* New York: Schocken Books, 1958.

Société Cantonale des Tireurs Fribourgeois. *Rapport de Gestion du Comité Cantonal pour l'Exercice.* Fribourg, Switz.: Hodel, 1940, 1941, 1942, 1943.

Soldatenbuch. Eidg. Militärdepartement, 1959.

Speer, Albert. *Inside the Third Reich.* New York: Macmillan, 1970.

Stanyan, Abraham. *An Account of Switzerland: Written in the Year 1714.* London, 1714.

Stapfer, Hans-Heiri, and Gino Künzle. *Escape to Neutrality.* Carrollton, TX: Squadron/Signal Publications, 1992.

Das Sturmgewehr 57 und die Gewehrgranaten 58. Schweizerische Armee, 1984.

Stüssi-Lauterburg, Jürg. *Das Schweizer Militärwesen des 17. Jahrhunderts in ausländischer Sicht.* Zürich: ADAG, 1982.

Stüssi-Lauterburg, Jürg, ed. *Entstehung und Wirken der Direktion der Militärverwaltung (DMV).* Brugg, Switz.: Verlag Effingerhof, 1989.

Stüssi-Lauterburg, Jürg. *Föderalismus und Freiheit.* Brugg, Switz.: Effingerhof, 1994.

Swiss Security Policy in Times of Change: Report 90 of the Federal Council to the Federal Assembly (1990).

Tagesbefehle des Generals, 1939–1945. Bern: Eidg. Militärbibliothek, n.d.

Thürer, Georg. *Free and Swiss: The Story of Switzerland.* London: Oswald Wolff, 1970.

Tschuy, Theo. *Carl Lutz und die Juden von Budapest.* Verlag: Neue Zürcher Zeitung, 1995.

United States Department of State. *Swiss Policies on Purge of Axis Supporters.* Washington, DC, 1945.

Urner, Klaus. *Der Schweizer Hitler-Attentäter.* Frauenfeld, Switz.: Huber, 1980.

Urner, Klaus. *Die Schweiz muss noch geschluckt werden!" Hitlers Aktionspläne gegen die Schweiz.* Zürich: Neue Zürcher Zeitung, 1990.

Vetter, Lorenz. *Das Grosse Buch der SIG-Pistolen.* Dietikon-Zürich: Stocker-Schmid, 1995.

Vögeli, Robert, et al. *Festungsmuseum Reuenthal.* Reuenthal, Switz.: 1989.

Wanner, Philipp. *Oberst Oscar Frey und der Schweizerische Widerstands-*

wille. Münsingen, Switz.: Tages-Nachrichten, 1974.

Wehrli, Edmund. *Wehrlose Schweiz, eine Insel des Friedens?* ASMZ, Schweizerischen Militärzeitschrift Nr. 9, 1973.

Weinberg, Gerhard L. *A World at Arms: A Global History of World War II.* Cambridge: Cambridge University Press, 1994.

Weinberg, Gerhard L. *Germany, Hitler, and World War II.* Cambridge: Cambridge University Press, 1995.

Werner, Harold. *Fighting Back: A Memoir of Jewish Resistance in World War II.* New York: Columbia University Press, 1992.

Wetter, Ernst. *Duell der Flieger und der Diplomaten.* Frauenfeld: Verlag Huber, 1987.

Wicht, Bernard. *L'Idée de Milice et le Modèle Suisse dans la Pensée de Machiavel.* Lausanne: L'Age d'Homme, 1995.

Wilson, Hugh R. *Switzerland: Neutrality as a Foreign Policy.* Philadelphia: Dorrance, 1974.

Windham, William. *A Plan of Discipline for the Use of the Norfolk Militia.* J. Millan, 1768.

Wingate, George W. *Why School Boys Should Be Taught to Shoot?* Boston: Sub-Target Gun Co., 1907.

Wyman, David S. *The Abandonment of the Jews: America and the Holocaust, 1941–1945.* New York: Pantheon Books, 1984.

Zubly, John J. *Great Britain's Right to Tax . . . By a Swiss.* London, 1775.

Zubly, John J. *The Law of Liberty: A Sermon on American Affairs.* Philadelphia, 1775.

ARTICLES

Barry, Griffin. "Swiss Democracy Goes into Action," in *Travel*, 73 (June 1939).

Bucher, Erwin, "Zur Linie Masson-Schellenberg," in *Schweizerische Zeitschrift für Geschichte*, Vol. 38 (1988) 359.

"Business at War," in *Fortune*, 29 (Feb. 1944).

Byng, Edward J. "If Switzerland Is Invaded," in *American Mercury*, 58 (April 1944).

Chable, J.E. "One Country, Four Languages," in *The Rotarian*, (Nov. 1935).

Chamberlain, William B. "Nazi Shadow Over Switzerland," in *Christian Century*, L (March 22, 1939).

Childs, Marquis W. "No Peace for the Swiss," in *The Saturday Evening Post*, 215 (May 1, 1943).

de Craon-Poussy, R. "Switzerland Is Ready," in *Commonweal*, 30 (July 7, 1939), 273.

Daniel, Anita. "The Miracle of Switzerland," in *American Mercury*, 54 (May 1942).

"Europe: 'Wir Machen Nicht Mit,' " in *Time*, 40 (Nov. 2, 1942).

Fehr, Joseph Conrad. "Fascism in Switzerland," in *Commonweal*, 27 (Jan. 28, 1938).

Friedman, R.A. "Switzerland Fights Against a New 'Anschluss,' " in *Contemporary Review*, 154 (Sept. 1938).

Friedrich, Carl J. "As Switzerland Sees It," in *Atlantic Monthly*, 178 (Dec. 1946).

Generaladjutantur, Sektion Heer und Haus. *Die Judenfrage*, Wehrbrief Nr. 26 (May 25, 1943).

Glenn, Jacob B. "The Jews in Switzerland," in *Contemporary Jewish Record*. New York: American Jewish Committee, 1941.

"Goods Still Move," in *Business Week* (Aug. 14, 1943).

Grieder, Heinrich. "Swiss Military Rifles," in *American Rifleman* (Jan. 1956).

Halbrook, Stephen P. "Swiss Schuetzenfest," in *American Rifleman* (May 1993).

Halbrook, Stephen P. "Switzerland's Feldschiessen," in *Gun Digest 1996*. Northbrook, IL: DBI Books, 1995.

Halbrook, Stephen P. "The World's Largest Rifle Shooting Match: Switzerland 1995," in *The 1996 Precision Shooting Annual*. Manchester, CT: Precision Shooting, Inc., 1996.

Hediger, Ferdinand. "The Fabulous Martini," in *Gun Digest 1996*. Northbrook, IL: DBI Books, 1995.

Hutson, James H. "Bombing the Sister Republic," in *Swiss-American Historical Society Review*, XXXI, 3 (Feb. 1995).

"Isolated Swiss," in *Newsweek*, 20 (Nov. 23, 1942).

Johnson, G.E.W. "Switzerland Is Next," in *North American Review*, vol. 237, 523 (June 1934).

Jolles, Paul R. "A Battle for Neutrality," in *Newsweek* (Sept. 1, 1997).

Kates, Don B. & Daniel D. Polsby. "Of Genocide and Disarmament," in *Criminal Law and Criminology* 86, 297 (1995).

Keller, Adolf. "Switzerland Will Fight," in *Christian Century*, LVI (May 24, 1939).

Köler, Jörg. "Switzerland as Champion for the Abolisment of Anti-Personnel Mines," in *Swiss Peace Keeper*, 8 (Sept. 3, 1997).

Kopel, David B. "Lethal Laws," in *New York Law School Journal of International and Comparative Law*, 15 (1995).

Kurz, Hans Rudolf, "In Hitler's Faust," in *Weltwoche Magazine*, 49 (Feb. 28, 1973).

Kurz, Hans Rudolf. "Vor vierzig Jahren: Aufstellung der Ortswehren," in *Der Fourier* (June 1980).

Kurz, Hans Rudolf, "Zu keiner ernsthaften Abwehr fähig," in *Der Bund* 7 (Aug. 1, 1981).

Lanius, Charles. "Switzerland, Axis Captive," in *The Saturday Evening Post*, 215 (Jan. 23, 1943).

Lippman, Walter. "The Faithful Witness," in *New York Herald Tribune* (Jan. 26, 1943).

Mandellaub, Max. "The Swiss Barometer," in *The Nation* (Nov. 13, 1943).

Memorandum by the Representatives of the British Chiefs of Staff, "Combined Chiefs of Staff Trade with Switzerland," C.C.S. 388/1 Washington, DC, November 29, 1943.

Mook, Hitelfer. "Training Day in New England," in *New England Quarterly*, XI (1938).

Moos, Malcolm. "Swiss Neutrality," in *Yale Review*, 33 (Sept. 1943).

Muller, Edwin. "Have Not and Prosper," in *Forum and Century*, 99 (May 1938).

"The New Lebensraum," in *Neue Volkszeitung*, in *Living Age*, (Aug. 1941).

"No Haven," in *Time,* 45 (Apr. 2, 1945).

Paulding, C.G. "Five Francs Swiss," in *Commonweal*, 41 (Feb. 23, 1945).

"Peaceful Switzerland," in *Literary Digest*, 124 (Aug. 14, 1937).

Rappard, William E. "Switzerland in a Changing Europe," in *Foreign Affairs*, XVI (July 1938).

Richardson, Donovan. "The Neutrals' Fight for Peace," in *The Christian Science Monitor* (Aug. 12, 1939).

Richter, Werner. "The War Pattern of Swiss Life," in *Foreign Affairs*, 22 (July 1944).

de Rougemont, Denis, and Charlotte Muret. "What Switzerland Teaches," in *Commonweal,* 34 (1941).

de Rougemont, Denis, and Charlotte Muret. "A Lesson from the Swiss Army," in *Reader's Digest*, 30 (Oct. 1941).

Rusch, J.B. "Swiss Forebodings," in *Living Age*, 354 (May 1938).

Schütz, W.W. "The Independence of Switzerland," in *Contemporary Review*, 159 (June 1941).

Senn, Hans. "Entre-deux-guerres et Seconde Guerre Mondiale," in *Forts et Fortifications en Suisse*. Lausanne: Payot, 1992.

de Sevin, B. "The European Importance of Switzerland," in *Contemporary Review*, 166 (July 1944).

"The Sister Republics," in *Rapport Annuel 1992*. Berne: Bibliothèque Nationale Suisse, 1993.

Snook, George A., "The Development of the Halberd," in *Man at Arms* 28 (May/June 1994).

Stoddard, Lothrop. "Europe's Balance of Neutrals," in *The Christian Science Moniter* (Apr. 14, 1937).

Stüssi-Lauterburg, Jürg. "The Swiss Military System and Neutrality in the Seventeenth Century as Seen by Contemporary Europe," in *War & Society* (Sept. 1984).

"Swiss Cherish Their Ancient Liberties," in *National Geographic*, 79 (Apr. 1941).

"Swiss Doors: European War-Scare Leads 'Isle of Peace' to Fortify Its Frontiers," in *The Literary Digest*, 123 (Jan. 23, 1937).

"Swiss-German Crisis Intensified," in *The Literary Digest*, 121 (February 29, 1936).

"Swiss Haven," in *Newsweek* (Oct. 26, 1942).

"Swiss Neutrality," in *Newsweek* (July 4, 1938).

"Swiss Trade," in *Newsweek* (Jan. 18, 1943).

"The Swiss War," in *Newsweek* (Jan. 15, 1945).

"Switzerland," in *Time* (July 4, 1938).

"Switzerland: Alone, Little & Tough," in *Time* (Dec. 7, 1942).

"Switzerland Sits Tight," in *Fortune*, 24 (Sept. 1941).

Thompson, C. Bradley. "John Adams's Machiavellian Moment," in *57 The Review of Politics*, 3 (Summer 1995).

"Three Minor Characters," in *Living Age*, 352 (Aug. 1937).

Urner, Klaus, "Der Kampf um die totale Einschliessung der Schweiz durch die Achsenmächte," in *Neue Zürcher Zeitung* 95 (June 17, 1990).

Vagts, Detlev F. "Switzerland, International Law and World War II," in *The American Journal of International Law* 91, 466 (1997).

Viola, Wilhelm, "The Position of Switzerland," in *Contemporary Review*, 156 (1939).

Whittlesey, Faith. "Switzerland on Trial," in *The Ambassadors Review* (Spring 1997).

Widmer, Paul, "Der Einfluss der Schweiz auf die Amerikanische Verfassung von 1787," in *Schweizerische Zeitschrift für Geschichte*, Vol. 38, 359 (1988).

Wiskemann, Elizabeth. "The Swiss Confederation and the War," in *Fortnightly*, 153 (April 1940).

Wiskemann, Elizabeth. "The Sword of Freedom," in *Fortnightly*, 156 (August 1941).

Index

Printed in the United States
96039LV00005B/84/A